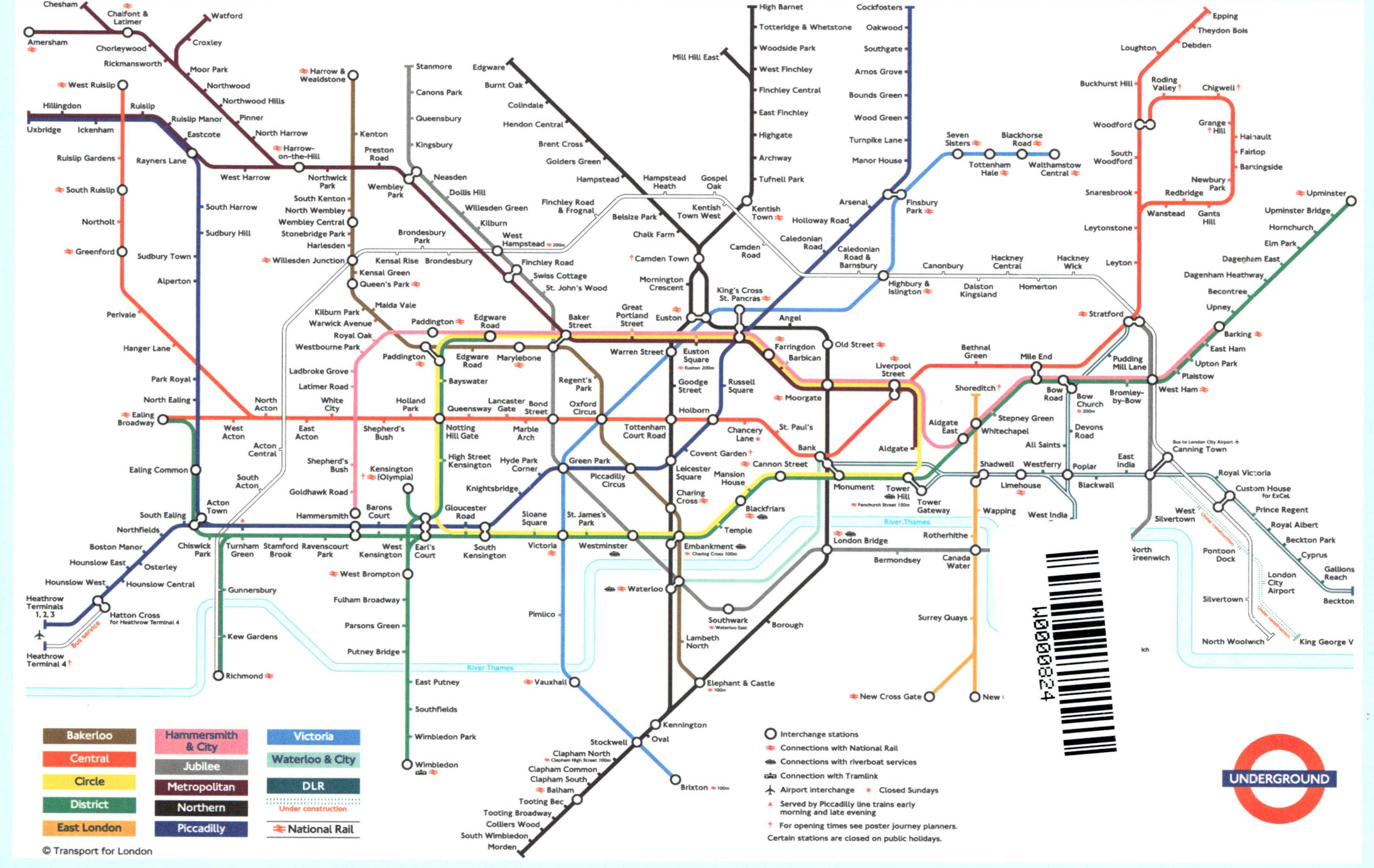
UNDERGROUND
Chesham
Chalfont & Latimer
Amersham
Chorleywood
Rickmansworth
Watford
Croxley
Moor Park
Northwood
Northwood Hills
Pinner
North Harrow
Harrow-on-the-Hill
West Harrow
West Ruislip
Ruislip
Ruislip Manor
Eastcote
Hillingdon
Uxbridge
Ickenham
Ruislip Gardens
Rayners Lane
South Ruislip
Northolt
Greenford
South Harrow
Sudbury Hill
Sudbury Town
Alperton
Perivale
Hanger Lane
Park Royal
North Ealing
Ealing Broadway
Ealing Common
South Ealing
Northfields
Boston Manor
Osterley
Hounslow East
Hounslow Central
Hounslow West
Hatton Cross
for Heathrow Terminal 4
Heathrow Terminals 1, 2, 3
Heathrow Terminal 4
Bus service
Harrow & Wealdstone
Kenton
Preston Road
Northwick Park
South Kenton
North Wembley
Wembley Central
Stonebridge Park
Harlesden
Willesden Junction
Stanmore
Canons Park
Queensbury
Kingsbury
Neasden
Wembley Park
Dollis Hill
Willesden Green
Kilburn
West Hampstead
Brondesbury Park
Brondesbury
Kensal Rise
Kensal Green
Queen's Park
Maida Vale
Kilburn Park
Warwick Avenue
Royal Oak
Westbourne Park
Ladbroke Grove
Latimer Road
White City
North Acton
West Acton
East Acton
Acton Central
South Acton
Acton Town
Chiswick Park
Turnham Green
Stamford Brook
Ravenscourt Park
Gunnersbury
Kew Gardens
Richmond
Edgware
Burnt Oak
Colindale
Hendon Central
Brent Cross
Golders Green
Hampstead
Finchley Road & Frognal
Belsize Park
Chalk Farm
Hampstead Heath
Gospel Oak
Kentish Town West
Camden Town
Camden Road
Mornington Crescent
Finchley Road
Swiss Cottage
St. John's Wood
Mill Hill East
High Barnet
Totteridge & Whetstone
Woodside Park
West Finchley
Finchley Central
East Finchley
Highgate
Archway
Tufnell Park
Kentish Town
Cockfosters
Oakwood
Southgate
Arnos Grove
Bounds Green
Wood Green
Turnpike Lane
Manor House
Arsenal
Holloway Road
Caledonian Road
Caledonian Road & Barnsbury
Finsbury Park
Seven Sisters
Tottenham Hale
Blackhorse Road
Walthamstow Central
Highbury & Islington
Canonbury
Dalston Kingsland
Hackney Central
Homerton
Hackney Wick
King's Cross St. Pancras
Euston
Great Portland Street
Baker Street
Paddington
Edgware Road
Marylebone
Bayswater
Regent's Park
Warren Street
Euston Square
Goodge Street
Russell Square
Angel
Old Street
Farringdon
Barbican
Moorgate
Liverpool Street
Holland Park
Queensway
Lancaster Gate
Bond Street
Marble Arch
Oxford Circus
Tottenham Court Road
Holborn
Chancery Lane
St. Paul's
Bank
Shepherd's Bush
Notting Hill Gate
High Street Kensington
Hyde Park Corner
Green Park
Piccadilly Circus
Leicester Square
Covent Garden
Cannon Street
Mansion House
Kensington (Olympia)
Goldhawk Road
Hammersmith
Barons Court
West Kensington
Earl's Court
Gloucester Road
Knightsbridge
South Kensington
Sloane Square
Victoria
St. James's Park
Westminster
Charing Cross
Embankment
Charing Cross 100m
Temple
Blackfriars
Monument
Tower Hill
Fenchurch Street 150m
Tower Gateway
Aldgate
Aldgate East
West Brompton
Fulham Broadway
Parsons Green
Putney Bridge
East Putney
Southfields
Wimbledon Park
Wimbledon
Pimlico
Vauxhall
Waterloo
Southwark
Waterloo East
Lambeth North
Borough
Elephant & Castle
London Bridge
Bermondsey
Canada Water
Rotherhithe
Surrey Quays
New Cross Gate
New Cross
Kennington
Oval
Stockwell
Brixton
Clapham North
Clapham High Street 100m
Clapham Common
Clapham South
Balham
Tooting Bec
Tooting Broadway
Colliers Wood
South Wimbledon
Morden
Bethnal Green
Mile End
Shoreditch
Whitechapel
Stepney Green
Shadwell
Limehouse
Wapping
Westferry
West India
All Saints
Bow Road
Bow Church
Devons Road
Poplar
Blackwall
East India
Pudding Mill Lane
Bromley-by-Bow
Stratford
West Ham
Plaistow
Upton Park
East Ham
Barking
Upney
Becontree
Dagenham Heathway
Dagenham East
Elm Park
Hornchurch
Upminster Bridge
Upminster
Leyton
Leytonstone
Snaresbrook
South Woodford
Woodford
Buckhurst Hill
Loughton
Debden
Theydon Bois
Epping
Roding Valley
Chigwell
Grange Hill
Hainault
Fairlop
Barkingside
Newbury Park
Gants Hill
Redbridge
Wanstead
Canning Town
Bus to London City Airport
Royal Victoria
Custom House
for ExCeL
West Silvertown
Prince Regent
Royal Albert
Beckton Park
Cyprus
Gallions Reach
Beckton
Pontoon Dock
London City Airport
Silvertown
North Woolwich
King George V
North Greenwich
Under construction
River Thames
Interchange stations
Connections with National Rail
Connections with riverboat services
Connection with Tramlink
Airport interchange
Closed Sundays
Served by Piccadilly line trains early morning and late evening
For opening times see poster journey planners.
Certain stations are closed on public holidays.
Bakerloo
Central
Circle
District
East London
Hammersmith & City
Jubilee
Metropolitan
Northern
Piccadilly
Victoria
Waterloo & City
DLR
Under construction
National Rail
© Transport for London
W0000824

Orange **Line**

Erweiterungskurs 3

Herausgeber: Frank Haß

Ernst Klett Verlag
Stuttgart • Leipzig

Orange Line 3 Erweiterungskurs

für Klasse 7 an allen differenzierenden Schulen

Im Auftrag des Verlags herausgegeben von:
Frank Haß, Kirchberg

Unter besonderer Mitwirkung von:
Harald Weisshaar, Bisingen

Erarbeitet von:
Marion Horner, Cambridge (*The Courier*);
David Lambert M. A., Cambridge (*The Hound of the Baskervilles, King Arthur, Canterville Ghost*)

Unter besonderer Mitwirkung von:
Hamida Aziz, Tübingen; Sheila McBride, Stuttgart

Beratung:
Anette Christiani, Dortmund; Ulf Degen, Braunschweig; Susan King-Köcher, Kassel; Margitta Kuty, Greifswald; Volker Pabst, Stade; Heike Parma, Halver; Annegret Preker-Franke, Bielefeld

1. Auflage 1 6 5 4 3 2 1 | 2011 2010 2009 2008 2007

Alle Drucke dieser Auflage sind unverändert und können im Unterricht nebeneinander verwendet werden. Die letzte Zahl bezeichnet das Jahr des Druckes.

Internetadresse: www.klett.de

Redaktion: Susanne Wilhelm M. A.; Cornelia Schaller, Lektorat editoria, Fellbach

Gestaltung: Ulrike Wursthorn
Illustrationen: David Norman, Meerbusch; Katja Hoppmann, Köln; Steffen Wolff, Düsseldorf
Umschlaggestaltung: Koma Amok, Stuttgart
Umschlagfoto: Corbis/Zefa/Graf
Reproduktion: Meyle + Müller, Medien-Management, Pforzheim
Druck: Firmengruppe APPL, aprinta druck, Wemding

Printed in Germany
ISBN 978-3-12-547531-1 (fester Einband)
ISBN 978-3-12-547631-8 (flexibler Einband)

Welcome back to Orange Line!

Nach zwei Jahren Englisch lernen mit Orange Line kommt nun der dritte Band.
Vieles wirst du wieder erkennen, aber manches ist auch anders.
Hier ein kurzer Überblick, um Bekanntes aufzufrischen und auf Neues einzustimmen:

In den fünf **Units** (Kapiteln) erfährst du viel Neues über Großbritannien – das Land und die Leute.
Band 3 hat folgende Unit-Teile (einige davon erkennst du auch gleich wieder):

Check-in	Neue Wörter und Landeskunde
Language	Sprache und Grammatik
Get fit!	Fertigkeitstraining
Overheard	Hörverstehen
Facts and fiction	Erlebnisse und Geschichten
Wordwise	Alles rund ums Wort!
Check-out	Prüfe, ob du alles verstanden hast.
Skills in action	Weiteres Fertigkeitstraining
Try it out!	Testaufgaben

Nach den Units gibt es eine kurze **Plus unit** mit Zusatzgrammatik.
In **Extras** findest du zwei Projekte:
A story: Eine spannende Geschichte
A radio play: Ein Hörspiel
Nach den Extras folgen **Mediation and communication** und **Grammar** (Grammatikanhang) mit vielen Beispielen, Regeln, Tipps und Übungen.
Am Ende des Buches findest du den Teil **Vocabulary** (Vokabelliste). Hier kannst du alle neuen Wörter nachschlagen und lernen.
Das **Dictionary** (Wörterbuch) listet die Vokabeln alphabetisch auf. Es ist auch zum Nachschlagen gedacht, wenn du einmal ein Wort vergessen hast.
Alles klar? Dann auf geht's in die Welt des Sports …

Erläuterungen:

Let's talk	Lasst uns reden
Let's listen	Lasst uns zuhören
Let's look	Lasst uns nachschauen
A role play	Verschiedene Rollen übernehmen
For my folder	Für meine Sammelmappe
L1, 22	Diese Teile sind auf den Begleit-CDs (Langversion) enthalten. (Beispiel: L1, 22: Lehrer-CD 1, Track 22)
(→ p. 14/ex. 4)	Workbook-Verweis zu passenden Übungsaufgaben
✲	Diese Übungen sind besonders knifflig.
	Partnerarbeit
	Gruppenarbeit
…………………	Diese Übungen kannst du machen, sie können aber auch wegfallen.
▶	Tipp zum Vokabellernen
▶	Tipp zur Grammatik
▶	Tipp mit Redemitteln

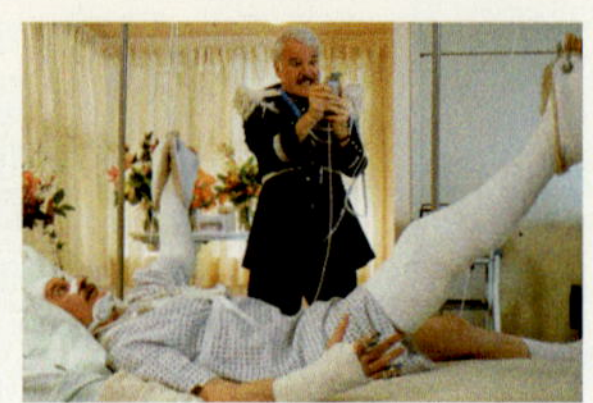

Unit 1 What's your game?

1 Twickenham: The home of rugby

DID YOU KNOW?

- In the 18th century in England a lot of schools played football but each school had its own rules.
- One of these schools was Rugby School and it gave its name to rugby or rugby football.
- They play on grass but rugby is different from football. It is more like American football but the players don't wear hard helmets during the game.
- A rugby ball is more like an egg than a football.
- Each team has 15 players and they can carry, pass, catch or kick the ball.
- England's home stadium is in Twickenham, London.
- There is a museum where you can learn more about this exciting sport.

1 Team sports

a) Rugby and baseball are team sports. *Which other team sports do you know? Which do you play and which do you watch?*

b) *Look at 'Did you know?' and photos 1, 2 and 3.*

1. What sports are they playing?
2. What are they doing/wearing?

WORDS

to bat [bæt] – *schlagen*
bat [bæt] – *Schläger*
glove [glʌv] – *Handschuh*
rugby boot [bu:t] – *Rugbyschuh, Stollenschuh*
at the front [frʌnt]/back [bæk] – *vorne/hinten, im vorderen/hinteren Teil*

2 Baseball: The batter wants to score a run.

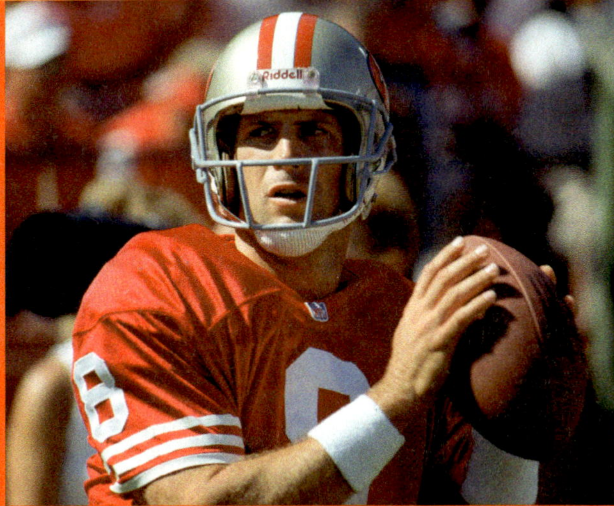

3 American football player in action

4 Stands on a roof near Wrigley Field Stadium

5 Wrigley Field Baseball Stadium

L1, 1 2 Let's listen: A souvenir of the game

Two young people, Nancy Cage and Dave Berry, came to Chicago from London to watch their favourite baseball team, the Chicago Cubs, in a game against the Cincinnati Reds.

Find out what happened. Listen to the radio reporter and look at pictures 4 and 5.

1. Where did Nancy and Dave watch the game from?
2. Why did they leave the game early?
3. Who is Derrek Lee? What did he do?

3 Let's talk: Other sports (→ p. 3/ex. 1–3)

a) *Find out more about one other sport on the Internet. These phrases can help you when you're surfing for information.*

b) *Tell your class about the sport.*

▶ **You use the simple present:**
- to say or ask what someone does regularly.
- to give facts about someone or something.

They **play** baseball every Wednesday.
He **watches** football at the weekend.
They **play** rugby for England.

Do they **play** rugby at your school?
Does he **play** baseball for the Cincinnati Reds?
Where **do** you **live**?
I **don't like** baseball.
She **doesn't play** rugby.

→ G1

1 Get it right! (→ p. 4/ex. 4–6)

Look at pages 8/9 again and correct these sentences about rugby and baseball.

1. Rugby players wear hard helmets.
2. A rugby team has eleven players.
3. A rugby ball looks like a football.
4. We call it rugby or 'Rugby School Ball'.
5. Rugby players wear long trousers.
6. Wrigley Field is a rugby pitch.
7. The Chicago Cubs play for New York.
8. Fans can watch the game from the road.

2 The accident (→ p. 5/ex. 7)

a) The reporter asks Dave and Nancy more questions. *Find their questions and answers.*

Example: Where do you live in London? – Near Twickenham Stadium.

What Which Why Where Who	+	does do	+	you live in London? they play there – baseball? you like better, baseball or rugby? no one in Britain watch baseball? your team play in London? you like best in our team? it say on his bat?	+	Baseball, but we don't play it. At our youth club. Sport is dangerous! Derrek Lee, of course! Near Twickenham Stadium. No! Rugby football. There are no national teams.

b) *You are a reporter. Interview Nancy or Dave. Find out about them and their accident.*

3 Beach volleyball

a) *Complete the text. Choose a verb and use the simple present.*

look, choose, use, like ✓, put, know, have, play, try, hit, watch, want, not play

A lot of young people **like** sports. They often … them on TV. But they … some games because they … to look fresh and 'cool' at the end of a match. So they … beach volleyball.
It … rules like volleyball. There is a net across the court. The players … on hard ground. They … sand on the court, so it … like a beach. They don't have a goal or goalkeeper. A player on one team … the ball from the back line. His or her team … to 'kill' the ball in the other team's court. The players … hand signals, so that the others in their team … what they want to do.

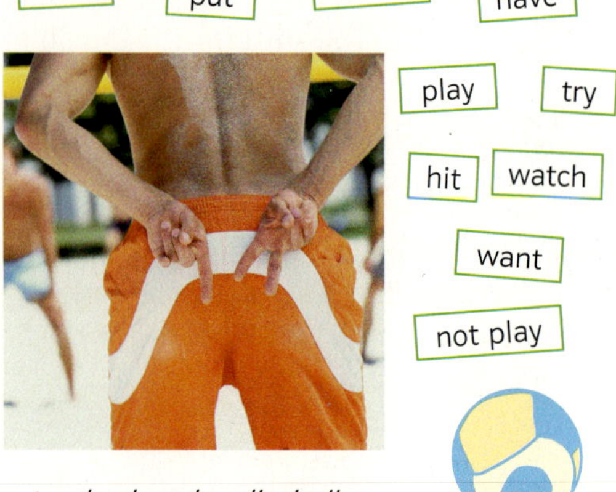

b) *Make notes on this sport and tell your partner how to play beach volleyball.*

4 Popular players (→ p. 5/ex. 8)

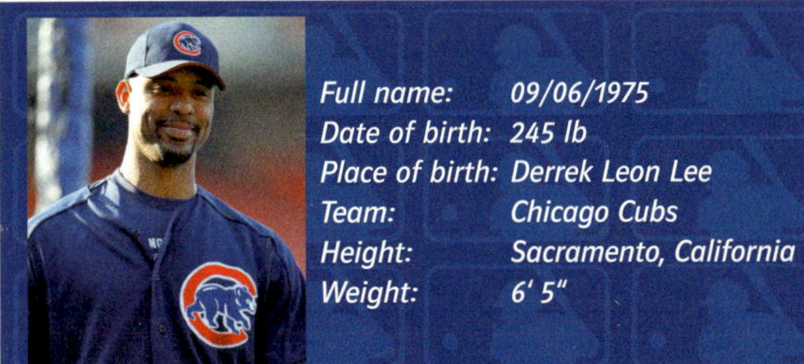

Full name: 09/06/1975
Date of birth: 245 lb
Place of birth: Derrek Leon Lee
Team: Chicago Cubs
Height: Sacramento, California
Weight: 6′ 5″

- 09/06 (AE + Internet) → 6th September
- 06/09 (BE)
- 6′ 5″ → 6 ft (feet) 5 in (inches)
- 1 lb (pound) → 450 g (grammes)
- 1 st (stone) → 14 lb (pounds)

a) *Look at Derrek Lee's profile. Put the information in the right order.*

b) *Read the text about Paula George. Make a profile for Paula.*

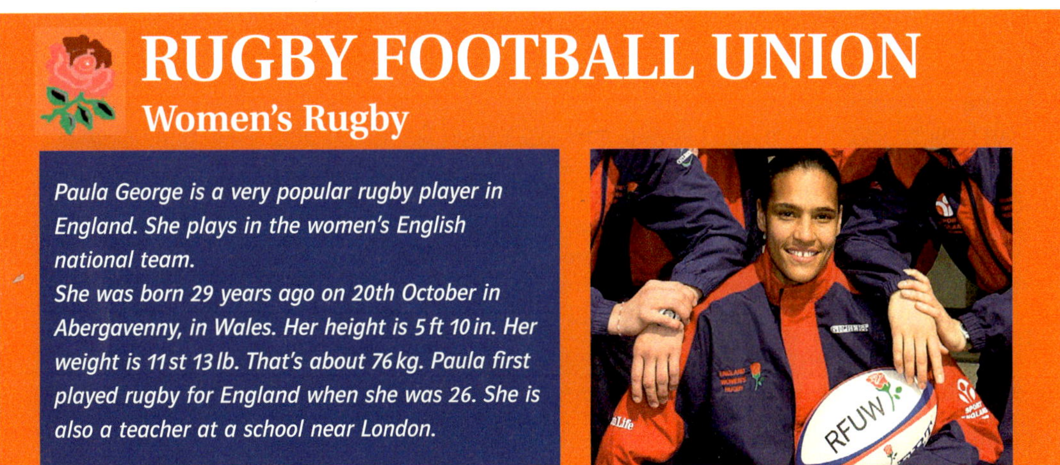

RUGBY FOOTBALL UNION

Women's Rugby

Paula George is a very popular rugby player in England. She plays in the women's English national team.
She was born 29 years ago on 20th October in Abergavenny, in Wales. Her height is 5 ft 10 in. Her weight is 11 st 13 lb. That's about 76 kg. Paula first played rugby for England when she was 26. She is also a teacher at a school near London.

c) *Close your books, ask questions about one of the players and test your partner.*

What's … 's full name? Where was she/he born? … ?

5 Some personal questions (→ p. 5/ex. 9)

Write a profile for your partner.
What questions can you ask?

What's your full name/height/weight/ … ? • What's your date of birth? • When were you born? • Where's your place of birth? • Where … ?

6 For my folder: My own profile

You want to find a chat partner from a partner school in the UK or the USA. They ask you for some information.

Write your own profile. Add more information about yourself. What about your hobbies? What about your favourite sports/film/colour? What are your plans for the future?

Name:
Age:
Date of birth:
Place of birth:
School:
Hobbies/sports:
Plans for the future:

▶ You use the present progressive to say what someone is doing at the moment.
What **are** you **doing** at the moment? **I'm** just **watching** a film.

→ G2

A couch potato

Me? Cycle to work? Never. OK, I'm a secretary for a firm which makes racing bikes. But that doesn't mean I have to cycle to the office, like my boss or some of my friends! I live near Wembley Stadium and it's terrible when there's a match there – all those people! And I hate football. In fact I don't like any sports, really. You could say I'm a bit of a couch potato: A walk in the park at the weekend is active enough for me. Sport isn't the only hobby a person can have. I love cooking and I often invite my friends for supper.
But sometimes I think maybe I should start to do some sports because, you see, a few weeks ago I had this strange dream. Just imagine, there I am: I'm sitting on a racing bike. I'm wearing yellow shorts, a jersey and a helmet. I'm going very, very fast …
Then suddenly everything changes in my dream and now I'm swimming in a pool. I'm wearing a wicked blue sports swimsuit and a cap. A lot of other women are swimming, too, but I'm the fastest. The funny thing is, in real life I can't even swim! And then the dream gets even crazier: I'm playing tennis like a tennis star! The umpire is smiling at me and we're all laughing. At the end of the dream I'm on a rugby field and it's half-time. The score is 16 to 20. Later I'm just passing a ball to another player and I see the referee. He's my boss! He's blowing the whistle. It's a draw.
Well, don't you think my dream is trying to tell me something?

1 Marcia's dream (→ p. 6/ex. 10)

Correct the sentences about Marcia's dream.

1. She is sitting in the bus.
2. She is wearing a long coat.
3. She is working at the swimming pool.
4. The umpire is laughing at her.
5. Her boss is passing the ball.

2 Marcia's friends (→ p. 6/ex. 11)

▶ He's **riding** a bike.
He **isn't playing** rugby.

→ G2

a) *What are they doing?*
Example: In picture 1 Rob is riding … . He isn't … . He's wearing … .

1 Rob: ride bike/jog

2 Jamie: swim/surf

3 Sue: play hockey/tennis

4 Barbara: play rugby/baseball

b) *Imagine you are dreaming. A friend phones.*
Tell him or her what you are doing. – You: Hi, … . I'm having great fun. I'm … .

 3 Rob and Sue's holiday (→ p. 7/ex. 12, 13)

Read what Marcia's friends usually do on holiday and what they are doing at the moment.

Usually Rob and Sue **visit** friends in Scotland. But at the moment they **aren't visiting** friends in Scotland. They **are visiting** friends in India. Usually they **ride** their bikes but at the moment they **aren't riding** … . *Go on, please.*

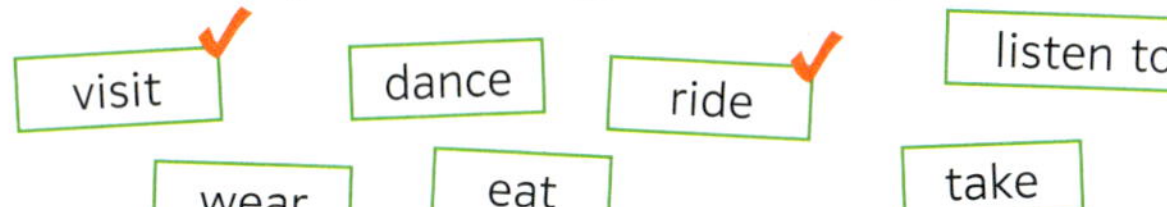

▶ They usually **visit** … , but at the moment they **are visiting** … .
→ G3

usually	at the moment
bikes	elephants
fish and chips	curries
Scottish music	Indian music
jackets and rubber boots	shorts and T-shirts
photos of castles	photos of the Taj Mahal
Scottish dances	Indian dances

4 Let's talk: Summer holiday plans (→ p. 7/ex. 14)

A: What are you doing at the moment?
Are you writing …/watching …/… ?
B: No, I'm not … . I'm … . What are you doing?
A: We're planning our holidays/talking about/watching … .
So what do you usually do in the holidays?
B: Well, I usually go to/visit/stay in … with … .
And what are you doing tonight?
A: I'm … . *Go on, please.*

At the moment? I'm talking to you, silly!

5 Let's talk: Snapshots

Bring in some snapshots of a holiday. Talk to a partner about them.

A: Look this is a photo of me with my … .
B: What are you doing/wearing/looking at/… ?
A: I'm/we're …ing.
B: And what are you doing/where are you going/… in this picture?
A: We're … . *Go on, please.*

6 For my folder: A sports photo

Find a sports photo. It can be of you or of someone else and you pretend you are in the photo. What's happening? What happens a few minutes later? Tell the class.

This is a photo of me in our team. I am playing for my club. I am hitting the ball. A few minutes later I get a goal for my team.

PRESENTATION

SKILLS

Preparing a talk

- Collect information, facts, pictures … . You can use the Internet.
- What could be interesting for your class? Collect three or four ideas.
- Make a plan:
  How long should your talk be?
  What pictures or diagrams can you use?
  What can you draw on the board?
- Look up 'special' words in a dictionary.
- Now write notes for your talk.
  What can you say at the beginning and at the end?

Giving a talk

- Check the things that you need: the cards with your notes, a pen, the poster, …
- If you use new words in your talk, write them on the board. The useful phrases in the box can help you.
- Tell the class what topic you want to talk about.
- Speak slowly.
- Look at your classmates while you are speaking.
- At the end of the talk ask the others in your class for questions.
- Answer their questions and say thank you to them.

1 A talk on sport (→ p. 8/ex. 15)

a) *Make a poster and prepare your talk about a sport.*

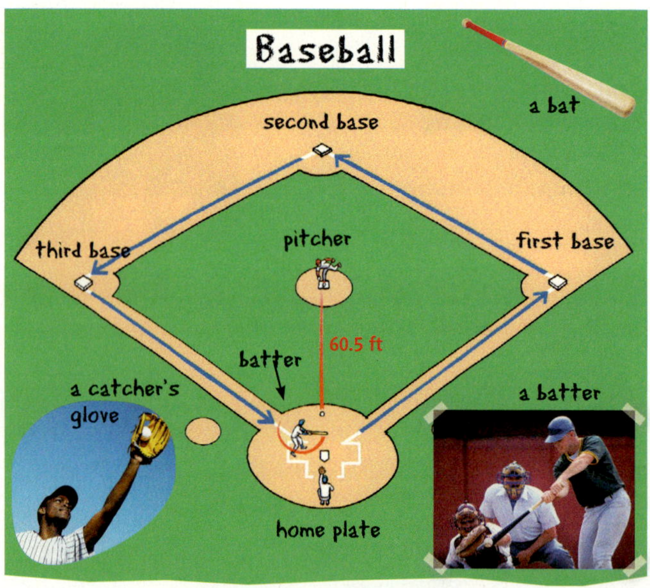

Useful phrases for a talk:

1. Today I'd like to talk about … .
2. My favourite team is … .
3. The players are wearing … .
4. The players must try to … .
5. At the top of the poster you can see … .
6. At the bottom, here, there's a … .
7. And on the left/right … .
8. I hope you liked the talk. Are there any questions?
9. Thank you to all of you.

b) *Present the sport to your class. Use the useful phrases in the box.*

2 How was it?

Discuss the talks in class.
Look at the box for ideas.
How can you make the talk better?
You can make suggestions but remember to be polite!

Did the speaker speak slowly/clearly enough?
Were the facts interesting?
Were important facts missing?
Could he/she answer the class's questions?
Were the pictures good?

L1, 2 1 Let's listen: Which game is it?

Listen to the three descriptions of games. Which games are the people talking about?

1. a. American football b. rugby c. football
2. a. rugby b. baseball c. hockey
3. a. badminton b. tennis c. beach volleyball

L1, 3 2 Let's listen: At the match (→ p. 9/ex. 16, 17)

a) *Look at the photos. Where are Tess and Trina? Which sport are they watching?*

Wembley Stadium

Twickenham

Wimbledon

b) *What happens to Tess and Trina?*

c) *Act the dialogue between Tess, Trina and the second young man. Use the phrases from the box.*

Excuse me! I think … .	I'm sorry but you're
But we've got … .	sitting in row … .
Could you check …, please?	Oh, no. Sorry!
Yes, of course. Row … .	No problem.

L1, 4 3 Let's listen: At a football match (→ p. 9/ex. 18)

Listen and answer the questions.

1. Why are the tickets half-price?
2. Why is the referee sending a player off?
3. What is the score at half-time?
4. What happened last time?

L1, 5 4 Sounds: Tongue twisters

1. Fifty famous football fans found foreign fields fantastic.
2. Brilliant British baseball batter bangs ball behind Boston bully's back.
3. Some surprising sports star's sister, Sheila, sings sad Scottish songs.

L1, 6 5 Let's listen: Football – facts and figures (→ p. 10/ex. 19)

Listen to the text. Use the numbers and figures in sentences about football.

Example: 1. There were 15 **English clubs in the FA Cup**.

1. 15 ✓	biggest stadium/Barcelona, Spain
2. in 1871	first football in Britain
3. 250 million	first rules of football
4. 90,000	seats in Wembley Stadium
5. 200 BC	height of goal posts
6. 98,800	football players
7. the 12th century	first FA Cup
8. in 1863	English clubs in the FA Cup ✓
9. 30 ft	football in China

L1, 7–12 A match to remember!

A Last Wednesday when Sarah came home from football practice with her friend Leo, it was nearly five o'clock. She put her hand in her jacket pocket. "Oh, no!" she said. "I've left the key in my other jacket." All they could do was to wait for her mum. But she always came home late on Wednesdays. They sat down on the doorstep, took out a magazine and started to read.

B Suddenly a voice said, "Hello, Sarah." They looked up. It was Mr Barnes. He lived in the house next door. Sarah didn't really like him. It wasn't because he was really ancient and he never smiled. Every week he moaned to Sarah's mum about something. Sarah's cat dug up his plants, Sarah's music was too loud or Sarah's friends made too much noise when they played football in the garden. But Sarah's mum said, "He's a nice old man. He's just very lonely." She felt sorry for him and sometimes gave him a pot of jam or some home-made cake.

C Sarah told him about the key and he invited them to wait in his living room until her mum came home. Sarah wanted to say 'No, thank you.' But it was cold and wet on the doorstep. She wrote a note for her mum and put it on the door.

Mum! I forgot my key.
We're next door with Mr Barnes.
Love, Sarah

Mr Barnes made them some hot chocolate and they sat on his big old sofa. Next to them was a table with a lot of photos. One was a picture of a football team. "Where are you in this picture, Mr Barnes?" Leo asked. "Oh, I didn't play for that team, Leo. That's Dynamo Moscow. I saw them in November 1945. They played against Arsenal at White Hart Lane. That was a match to remember."

Dynamo Moscow

D "Why?" asked Sarah. She felt happier now. Maybe her mum was right about him. "Well, it all started very well," said Mr Barnes. He smiled as he remembered. "But then one of the Arsenal players had a fight with one of the Russian players. The referee sent the Arsenal player off the field. Suddenly a really thick fog came down. We had a lot of fog in London when I was a boy. The referee couldn't see the pitch, and the Arsenal player came back onto the pitch again."
"That's not fair play," said Sarah.
She laughed and Mr Barnes smiled again. He didn't look so old now.

Before the fog came down

E "No," he said. "But the Russians didn't play fair either. They substituted a player. But they didn't send the first man off so they had twelve players instead of eleven. In fact some people say they had 15 players on the field at the end of the match."
"What a laugh!" said Leo.
"But that wasn't all," said Mr Barnes. "The Arsenal goalkeeper had an accident. He couldn't see the goal post because the fog was so thick. He ran into it and knocked himself out."
"So Arsenal had one player fewer again." said Sarah. She couldn't stop laughing now.
"No!" said Mr Barnes. "They took him off the field and a man from the crowd played in goal for the rest of the match."

A goalkeeper in the fog

F "And was it a draw?" asked Leo. "No," said Mr Barnes. "The Russians won."
"What was the score?" asked Sarah. "Four goals to three," said Mr Barnes. Suddenly the doorbell rang. It was Sarah's mum. They thanked Mr Barnes and went to Sarah's house.
A week later Sarah asked, "Mum, can I take this pot of jam to Mr Barnes this afternoon after football?"

1 Before you read: Think back!

Have you ever seen a 'match to remember'? Where and when was it? What happened?

2 New words

What do you think these words from the text mean?
Example: I think 'nearly' means 'beinahe' ('fast') because 'near' means 'nah an'.

practice (*l. 2*) • home-made (*l. 22*) • fair (*l. 50*) • rest (*l. 69*)

3 Two stories (→ p. 11/ex. 20)

Sort the sentences. Which belong to the 'Sarah' story? Which belong to the 'football' story?

1. Suddenly a really thick fog came down.
2. He didn't look so old now.
3. She put her hand in her jacket pocket.
4. They substituted a player.
5. Mr Barnes made them some hot chocolate … .
6. The referee couldn't see the pitch … .
7. They thanked Mr Barnes … .
8. They played against Arsenal … .

4 Change your mind!

a) Sarah changes her mind about Mr Barnes.
What did the old man do? Collect words and phrases which show how she feels about him before and after she forgets her key.

Before	After
She didn't really like him.	She felt happier now.
…	…

b) *Have you ever changed your mind about someone? Why did you change your mind? What happened?*

I thought he/she was horrible/really nice/… .
He/she never spoke/smiled/… .
One day he/she sent me/gave me/… .
Then he/she said/took/asked me/… .
I was happy/surprised/angry/fed up/… .

1 Mind maps (→ p. 12/ex. 21)

a) *Complete the mind maps for the four sports.*

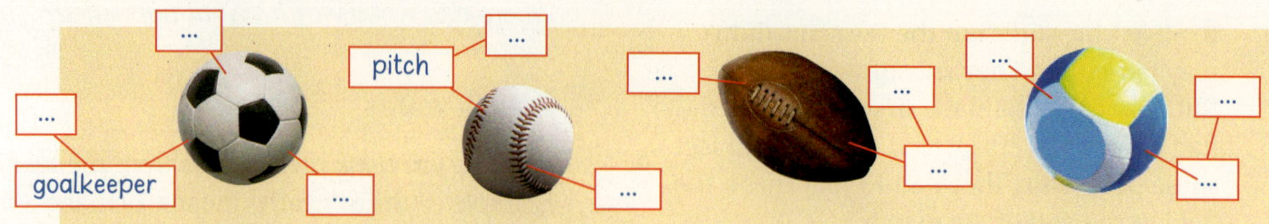

b) *Choose a sport which you know. Write three or four sentences about it. Don't use the name of the sport. Read your text to your partner. Can she/he guess the sport?*

2 Let's look: A crazy game

Look at the picture of a football match. What is wrong?

3 Verbs and nouns (→ p. 12/ex. 22)

a) In English a lot of 'sports' verbs have a noun which is the same.
Find more words and make a list.

verb	noun
to kick	a kick
to throw	a throw
to pass	a ...
...	...

b) Words for people often add '-er' or '-or' to the verb (scor~~e~~ → scor+er, bat → batt+er).
Find more words and make a list.

verb	noun
to play	a player
to report	a reporter
to ride	a ...
...	...

4 The right preposition

a) *Complete the phrases. Use 'of' or 'from' and match them with the pictures.*

Example: the website **of** the Chicago Cubs

1. a player … Chicago
2. fans … the Chicago Cubs
3. the roof … a friend's house
4. a reporter … a newspaper
5. the name … the stadium
6. date … birth

b) *Match the adjectives and prepositions and use them in sentences.*

Example: 1. excited + d. about the match: Jane was very **excited about the match**.

1. excited	a. for the fans
2. different	b. in America
3. interested	c. with the game
4. interesting	d. about the match
5. sorry	e. in cricket
6. bored	f. for young players
7. popular	g. from other games

c) *Choose the right prepositions from the box and complete the sentences.*

Example: The game ended **in** hospital.

in ✓ • to • about • about • on • at • on

1. They came … Chicago to watch the match at Wrigley Field.
2. They were … the roof of a friend's house.
3. He told Derrek … the accident.
4. You can learn … this exciting sport on their website.
5. He lives … 3621 North Field, so he can often watch the matches.
6. You can find out more … the Internet or from sports magazines.

5 A game: Sports words (→ p. 12/ex. 23)

a) *Match the verbs and nouns. Example:* **score a goal**

kick | win | break | wear | score ✓ | send off

goal ✓ | player | match | leg | helmet | ball

b) *One of the group thinks of a sport and a word from it.*
The others have to use a verb with this word.

A: The sport is football. – The word is a **football**.
B: You can kick a football.
C: You can throw a football.
D: You can catch a football.
E: You can eat a football.
A: No, you can't. Now it's your turn.
E: OK. The sport is **swimming**. The word is a **swimsuit**.
A: You can … . *Go on, please.*

1 Things people do (simple present → G1) (→ p. 13/ex. 24)

Look at the pictures. Write the questions and the answers.

1 Derrek/watch/sometimes

2 Sue and Barbara/play/often

3 Marcia/enjoy/always

4 Mr Brown/buy/usually

5 Rob/ride bike to/at weekends

6 Fans/take flags to game/always

1. Does Derrek **watch** football on TV? – No, but he **sometimes** watches rugby.
2. Do Sue and Barbara **play** ... ? – No, but they ... . *Go on, please.*

2 Wrong facts (simple present → G1)

Correct these facts about different sports.

Example: Rugby players always wear hard helmets. – That's wrong. Rugby players **never** wear hard helmets. **American football players** wear them.

1. A football team has 15 players.
2. Derrek Lee plays for the Cincinnati Reds.
3. Beach volleyball players often use arm signals.
4. In baseball the pitcher tries to hit the ball with a bat.
5. Volleyball players always wear helmets.
6. In football the players can pass and catch the ball.
7. They play beach volleyball in a field.
8. In tennis a referee says the score.

3 A description: A crazy tennis match (present progressive → G2) (→ p. 13/ex. 25)

Describe this picture. What are the people doing/wearing/saying … ?

4 Mixed bag: No test tomorrow! (present tenses → G3) (→ p. 13/ex. 26)

Find the missing words. (Choose between the simple present or present progressive.)

On Mondays Rob usually (1) to the sports club after school. But today he (2) in his room and (3) all about the history of England for a History test.
He (4) not always (5) at the last minute but he forgot all about this test so now he (6) not (7) sports with the others.
At the moment he (8) to forget sports. Suddenly his mobile phone rings.
It's his friend's mum. She says there's no History test! So what (9) Rob (10) now?
He (11) his sports things into his bag, of course!

NOW YOU CAN

✓ describe a person.	→ *Describe someone in five sentences.*
✓ give information about yourself.	→ *Give five facts about yourself.*
✓ present a topic.	→ *Talk for two minutes about an interesting topic.*
✓ explain how you play a sport.	→ *Explain to your partner how you play baseball.*
✓ describe a picture.	→ *Describe the picture on page 10.*

1 New English words

DICTIONARY SKILLS

1. If you don't know the meaning of an English word, use an English-German dictionary.

   Example: A rabbit ran across the pitch.

2. Remember: The words in a dictionary are in alphabetical order. This means you must look at the letters after the first letter, too.

   Rabbit → rabies → race → racer →

rabbit ['ræbɪt] Kaninchen
rabies ['reɪbi:z] Tollwut
race [reɪs] ❶ Rennen; [Wett]Lauf

A rabbit without rabies won the race in his racer.

a) *Put these words in the right alphabetical order.*

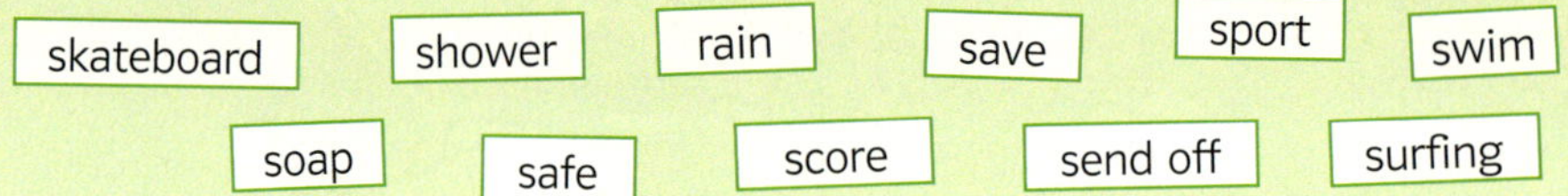

skateboard
shower
rain
save
sport
swim
soap
safe
score
send off
surfing

b) *Use a dictionary and find the meanings of 'safe'.*

2 Check the pronunciation[1]

If you don't know how to say a new word, look at the symbols in brackets[2] after the word. Most of the letters in the phonetic[3] alphabet are the same as the letters which you already know, so don't worry. There's a list in every dictionary.
Here is a secret[4] message. Can you read it?

haɪ nɪ'kəʊl. aɪ dʒʌst 'wɒntɪd tə seɪ ðæt wi: ɑ:r ɔ:l 'mi:tɪŋ æt ðə 'sɪnəmə æt sɪks ə'klɒk ðɪs 'i:vnɪŋ. həʊp ju: kæn bi: ðeə. 'rɒdʒə.

Here are some clues:
nɪ'kəʊl = Nicole
'sɪnəmə = cinema
sɪks ə'klɒk = six o'clock

3 Which meaning? (→ p. 14/ex. 1, 2)

Which meaning for 'fan' is correct in this sentence? Look in an English-German dictionary.

We had a big fan in our room so we felt nice and cool there.

4 Practise

Find the right translation[5] of the words in bold[6]. Use an English-German dictionary.

1. I **do** two miles in the pool every day.
2. He is in good **form** at the moment.
3. He tried to **head** the ball but it **hit** his arm.
4. Here is my **watch**. Can you **time** me, please?

[1]pronunciation [prəˌnʌnsi'eɪʃn] – *Aussprache,* [2]bracket ['brækɪt] – *Klammer,* [3]phonetic [fən'etɪk] – *phonetisch,* [4]secret ['si:krət] – *geheim,* [5]translation [trænz'leɪʃn] – *Übersetzung,* [6]in bold [bəʊld] – *fett*

5 The right meaning

Imagine you want to say 'We can meet (auf dem Platz) in front of the station', but you don't know the English word for 'Platz'. First find the meanings in a German-English dictionary. Then look at the sentences and pictures. Which meaning is right in your sentence?

1. The referee sent him off the field.

2. Sorry! There's no room for you here!

3. We can watch the match in the town square.

6 The right translation

Use a German-English dictionary and choose the right translation for the words in bold.

1. Er **hat** den Torpfosten **getroffen**.
   a. He hit ... / b. He met ... / c. He hurt ... → ... the goal post.

2. Der Torwart konnte den Ball nicht **halten**.
   The goalkeeper couldn't ... → a. ... support the ball. / b. ... stop the ball. / c. ... keep the ball.

3. Das Spiel war **schlecht**!
   The game was ... → a. ... bad. / b. ... badly. / c. ... sick.

4. Wir haben **Karten** für das Spiel morgen.
   a. We have maps ... / b. We have cards ... / c. We have tickets ... → ... for the game tomorrow.

7 More translations

Use a German-English dictionary and find the correct meanings.

Last week our youth club organized a dance competition for young people under/below/underneath [**unter**] 16. My friend and I took part[1]. We didn't win/gain [**gewinnen**] but it was/made [**machen**] a lot of fun. The price/reward/prize [**Preis**] for the best dancers[2] was five dancing[3] hours/lessons [**Stunden**] with a professional[4] teacher. But the worst dancers got something, too. It was two maps/tickets/cards [**Karten**] for a rugby game/play/set [**Spiel**] at Twickenham. The boy from the couple/pair [**Paar**] that won the competition was not very happy/lucky [**glücklich**]. He was a real rugby fan. But the girl from the other pair/couple [**Paar**] didn't like rugby, so they made/did [**machen**] a swap.

[1]to take part [teɪk 'pɑ:t] – *teilnehmen*, [2]dancer ['dɑ:nsə] – *Tänzer/in*, [3]dancing ['dɑ:nsɪŋ] – *Tanz*, [4]professional [prə'feʃnl] – *professionell*

THE TOUR[1]

When cycling fans talk about 'the Tour', they always mean the Tour de France. What's that, some of you ask? Well, it's the most famous bike race in the world. You know what the World Cup is, don't you? Well, for cycling fans the 'Tour' is like a World Cup.
It's very dangerous, too. Every year there are accidents. Most of them are not really bad.

But sometimes riders die[2]. In 1995 for example an Italian rider crashed[3] at 88 km[4] an hour. He died and they think this was because he didn't have his helmet on.
Now all riders must wear helmets at all times during the race. The 'Tour' is the most difficult bike race in the world and the rules are difficult, too. But we'll try to explain some of them. There is a race nearly every day during three weeks in July. The men ride in teams. The teams cycle more than three thousand kilometres before the race ends in Paris. Sometimes the tour goes into other countries, for example to Spain, Germany or the UK.

There are three different groups of races:

1. A race where all riders start at the same time.
2. A time race for each rider.
3. A time race for each team.

There are other competitions in the Tour, too. One of them is the points competition. Riders get points for their position[5] in a race. The man with the most points after all the races gets a green jersey. But the race for the yellow jersey is more important. The man with the shortest time for all the races together wears it in the next race.

[1]tour [tʊə] – *Rundfahrt, Tour,* [2]to die [daɪ] – *sterben,* [3]to crash [kræʃ] – *stürzen,*
[4]kilometre (km) ['kɪləʊˌmiːtə; kɪ'lɒmɪtə] – *Kilometer,* [5]position [pə'zɪʃn] – *Position,* [6]serious ['sɪəriəs] – *ernst*

A Reading

1 Read the text and complete the sentences.

a. The 'Tour de France' is a famous … .
b. In 1995 there was a serious[6] … .
c. The race is always in the month of … .
d. The Tour goes into other … .
e. There are three groups of … .
f. In the Tour there is a points … .
g. The man with the most points wears … .
h. The race for the yellow jersey is more … .

2 Complete the sentence.

The rider who gets the yellow jersey is …

a. the rider with the most points.
b. one of the riders in the fastest team.
c. the fastest French rider.
d. the man with the shortest time for all the races.

3 Look at the photo and text and find the missing word in each sentence.

a. The men in the photo are wearing … on their heads.
b. They must wear them at all … when they are in a race.
c. They have had this rule since an Italian rider … and died.

B Language

Find the right prepositions in the text.

a. cycling fans talk … the 'Tour'
b. the most famous bike race … the world
c. most … them are not really bad
d. crashed … 88 kilometres an hour
e. must wear helmets … the race
f. different groups … races
g. the man … the most points
h. the race … the yellow jersey

C Mediation and communication

Help your English friend, Tom, in a cycle shop.

Tom: Please tell the shop assistant that I need a helmet. But I don't want to buy one. I only want to borrow one for the weekend.
You: …
Assistant: Kein Problem. Wir haben hier einige alte. Probier sie mal!
You: …
Tom: The blue helmet is too big but the red helmet fits really well. Can I borrow it until Monday?
You: …
Assistant: Montags bin ich nicht hier. Aber Dienstag ist auch o.k.
You: …

, 13
D Listening

Listen to the radio report[1] and answer the questions.

a. Where are the riders?
b. What is the weather like?
c. Why will two riders lose even more time?

E Writing

1 An article for a school magazine

Think about a sports event that you have been to. Write 35–40 words about it. Write down:
– what sport it was.
– where it happened.
– who won.

2 Your opinion

"People shouldn't do dangerous sports."
Say why you think this opinion is right or wrong. Give two reasons.

[1]report [rɪ'pɔːt] – *Bericht*

Unit 2 Out and about in London

DID YOU KNOW?

- From a capsule on the London Eye you get spectacular views of the Palace of Westminster and Big Ben.
- The Royal Family are just some of the famous people who live in London. Their London home is Buckingham Palace.
- In the scary London Dungeon Museum you can relive some of the most terrible events in the history of London – even the Great Fire of 1666.
- Don't wait in bus queues or traffic jams. 'Tube' trains are much faster. On the Tube you'll go far!
- Most people have heard of Harrods but London has over 40,000 other shops – some of the trendiest are in the King's Road.
- They built the Tower in the 11th century. It's one of the oldest buildings in London. You can see the most valuable jewels in the world there: the Crown Jewels.

1 Remember London

a) *What do you remember about London? Make a mind map.*

b) *Match the captions with the photos.*

L1, 14

2 Let's listen: Sounds of London

Look at the photos and listen. Where are the people?

Example: 1. The people are at **Buckingham Palace**.

At the London Dungeon Museum
On the London Eye
At the Tower of London
In the London Underground (Tube)
In a department store
The Royal Family at Buckingham Palace

3 Facts and photos (→ p. 17/ex. 1, 2)

a) *Describe the nouns and match them with the photos.*

Example: Photo 5: Some of the shops are trendy.

shops ✓ • Tube trains • museums • buildings • views • jewels • people

b) *Choose one photo and talk about it.*

4 A city of superlatives

scariest | … | most valuable

Collect superlatives for London.

Example: London has one of the **scariest** museums in Britain. It also has some of the … .

5 Let's talk: Let's spend a day in London

What do you want to do, see or visit in London? Plan the day and discuss it.

A: Let's have breakfast at … . – B: OK. Then we can … . / Oh, no. Let's … .

8:00 – have breakfast
9:00 – go to Tube station
9:30 – visit the Tower
…

You use **the simple past** to describe what happened in the past.
The tourist **was** in a queue.
The police **stopped** the pickpocket.
He **got onto** the Tube at Monument.
How **did** he **do** it?
What **did** the pickpocket **get**?
There **wasn't** any money in the wallet.
The pickpocket **didn't escape** from the police.
Did he **steal** any money?
Were the police faster than the pickpocket?

→ G4

1 How did he do it? (→ p. 18/ex. 3–5; p. 19/ex. 6, 7)

a) This story was in a local newspaper in London.
Read the text.

b) *Where was the pickpocket? Find all the places on the map at the front of your book.*

c) *Read the text again. Describe the pickpocket's route on the Underground. Start like this:*
He **got onto** the Tube at Monument. He **took** the Circle Line to Embankment. Then he **changed** to the Bakerloo Line. He **got off** at … .

to get onto
to take the … Line to …
to change to …
to get off at

The fastest pickpocket in London

Today the police stopped the fastest pickpocket in London, James R. (15).
Thanks to the Underground, he robbed five people at five different places in London within two hours. How did he do it? He left home at 9 o'clock and got onto the Tube at Monument and stole a baseball jacket from another teenager. At half past nine the pickpocket stole again at Piccadilly Circus. He pushed a young woman on a busy Tube train and ran away with her handbag. Half an hour later he stole a businessman's wallet at Covent Garden. At half past ten he stole a rucksack from a young tourist who was in a queue at Marble Arch station. At 11 o'clock the police finally caught James R. when he tried to steal a camera from a boy at St Paul's Cathedral. And what did the pickpocket get for his trouble? A jacket which was too small, a handbag with ten different lip balms, a wallet with four bills and no money, a rucksack with dirty clothes and a toy camera. And what else did he get? A £100 fine and he has to collect rubbish in St James's Park for the next two months. Sometimes the police are faster than the Underground.

famous ones

London people

A lot of rich women have homes in or near London. The ones in the pictures here are not only rich, they are famous, too.

Only the Queen was born rich. The other younger ones have all worked to become rich. The blonde-haired one on the left is a singer.

There are four women in the pictures. The oldest one is the Queen. She's the one on the right with the big hat.

The dark-haired one next to the Queen is an actress and the other one who is smiling is a model.

2 Who's who? (→ p. 19/ex. 8)

Naomi Campbell
Queen Elizabeth II
Madonna
Angelina Jolie

a) *Do you know the names of the four famous women in the pictures? Who's who?*
Example: Naomi Campbell is **the one** who is … . She is between … .

b) *Now write a short text about the men in the pictures.*
Example: A lot of rich men … . **The ones** in the pictures … .

the youngest • the sportiest • the trendiest • the tallest one(s) …

▶ **The ones** in the pictures … .
… is the youngest **one.**

G5

Robbie Williams

David Beckham

Prince William

Prince Harry

3 A role play: Shopping at Harrods

Your partner is the shop assistant. *Complete the dialogues.*

A: Good morning. I'd like to buy some souvenirs for my family.
B: What about some posters? There are some interesting **ones** over there.
A: This **one** is great but it's too big.
B: What about that **one**? *Go on, please.*

people	things	☺	☹
family Dad friends sisters brother aunt	some posters a book about the Tower some CDs a T-shirt … …	interesting great lovely …	long big expensive …

The Eye-dea

The idea for the London Eye (1) began on a kitchen table in a flat in London in 1993. Julia Marks and David Barnfield (2) read about a millennium competition. After they had talked about it, they decided to enter it. They wanted to build a landmark which gave people a new and exciting view of London from the sky. They didn't win the competition but after they had worked so hard on it, they didn't want to give up their dream. They talked to reporters about it. After they had explained their idea, the reporters wrote articles for their newspapers and soon British Airways (BA) heard about it. The dream began to come true.

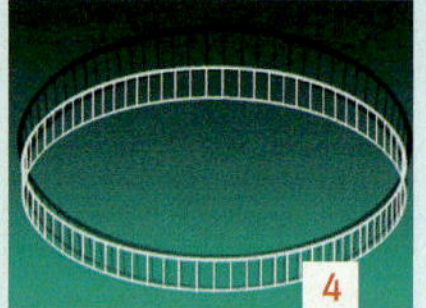

The two architects made a model (3) before they started to work on the real 'Eye'. They built the rim (4) first from four large pieces. When they had completed the wheel, they slowly lifted it (5). After they had lifted it, they added a platform for visitors and fixed capsules to it. The London Eye is like the wheel of a huge bike but the rim is 400 times larger than the rim on a normal bike. It is now one of the most popular landmarks in the world.

1 First things first

Read the text and look at the pictures. How did the architects make the wheel?
Start like this: First they designed the wheel for a competition. Then they … .

2 Towards a dream (→ p. 20/ex. 9–11; p. 21/ex. 12)

What did the architects say? Match the parts and make sentences.

Example: 1. After we **had heard** about the competition, we **decided** to enter it.

1. After we had heard about the competition,
2. When we had talked about it,
3. After we had worked so hard on the plans,
4. After a man from BA had read about it,
5. After we had made a model,
6. When we had put the rim pieces together,
7. After we had lifted the wheel,
8. After we had finished it,

a. he phoned us.
b. we first saw London from it in 1999.
c. we added a platform and capsules to it.
d. we decided to enter it.
e. we didn't want to give up our dream.
f. we drew our plans for the 'Eye'.
g. we constructed the real 'Eye'.
h. we completed the wheel.

3 From fortress to museum (→ p. 21/ex. 13)

1 fortress

2 royal palace

3 castle

4 prison

5 menagerie

6 museum

Look at the pictures and complete the text. Use the simple past or the past perfect.

After William the Conqueror **had become** (*become*) king in 1066, he **decided** (*decide*) to build a fortress in London. After he … (*design*) it, his men … (*start*) to build it in 1078. But William … (*die*) before they … (*finish*) it. When they … (*finish*) it, the people … (*call*) it the Great Tower. William never … (*live*) there but later kings … (*use*) it as a royal palace. In the 13th and 14th centuries they … (*add*) a lot of towers and buildings. After they … (*build*) these, the tower … (*become*) a castle and a prison. From the 13th to the 19th century there … (*be*) also a menagerie in the Tower with lots of wild animals. But they … (*close*) it in 1835 after they … (*build*) London Zoo. Visitors first … (*come*) to the Tower in the 16th century. Today the Tower is a museum.

▶ After he **had become** king, … .
When they **had finished**, … .
→ G6

4 For my folder: Different uses

a) *Complete the text. Use the verbs from the box.*

had used • became • built • had died • sold • married • opened • decided

This is a photo of the Lutherhaus in Wittenberg. They … it as a monastery in 1504. When Luther … Katharina von Bora, it … their home. After Luther … , his family … the house to Wittenberg University. After the university … it for many different things, they … to put the museum there. In spring 2003 they … the Luther exhibition there.

 b) *Think of a building in your town. Write about it.*

READING

Skimming:
Finding the main ideas

1. Before you read:
   Look at the picture. What does it show?
   Read the title. What does it mean?
   Think. What could the text be about?
2. Skim the text. Don't read every word.
   Just look out for key words.
3. Ask: When? Who? What? Where? Why?
   Write notes. *Example:*

A landmark in London

In the **11th century William built the Tower** on the river Thames **to protect the city of London** from its dangerous enemies.

One of the most frightening events in the history of London was the Great Fire of 1666. You can relive it at the London Dungeon in the exhibition 'Firestorm 1666'. *Use the skills box and find out more.*

4/5 = four fifths
3/4 = three quarters

The 1666 Great Fire of London (→ p. 22/ex. 14)

In 1666 the Great Fire of London destroyed four fifths of the old city of London and many buildings outside the walls. At that time people usually built houses with wood and straw. On 1st September 1666 in Pudding Lane, near the Tower of London, the king's baker finished the bread for the king and his family and went to bed. But he forgot to put out the fire in his kitchen. Early the next morning he woke up suddenly. He could smell smoke. Sparks had jumped onto some straw and a fire had started in the kitchen. He woke his family and they escaped over the roof of the house. Soon all the houses in Pudding Lane were in flames. A wind from the east blew the flames across the old city and the fire burnt for four days. There was no fire brigade at that time but people tried to stop the fire. They used water from the Thames. Some of them even destroyed their own houses before the fire came near them but that didn't help. The fire didn't damage many stone buildings like the Tower of London. But it destroyed 13,200 houses. It even destroyed half of London Bridge. It was a stone bridge but there were houses on it and they burnt very quickly. Most people in London were lucky. The fire killed only six of them. Many people escaped. They went down the river in boats. Or they went to the country around London with their families and animals.

L1, 15 1 Let's listen: Out and about in London (→ p. 23/ex. 15)

a) *Before you listen: What can you see in the pictures? What can you say about the places?*

b) *Listen and match the pictures with the announcements.*

1 in the Tower

2 at a museum

3 on a boat

4 at a station

c) *Listen again. What is wrong in these sentences?*

1. This train is for Greenwich only.
2. Jane White's sister got lost in the Great Tower.
3. The visitors should leave now because there is a fire in the museum.
4. The Tower of London is between Tower Bridge and Buckingham Bridge.

L1, 16 2 Let's listen: What does it mean here?

a) *Write these words in English:*

1. [faɪn] ❶ o.k. ❷ Geldstrafe
2. [breɪk] ❶ Pause ❷ zerbrechen
3. ['faɪə] ❶ Brand ❷ Kaminfeuer
4. [tʃeɪndʒ] ❶ Änderung ❷ Wechselgeld

b) The English words in part a) can have different meanings.
Listen to eight dialogues. Which meaning of which word is correct?

L1, 17 3 Let's listen: Could I have your attention, please? (→ p. 23/ex. 16, 17; p. 24/ex. 18)

a) *Listen. Where are we?*

b) *Listen again. Can you guess what 'ladies and gentlemen' and 'customer' mean?*

c) *What is 'the black one'? What is in it?*

L1, 18 4 A song: Landing in London

(Text: B. Arnold, R.T. Harrell, Chr. L. Henderson, M. D. Roberts © Songs of Universal)

I woke up today in London
As the plane was touching down[1]
And all I could think about was Monday
When maybe I'd be back around.
If this keeps me away[2] much longer
I don't know what I would do.

You've got to[3] understand it's a hard life
That I'm going through[4].
And when the night falls in[5] around me
I don't think I'll make it through[6].
I'll use your light to guide[7] the way
'cause all I think about is you.

Which lines tell you that the singer has problems, hopes he will be back on Monday, is missing someone?

[1]to touch down [tʌtʃ 'daʊn] – *landen,* [2]to keep s.o. away [ˌki:p‿ə'weɪ] – *jdn. fernhalten,* [3]you've got to [ju:v 'gɒt tə] – *du musst,* [4]to go through [gəʊ 'θru:] – *durchmachen,* [5]to fall in [fɔ:l‿'ɪn] – *hereinbrechen,* [6]to make it through [ˌmeɪk‿ɪt 'θru:] – *durchhalten,* [7]to guide [gaɪd] – *führen*

L1, 19–22 Voices of London

A "My name is Suzanne. I'm training to be a gardener and in the summer months I work as a bike courier. The job is great but I sometimes have to get to a place very quickly and there's a lot of pollution in the city. It can be really dangerous because car drivers often don't see me on my bike. I hated helmets until I got this job. Now my helmet has become a part of me. Once it even saved my life! If you're on a bike, believe me, you don't argue with a big red London bus! I've carried some really strange or funny things as a courier: a tin of *Sauerkraut*, pink rubber boots, a bag of rubbish, a sponge, a judge's wig, cat food – and there are many more on my list."

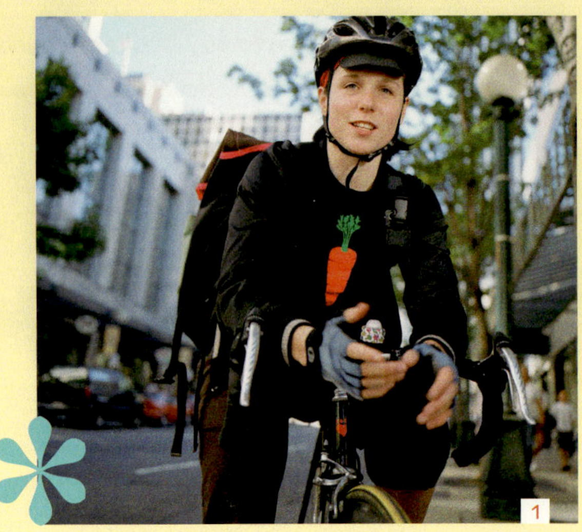
1

2

B "Hi, I'm James Cartwright! What's my job? I'm a milkman. It's true! I have a milk round in Acton. There aren't many of us left now in London. My grandad was a milkman and so was my dad, so it's something like a family tradition. Of course, the job is a bit different today: They worked for a dairy but I've started my own one-man company. I have to do much more than just deliver milk. I have to get up at the crack of dawn but the job is, in fact, really interesting because I meet so many people. A lot of my customers have known me since I was a kid. And when I come to collect the empty milk bottles, I often find little cakes or sweets at the door!"

C "I'm Reg, and I drive one of those London taxis. If you want to be a taxi driver in this city, you have to spend six months just learning where all the streets are! I've done this job for 15 years so I know London like the back of my hand! I love my job. All kinds of people take taxis so I meet some interesting people. Last week I took David Beckham to the airport. I asked him for his autograph. Not for me, for my kids, of course. My job can be boring, but I listen to CDs when I'm in a queue of traffic. I also have a CD 'Deutsch in 20 Tagen'. When I drive German tourists, I practise my German on them. You should see their faces! They don't expect a London taxi driver to say, *Guten Tag! Wohin möchten Sie?*"

3

D "Hi, I'm Pru. No, I'm not a punk! I'm a hairdresser at Accent in Shoreditch – I only began there last year but I've already learnt to do some fantastic styles – and I learn more every day. I really love my work there. It is more like a hobby to me. When I left school, I worked in a post office but it was a bit boring. This job is different. You know, a few of my regulars are big names on TV and they chat to me about their lives. I can tell you, it's as exciting as any of those TV soaps! I once got so interested in a spicy story that I made a real mess of the woman's hair. But I was lucky – she just thought it was a cool, new style!"

1 Before you read: Jobs

a) *Look at the pictures. What do you think these people do in their jobs?*

b) *What jobs do you know? Make a mind map.*

2 Things they said

Read these sentences.
Who said the same things in different words?

1. My customers often tell me interesting stories.
2. They're surprised when I speak German.
3. I only do this job in July and August.
4. You don't see many people now who do my job.
5. The air where I work is very unhealthy.
6. I know London really well.

3 A day from a diary (→ p. 25/ex. 19)

Imagine you are one of the people in the texts. Write a diary entry for one day.

Thursday 16th.
I got up late because … .
I ate cornflakes and … for breakfast.
My first customer was … .
At … I had lunch.

4 More information

Choose one of the people and write what he/she likes to do in his/her free time. You can start like this:
After work I like to … .
At the weekends I often … .

5 For my folder: A dream job

Find a picture of someone who is doing your dream job. Write about his or her day. What does he or she do? When? Where? Why is it your dream job?

This is …. He's a DJ in the …. He works from Friday to Sunday. He always starts in the evening at ….

1 London words (→ p. 26/ex. 20)

a) *Collect words, phrases and photos and make a mind map for London.*

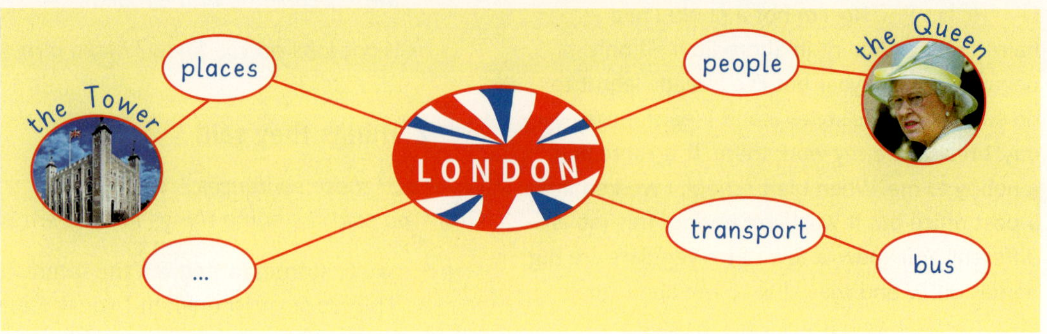

b) *Tell your partner about one of the topics in part a).*

2 Words from words

Copy the grids into your exercise book. Complete them. Use your dictionary and add more words to the lists.

1.

to ...	married
to frighten	...
to worry	...

2.

interested	interesting
bored	...
...	exciting

3.

sport	sporty
rain	...
...	funny

4.

happy	happily
quick	...
...	slowly

3 How do they feel? (→ p. 26/ex. 21)

a) *Match the sentences with these words.*

excited | sick | bored | angry | frightened

1. These pictures are really scary.
2. I don't think this place is very interesting.
3. That was a really stupid and dangerous thing to do.
4. Let's go home, my stomach hurts.
5. Look, there's the Queen! She's waving at us!

b) *Collect more words which say how people feel. Put them into one of these lists.*

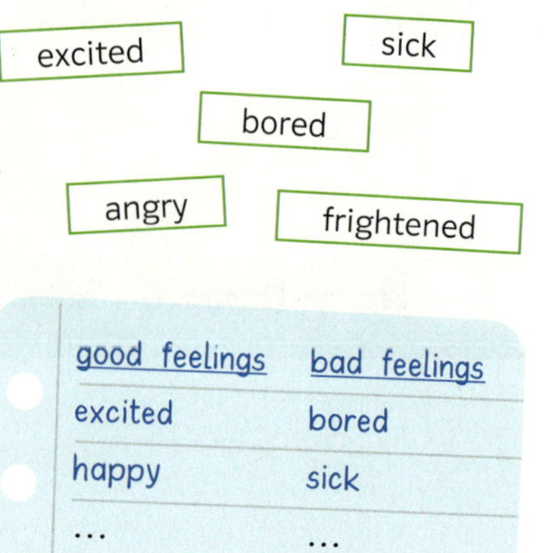

c) *Talk to a partner.*

A: When do you feel excited?
B: I feel excited when it's my birthday.
When do you feel bored?
A: I feel bored when ... .

4 Let's look: Questions from visitors

What do the people ask? What can you answer?

Example: 1. Excuse me. How do I get to the nearest … ? – The nearest … is/are in … . Go down … .

5 Numbers

Fill in the missing numbers and say the sentences.

1. In the … century there was a really big fire in London.
2. It started on … September.
3. This fire destroyed … of the city.
4. They built the Tower in the … century.
5. The rim of the 'Eye' is … times larger than the wheel of a bike.
6. Taxi drivers learn the street names for … a year.

1st | 4/5 | 400 | ½ | 11th | 17th

6 What's the word? (→ p. 26/ex. 22, 23)

Find the right word.

1. A fashion which is new is a … .
2. This is lots of people in a line.
3. A woman actor is an … .
4. A … person is someone with a lot of money.
5. He/she makes plans for buildings.
6. This means 'to bring things to a house/shop'.

1 At the Science Museum (simple past → G4)

a) *Read the text and put the verbs in the simple past. Start like this:* Last Saturday it **was** … .

On Saturday it is Jamie's birthday. Jamie and his friends go to the Science Museum. They take the Underground there. The trip isn't long so they get to the museum early. They buy their tickets and decide to go to the flight lab first because they don't want to wait in the long queues later. They really like it.
Then they want to see the old Concorde but they can't find it. They ask a man in uniform. He's very nice and shows them where to go.
Before they leave, they visit the museum shop. There are lots of interesting things there and fantastic posters, too. Jamie's friends give him a great present: He can choose something from the shop!
He chooses a model of his favourite car.

b) *What's wrong in the sentences?*

1. It wasn't **Jamie's friend's** birthday, it was **Jamie's** birthday.
2. They didn't watch …, … . *Go on, please.*

1. It was Jamie's friend's birthday.
2. They watched a science film.
3. They went there by bus.
4. They stole the tickets!
5. They wanted to have a snack first.
6. They hated the flight lab.
7. They visited the toilets.
8. Jamie got a poster from his friends.

2 Can you remember? (simple past → G4) (→ p. 27/ex. 24)

a) *Make questions. Example:* 1. When did the Great Fire happen?

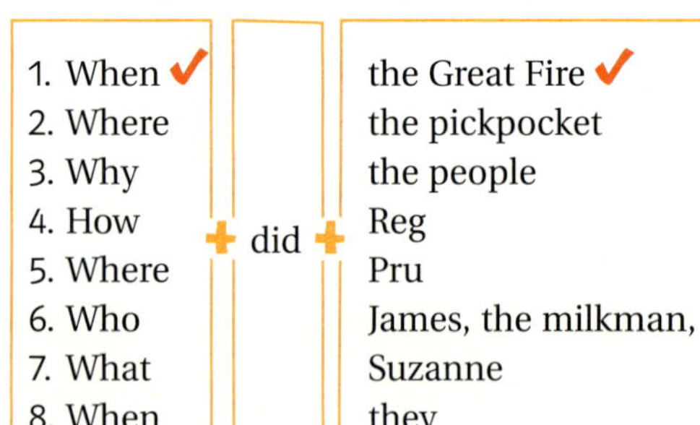

	+		+	
1. When ✓		the Great Fire ✓		steal the rucksack?
2. Where		the pickpocket		go to the river?
3. Why		the people		build the Tower of London?
4. How	did	Reg		get cakes or sweets from?
5. Where		Pru		hate until she became a courier?
6. Who		James, the milkman,		work before she started at Accent?
7. What		Suzanne		happen? ✓
8. When		they		meet David Beckham?

b) *Look at the key words in the box. Write the answers.*

Example: 1. The Great Fire happened in … .
2. He stole it at … . *Go on, please.*

post office • Marble Arch • escape from the fire • helmets • 11th century • customers • take to airport • 1666

3 A class photo

(one, ones → G5) (→ p. 27/ex. 25)

Fill in 'one' or 'ones'.

We took some great photos on our trip to London. The most spectacular … were from the London Eye but this … in the London Dungeon is my favourite. On the left you can see our teacher. She's the … with blond hair. The pupils here are all in my class. I'm the … on the right with the brown sweatshirt. The … at the front are my best friends. The two tall … at the back are idiots. They're always in trouble. And the … in the centre is the worst kid in the school.

4 Mixed bag: A terrible trip to London

(simple past + past perfect → G6) (→ p. 27/ex. 26)

Choose the right tense and complete the text.

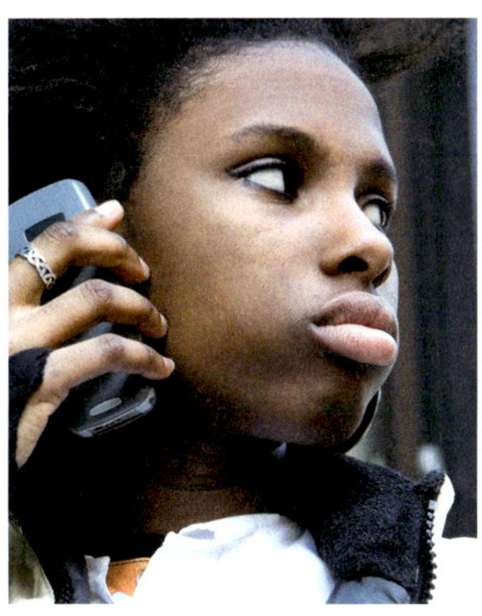

Yesterday I (1) (*come*) back from a school trip to London. We all (2) (*have*) a terrible time. The journey there (3) (*be*) really boring but a bit later we (4) (*forget*) about that. It (5) (*get*) worse and worse.
On the first day we (6) (*go*) on the London Eye. The weather was bad – worse than in Manchester. It (7) (*be*) rainy and foggy. We (8) (*get*) better views than that in Manchester last winter! After we (9) (*see*) a few boring buildings from our capsule, we then (10) (*go*) to visit them.
Some of them (11) (*be*) more spectacular in photos. I (12) (*not/like*) the Tower of London. There (13) (*be*) people everywhere. After we (14) (*leave*) it, we (15) (*go*) to the London Dungeon. I thought this (16) (*be*) the best part of the trip. But one or two of the girls (17) (*not/feel*) very well, so we (18) (*go*) back outside again. They (19) (*not/look*) really sick. I think they just (20) (*want*) something to eat. After the teacher (21) (*buy*) them an ice-cream, they suddenly (22) (*look*) happier. But the rest of us (23) (*be*) fed up.

NOW YOU CAN

- ✓ describe an interesting place. → *Describe an interesting place in your town in five sentences.*
- ✓ say how to get from 'A' to 'B'. → *Tell your partner how to get to places in your town.*
- ✓ describe a photo of a group of people. → *Describe a photo of your class or family.*
- ✓ use 'after' and 'when' to talk about actions and events. → *Tell your partner in five sentences about what you did last Saturday. Use 'after' and 'when'.*
- ✓ collect important facts from a text. → *Give your partner a short summary of the text on page 28.*

1 The pictures

Look at the pictures. What's happening? What do you think?

2 The texts (→ p. 28/ex. 1)

a) *Read texts 1–3 without a dictionary. What do you think is in the bag?*

1. Last Saturday Sue Brady, a bike courier, was in South Kensington when her mobile rang. A customer needed something from Harrods at once. That wasn't a problem because Sue was near it. She set off quickly.

2. Two minutes later she arrived at Harrods. But she didn't know what to do with her bike. She couldn't carry it into the shop so she left it with the doorman who was a bit surprised. The young man just said, "No problem!"

3. Ten minutes later the girl came out again with a huge bag in her arms. It was heavy but the doorman said, "Let me help you." They fixed it onto the bike which Sue then pushed. She felt stupid but she couldn't ride it.

b) *Read the texts again and look up any new words in your dictionary.*

c) *What important information does each part give you?*

part	Who?	Where?	When?	What?	Why?
1	Sue Brady	South ...	last ...	mobile ...	...

3 The language (→ p. 28/ex. 2, 3)

a) *Look at the verbs in the texts. Most of them are in the 'simple past'. Why?*

b) Conjunctions[1] are important when you write a story. *Find more of them in the story.*

c) Adjectives and adverbs can make a story more interesting. *Make two lists.*

d) *Find pronouns[2] in the text.*

e) *What do you think the customer and Sue said in part 1?*

WRITING A STORY SKILLS

1. Story about sth. in the past = simple past
2. Use conjunctions and relative clauses[3]: but, because, so, who, …
3. Use adjectives and adverbs: young, quickly, …
4. Use pronouns and other words:
   Sue Brady → the courier, the girl, she
   the doorman → the young man, he
5. Use direct speech[4]:
   He just said, "No problem!"

[1]conjunction [kən'dʒʌŋkʃn] – *Bindewort*, [2]pronoun ['prəʊnaʊn] – *Pronomen*, [3]relative clause ['relətɪv ˌklɔːz] – *Relativsatz*, [4]direct speech [ˌdɪrekt 'spiːtʃ] – *direkte Rede*

4 The next parts of a story

a) *Look at the next pictures from the story. Write notes and look up words which you need.*

4. push bike
   outside …
   hot …
   …

5. at gates
   talk to guard[1]
   …
   …

b) *Now write a short text for pictures 4 and 5. Check your tenses. Have you used enough conjunctions? Have you got some adjectives and adverbs? What about pronouns? Where could you use direct speech?*

5 The end of the story

a) *Look at picture 6. What do you now think was in the bag? Why do you think this?*

b) *Read the two endings. Which text is better English and why?*

1. They went into the kitchen. The Queen was there. There were a lot of dogs there, too. The dogs were very loud. The dogs were very hungry. The servant[2] opened the tins. The servant gave the food to the dogs. The dogs were very happy. The Queen was very happy, too. The dogs only liked this food.

2. Ten minutes later Sue entered the palace kitchen with a servant. The Queen was there but she looked unhappy. Her dogs were really noisy[3] because they were very hungry. Sue nervously gave the huge bag to the servant who quickly opened the tins and gave the food to the hungry dogs. They ate it noisily but that didn't worry the Queen. She was happy again and she said to Sue, "Thank you! They don't like any other dog food. Now let's have a cup of tea!"

c) *Find a good title for the story.*

6 For my folder: Sue's story

What do you think Sue told her friend that evening? Write at least five sentences.
Start like this: This afternoon I was on my bike in … .

[1]guard [gɑːd] – *Wachmann,* [2]servant ['sɜːvnt] – *Diener/Dienerin,* [3]noisy ['nɔɪzi] – *laut*

Young people in London

Did you know that there is a new website for young people in London? It is for young people and young people helped to make it. One part of the website is just for teenagers. 16-year-old Toni Ann helped to put the website together. She told our reporter, "It's a great idea. We usually know about events and activities near where we live. But London is a really big city. On the website you can find out about other places, too."

She says that she and her friends will use the website in the future. "The website is fun and it has lots of information on things like buses, trains and special events. But it isn't only for information. Many young people in London have difficult lives. They have problems at school with teachers or with bullies or at home with parents or with friends. Some come from other countries and don't speak English well. So they can write about their problems and ask for advice."

15-year-old Terry said, "I feel the website is important. I know lots of people who worry about things like drugs[1], bullying[2] and healthy food. They don't always want to talk to their parents or teachers. Here they can find telephone numbers and addresses of people who can help them."

Kingsley, 13, thinks that young people will find it interesting. "We've sent information about the website to every school in London. All young people should know about it. If they need information or help, they can ask questions. But the website can only work if young people know about it," says Kingsley.

[1]drugs [drʌgz] – *Drogen*, [2]bullying ['bʊlɪŋ] – *Tyrannisierung*

A Reading

1 Read the text. Are the sentences right or wrong?

a. London is a really big city.
b. Toni Ann helped to make the website.
c. The website is only for information.
d. The website is for parents.
e. Terry feels it is important.
f. All schools in London know about it.

2 Answer the questions.

a. Who is the website for?
b. What does Toni Ann think about the website?
c. What do many young people worry about?

B Language

Find words in the text which mean the opposite:

a. boring
b. old
c. terrible
d. unhealthy
e. enemies
f. answers

C Skills

Read the page from a dictionary and translate[1] the underlined words.

a. She works every evening.
b. This computer doesn't work.
c. He is fit for work now.
d. My mum is out of work.
e. I don't like office work.

work[1] [wɜːk] ❶ Arbeit; **at work** bei der Arbeit; **casual work** Gelegenheitsarbeit; **clerical** [*oder* **office**] **work** Schreibarbeit, Büroarbeit; **fit for work** arbeitsfähig; **be in work** Arbeit [*oder* einen Stelle] haben; **be out of work** arbeitslos sein ❷ [Arbeits]Leistung; **his work is very thorough** er arbeitet sehr gründlich ❸ (*geistlich*) Werk; **works of Shakespeare** Werke von Shakespeare;

work[2] [wɜːk] ❶ arbeiten (**on** an) **who does he work** for) wo ist er beschäftigt [*oder* bei wem arbeitet er]?; **she works at Smith's** sie arbeitet bei Smith's; **work towards something** auf etwas hinarbeiten; **work oneself hard** hart arbeiten, sich viel abverlangen; **work one's way through something** sich durch etwas durcharbeiten ❷ *Gerät, Plan*: funktionieren; **it won't work** das klappt nicht; **he worked it so th...**

D Mediation and communication

A friend from London is in your school. She has a question for the school secretary, who doesn't speak English. You help her.

Visitor: I need to find out about transport to the stadium tomorrow.
You: …
Secretary: Frage deine Freundin, wann sie von hier abfahren will.
You: …
Visitor: I need to be at the stadium by 2 o'clock.
You: …
Secretary: Dann kann sie mit dem Bus fahren, der um 13:24 vor der Schule abfährt.
You: …

23 ◎
E Listening

Listen to two young Americans. Which four problems in London do they talk about?

traffic jams | bullying | drugs | healthy food | noise | pickpockets

F Writing

1 An e-mail to a friend

Tell your friend (5–6 sentences) about the website for young people in London. Start like this:
Hi, … ! I have just read about a new website for … .
Finish like this:
I'll send you the address if you like.
Yours, (*your name*)

2 Your opinion

"Every school should have its own website."
Is this right or wrong? Why? Write two sentences.

[1]to translate [træns'leɪt] – *übersetzen*

Unit 3 Here we come!

1 Places on the map of the British Isles

a) *Which places do you already know? What do you know about them?*

b) The places in photos 2–4 are in South England. *Where are they on the map? What can you see and do there?*

2 Facts on the British Isles (→ p. 29/ex. 1)

1. Which is bigger – the British Isles or the UK?
2. The coastline is very long. What is good about this? What is bad?
3. How can you travel to the UK?

1 Map of the British Isles 2 The beach in Brighton 3 The White Cliffs of Dover 4 An ancient circle of stones: Stonehenge

DID YOU KNOW?

- The British Isles = The United Kingdom (UK) + The Republic of Ireland and some smaller islands. The United Kingdom = England, Northern Ireland, Scotland, Wales
- Together the islands have a coastline of almost 50,000 km (Germany has 2,389 km). Of course this makes it more difficult for UK Customs officers to catch smugglers. But the good thing is that it doesn't take more than 1 ½ hours by car from anywhere to the coast!
- You can't travel to the UK by car. At Calais, in France, you can drive onto a train which goes across the Channel through the "Chunnel" (Channel Tunnel) to Folkestone.
- You can also go by ferry – but most people fly and land at Heathrow Airport, the airport with the highest number of international passengers in the world.
- Southampton is an important port for cruise ships and ocean liners. The Titanic sailed from here on 10th April 1912.

L1, 24

3 Let's listen: Voices from the south (→ p. 29/ex. 2)

You will hear five dialogues. The people are on or near the south coast of England.

a) *Listen and look at the map. Where are the speakers?*
In dialogue 1 the speakers are … .
Go on, please.

b) *Listen again and find the answers.*

1. Where does the swimmer want to go?
2. What can you see from the plane?
3. Why do the women take the ferry? What do you think?
4. How long is the Channel Tunnel?

c) *How would you like to travel to the British Isles? Why?*

4 For my folder: South England

Find out more about one of the places in South England on the Internet. Make a poster and present it to the class.

Visit Dover!
See the famous White Cliffs
or visit Dover Castle!

▶ **Can/can't (cannot)** and **must/mustn't** are **modal auxiliary verbs.**
You use **can/can't** to talk about a skill or a rule, or to say what is possible:
– I can swim. You **can't** swim here. It **can** be dangerous.
You use **must/mustn't** to give a rule about something:
– You **must** listen to the lifeguard. You **mustn't** swim when the red flag is flying.
Remember: mustn't = nicht dürfen, **needn't** = nicht müssen

→ G7

Water, water, everywhere!

So you love sand, sun and sea air? Then you can have a great time on the south coast of England. It's a real paradise for fans of water sports. Of course, it rains more often than in Spain. And you can't always run around in a swimsuit, but it can get very warm in the summer. The highest temperature on record is 38.5 °C.

There are hundreds of clean, sandy beaches. Many of them have lifeguards and flags because the sea can be dangerous. You can't just swim in it like in a big swimming pool. You needn't worry but you must be sensible: When the red flag is flying, you mustn't swim. And you must listen to the lifeguard. When it isn't safe, he'll tell you to leave the water.

You can learn to surf, windsurf, sail or canoe. You can also go fishing and you may play beach volleyball. There is something for all ages.

1 You can have a great time but ...

Read the text. Make a grid and put in what you can/can't, must/mustn't or needn't do.

2 Things to do (→ p. 30/ex. 3–5)

a) *Look at the signs on a beach in England. What can/can't you do here?*

1 

2

3 

4 

5 

6 

b) *What must/mustn't you do on the beach?*

Example: 1. You **must put** your rubbish in the bin.

1. Put your rubbish in the bin!
2. Don't throw bottles into the sea!
3. Bring lost children to the lifeguard.
4. Don't go into the water at night.
5. Don't walk your dog on the beach!
6. Tell the lifeguard if someone needs help.
7. The red flag is flying so don't go swimming.
8. Don't swim just after a meal.

c) *Think of more rules for the beach or swimming pool. What must/mustn't you do?*

3 Summers in Brighton (→ p. 31/ex. 6, 7)

Since he was a small boy, Fred has spent his summers on the south coast of England. He learnt to swim at Brighton Beach.

Match the pictures of Fred with his mum's speech bubbles.

1 When I was five:

2 When I was eight:

3 When I was nine:

4 When I was ten:

5 When I was twelve:

6 When I was thirteen:

a. You can dive in some places but you must be very careful. And you must follow the signs.

b. I know you can swim but you really mustn't swim alone.

c. You can swim all day if you like. But you can't swim just after lunch.

d. Well done, Fred! So now you can swim very fast but you mustn't swim with strangers!

e. Now Fred, as long as you can't swim, you must wear a rubber ring.

f. You can swim alone but you know you can't swim very far.

4 Let's talk: But we mustn't … (→ p. 31/ex. 8)

Three of you are in town on the south coast. *Talk about what to do next.*

A: Well, we **can** go down to the beach.
B: Good idea! But we **mustn't** swim yet. We've just had lunch.
C: OK. So we **must** … .

Go on, please.

can	mustn't	must
go down to the beach	eat them on the bus	get some stamps, too
buy some postcards	miss the bus home	get some wood
make a fire on the beach	forget to put it out	eat them quickly now
visit a smugglers' museum	forget to send them	stay on the cliff path
go up to the cliffs	dive from them	wait for an hour
get some fish and chips	swim yet	leave at 6 p.m.

▶ **Who** and **which** are relative pronouns. You use **who** for people and **which** for things.
Many of the visitors **who** fly to the UK land at Heathrow.
That circle of stones **which** you can see is Stonehenge.

→ G8

1 Languages in the British Isles

(→ p. 32/ex. 9)

Read the text and put in 'who' or 'which'.

1 mile	= 1760 yards (1 yard = 91,44 cm)
	= 1609 metres

When you leave the Tunnel at Folkestone or the airport buildings at Heathrow, you will notice at once that you are in a foreign country. All the signs … (*who/which*) you see around you are in English. People will speak to you in English, too, but does everyone … (*who/which*) lives here speak English? In the Republic of Ireland most signs, for example, are in Irish with the English names below them. Some of the people … (*who/which*) live in the west of Ireland still speak Irish, and teachers … (*who/which*) want to work in the Republic must learn Irish, too.

A language … (*who/which*) you can still hear on the islands to the west of Scotland is Scottish Gaelic. In parts of Wales you will still find people … (*who/which*) only speak Welsh at home. Cornwall in the southwest of England has its own language, too. They call it Cornish.

But don't worry! English is still the official language on these islands. And they all have Greenwich Mean Time, so everyone hears the six o'clock news at six o'clock. And at midnight on 31st December Big Ben signals the New Year to everyone.

Irish road signs

2 English, Irish, Scottish, Welsh …

(→ p. 32/ex. 10)

a) *Make sentences.*

▶ All passengers **whose** flight has just arrived please go to customs.

→ G8

Example: A passenger **whose** plane lands at Heathrow will see signs in English.

1. A passenger 2. A teacher 3. Some people 4. A person 5. Visitors 6. Tourists	+ who whose +	plane lands at Heathrow will see signs in English. job is in the Republic must learn Irish. live in the west of Ireland speak Irish. home is on an island to the west of Scotland may speak Scottish Gaelic. speak some English needn't worry. visit London can hear Big Ben.

b) *Define these jobs: a teacher, a customs officer, a policeman, a secretary, a milkman.*

Example: A teacher **is a person whose job is** to teach pupils.

One of South England's big mysteries

The beginnings of Stonehenge go back to the New Stone Age, (around 3,100 BC). Then it was a circle of wooden posts.
Around 600 years later the people that rebuilt it used huge stones that came from nearly 250 miles away, from South Wales.
Each stone had a weight of about five tons so it is hard to imagine how they brought them across the country.
After two centuries they replaced these stones with even bigger stones (up to 40 tons) that they found not far from Stonehenge.
The way the stones stand they show, for example, the position of the sun on the shortest and longest days of the year. So people think Stonehenge was once a kind of observatory. But who exactly were these people who built Stonehenge? How did they have the power to pull up stones of up to 45 tons so they could stand? Why did they go to the trouble to do this? Will we ever know?
The big mystery around Stonehenge has made it a spectacular attraction for people from all over the world. But visitors have damaged the stones in the past. So today there are rules that protect them.

3 When? (→ p. 32/ex. 11; p. 33/ex. 12)

a) *Match the information about the stones with the correct time.*

Facts	Time
a circle of posts	in the past
huge stones	after two centuries
bigger stones	today
damaged stones	around 600 years later
rules to protect stones	around 3,100 BC

▶ Sometimes you will find **that** instead of **who** or **which**.
→ G8

▶ Phrases of time go at the beginning or the end of the sentence:
… the stones in **the past**.
Then it was a circle … .
→ G9

b) *Write about the stones with the correct phrases of time. Be careful with the word order.*

Example: Around 3,100 BC Stonehenge was a circle of wooden posts.

4 A weekend trip (→ p. 33/ex. 13)

Find the right order. Write down the sentences and get a summary of a tourist's trip to Stonehenge.

1. to Stonehenge / we / last weekend / went
2. at 7:20 a.m. / to Salisbury / got the train / first / we / from London
3. in Salisbury / two hours later / arrived / we
4. in a queue / we / at Stonehenge / for hours / stand / had to
5. never / to Stonehenge / go / at the weekend again/ we'll

▶ I went **to London two years ago.**
What's the word order of place and time in a sentence?
Make the rule.
→ G9

5 For my folder: My trip

Write about a weekend trip. Where did you go? What did you do?

SPEAKING SKILLS

Being polite

You should always be polite. How do you do this in English? Here are some useful phrases:

Excuse me. Could you …?	–	Yes, of course.
Sorry, but could I …, please?	–	Yes, of course! Let me help you.
Could you help me, please?	–	Well, I'll try. What's the problem?
Would you like … or …?	–	…, please!
Would you like …?	–	Yes, please. / No, thank you.
I'm sorry to bother you, but … .	–	That's no problem.

L1, 25 1 Let's listen: On the flight (→ p. 34/ex. 14)

a) *Listen to some people on a flight to London. What questions do they ask? Write notes.*

b) *Listen again and match their questions with the right answers.*

Example: Question 1 matches answer g: Yes, of course. Here you are.

a. Cheese, please. I don't eat meat.

b. We must go through passports and customs.

c. Yes, of course. What colour is it?

d. It's no problem. I'll just close my laptop.

e. Well, I'll try. What's the problem?

f. Oh, yes. Thank you. I'm hungry because I didn't have any lunch.

g. Yes, of course. Here you are!

c) *Now practise the dialogues with a partner.*

2 Be friendly! (→ p. 34/ex. 15)

You are waiting to collect your luggage at the airport. *What do you say in these situations? Look at the skills box for help.*

1. You can't see any trolleys in the hall.
2. A man has got your bag (his bag looks the same). You want him to check the name on it.
3. A woman asks you to help her with her heavy luggage.
4. You can't find a phone box.
5. A boy has just dropped his mobile.
6. You need to use the toilet.

A trolley? That's no problem. They're just down there, on the right.

3 A role play: At the airport

One of you is a tourist, the other one works at the airport.
Make dialogues for the situations in exercise 2 and practise them with a partner.

L1, 26 1 Let's listen: Your passport, please! (→ p. 35/ex. 16)

a) *Listen. What is Steffi's problem?*

b) *Listen again. What does the officer ask Jens to do?*

c) *Could this be a picture of Jens at customs?*
Why or why not?

L1, 27 2 Let's listen: A cigarette smuggler? (→ p. 35/ex. 17, 18)

a) *Listen to the conversation. Read the message.*
What did Mr Robbins forget to tell his son, Dave, in it?

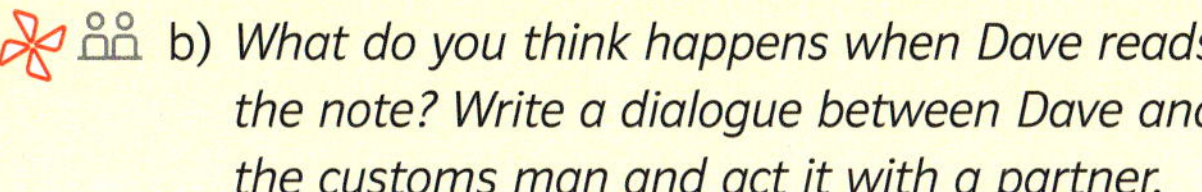

b) *What do you think happens when Dave reads the note? Write a dialogue between Dave and the customs man and act it with a partner.*

Hi, Dave!
A customs officer from Dover called. Someone found your bag in the toilets. They wanted to know if everything was still in it. Please ring them when you get home. The number is ...

L1, 28 3 Sounds: [f] and [w] (→ p. 36/ex. 19, 20)

1. Fresh French fish on Fridays for fourteen frightened football fans.
2. We'll wash the windows well with warm water on Wednesdays.

L1, 29 4 A song: Message in a bottle

(Text: Sting © GM Sumner)

Just a castaway[1], an island lost at sea, another lonely day,
no one here but me
More loneliness[2] than any man could bear[3],
rescue me before I fall into despair[4]

I'll send an SOS[5] to the world,
I'll send an SOS to the world

I hope that someone gets my I hope that someone gets my,
I hope that someone gets my message in a bottle.
A year has passed[6] since I wrote my note,
but I should have known this[7] right from the start[8]
Only hope[9] can keep me together,
love can mend[10] your life, but love can break your heart[11]

I'll send an SOS to the world,
I'll send an SOS to the world

I hope that someone gets my I hope that someone gets my,
I hope that someone gets my message in a bottle.

1. Is this a picture of the person in the song? Why? Why not?
2. What could the message in the song be about?
Write your own message.

[1]castaway ['kɑ:stəweɪ] – *Schiffbrüchiger/Schiffbrüchige,* [2]loneliness ['ləʊnlɪnəs] – *Einsamkeit,* [3]to bear [beə] – *aushalten, ertragen,* [4]despair [dɪ'speə] – *Hoffnungslosigkeit, Verzweiflung,* [5]SOS [ˌesəʊ'es] – *SOS,* [6]to pass [pɑ:s] – *vorübergehen,* [7]I should have known this [aɪ ˌʃʊd‿həv 'nəʊn ðɪs] – *ich hätte es wissen müssen,* [8]right from the start [ˌraɪt frɒm ðə 'stɑ:t] – *von Anfang an,* [9]hope [həʊp] – *Hoffnung,* [10]to mend [mend] – *hier: heilen,* [11]heart [hɑ:t] – *Herz*

L1, 30–36 ◎
The courier

A At Moscow Airport two men waited for the announcement of their flight to London.
"Try not to look so nervous," the taller one said. "People will notice us."
"But I am nervous. What if it doesn't work?" his friend answered.
"It'll work fine. Trust me! Ah! …"

B "There she is! Hi, Sue! We're here!"
Sue Clarke was really happy when she heard her parents' voices at Heathrow Airport. She had enjoyed her trip to Moscow but it was good to be home again. She thanked the woman with whom she had walked from the plane and through customs. She took her mother's arm and walked with her to the car. Her father came behind with her luggage. Suddenly he shouted, "Hey!"
Sue felt a tug on her handbag.
"What's happening?" she wanted to know.
"Some bloke tried to put his hand into your bag," her dad explained. "You should close it, Sue. It's lucky I saw him."

C When they arrived at their house, none of them noticed the car which stopped on the other side of the street.
Sue took off her shoes and her mum put them away. "I'm sorry that we have to go back to work now," she said.
"Don't worry," Sue answered. "I can rest and we can talk later this evening."
"I'll just take your bags down to your flat," said her dad.
Sue had her own small flat in the basement. She had been blind since birth. But although she had always needed help, she wasn't helpless. In fact she was as independent as most young women.

D She put her handbag on a chair in the bedroom and lay down on her bed. Then she remembered that her mobile was still turned off. She picked up her bag and felt for the phone in it. Something small and heavy fell into her hands but she had no idea what it was.
Then she heard the door at the top of the stairs to the basement, then footsteps. It wasn't her mother or father – these footsteps were different: two men, one heavier than the other. Sue was scared but she went into the hall and shouted, "Who's there? What do you want?"

E Both men were near her now. Where had she smelt that aftershave before? At the airport in Moscow! And again, in Heathrow!
"Who are you?" Sue asked again.

But they didn't speak. She tried to push past them, but the bigger one took her arm and pushed her onto the floor. Then the men went into the bedroom. Sue was really frightened. She had to get out! She touched something on the wall behind her. It was the fuse-box.

F The lights went out and suddenly one of the men shouted. He was furious. He had fallen over something.
Sue started to crawl down the hall.
"Oh no, you don't!" The other man tried to grab her now, but Crash! He had forgotten about Sue's luggage. She took her chance and ran upstairs and locked the basement door behind her. Then she ran out of the house and shouted for help. A neighbour heard her and came out into the street.

G "It's a Russian icon, small but very valuable," the police officer told the Clarkes. "Those smugglers didn't want UK customs to catch them. So they looked for someone to be their courier. Someone whose bags the customs officers wouldn't check. Of course, they planned to take it back again at Heathrow. But you stopped them, Mr Clarke. So they followed you back here and waited until Sue was alone. They thought she would be helpless. How wrong they were!"
"I've always thought it must be exciting to be a courier," laughed Sue. "But now I understand just how exciting it can be."

1 Before you read: Couriers

1. What does a courier do?
2. What kind of people often do this job?

2 At the airport

Look at pictures 1 and 2.
Read parts A and B.

1. How did the icon get into Sue's bag?
2. Who put it there?
3. Why did they pick Sue?

3 Evidence

a) *What hints are there before line 34 that Sue is blind?*

b) *What do you think Sue can/can't do that you can do? Think about activities (things at home, different sports, …). Look for clues in the story.*

4 The story (→ p. 37/ex. 21)

Write a summary of 'The courier'.
The tips in the skills box can help you.

WRITING    SKILLS

Tips for a summary:
1. Write down the important facts or key words for each part of the story: the people (Who?), the time (When?), the place (Where?).
2. Now use your key words to make sentences for your summary.
3. Use the simple present for the whole summary.
4. Keep your text short but remember: A person who doesn't know the story should understand what it's about.
You can start like this: The text … is about … .

5 A role play: In the street

a) *Discuss what happened between parts F and G.*

b) *Write a dialogue between Sue and her neighbour and act it with a partner.*

1 Holiday words (→ p. 38/ex. 22)

Collect words for the two kinds of holiday. Some words can be for both.

a wet week on the moors	both	a sunny week at the beach
rubber boots	a hat	a swimsuit
a map ...	a rucksack ...	ice-cream ...

2 Let's look: On the beach!

Look at the picture. What can you see? Where are the people? What are they doing?

Example: I can see a man **who** is lying on a bed in the sea. He is drinking out of a glass.

3 Holiday information (→ p. 38/ex. 23)

Find the right prepositions for these sentences.

1. You can't drive your car … *(over/through/under)* the Chunnel. But you can drive it … *(onto/below/between)* a train.
2. You must drive … *(at/in/on)* the left … *(in/on/over)* Britain.
3. From Heathrow you can get the Tube … *(of/into/at)* London.
4. You can take good photos … *(from/by/of)* Stonehenge if there are no crowds.
5. There are many famous old castles all … *(before/around/about)* South England.
6. Huge ocean liners sail … *(around/from/between)* Southampton and New York.
7. You will find many interesting towns all … *(for/in/along)* the south coast.
8. Hastings has got a museum that is all … *(over/around/about)* smugglers.

4 Measurements everywhere (→ p. 38/ex. 24)

Britain is in the EU (European Union) but people on these islands still do a lot of things in their own way. They still use pounds (lb) and stones (st), and inches (in), feet (ft), yards (yd) and miles (ml).

a) *Copy the grids and find the answers. The box on the left can help you.*

1 pound	=	450 g
1 stone (14 pounds)	=	6.348 kg
1 inch	=	2.54 cm
1 foot (12 inches)	=	30.48 cm
1 yard (3 feet)	=	91.44 cm

? lb	=	900 g
20 st	=	? kg
10 in	=	? cm
2ft	=	? cm
? yd	=	9.144 cm

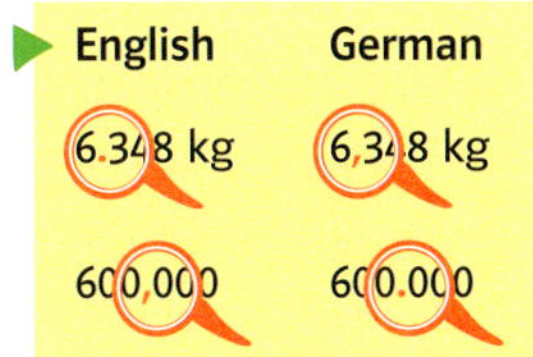

b) *Find out your height in feet and inches and your weight in stones and pounds.*

c) *Look at the pictures and answer the questions below.*

	£
MINCED LAMB	2.58
CARRS MELTS	0.68
BANROCK MAT/SH*	13.99
BANANAS LOOSE	
1.165 kg £0.74/kg	0.86
TOTAL	18.11
CASH	20.11
CHANGE DUE	2.00

1

2

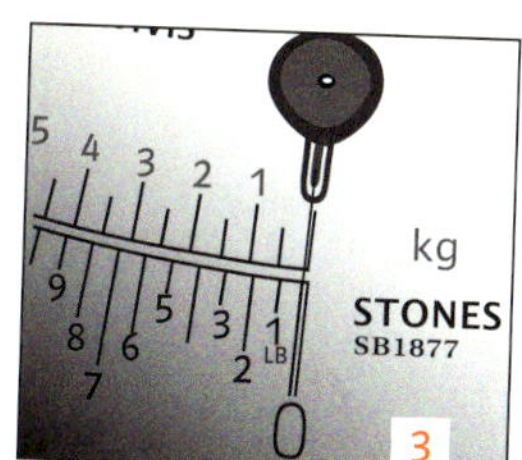

3

4

1. What is 11' 9" in metres?
2. The bananas are 34p per pound. How much are they per kilo?
3. Is 6 pounds more than 3 kilos?
4. How far is 225 yards in metres?

L1, 37
5 Let's listen: Hello!

Scottish Gaelic | Irish | Welsh | Cornish

Listen to the people who are saying 'hello' in their own language. Match the photos with the languages.

Example: The women who are in picture 1 are speaking Welsh. They are Welsh.

1

2

3

4

1 A day trip (can, can't, needn't → G7)

Sue's parents are talking about a day trip to Calais. *Make sentences.*

1. I bought tickets so we 2. It isn't raining now. We 3. The traffic jams are terrible. Why 4. Well, if we go by car we 5. I've got a digital camera so we 6. I really hope we 7. If not, I think we 8. I'm getting hungry. Where 9. I've packed lots of snacks so we 10. You're right. Then we	+ can can't needn't +	go to Calais on the ferry. take our umbrellas. we get on a train to Dover? be in a hurry to get the last train back. take your old camera with us. get a view of the White Cliffs! buy postcards of Dover on the ferry. we get some snacks? spend all our money on food! bring home lots of souvenirs.

2 Rules on a ferry (must, mustn't → G7)

Look at the pictures. What must you or mustn't you do on a ferry?

1. You mustn't lean out too far. 2. You … … to the announcements. *Go on, please.*

1 lean out

2 listen

3 put on seat

4 keep out of

5 throw away

6 take back

7 leave

8 keep

9 dive off

10 carry

3 Must I? (must, needn't → G7) (→ p. 39/ex. 25)

a) *Your mum wants you to do something. You ask your dad if you must do it now. Make dialogues.*

You: Mum says I must learn my French. Must I do it now?
Dad: No, you needn't. You can learn it … .

learn my French ✓	next week ✓
wash the car	tomorrow
clean my shoes	this afternoon
do the shopping	after lunch
walk the dog	after supper
feed the cat	in an hour

b) *Your mum reminds you about other things. What does she answer? Use the sentences from part a).*

You: Dad says I can learn my French next week.
Mum: No, you can't. You must … .

help the neighbour • do a test on Monday • go to bed early • go swimming • do it at once • buy some things for lunch

4 A word puzzle (who, which, that → G8) (→ p. 39/ex. 26)

Find the words and make clues for them.

1. A … ship is a ship where people spend a holiday.
2. A … is a person who … .
3. A … is a … that … .

Go on, please.

S	H	[1] C	R	U	I	[2] S	E	G
F	G	J	A	D	R	M	I	[3] P
O	[4] C	Y	W	[5] F	E	U	C	O
[6] P	A	S	S	E	N	G	E	R
U	N	I	L	R	B	G	A	T
J	O	L	Q	R	I	L	X	R
[7] S	E	A	V	Y	K	E	Z	E
A	R	B	H	O	K	R	E	Y

5 Mixed bag: English isn't always English (whose, that → G8)

Read the text and fill in 'whose' or 'that'.

On the islands (1) they call the British Isles everyone speaks English but English isn't always English. You will often hear an English (2) is different from the English (3) you learn at school. A person from London will not always understand someone (4) comes from the North of Scotland. The language (5) everyone speaks is English but not everyone from the British Isles is English. A person (6) parents come from the Republic of Ireland will have a passport (7) says that they are Irish. A lot of people (8) passports say 'British' will say that they are Scottish or Welsh. People on the west coast of Scotland may even speak a strange language (9) they call Scottish Gaelic. Some of the words (10) they use are very like German words. A 'loch' in Scotland, for example, is a 'lake' in England.

6 A visit to Leeds Castle (word order with phrases of time and place → G9) (→ p. 39/ex. 27)

Put the words in the right order to find the sentences.

1. to South England / last summer / for a holiday / we went
2. rainy / after we arrived / on the day / it was
3. take the train / didn't want to / so we / on that day / down to the coast
4. we went / instead of that / in the morning / to Leeds Castle
5. showed us / the different rooms / at ten o'clock / of the castle / the owner
6. the first castle buildings / over a thousand years ago / they built / there
7. in Kent / visit / today / from all over the world / this fantastic castle / people

NOW YOU CAN

✓ talk about the British Isles.	→ *Give a short talk on the British Isles.*
✓ say what you can, must or needn't do.	→ *Say what you can, must or needn't do at the weekend.*
✓ define people, their jobs and things.	→ *Define four jobs that people do and four things.*
✓ use phrases of time.	→ *Make a list of phrases of time that you know.*
✓ write a summary.	→ *Write a short summary of the text on page 30.*
✓ be polite in English.	→ *Imagine three situations and write dialogues for them.*

Two adverts[1]

SURF BEACH
Did you know that the best windsurfing school in Britain is on the Isle of Wight?
WWW means Wight Windsurfing Wizards.
After one week of lessons with us you'll be one of the world's best wind-surfers[2]. Guys[3] who can windsurf get all the girls!
For more information just check our website.

Huge burger with chips!
Visit Burts for the best burgers in Brighton!
Only 50 p with chips! Two for the price of one!*
*If you buy more than 6 burgers.

[1]advert [ˈædvɜːt] – *Werbeanzeige*, [2]windsurfer [ˈwɪndˌsɜːfə] – *Windsurfer/Windsurferin*, [3]guy [gaɪ] – *Kerl, Typ*

1 Good adverts (→ p. 40/ex. 1)

Look at the two adverts on the opposite page. Answer the questions. Look at the language skills below for help.

1. What do they want to sell? Who should buy it?
2. What do the photos show? Are they interesting?
3. Is there enough information? Are the texts short enough and interesting?
4. Do you think the adverts are good? Why or why not?
5. In which advert can you find which feature[1]?

2 Let's talk: An interesting advert

Adverts usually want to sell something. *Think about an advert which you found interesting. What was it for? Where did you see it? Why was it interesting? Talk to your partner about it.*

A: I saw an interesting advert yesterday/last week/on Saturday/... .
B: What was it for?
A: It was for a new ice-cream/jeans/German lessons/... .

3 For my folder: My own advert (→ p. 40/ex. 2)

a) *Look at the skills box and design an advert.*

DESIGNING ADVERTS 

1. You must think about What? and Who?
   What is the advert for? (Food? Clothes? ... ?)
   Who is it for? (Old people? Young people? ... ?)
2. You must choose interesting photos or pictures.
3. You must write a short, interesting text.
   You needn't write full sentences.

LANGUAGE 

In adverts you often find features like
- imperatives[2],
- questions,
- short sentences with exclamation marks[3],
- big pictures.

b) *Show it to the other groups. Which advert is the best and why?*

TASTY!
The chocolate that you can't say 'no!' to.

[1]feature ['fi:tʃə] – *Kennzeichen, Merkmal,* [2]imperative [ɪm'perətɪv] – *Befehlsform,* [3]exclamation mark [ˌekskləˈmeɪʃn mɑːk] – *Ausrufezeichen*

Two travel brochures

Are you ready to be scared? Yes? Are you sure? OK! Then you should visit 'Smugglers' Adventure'. It's a really exciting museum in Hastings on the south coast of England. You can spend a day there and we promise that you'll never forget it! In this labyrinth[1] of dark halls and tunnels you can learn all about the history of smuggling[2] on this coast. You can relive the dangerous life of a smuggler hundreds of years ago. You can visit the caves[3] that the real smugglers used. There is a film about smuggling in one of them. In other caves there are information boards with life-sized[4] smugglers. They will show you what a smuggler's life was really like in past[5] times. You can meet the 'ghost' of a smuggler who died here many years ago. If that doesn't scare[6] you, then don't worry. A smuggler's life was hard and often very frightening. You will find out why. The caves are full of surprising things. You can hear strange noises and spooky lights will frighten[7] even the 'coolest' of your friends!

The Isle of Wight is the largest island of the south coast of England. It is very popular with visitors who like to walk or cycle. Cowes, a town on the north side of the island, is famous all over the world with people who sail. The island has its own royal palace, too. It is Osborne House. Queen Victoria and Prince Albert spent a lot of time there and the Queen died there in 1901. There are more than 70 other interesting places for foreign visitors. So there's something for everyone. One of them is the Smuggling Museum. Here you can find out how smugglers have brought things into Britain over the last 700 years. In the past they smuggled[8] brandy[9], gold, and even slaves[10]. Today tobacco[11], drugs and wild animals are at the top of their lists, but they smuggle people, too. The museum also tells the story of pirates[12] who often attacked[13] ships in the Channel.

[1]labyrinth ['læbərɪnθ] – *Labyrinth*, [2]smuggling ['smʌglɪŋ] – *Schmuggel*, [3]cave [keɪv] – *Höhle*, [4]life-sized ['laɪfsaɪzd] – *lebensgroß*, [5]past [pɑːst] – *vergangen*, [6]to scare ['skeə] – *erschrecken*, [7]to frighten ['fraɪtn] – *erschrecken*, [8]to smuggle ['smʌgl] – *schmuggeln*, [9]brandy ['brændi] – *Weinbrand*, [10]slave [sleɪv] – *Sklave/Sklavin*, [11]tobacco [tə'bækəʊ] – *Tabak*, [12]pirate ['paɪrət] – *Pirat/Piratin*, [13]to attack [ə'tæk] – *angreifen*

A Reading

1 Which place are the sentences about, Hastings or the Isle of Wight?

a. The museum is in caves.
b. You can find out about pirates.
c. Queen Victoria died here.
d. People come here to cycle.
e. You can see spooky lights.
f. It has a royal palace.

2 In the museum in Hastings you can …

a. spend … b. relive … c. learn about … d. visit … e. meet … f. hear …

B Language

Find words in the texts which mean the same as …

a. frightened b. difficult c. sounds d. biggest e. ride a bike

C Skills

1 Look at the texts and find the words for these definitions.

a. Someone who hides things when he or she goes through customs is a … .
b. Something that is as big as a person is … .
c. Someone who has to work for another person for no money is a … .

2 Write definitions for …

a. museum b. pirate c. labyrinth

D Mediation and communication

Answer an English visitor's questions about this museum.

a. Where is the museum?
b. Can we visit it on 10th April?
c. What can we learn about in the museum?
d. What can we do there?
e. Can we get there by train?

Am Sonntag, 13. April ist Saisoneröffnung im schweizerischen Zollmuseum in Gandria. Im ehemaligen Grenzwächterhaus erhalten Besucherinnen und Besucher einen Einblick in die Zoll- und Grenzgeschichte von der Mitte des 19. Jahrhunderts bis in die Gegenwart. Moderne Technik und Interaktivität machen aus dem Zollmuseum in Gandria eine lebendige Ausstellung für Jung und Alt. Wer will, kann seinen Pass, seine Kreditkarte oder eine Banknote auf ihre Echtheit prüfen oder in einem Auto nach versteckten Schmuggelwaren suchen. Das Schmugglermuseum – wie es im Volksmund auch heißt – ist nur mit dem Schiff erreichbar.

38 E Listening

Use the right word to complete the sentences.

a. Last year Fabian and his parents went to:	1 Ireland	2 England	3 Scotland.
b. Mark's suggestion is:	1 London	2 Hastings	3 Dover.
c. His mother likes:	1 museums	2 castles	3 palaces.
d. Last year his dad learnt:	1 English	2 to drive	3 to windsurf.
e. Fabian wants to:	1 learn English	2 sail	3 windsurf.

F Writing

1 A report[1] on smuggling

Collect facts on smuggling from the two texts.
Write a short report (5–6 sentences) on the topic.

2 Your opinion

"Some museums are very interesting."

Say why you think this opinion is right or wrong. Write two sentences.

[1]report [rɪ'pɔːt] – *Bericht*

Unit 4 Let it out!

1 Let's talk: What's happening? (→ p. 43/ex. 1)

Look at photo 1. What's happening?
Make up a reason for the situation.
Talk to your partner about what you think.

WORDS

tattoo [tæt'u:] – *Tätowierung*
disappointed [ˌdɪsə'pɔɪntɪd] – *enttäuscht*
frustrated [frʌs'treɪtɪd] – *frustriert*
strict [strɪkt] – *streng, strikt*
to have an argument ['ɑ:gjəmənt] – *sich streiten*

L1, 39 2 Let's listen: That's so unfair!

Dave and his parents are talking about a problem. They are all getting more and more angry.

a) *Look at the photo again and listen.*

1. How old is Dave? What does he want?
2. Why does he want this? *Give three reasons.*
3. Does he get what he wants in the end?

b) *What do you think about Dave's idea? Say why you think this.*

c) *Have you ever been in a similar situation? What happened?*

I wanted a …/my (eyebrow/tongue/…) pierced.
I had a problem with … .
My parents said … .

RESPECT POETRY SLAM AT CRAWFORD PARK

Open to 12–18 year-olds

•

Enter through your school or youth group.

•

Winners of this round will take part in workshops with big names in hip hop and performance poetry.

DID YOU KNOW?

- The first poetry slam took place in Chicago in 1985. The poet Marc Smith invented this event because he wanted more people to see and hear poetry live.
- A lot of teenage slam poems are about dreams, wishes or problems, for example with a girlfriend or boyfriend.
- There are special slam rules:

1. You perform one or more poems but you've only got three minutes in all.
2. The organizers pick judges from the audience.
3. The judges can give a slamster up to 30 points (ten points each for content, performance and audience response).

3 Poetry slam (→ p. 43/ex. 2)

1. What do you know about poetry slams? *You can look at 'Did you know' for help or use the Internet to get more information.*
2. What do teenage slamsters write about?
3. Think of other topics for slam poetry.

4 Let's talk: When I'm frustrated

What do you do to 'let it out' if …

- you get a bad mark at school (parents angry)?
- you can't see a film (you're under 16)?
- your team lost an important match?

Talk to a partner.

▶ You use the **will-future** to talk about what you think will happen next or in the future:
– Take my umbrella. I'm sure it'**ll rain**. – No, thanks. I've got an anorak so **I won't get** wet.
You also use this form when you suddenly decide to do something, or for promises:
– I'm tired. – OK, we **won't walk**, we'**ll take** the bus.
– I promise I **won't be** late again. / I'**ll do** my best, I promise!
You use this form, too, when you offer to help someone:
– Those boxes are too heavy, Mr Morley. I'**ll carry** them into the shop for you.

→ G10

L1, 40 Dear diary

Lauren is 14. She has just heard that her dad has got a new job in Cornwall. So they'll have to move away from London. This is what she writes in her diary:

What a disaster!
OK, it's cool that Dad has now got a job again. But why down in Cornwall? I'm sure we'll live in a tiny village in some stupid cottage in the middle of nowhere – and we won't even have any neighbours. I know that Mum wants a garden (but that'll mean more work)! I bet we'll all have to help her with it. And my new school will probably be miles away – so I'll have to get up early and take a bus to school.
Oh, no – a new school, new teachers. It'll drive me crazy! I won't have my friends there, so who will I hang out with? What about Nyla, Carrie and the others – what will it be like without them? What will they say when they find out?
I bet there won't even be a rap club at the new school. And I can forget about my steel band, I'm sure they won't like loud music out in the country: It'll upset the cows! No, this is not funny …
I'm not even there yet and I already have the feeling I want to run away! And I almost forgot old Mr Morley. I know it was only a Saturday job and he's only my boss. But he's almost like a grandad to me. So who will help him in the shop with all those heavy boxes now? I'm sure he'll miss me.
I think Mum's sad, too, but she tries to hide it. She says we'll have a bigger house. OK, so Daisy and I'll have our own rooms. But I won't need my own room with no friends to hang out with!
Please, why can't we just stay here?
Oh, it's useless. I feel terrible.
What can I do? I know what – I'll text Nyla now. Maybe she'll come over and we can talk …

1 Lauren's worries (→ p. 44/ex. 3)

What are Lauren's worries? Make a grid like this:

What does she think will happen? What will there be?	What won't happen? What won't there be?
They'll live in a tiny village … . …	They won't have any neighbours. …

2 A role play: It won't be that bad! (→ p. 44/ex. 4)

Look at your grid from exercise 1. You are Lauren's friend. What can you say to help her?

Lauren: **I'm sure** we'll live in a tiny village/some stupid cottage.
Friend: But **maybe** you won't, Lauren. **Maybe** you'll live in town, near your dad's work/… . And I'll write to you every day!
Lauren: My new school will **probably** be … .
Friend: No, **I'm sure** it … . It … .
Go on, please.

▶ probably
maybe
I'm sure
I think
I don't think

3 We'll all help! (→ p. 44/ex. 5; p. 45/ex. 6, 7)

Lauren is getting ready to move. All her friends offer to help her. *What do they say?*

1. Nyla: I'll put out the bags of rubbish. 2. Nyla and Carrie: We'll … . *Go on, please.*

1 Nyla / put out

2 Nyla and Carrie / push

3 Alison / take down

4 Jamal / order and get

5 Ruby / clean

6 all her friends / paint

 4 A role play: In the new house (→ p. 45/ex. 8)

Lauren makes suggestions to help her sister Daisy with her new room. *Make dialogues.*

Lauren: Hey, little sis, I've got some time.
So shall I help you with your room?
Daisy: Oh, yes. Thanks, Lauren.
Shall we paint the walls green?
Lauren: OK, that's a good idea.

▶ I've got some time.
So **shall** I **help** you with your room … ?
→ G11

room	paint the walls green
box of clothes	put them in the wardrobe
books	put up the shelves
computer	get the things off my desk
pictures	…
poster	…

5 For my folder: A change of place?

Have you ever moved to a different house/flat/town? How was it? If you have never moved, would you like to? Why? Why not?

Survival tips for pupils

1. Need a key for a locker? ☞ Buy one from the school shop.
2. Don't know a room number? ☞ Look on the main notice board.
3. Can't find your bag? ☞ Go to the secretary's office.
4. Vending machine is broken? ☞ Tell the caretaker.
5. Haven't any sandwiches for lunch? ☞ Don't miss lunch, have a school lunch!
6. Haven't got your homework with you? ☞ Don't copy from a friend!

1 What will Lauren do if … ? (→ p. 46/ex. 9)

Lauren's new school has sent her a leaflet about Kingsdale.
Look at the leaflet. Make sentences.

Example: 1. **If** Lauren **needs** a key for a locker,
she**'ll buy** one from the school shop.

▶ If she **needs** …,
she**'ll buy** … .
If she **hasn't got** …,
she **won't copy** … .
→ G12

2 Unhappy Lauren (→ p. 46/ex. 10, 11)

Hi Nyla,

Monday will be my first day at Kingsdale. On their website it says: I'll feel at home there quickly as long as I follow the school rules! But rules don't give you friends! And what if I don't feel happy, what will they do about it?
Can you imagine: On Monday I have to be there by 8 a.m.? So I'll probably sleep through our first lesson! But if I don't arrive early, I won't know where to go.
Can you guess the colour of their school uniform? It's a really yukky dark purple.
Don't even think of it – you won't get a photo of me in that thing!
Where are you all hanging out? Rap session? Although I'm tired, I think I'll just watch a film on TV. As soon as the film has finished, I'll text you.

So bye now,
Lauren

a) *Imagine you are Nyla. Answer Lauren's e-mail.*

b) *Would you like to go to Kingsdale Comprehensive School? Why? Why not?*

▶ don't worry/not shy, find new friends
if – look on club notice board, find … .
if – have time, send new raps/ … .

3 My cat loves me (→ p. 47/ex. 12)

Lauren is sad but at least she has got her cat.
Say this sentence out loud. Then use the other pronouns.

I love my cat and my cat loves me.
You love your … .
Go on, please.

4 A rap: Myself, yourself (→ p. 47/ex. 13, 14)

L1, 41

Teach yourselves this rap. Use the reflexive pronouns and perform it.

I get up in the morning and I wash myself.
I go back into my bedroom and I dress myself.
I go into the kitchen and I feed myself.
I look into the mirror and I scare myself!

You get …, and you wash yourself … . *Go on, please.*

I	me	**my**	**myself**
you	you	**your**	**yourself**
he	**him**	his	**himself**
she	her	**her**	**herself**
we	us	**our**	**ourselves**
you	you	**your**	**yourselves**
they	**them**	their	**themselves**

→ G 13/14

5 Let's talk: Their schools – our schools (→ p. 48/ex. 15, 16)

This is the Kingsdale website for their partner schools:

For our partner schools abroad:

WELCOME TO KINGSDALE COMPREHENSIVE SCHOOL

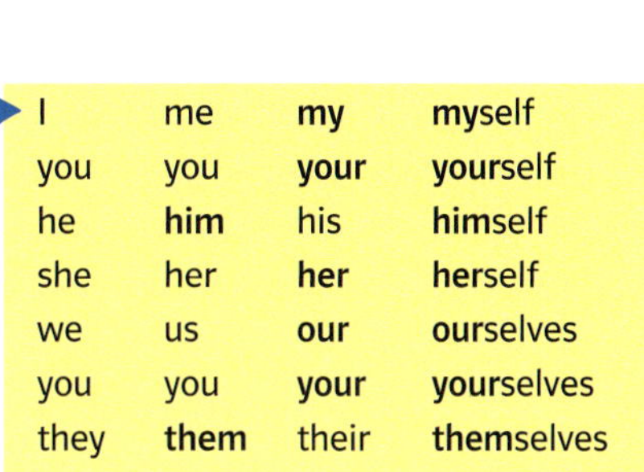

If you compare your school system with the British system, you'll see that some things are different. Here, school is compulsory from 5 to 16 years of age – and we have state schools as well as private schools.
If you want to know more, the following grid will give you an idea:

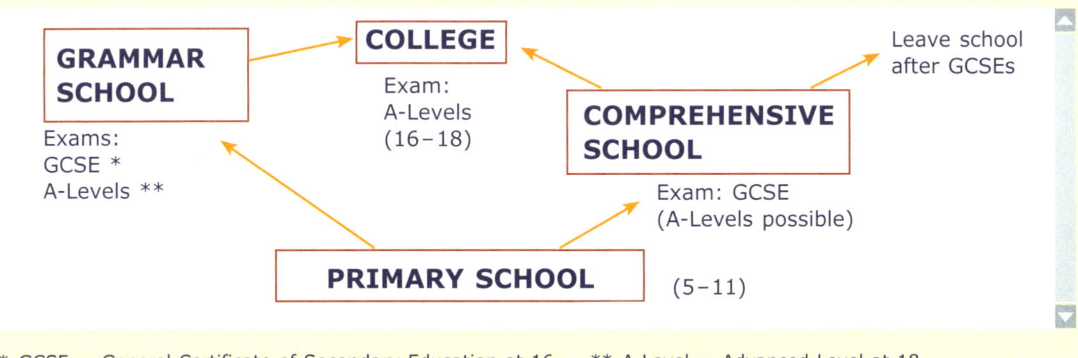

* GCSE = General Certificate of Secondary Education at 16 ** A-Level = Advanced Level at 18

a) *Compare schools.*

1. At what age do children start school in Britain? – When do you start in Germany?
2. When can they leave school? – When can you leave school?
3. Which exams can they take? When? – Which ones can you take?

b) *Make a grid like the one above about your school and the school system in Germany.*

WRITING 

Personal writing:

1. **Diary:** You are free to write as you like because a diary is usually for your eyes only. Some people use a kind of code (for example, short forms for names) so things stay secret.
2. **Text message:** You don't have to write whole sentences or words and you can use numbers for words.
3. **Note:** Use the person's name and write short phrases or sentences with the information that you want to give.
4. **E-mail or letter** (to friends or family): Use full sentences. Don't forget the beginning, the ending and the date (in a letter).
5. **A poem, rap or rhyme:** Use simple words to say how you feel and try to find a rhyme.

1 Good news (→ p. 49/ex. 17)

Read the texts. What sort of texts are they? How do you know? (The tips above can help you.)

I think that text A is a … because … . *Go on, please.*

A

GOT GR-8 NEWS 4
U! I'M ON THE
FBALL TEAM.
CU AFTER PRAC.
BFN. LAUREN

B

Dear Uncle Ray,
You won't believe it!
I'm now on the school football team and they want me to play on Sunday – I'm so glad I put in all that extra training …
Lots of love, Lauren

C

Thurs. 25th
YES!!! Wicked! I'm on the team. Ha! I've shown that idiot you-know-who. Bet she won't argue with me again. I wish I had a photo of her face, when she heard the news! Really must write Uncle R. – won't he just be proud of ME!!!

D

Hi Mum, I've made it
(just like you said):
I'm on the team!!!!
Will be home just after 8 p.m.
See you later, Love Lauren

E

I want to shout
And jump about:
I've got my dream,
I'm on the team!
Lauren Akodu

2 Quick info (→ p. 49/ex. 18)

a) *Think of a situation or choose one of these: Write a text message. Your partner can write out the full message.*

b) *Write an e-mail to someone who you like and describe the situation.*

You've won tickets for a concert.

You've got the best mark ever in English.

You scored the winning goal in an important match.

You're going on a camping weekend with your youth group.

L1, 42 ◎

1 Let's listen: Strict parents? (→ p. 50/ex. 19)

a) *Before you listen: Give three examples of strict parents.*
Example: Strict parents are parents who … .

b) *Listen to the radio helpline. Write notes on the callers Andy, Sally and Ross (age, what problem, …).*

c) *Which sentence is about which caller?*
1. Her friend has no time for her. That's … .
2. He doesn't want his parents to fight all the time. That's … .
3. His parents are strict. That's … .

d) *Listen again. What advice does DJ Jenna give?*

1. She tells Andy to	a. forget about it.	b. stay out late.	c. talk to his parents.
2. Jenna thinks Sally should	a. wait for some time.	b. tell a friend.	c. do her homework.
3. She advises Ross to	a. try not to worry.	b. talk to an aunt or uncle.	c. leave home.

e) *What do you think of Jenna's advice? Have you got any other ideas about how to help?*
I think he/she should … ./I don't think he/she … .

L1, 43 ◎

2 Let's listen: A new friend (→ p. 50/ex. 20, 21)

Lauren left a message on Reece's answerphone, so he calls her back.

a) *Listen and answer the questions.*
1. What does Lauren want to ask Reece?
2. Where does she suggest they can meet?
3. What information does she almost forget to give him on the answerphone?
4. Is Reece happy about Lauren's suggestion? How do you know?
5. When and where are they meeting? Write down the spelling of the road.

> Hi, it's … .
> Hello. It's … speaking.
> Of course we can … . Shall we … ?
> Can you spell that, please?
> OK. See you then. Thanks. Bye.

b) *Write a telephone dialogue. You can put in a difficult name or two that you have to spell. The phrases in the box can help you. Act the dialogue with your partner.*

L1, 44 ◎

3 A song: Beautiful

(Text: L. Perry © Famous Music)

Don't look at me
Every day is so wonderful[1]
And suddenly it's hard to breathe[2]
Now and then, I get insecure[3]
From all the fame[4], I'm so ashamed[5]

I am beautiful no matter what[6] they say
Words can't bring me down[7]
I am beautiful in every single[8] way
Yes, words can't bring me down

Find the word in the text that means:

fantastic • each • not sure • difficult

[1]wonderful ['wʌndəfl] – *wunderbar,* [2]to breathe [bri:θ] – *atmen,* [3]insecure [ˌɪnsɪ'kjʊə] – *unsicher,* [4]fame [feɪm] – *Ruhm,* [5]to be ashamed [ə'ʃeɪmd] – *sich schämen,* [6]no matter what ['mætə] – *ganz gleich was,* [7]to bring down [brɪŋ 'daʊn] – *runterziehen,* [8]single [sɪŋgl] – *einzeln*

L1, 45–48

Slam stars

Listen to some examples of young slamster poetry.

A

I'm just finding a way back
Into my dream
When my mum's loud voice
Leaves me no choice.

What does she want?
What's all the fuss ...?
"You'd better get up –
Or you'll miss your bus!"

I'm just moving along
Like a cloud of smoke
But the sun's sudden glare
Is now everywhere.

What does she want?
What the heck ...?
'You'd better wake up –
You look such a wreck!"

I'm just trying hard
To forget last night
And my stupid head
Feels as heavy as lead.

What does she want?
Is this a joke?
"Get up right now
Or you'll give me a stroke!"

I'm just doing my best ...
... To get up!

Leroy Glenn, 15

B

He said: No tattoo and that's that!
Oh, Dad, I said, there's no harm.
What do you mean, no harm?!
And to that Mum added,
Now, dear, stay calm!

No is no, get that into your head
But Dad, I said, Tony's got one ...
What's Tony got to do with it!
Be quiet, Mum said,
Stop having a fit!

But I say, it's not fair
I don't think they really care
How it feels when you have to wait.
It's such a tiny little thing
And they get into such a state!

Daniel Jones, 16

C

WHY
did he drink
to the brink?
WHY
did Ann leave
with Steve?
WHY
did he swerve
in the curve?
WHY
didn't he see
the tree?
WHY
didn't they arrive
alive?

Mark Wilkins, 16
(For my sister Ann)

D

When he looks at me,
I shake like leaves on a tree.
When he smiles at me,
I'm all waves in the sea.
When he stands next to me,
I go weak in the knees.
When he talks to me,
I could choke with glee.
Please help me – please!
How can I tell him
What he means to me?

Lauren Akodu, 14

1 Pictures in poems

POETRY SKILLS

Picture language
Poems put words together to say something in a different way. So poems are often like pictures.

Example:
The person is very sleepy. It's from poem A: 'I'm just moving along/Like a cloud of smoke'.

Match these pictures with the right phrases from the poems:

1

2

3

4

5

6

2 The title helps (→ p. 51/ex. 22)

a) *Find your own titles for the poems.*

b) *Look at the titles in the boxes. Which title goes with which poem? Which are better – your titles or the ones in the boxes? What does your partner think?*

c) *Which poem do you like best? Is there one that you don't like? Give reasons.*

Help!

Why?

Monday morning, 8 a.m.

Such a tiny little thing

3 What's it about? (→ p. 51/ex. 23)

PRESENTATION SKILLS

Presenting a poem
1. Choose a poem.
2. What are the feelings in the poem? (Remember them when you read it.)
3. Practise the poem: Listen to the CD, read it to a partner, practise it in front of a mirror.
4. Present the poem in class.

a) *Choose one of the slamster poems.*

b) *Make a poster with the poem for your classroom to show the ideas in the poem.*

c) *Present your poem to your class.*

1 Let's look: The same or different? (→ p. 52/ex. 24)

Pictures A and B look the same but they aren't. What's different? Find six more things.

Example: In picture A the slamster is reading from … . In picture B he's … .

2 Which one?

a) *Look at each adjective and decide if it describes something good or bad. Make a grid.*

b) *Find the right adjective. Use each adjective only once.*

useless | angry | frustrated | wicked | scared | unhealthy | surprised | scary | funny | strict

1. I didn't know what the present was. So I was … when I opened it.
2. My younger sister never reads … ghost stories before she goes to bed.
3. This knife is … . You can use it for butter but not for tomatoes.
4. Julie had to do her Maths homework again: Her teacher is so … .
5. I've just bought my favourite group's new CD. It's really … !
6. "Charlie Chaplin films are so …," says Mike, and laughs loudly.
7. I want a tattoo but my dad has said no. So I'm really … now.
8. I'm too … to walk across the fields at night without my dog.
9. Food that is … often tastes good but it is bad for you.
10. You know, I'm so … . I've tried to call my dad at least 20 times!

3 The odd one out (→ p. 52/ex. 25)

Find the word or phrase that doesn't fit in the group. Say why it's the odd one out.

1. house – flat – cottage – tent
2. frustrated – excited – disappointed – sad
3. caretaker – secretary – locker – school nurse
4. locker – poet – notice board – vending machine
5. CD – diary – poetry book – text message
6. cafeteria – registration – classroom – gym
7. audience – organizers – workshop – judges
8. knee – hair – eyebrow – tattoo

'Tent' is the odd one out because it isn't a building!

4 The fourth word

points ✓ · argument · event · enemy · audition · a poem · message · country · website · slam · DJ · microphone

Find the missing word.
Example: 1. pupil – marks; slamster – **points**

1. pupil – marks; slamster – …
2. listen – headphones; speak – …
3. laugh – joke; shout – …
4. buildings – city; farms – …
5. help – friend; fight – …
6. newspaper – reporter; radio – …
7. act – a play; perform – …
8. job – interview; song – …
9. music – concert; poetry – …
10. book – page; Internet – …
11. write – e-mail; text – …
12. manager – company; organizer – …

5 Little words (→ p. 52/ex. 26)

Find the right prepositions for the verbs in these sentences:

1. Oh, no! The alarm has **gone off** ! – Perhaps there's a fire! We must go out quickly!
2. If you're **looking** … a rap club, **look** it … in the phone book.
3. My pen is broken! – Don't **look** … me! I always **look** … the things that I borrow!
4. I'll **put** … the cupboard if you **put** … the shelves.
5. **Hang** …! I'd like to come, too! – Oh, well, I'm just **hanging** … with a friend in town.
6. Hey, Tiger, **get** … my bed. I want to **get** … now.
7. If our new neighbours **come** … to say hello, ask them to **come** … for a cup of tea.
8. The father **jumped** … because his kid started to **jump** … in the bus.
9. What about lunch? You shouldn't **go** … a meal! – I'm not hungry. Let's just **go** … together.

6 Little poems

Complete these little poems.

The best day is …
Because …

I like you,
You like me
Together we can … !

Our show
will be great!
You don't have to … .
Here's the time
and the …
Now just
don't be …!

Friday/… • it's the first day of the holidays • my friends come and stay • there's time to play • what more can you say? • we're going away

skate • wait • late • date • great • plate • gate • mate • hate • eight • ate

climb a tree • watch TV • buy a CD • be happy • have some tea • swim in the sea • have a party

1 Work for it! (will-future, if-clauses → G12) (→ p. 53/ex. 27)

You want your eyebrow pierced. Your parents say yes. But you haven't got enough money for it. Your family and neighbours will help you to get the money together.

a) *Make sentences.*

Example: Mr Brown: If you **help** me in the garden, I'**ll give** you four pounds.

1 Mr Brown / help
£4.00

2 dad / paint
£5.00

3 aunt + uncle / do shopping
£3.00

4 brother / deliver
£5.00

5 grandma / clean
£4.00

6 Mrs Howard / read
£3.00

b) *In the evening you tell a friend about this on the phone. Use your sentences from a).*

Example: If I **help** Mr Brown in the garden, he'**ll give** me four pounds.

2 If, if, if ... (will-future, if-clauses → G12) (→ p. 53/ex. 28)

Make sentences.

Example: If you shout at me again, I won't listen to you!

If +	you shout at me again, Mum's still at work, you're busy, you aren't careful, my parents are angry, you're sad, you take my CD once more, she doesn't turn off that yukky music,	+ you'll have an accident on your bike. I won't ask for your help right now. I won't help her with her homework! we'll go and see a funny film. they won't give me my pocket money. I won't listen to you! I'll do the shopping for her. you'll be sorry!

3 Myself, yourself … (reflexive pronouns → G14) (→ p. 53/ex. 29)

Look at the pictures and answer the questions.

1. What should I teach myself? – Maybe I should teach **myself** … . *Go on, please.*

1. What should I teach myself?
2. When do you wash yourself?
3. Where does she dress herself?
4. Where can he see himself?
5. When do they hear themselves?
6. How can you hurt yourselves?
7. Where can we help ourselves?
8. What does it do itself?

4 Mixed bag: She'll be surprised! (→ G12–G14)

Find the missing words and find out about Glinda's next poetry slam.

The next poetry slam that Glinda takes (1) in will be in Bristol. She (2) the first two rounds – at her (3) school and in the town where (4) lives. Now most of her class (5) to be there and watch her (6) at the big event. So her (7) have organized a bus to get (8) to Bristol. They have also made (9) of flags to wave at their (10) poet when it's her turn to (11).
Glinda is also in a steel (12) and the other kids have promised (13) they'll come, too. What Glinda doesn't (14) is that her steel band will (15) in the break just before her (16). They are sure that the audience (17) then enjoy Glinda's poem 'My steel band' even more!

won • band • friends • lots • will • part • she • that • play • perform • favourite • across • know • grammar • performance • slam • want

NOW YOU CAN

- ✓ talk about a difficult situation. → *You want (to buy) something. What do you say to your parents?*
- ✓ say what will happen in the future. → *Say what you think you'll do in your next school holiday.*
- ✓ say what will happen if … . → *Say what will happen if you're sick next weekend.*
- ✓ talk about a song, rap or poem. → *Talk about a song that you like.*

1 Jobs for children

All children in Europe[1] must go to school but a lot of them have jobs in the evenings or at the weekend. They want to earn[2] money because they think that they don't get enough pocket money.

a) *What about you? Do you have a job? What do you know about jobs for children in Germany? You can find out more on the Internet. Look at: Jugendschutzgesetz.*

b) *Read the facts about the UK. Compare them with Germany. What is different?*

Facts on jobs for children in the UK

- A lot of school children in the UK have jobs.
- They cannot work during school hours.
- For most jobs they must be 14 or older.
- They cannot work before 7 in the morning or after 7 in the evening.
- On school days and Sundays they can only work for 2 hours.
- On Saturdays they must not work more than 8 hours (5 hours if under 15).
- In school time they should not work more than 12 hours a week.

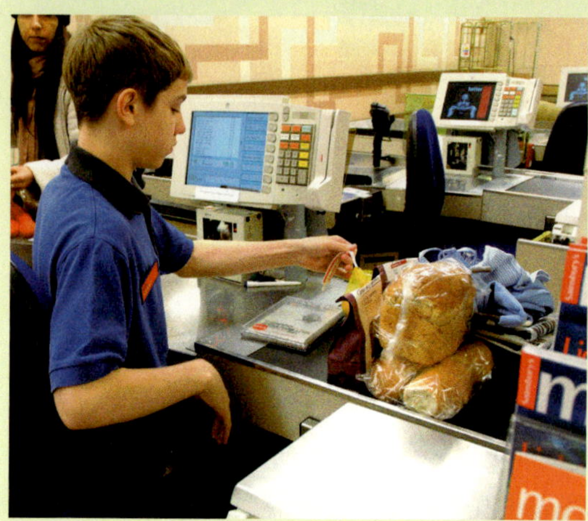

2 Child labour[3]

At the same time there are millions of children all over the world, who can't go to school. They have to work because their families are very poor[4]. This 'child labour' is very different from the 'Saturday jobs' or 'holiday jobs' which we know.

Read the facts on 'child labour'. Which do you find is the most terrible?

Facts on child labour

- 246 million children (14 and under) do child labour.
- 73 million of them are under 10 years old.
- Many children work 15–18 hours a day.
- They only earn half of what an older person earns.
- 8.4 million children have dangerous jobs.
- Every year 22,000 children die in accidents at work.
- There are international laws[5] to protect children but many countries ignore[6] them.

[1]Europe [ˈjʊərəp] – *Europa*, [2]to earn [ɜːn] – *verdienen*, [3]child labour [ˌtʃaɪld ˈleɪbə] – *Kinderarbeit*, [4]poor [pɔː] – *arm*, [5]law [lɔː] – *Gesetz*, [6]to ignore [ɪɡˈnɔː] – *ignorieren*

L1, 49

3 Let's listen: React[1] to opinions

In a discussion[2] you react to other people's opinions. You can agree[3] or disagree[4] with them.
*Listen to a discussion and look at the phrases in the box. Which two do they **not** use?*

- Sorry, but I disagree.
- I can't agree with you.
- You're right, … .
- That isn't fair.
- Yes, I agree.
- Yes, I know.
- I know that's a problem.
- No, that isn't right, … .

4 Say what you think (→ p. 54/ex. 1)

a) *Here are some sentences about children who work. Use the phrases in the box and give your opinion.*

Example: In my opinion children should … .

Yes!	No!
In my opinion[5] … should … .	In my opinion … shouldn't … .
I think that … .	I don't think that … .
I believe that … .	I don't believe that … .
I think it's right that … .	I think it's wrong that … .

1. Children should (shouldn't) go to school even if their family is poor.
2. Children should (shouldn't) work if they need more pocket money.
3. Children should (shouldn't) do heavy, dangerous work.
4. Older people should (shouldn't) earn more than children for the same work.

b) *Say why these are your opinions.*

Example: 1. In my opinion children should … **because school is important.**

5 Let's talk: A discussion (→ p. 54/ex. 2)

Look at exercises 3 and 4 again and discuss.

A: In my opinion children should … .
B: Sorry, but I disagree. Children shouldn't … . / You're right. Children should … .

DISCUSSION SKILLS

Rules for a discussion:
1. Always be polite.
2. Speak loudly and clearly.
3. Don't speak when someone else is speaking.
4. Use the phrases from exercises 3 and 4.

6 Let's talk: A new discussion

a) *Plan a discussion on an interesting topic. Each person in the group writes two or three opinions about it.*

b) *One person starts the discussion. The others agree or disagree and say why.*

A: In my opinion … .
B: You're right. I think …, too, because … .
C: Sorry, but I disagree. I think that … because … .

[1]to react [rɪ'ækt] – *reagieren,* [2]discussion [dɪ'skʌʃn] – *Diskussion,* [3]to agree [ə'griː] – *übereinstimmen,* [4]to disagree [ˌdɪsə'griː] – *nicht übereinstimmen,* [5]in my opinion [ɪn 'maɪ əˌpɪnjən] – *meiner Meinung nach*

Cheap children

This is Sindhu. She's twelve years old and she comes from Tamil Nadu in India. In the photo she isn't playing, she's working. She's making matches[1]. Sindhu is just one of millions of children in India who have to work. She has four younger brothers and sisters.

"My father had a bad accident and now he can't work. So I must earn[2] some money. I come here every day with my mother," she explains.

The children have to work in a room without windows for 13 hours every day. Sindhu earns 30 rupees[3] a day. That's about 50 cents. With the money she has to buy food for all the family. "My fingers hurt and I feel very tired but we need the money," she tells our reporter as she puts the sticks into hot sulphur[4].

The smell[5] of sulphur in the air is very strong[6].

One boy's grandma borrowed money from the factory[7] owner.

"She couldn't pay[8] it back," the boy explains, "so she took me out of school and sent me to the factory." That was two years ago. He's still there.

Suddenly the owner of the match factory comes in and tells our reporter to leave.

This is just one of many factories in this part of India where children under 14 work. They should not be here. They should be in school. All the owners know this but children are cheap, much cheaper than their parents.

India is not the only country in the world where things like this still happen. More than 200 million children in the world do child labour[9]. Many people are trying hard to stop this. The number of children who do dangerous work has fallen and life for millions of children is better now than it was ten years ago. But it will take many years before they can say that there is no more child labour in the world.

[1]match [mætʃ] – *Streichholz*, [2]to earn [ɜ:n] – *verdienen*, [3]rupee [ru:'pi:] – *Rupie (indische Währung)*, [4]sulphur ['sʌlfə] – *Schwefel*, [5]smell [smel] – *Geruch*, [6]strong [strɒŋ] – *stark*, [7]factory ['fæktri] – *Fabrik*, [8]to pay [peɪ] – *zahlen*, [9]child labour [ˌtʃaɪld 'leɪbə] – *Kinderarbeit*

A Reading

1 Read the text and complete the sentences.

a. Sindhu comes from … .
b. She makes … .
c. She has to work in a room without … .
d. Her fingers … .
e. The smell of sulphur is very … .
f. One boy's grandma borrowed … .
g. Children under 14 should be in … .
h. Children are cheaper than their … .
i. More than 200 million children do … .
j. Life is better than it was … .

B Language

1 Replace each of these verbs with another verb from the text.

a. She **is** from Tamil Nadu.
b. … children in India who **must** work.
c. They **get** about 50 cents a day.
d. I **am** very tired.
e. … and tells us to **go away**.
f. … where things like this still **take place**.

2 Read the text again. Find the words for:

a. a place where people make things
b. sticks which you use to burn something
c. father and mother
d. work that children do for money

C Mediation and communication

You show your friend the photo of Sindhu. Answer his or her questions.

a. Wo ist sie?
b. Was macht sie?
c. Warum geht sie nicht in die Schule?
d. Wie viel verdient sie?
e. Passiert so etwas nur in Indien?

50 ## D Listening

What four 'problems' does Lorna have?

E Skills

Copy the mind map and complete it.

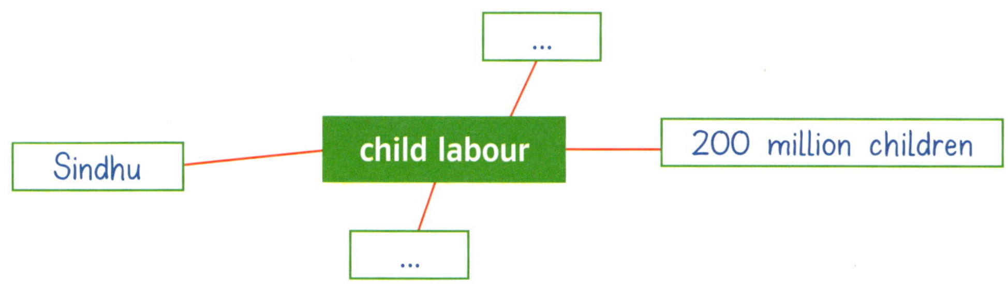

F Writing

1 A text about cheap children

Use your mind map from part E and write 4–5 sentences about 'child labour'.

2 Your opinion

"Sindhu has a very difficult life."

What do you think? Why? Write two sentences.

Unit 5 Screen shots

Programme 1: A tough hero and a fair heroine

DID YOU KNOW?

- The average British teenager watches 2–3 hours of TV daily, most watch between 3:30 p.m. and 9 p.m. Favourite programmes are sports, drama, talk or reality shows and soaps. In Britain some soaps have over ten million viewers per week.
- Bollywood films are very popular with British teenagers.
- Bollywood, the world's largest film industry, comes from India. It makes over 1,000 films per year – twice as many as Hollywood.
- Most Bollywood films are musicals that are at least three hours long. Their recipe for success is: catchy songs, colourful dances, dramatic fights, scenes of love, but in contrast to Hollywood, they seldom kiss on screen!

1 What's on? (→ p. 55/ex. 1)

1. What can you see in the picture for programme 1?
2. What is he saying? What is he thinking? What kind of film is it? What do you think? Why?
3. What kind of programmes are P2 to P5?
4. Which of these programmes would you like to watch? Why? *Discuss with a partner.*

WORDS

cartoon [ka:'tu:n] – *Cartoon, Zeichentrickfilm*
comedy ['kɒmədi] – *Komödie*
detective story [dɪ'tektɪv ˌstɔ:ri] – *Krimi*
documentary [ˌdɒkjə'mentri] – *Dokumentarfilm*
docu soap ['dɒkju səʊp] – *Dokusoap*
reality show [ri'æləti] – *Realityshow*
science fiction [ˌsaɪəns 'fɪkʃn] – *Sciencefiction*
talk show ['tɔ:k ˌʃəʊ] – *Talkshow*
thriller ['θrɪlə] – *Thriller*

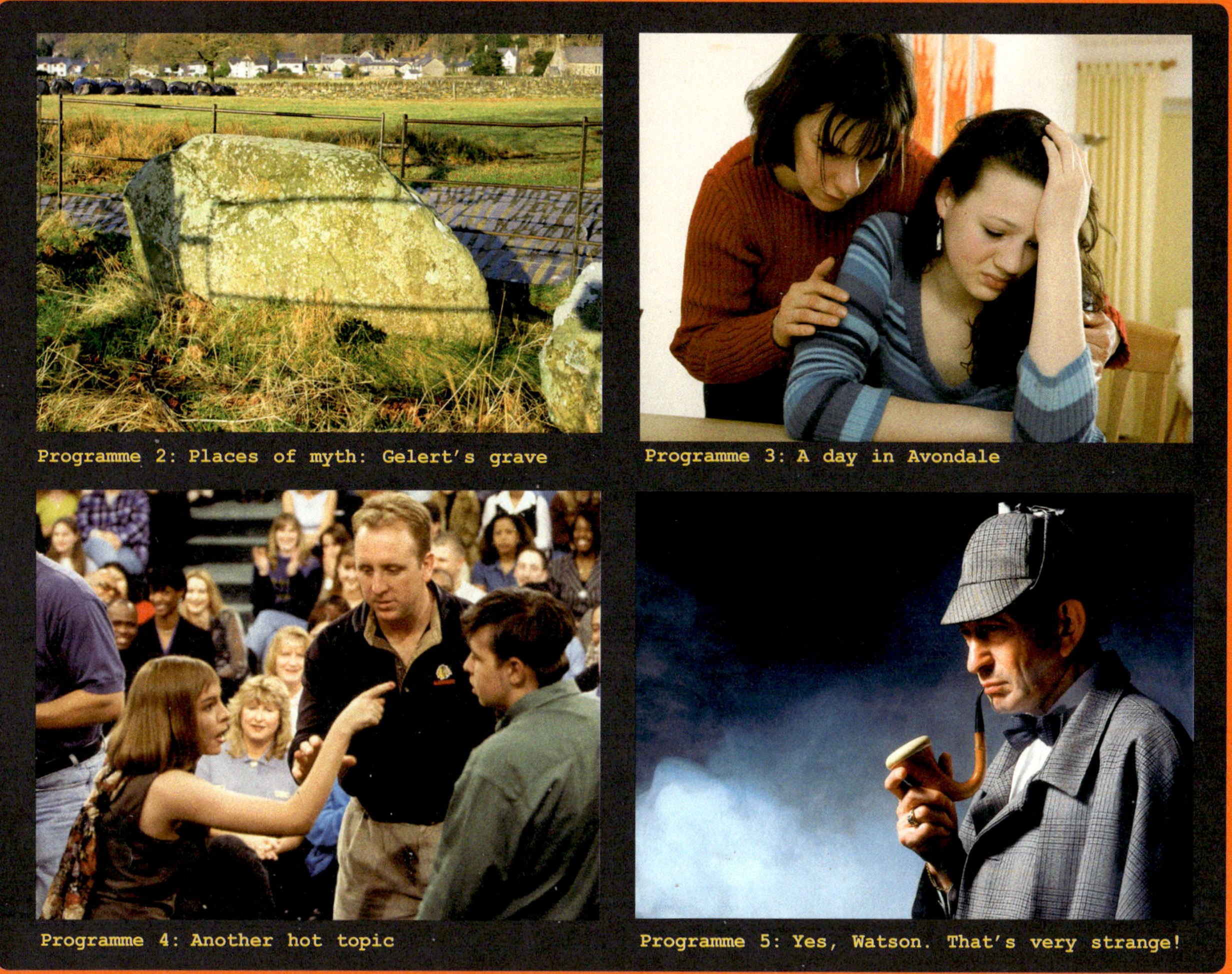

Programme 2: Places of myth: Gelert's grave

Programme 3: A day in Avondale

Programme 4: Another hot topic

Programme 5: Yes, Watson. That's very strange!

L2, 1 2 Let's listen: The script

Look at the photos. Listen to the four bits of script. Which could go with which programme?

Script 1 could go with programme … .
Script 2 could go with … . *Go on, please.*

3 Film and TV facts (→ p. 55/ex. 2)

1. How much TV do teenagers watch daily?
2. When do teenagers watch TV?
3. What programmes do they like best?
4. How many viewers do some soaps have?
5. Which is the world's biggest film industry?
6. How many films do they make per year?
7. What is different from Hollywood films?
8. What do you often find in Bollywood films?

4 Let's talk: The best film!

You want to go to the cinema or watch a DVD together.
Each chooses a film that you want to see. Write notes.
Try to convince the others that your idea is the best.

A: I'd like to see … because … .
B: But … is better because … .
C: You're right, but … .

You use **some** and **any** with nouns when you don't give a number.
In negative statements and questions you use **any**:
– I haven't got **any** homework today. Are there **any** good films on TV this evening?
In statements you usually use **some**: – Yes, there are **some** good films on later.

→ G15

	BBC1	BBC2	ITV	Channel 4
4 p.m.	4:15 – 4:35 children **Pet Tips** 4:35 – 5:00 sports **Final Score** (football and more …)	4:30 – 5:15 cooking **Ready Steady Cook** (famous cooks have 20 minutes to make a tasty meal)	4:30 – 5:30 detective story **The Adventures of Sherlock Holmes** (drama series, today: The Hound of the Baskervilles)	4:30 – 5:00 game show **Countdown** (words and numbers game where you run a race against the clock)
5 p.m.	5:00 – 5:30 children **Blue Peter** (how they make windows) 5:30 – 6:00 soap **Neighbours**	5:15 – 6:00 game show **Weakest Link** (… and you won't get any help from game show host, Ann!)	5:30 – 6:00 sitcom **My Parents are Aliens** (Dad has a new job … as a burglar!)	5:00 – 6:00 drama series **Emergency Room** (Dr Carter has three problem patients in one afternoon)
6 p.m.	6:00 – 7:00 news **BBC 1 News** and weather	6:00 – 7:00 sports **Sports special** (A new team player for Man U?)	6:00 – 6:30 news **London Tonight** 6:30 – 7:00 news **ITV News**	6:00 – 6:30 cartoon **The Simpsons** 6:30 – 7:00 soap **Hollyoaks** (teen series)
7 p.m.	7:00 – 8:00 soap **OC California**	7:00 – 7:35 music **Top of the Pops** (charts and number one hit)	7:00 – 7:30 soap **Avondale** (Is Rob in trouble?)	7:00 – 8:00 news **Channel 4 News**
8 p.m.	8:00 – 8:30 docu **Seaside rescue** (the work of rescue teams on the Cornish coast)	7:35 – 10:40 film ★★★ **Chalte Chalte** (Best of Bollywood – so get ready to cry for three hours …)	7:30 – 9:30 film ★★★★★ **The Diamond Hotel** (Who has stolen the jewellery? Some great stars in this comedy-thriller!)	8:00 – 9:00 travel docu **Places of Myth: Wales** (a small but special village …)

1 We've got that, too! (→ p. 56/ex. 3)

1. Look at the TV magazine. Which of the programmes have you got in Germany, too?
2. Which other British programmes are like programmes in Germany?
3. Which would you like to watch? Why?

2 Things to do (→ p. 56/ex. 4, 5)

Put in 'some' or 'any' and say which programmes they are.
Example: 1. Have you got any questions about pets? Well, watch **Pet Tips on … at** … .

1. Have you got 2. There are 3. You won't get 4. Find out about 5. You can watch 6. For 7. Are there	+ some any +	questions about pets? Well, watch … . great stars in this film. That's … . help from the game show host, Ann, in … . Welsh villages and the myths around them in … . rescue teams on the job in the documentary … . fun in a family with crazy parents don't miss … . new songs in the charts this week? Find out on … .

L2, 2 ## A runaway from Avondale

PC Burns: Has anybody seen this teenager?
Man: Wait a minute, I think I saw the lad somewhere. Yes, it was this morning: He was at the train station.
PC Burns: Did he have anything with him?
Man: Yes, he had something in his left hand: a rucksack. No, a big blue sports bag.
Jenny: Hello, Officer. Is there anything wrong?
PC Burns: Hi, Jenny. Have you seen your younger brother anywhere today?
Jenny: Rob? He's not in trouble, I hope.
PC Burns: Well, we don't know. Somebody called just an hour ago. Your dad, I think. Rob didn't come home from school yesterday.
Jenny: Oh, no! But he has to be somewhere! I'm sure he hasn't got anything to hide, but I think he had something on his mind.

Wait a minute!
...
POLICE

3 Work it out!

a) *Who is the runaway in this TV soap? Where could he be? What do you think?*

b) *Which of the words with 'some' and 'any' do you use in statements, negative statements and questions?*

I have **some** information about **some**body or **some**thing, **some**where.

He hasn't got **any** information about **any**body or **any**thing, **any**where.

→ G16

4 He must be somewhere! (→ p. 57/ex. 6, 7)

Choose the right words and find another clue about Rob.

PC Burns talked to Rob's teachers but they couldn't tell him **anything**. He was sure that one of Rob's friends knew … but he couldn't get … information from him.
The police couldn't find Rob … so they asked … people at the train station. At first they didn't find out … .
Then … remembered that they saw a young man who looked like Rob on the 7:30 train to London that morning.
So perhaps Rob was now … in London.
Later Jenny told the police … that was really interesting!

some | any | anywhere | something | somewhere | somebody | anything | anything ✓ | something

5 For my folder: A runaway story

a) *Make up a story about Rob.*

What kind of person is he?
Why did he run away from home?
Where did he go to?

b) *Present your story to the class.*

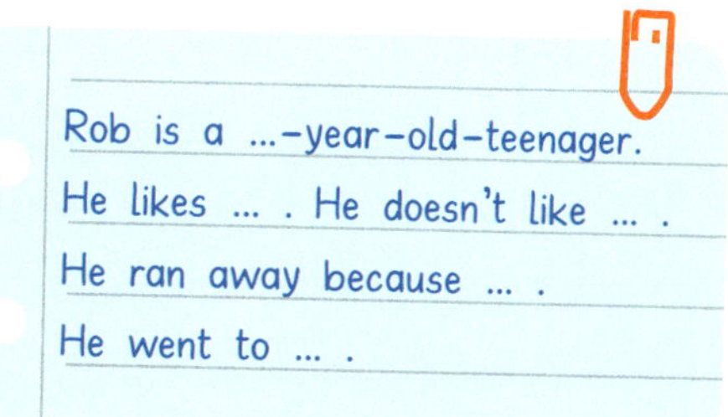

Rob is a ...-year-old-teenager.
He likes ... . He doesn't like ... .
He ran away because ... .
He went to ... .

The Diamond Hotel

In the film 'The Diamond Hotel' Lady Richstone's jewellery is missing from the hotel safe and somebody has attacked the hotel manager.

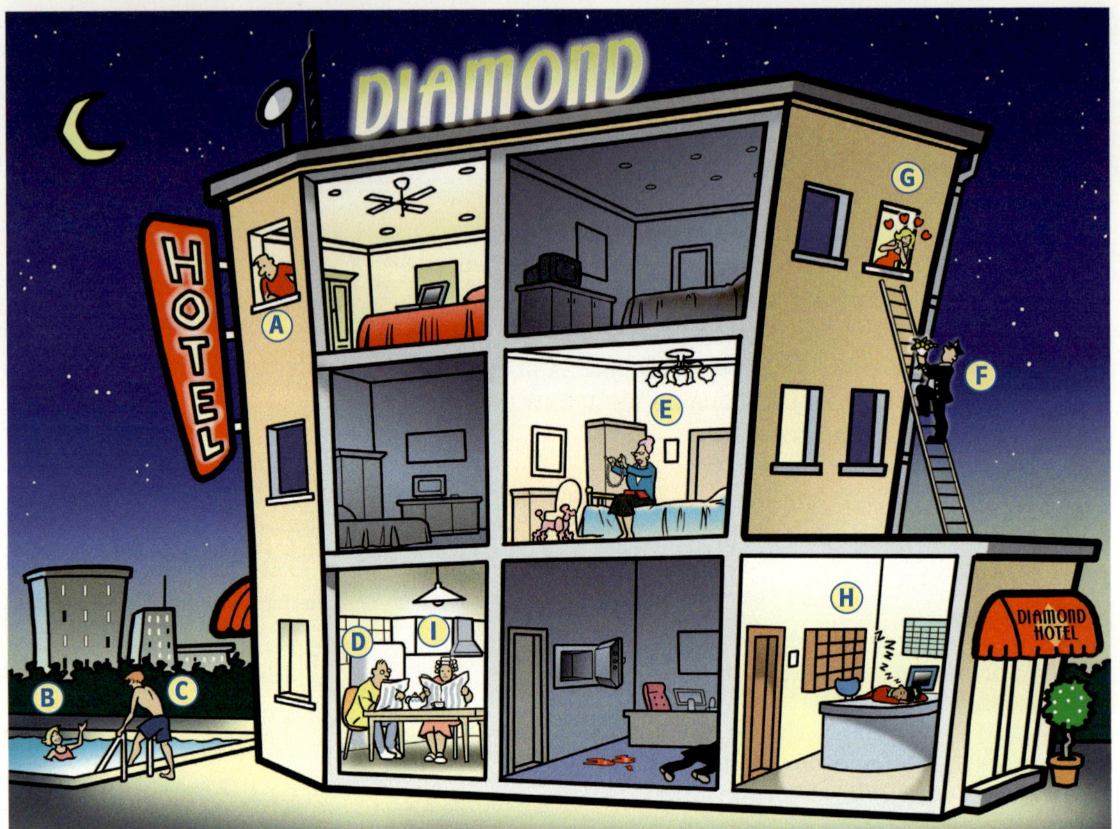

1 Inspector I. Newitt (→ p. 58/ex. 8, 9)

Inspector I. Newitt is interviewing people at the hotel about the crime.

Complete the dialogues.

Inspector: What **were** you **doing** at midnight?
Suspect A: I **was writing** an e-mail to a friend.
Inspector: And what were you doing?
Suspects B + C: We were … in the TV room.

Go on, please.

2 That's not true! (→ p. 58/ex. 10)

Look at the picture. What were the suspects really doing?

Suspect A wasn't … . He was … .
Suspects B and C weren't … . They were … . *Go on, please.*

I was/wasn't writing an e-mail.
They **were/weren't watching** TV.
→ G17

Suspects say:

A:	write e-mail
B + C:	watch TV
D + I:	clean kitchen
E:	walk dog
F:	smoke pipe in gardens
G:	dance at disco
H:	sit at reception

A:	→ watch	F:	→ climb
B + C:	→ swim	G:	→ wait for
D + I:	→ read	H:	→ sleep
E:	→ look at		

3 What was happening when ...? (→ p. 59/ex. 11)

Polly works at the hotel. She found the manager in his office in the morning.
What did she see? *Look at the grid. Use the headings and the inspector's notes.*

Example: 1. When Polly **came** downstairs, Lady Richstone **was walking** upstairs. She **was** ... and ... .

When Polly ...	was (wasn't)/were (weren't) ...
1. come downstairs,	Lady Richstone/walk upstairs/ not carry stick/dog follow her
2. reach reception,	Marg (receptionist)/sleep at desk
3. pass TV room,	nobody/sit in there
4. come into office,	Mr Mangold (manager)/lie on floor!
5. call the police,	others talk about crime
6. go out of hotel,	guard/not check gardens
7. look around the gardens,	two people/hide behind tree!
8. walk around hotel,	somebody/climb down a ladder!

▶ When Polly **heard** the strange noise, she **was putting** her cleaning things away upstairs. → G18

4 While ... (→ p. 59/ex. 12)

While the ambulance was taking Mr Mangold to the hospital, what were the people in the hotel doing? *Make sentences.*

1. While the ambulance **was taking** ... , Lady Richstone **was packing** ... .
2. While Lady Richstone **was packing** ..., Polly **was** ... . Go on, please.

▶ While they **were taking** him to the hospital, a guest **was having** breakfast. → G18

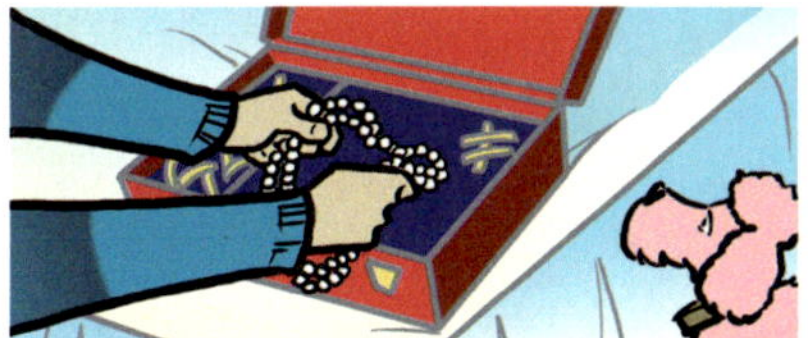
1 Lady Richstone / pack

2 Polly / look at

3 I. Newitt / look for clues

4 policemen / check rooms

5 receptionist + guest / talk

6 guard / sleep

5 For my folder: A detective story

Inspector I. Newitt knows who attacked the hotel manager. Who was it?
Look at the clues and write what happened.

READING SKILLS

Expressive reading
Make your reading expressive and interesting for your audience. How can you do this?
Understand the text: Read the story to yourself. What is it about?
Say the words correctly: Look up any new words in the dictionary. Can you say all the words?
Check your intonation: Look at the story again. Listen to it on the CD. Where should your voice go up or down? Which words should you stress?
Relax: Take a deep breath. If you enjoy the story, then others will, too.
Read: Don't read too fast. Can your audience understand everything?

1 A great story (→ p. 60/ex. 13–15)

a) *Make a copy of the story. Read your text and prepare it:*
- *Look up the new words.*
- *Look at the phonetic symbols on p. 141. Write them above the words.*
- *Mark where your voice goes up or down in a sentence:*

  What have you done with my son? You've killed him.
- *Mark the words that you find difficult to say. Write the intonation above the word.*

> **Remember:**
> . = stop
> , = pause

L2, 3

A terrible mistake

There was once a Welsh prince called Llywelyn. He had a very good, brave friend – Gelert, his big, white dog.
One day, when Llywelyn's wife was not at home, he wanted to go hunting. He couldn't leave his son all alone in the castle so he left Gelert at home to look after the baby.
He said goodbye to his son and dog, got on his horse and took the road along the river.
At the castle the baby slept all morning and Gelert stayed with him. Suddenly there was a sound and the door opened. Gelert got up quickly, picked up the baby in his mouth and put him under the bed in the next room.
Then he turned and looked at the visitor: It was a strong, hungry wolf with very big teeth. But Gelert was not afraid and attacked it. They fought hard for almost an hour. Later, when Llywelyn came home, Gelert was waiting at the door. There was blood all around his mouth. Llywelyn couldn't find his son in his little bed so he began to shout, "What have you done with my son? You've killed him!"
Llywelyn was so angry that he took out his knife and killed Gelert. At that moment he heard a cry. He looked under the bed and found the baby safe, not hurt at all.
Then he turned and saw the dead wolf behind the door. He was shocked because he now understood: The blood on Gelert's mouth was from the wolf, not from the baby. "Oh, no, what have I done?" he cried, "Gelert killed the wolf and now I've killed my best friend!"
Llywelyn felt so sad that he buried his brave dog in a special place. He made a gravestone and wrote Gelert's name and his story on it.

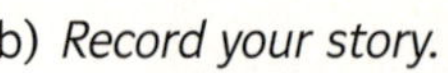

b) *Record your story.*

c) *Now listen. Compare your reading with the one on the CD and check what's different.*

d) *Listen again. Try to copy the voice on the CD so that your reading sounds better.*

e) *Now choose another story, for example p. 16/17 or p. 46/47. Use the skills box and read the story to the class.*

L2, 4 1 Let's listen: An interesting role (→ p. 61/ex. 16, 17)

a) Star guest on Ian Hall's talk show today is Amanda Willis. *Listen to the interview and look at the key phrases. Find the four phrases that have to do with Ian's questions.*

make up lines? • meet new stars? • no more TV dramas? • learn to swim? • live in London? • first big film part? • was anything difficult? • like your hotel?

b) *Listen again. Correct the sentences.*

1. Amanda got the part because she flew to Paris.
2. She just walked up to the director and thanked him.
3. Amanda's assistant gave her three days to learn her lines.
4. While they were filming, she fell off her horse.
5. Her make-up assistant helped her to get on the horse again.
6. Amanda doesn't want to do any more TV dramas.
7. She thinks that it's difficult to keep secrets.

L2, 5 2 Let's listen: Is it a draw?

Do the TV quiz with the players on the game show.

1st question:
a. James Bond
b. Sir Arthur Conan Doyle
c. Shakespeare?

2nd question:
a. General Hospital
b. Chicago Hope
c. Emergency Room?

3rd question:
a. Spiderman
b. Batman
c. Superman?

4th question: *(Use the photo.)*
a. dirty hands
b. thinking
c. saying hello?

L2, 6 3 Sounds: [əʊ], [aʊ], [eə] and [ɪə] (→ p. 61/ex. 18)

Listen to the sentences. Look at the words and write down the ones that you hear.

1. shown/phone/won't/goal
2. known/now/sound/crowds
3. hear/ear/clean/hair
4. clear/wear/just/chairs

L2, 7 4 A poem: Films (→ p. 61/ex. 19; p. 62/ex. 20)

(William Sears)

Some films are sad – you watch them and cry.
You know that the hero is going to[1] die.
Some films have spies[2] – they fight, run and jump.
When they crash[3] their cars, there's a very big bump[4]!
Sometimes aliens come down from space[5].
That often means trouble for the human race[6].
And then there are ghost films – ghosts come out at night
And give everybody an awful fright[7].
But the worst films are love films where all the stars kiss.
Those are the films that I want to miss!

What sort of films does the poem talk about? What are the worst films? Do you agree?

[1]is going to ['gəʊɪŋ ˌtə] – *wird,* [2]spy [spaɪ] – *Spion,* [3]to crash [kræʃ] – *einen Unfall haben mit …,* [4]bump [bʌmp] – *Knall,* [5]space [speɪs] – *Weltraum,* [6]human race [ˌhjumən 'reɪs] – *menschliche Rasse,* [7]to give s.o. an awful fright [ˌɔ:fl 'fraɪt] – *jdm. furchtbaren Schrecken einjagen*

The Hound of the Baskervilles

A No one knew who murdered Sir Charles Baskerville at his old house, Baskerville Hall, on Dartmoor in the southwest of England. People said that it was a huge and terrible hound that glowed in the dark. They called it the Hound of the Baskervilles.
Sir Charles had no wife and no children. So the only inheritor of the big house was Sir Charles' nephew, young Sir Henry Baskerville. Sir Henry arrived from Canada, but before he moved into Baskerville Hall, he visited the famous detective, Sherlock Holmes, and his assistant, Dr Watson, at 221b Baker Street, London.

B When he entered Holmes' flat, Henry was so scared that he was shaking.
"What's the matter, Sir Henry?" asked Holmes. "Quick, Watson! Give this man a cup of tea!"
"I'm the only inheritor of Baskerville Hall, but I'm too scared to live in it. A huge and terrible hound that glows in the dark kills Baskervilles, they say. Now I'm the last one left. I need to know: Is this hound real? You are the only man who can solve this mystery, Sherlock Holmes."

Holmes thanked Sir Henry for his trust and he and his assistant agreed to go with poor Sir Henry to Dartmoor the following day.
"Did you notice his boots, Watson?" asked Holmes after Sir Henry had left the flat.
"Yes, I did," said Watson. "One was black and one was brown!"
From the window Holmes and Watson saw Sir Henry in Baker Street. A tall man with a black beard was following him.
"Very strange," said Holmes.

C On the next day Holmes, Watson and Sir Henry arrived on Dartmoor. At Baskerville Hall, the servant Barrymore took their bags.
"Holmes!" whispered Watson. "Barrymore has got a black beard … !"
"You should leave this place, Sir Henry!" said Barrymore. "The Hound of the Baskervilles will kill you like it killed your poor uncle!"
Just then they all heard loud barking.
"W-what's that?" cried Sir Henry. He started shaking again.
"It's only my hunting dogs," said Barrymore. "They can smell visitors, you see. Dogs have a very good sense of smell."

D The following day Holmes, Watson and Sir Henry went for a walk on Dartmoor.
"Sir Henry," said Holmes, "why do you always wear one black boot and one brown boot?"
"They're the only boots that I have now," said Sir Henry. "First, someone stole one black boot from my hotel room in London. I had never worn them, they were new. Next morning I found that one of my old brown boots was missing!"
Suddenly they heard a terrible noise. It sounded like a huge hound which was barking, but they could see absolutely nothing on Dartmoor.

E When they got back to Baskerville Hall, a visitor was waiting for Sir Henry. He had fair hair and grey eyes and he wore a white coat like a scientist.
"Hello, neighbour!" the man said. "Stapleton is the name!"
"We heard a terrible noise when we were walking out on the moor, Mr Stapleton. What was it?" asked Sherlock Holmes.
"Stupid people believe it's a big dog which glows in the dark," laughed Stapleton.
Holmes went over to a painting of a man above the fireplace.
"Hmm," he said. "Who's this?"
"It's my other uncle, Rodger Baskerville, who died in South America. He had no children," said Sir Henry.
"Hm," said Holmes to himself. "Fair hair, grey eyes …"
"I'd like to invite you all to supper tonight," said Stapleton.
"Thank you, Mr Stapleton," said Sherlock Holmes, "but Dr Watson and I must go to the station right away."
"But Holmes," said his assistant, "we've only just …"
"Right now, Watson. Please hurry up."
"Thanks for the invitation, Mr Stapleton," said Sir Henry. "But I'm afraid to walk on the moor after dark."
"You aren't scared of the Hound of the Baskervilles, are you, Sir Henry?" laughed Stapleton. "There is no hound. But come at six, it doesn't get dark until seven."

F "Did you notice Stapleton's hands?" Holmes asked on their way to the station.
"Yes, I did, Holmes. There was a white powder on them. Stapleton is a scientist, I'm sure the powder is from one of his experiments."
"Hmmm …" said Holmes. "It's very strange."

1 Before you read: Be a detective

a) *What do you know about Sherlock Holmes?*

b) *Where is he at the moment?*
What do the clues in the picture tell you?

2 Up to now (→ p. 63/ex. 21)

Holmes and his assistant know that dogs don't usually glow in the dark!
What else do they find strange?
The key words can help you.

In part B a man with a black beard … .
In part C we find out that Barrymore has got …, too.
In part D we learn that someone … . Then … .
Go on, please.

▶ black beard	fair hair, grey eyes
black boot/brown boot	white powder/scientist

G At six o'clock Sir Henry knocked at Stapleton's door, but no one answered. Then he saw his neighbour's face in an upstairs window.

"Hello!" said Sir Henry. "It's getting dark out here. Let me in …"

Suddenly there was a terrible sound. It was a very big dog. It was coming across the moor and it was getting closer.

"The Hound of the Baskervilles is coming to get you, Cousin!" laughed Stapleton.

"Help, help!" shouted Sir Henry. "Hang on, I'm not your cousin …"

"Oh, yes, you are!" said Stapleton. "You thought Sir Rodger Baskerville didn't have any children, but he had me! So Baskerville Hall belongs to both of us."

"But that's no problem," said Sir Henry. "We can share it. Just let me in!"

Stapleton just laughed. "Why share the Hall with you when I can have it all to myself?"

The sound was very near now. When Sir Henry turned, he saw a terrible hound. It was the size of a horse. It was sniffing the ground where Sir Henry had walked. Its enormous body glowed and its eyes were like fire! It ran towards Sir Henry and jumped. Sir Henry closed his eyes.

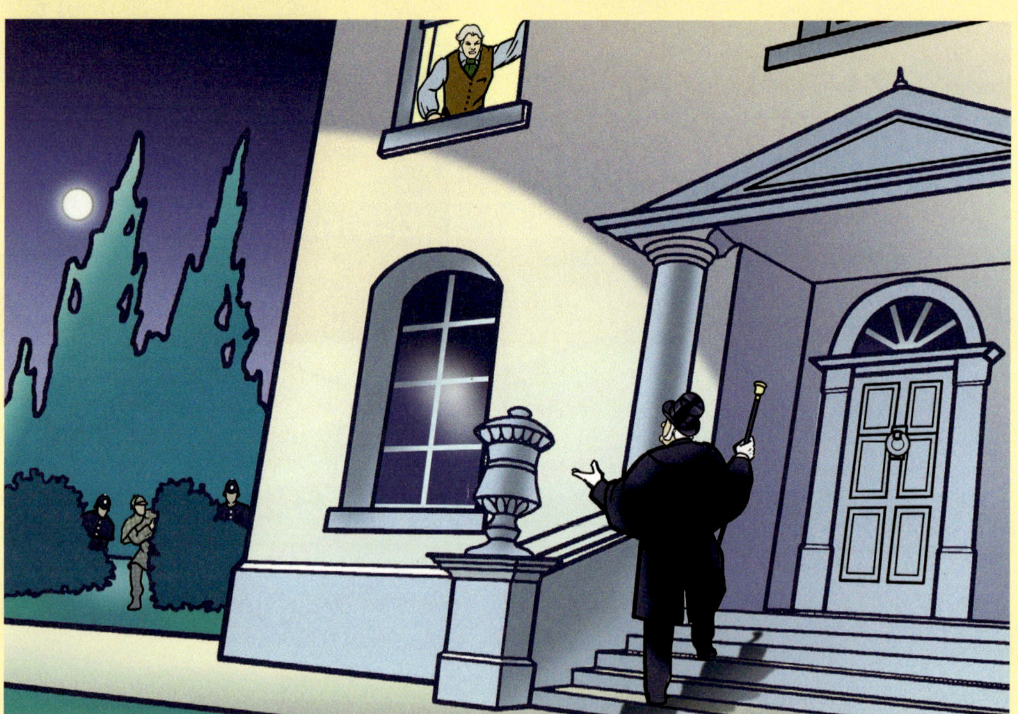

H BANG! A gunshot echoed across the moor. BANG! BANG! The terrible hound fell to the ground. Stapleton could not believe what he was seeing from the window: Three London policemen came out of the bushes with guns. Behind them came Sherlock Holmes and his assistant, Dr Watson.

"Arrg! Holmes!" cried Stapleton. "I thought that you wanted to go to the train station!"

"Oh, I did," said Holmes calmly. "But only to meet Her Majesty's three finest policemen. He turned to the policemen. "Arrest him." The policemen went into Stapleton's house and took him away.

"You solved the mystery, Sherlock Holmes!" said Sir Henry. "The Hound of the Baskervilles is dead. Now it's safe to live here again!"

3 How does it end?

Match the right picture with the ending of the story.

4 Parts of the story

Look at parts A–H of the story again. Find a title for each part.

5 Who's who? (→ p. 63/ex. 22)

1. Who died at Baskerville Hall?
2. Who came to England from Canada?
3. Who did Sir Henry visit in London?
4. Who was at Holmes' flat, too?
5. Who was a servant at Baskerville Hall?
6. Who was Sir Henry's neighbour?
7. Who was Stapleton's father?
8. Who did Holmes meet at the station?

6 How did you do it, Holmes?

Dr Watson asks Holmes how he solved the mystery.
Match the parts and find his answers.

	+
1. Someone stole a black boot	because Stapleton put white powder on it.
2. So he then stole an old brown boot	but the man who followed Sir Henry was taller.
3. Barrymore had a black beard, too,	but it was new, so it didn't 'smell' of Sir Henry.
4. Stapleton had fair hair and grey eyes	and the hound got Sir Henry's 'smell' from it.
5. The hound glowed in the dark	so maybe he was the son of Sir Rodger.

7 For my folder: An exciting report (→ p. 63/ex. 23)

Imagine you are a newspaper reporter. Write an exciting report for your readers.
Look at the skills box on page 40 for help.

1 Media and programmes (→ p. 64/ex. 24)

Make a mind map for 'media' and 'programmes'.

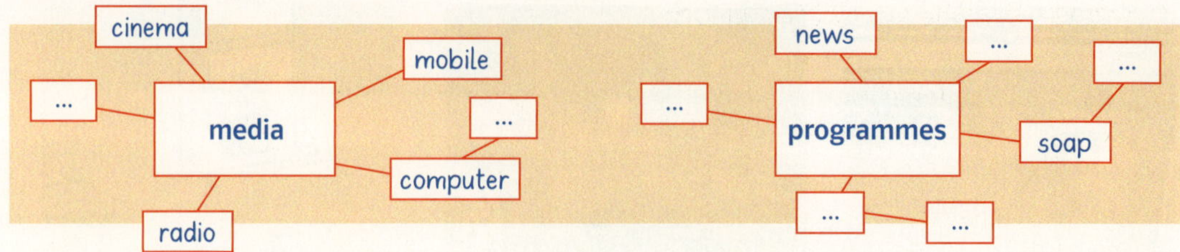

2 Let's look: Sherlock's room

a) *Look at the picture of Sherlock's room for ten seconds. Close your book. How many things can you remember?*

b) *Look again. What could Holmes not have had in his room?*

3 Bollywood words (→ p. 64/ex. 25)

Find the words (adjectives) that can describe Bollywood films. Look at pages 80/81 for help.

1. Bollywood: It's a very **large** film industry.
2. The films are very … (with teenagers).
3. They're at least 3 hours … .
4. You remember the songs because they're … .
5. And the dances are … .
6. The films have many … fights.
7. The heroes are strong and … .
8. The heroines are beautiful and … .

4 Words that go together (→ p. 64/ex. 26)

a) *Find the pairs.*
Example: **Look at** goes with **a picture**.

look at ✓ • interview • take • tell • watch • go to • listen to • make • learn • do	a grid • a survey • photos • TV • a star • a picture ✓ • the cinema • a story • your lines • the radio

 b) *Choose one of the verbs from the first box and find more words to go with it.*
Example: **learn English, …**

5 Say it right

a) *Say the words in the box out loud to a partner.*

out • but • sound • mouth • shout • around • found • up • hunt • once • blood • done • one • son • under • looked • took • good • put • wolf • horse • called • fought • all • saw • strong • story • want • dog • what • was

 b) *Your partner can put the words under the right heading in a grid like this:*

aʊ (as in 'now')	ʌ (as in 'bus')	ʊ (as in 'book')	ɔ (as in 'ball')	ɒ (as in 'box')
out	but	...	...	...
...	...	...	...	...

6 Be a word detective

a) *Find the right word.*

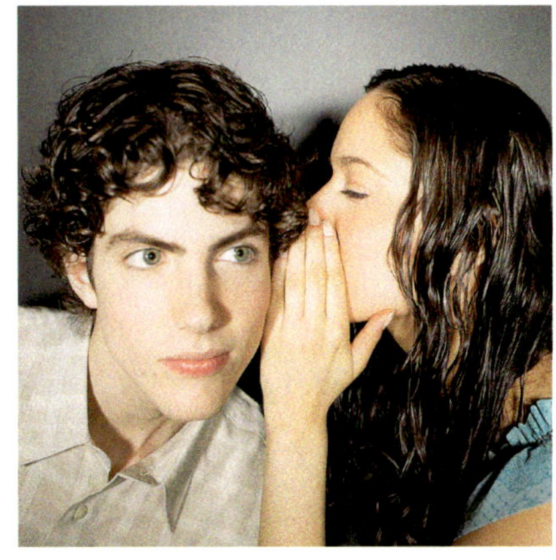

1. When something …, it's like a light in the dark.
2. An … is somebody who gets something from his or her parents when they die.
3. An inspector looks for … at the scene of the crime.
4. If you find out who did it, you have … the mystery.
5. If you catch the wrong person, you have made a terrible … .
6. A person who does experiments in science is a … .
7. When the police catch a burglar, they usually … him.
8. A person who runs away from home is a … .
9. You ask somebody to keep a … if you don't want other people to know about it.
10. A … is when two teams have the same number of points.

b) *Make sentences for five words from the unit. Can your partner guess your words?*

1 Have they got any ...? (some, any → G15)

a) In the shop they've got some things, but they haven't got other things.
Write 11 questions. Use the words from the box.

Example: Have you got **any** biscuits?

biscuits? • DVDs? • newspapers? • books? • sports posters? • birthday cards? • exercise books? • coke? • camera batteries? • banana ice-cream? • pencils?

b) *Now turn your book around, look at the picture and answer with 'some' or 'any'.*

Example: No, sorry, we haven't got **any** biscuits but we've got **some** crisps.

2 Anybody for a cup of tea? (compounds of some/any → G16) (→ p. 65/ex. 27)

Choose the right word and complete the sentences.

1. I'm just making some tea – *(somebody/anybody)* else for tea?
2. Did you see Derek with Fiona? I'm sure there's *(something/anything)* in the air!
3. You're not going *(somewhere/anywhere)* until you've cleaned your room!
4. I'm still hungry. Isn't there *(something/anything)* left to eat?
5. If you don't have *(somebody/anybody)* who can help you, just call me at the weekend.
6. I know *(somebody/anybody)* has to lose. But why must it be me?
7. I've lost my TV magazine. Have you seen it *(somewhere/anywhere)*?
8. We won't tell *(somebody/anybody)* our plans yet because we want them all to be surprised.
9. I dropped my mobile down the toilet – and there isn't *(something/anything)* funny about that!
10. I saw a great poster of that film *(somewhere/anywhere)* in town.
11. *(something/anything)* strange happened to Dave when he was on his way to the cinema.
12. I don't think *(something/anything)* has gone wrong. They've probably just missed their train.

3 While the burglar was stealing … (past progressive → G17) (→ p. 65/ex. 28, 29)

a) A burglar broke the window and climbed into the Bells' house. What were the Bells doing while he was stealing their things?
1. Mrs Bell **was flying** to Australia. 2. Mark and his girlfriend **were** … . *Go on, please.*

1 Mrs Bell / fly

2 Mark & girlfriend / dance

3 Mr Bell / drive

4 Jenny / sit

5 Grandpa Bell / walk dog

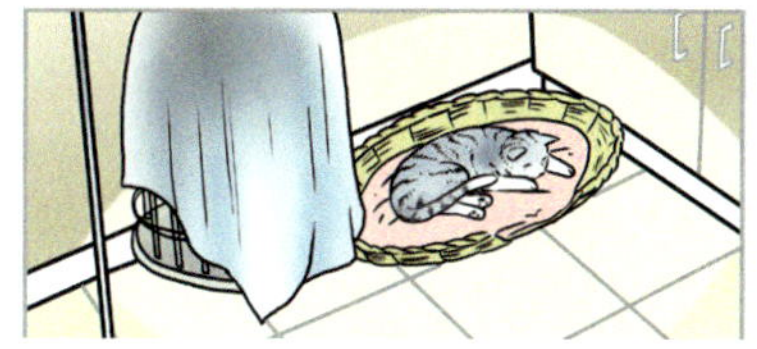
6 Kitty and Birdy Bell / sleep

b) The Bells' neighbour tells the police the wrong facts. *Correct his statements.*
Mrs Bell **wasn't visiting** … . She **was** … . *Go on, please.*

1. When the burglar came, Mrs Bell was visiting her sister in Cornwall.
2. Mark and his girlfriend were having a meal at an Indian restaurant.
3. Mr Bell? Oh, he was walking their dog.
4. Jenny was staying at a friend's house that night.
5. And I'm sure old Mr Bell was sleeping upstairs.

4 Mixed bag: The story never ends (→ G15–G17)

Find the missing words and find out what happened next in 'Avondale'.

When Rob arrived in London, it was raining hard. Tess, (1) he knew from his last holiday job in Devon, wasn't (2) the station to meet him. Perhaps she was late, he (3), a bit worried. The battery of his mobile was now (4), so he looked around for a phone and called her. (5) he was doing this, he had his back to his (6) bag. There was no answer from Tess. Rob decided to (7) back to the place where they planned to meet. He (8) to pick up his bag – but it wasn't there! He couldn't (9) to the police because he was a runaway. And now he (10) have any clothes or anything – and he hadn't a lot of money! What if she (11) come? He waited for two hours and he was (12) more and more fed up. Now what?

NOW YOU CAN

- ✓ talk about films and TV programmes. → *Describe a programme that you saw on TV.*
- ✓ use 'some'/'any' with '-body', '-where', etc. → *Talk about different places, things and people.*
- ✓ describe things that were going on. → *Write about five things that were happening when you were in the park, playground or on the bus.*
- ✓ read out loud and make it interesting. → *Practise and read the text from ex. 4 out loud.*

A long way from home

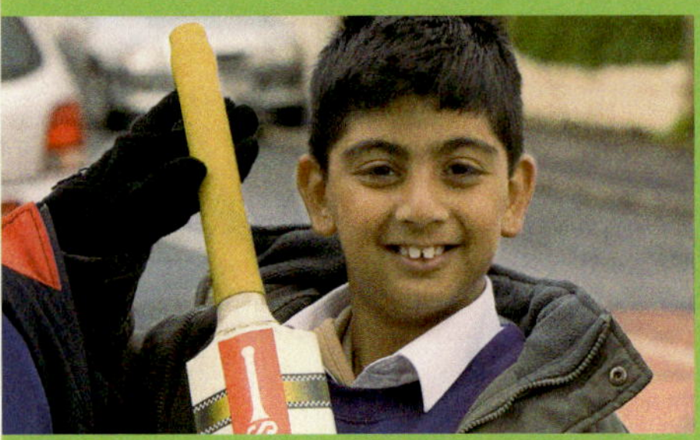

Every year thousands of people come to the UK as refugees[1]. Many of them are young and some of them come alone, without their parents or family. Every week in 'Cool' Magazine one of these young people tells you his or her own story. This week our story is about Rizwan[2].

This is Rizwan. He's from Pakistan[3] and he's 14. He came to England when both his parents died in an earthquake[4]. His aunt and uncle in Wolverhampton[5] adopted[6] him. He told our 'Cool' reporter: I didn't like it here at first. It was November and when we landed in Heathrow, it was cold and foggy. A friendly lady collected me from the flight and brought me to my aunt and uncle, who were waiting for me with a huge box of chocolates and a warm coat. I remember a lot of strange faces and funny smells. I was a bit frightened but my aunt was really nice. While my uncle was driving home, she told me about my new school.

That was another big problem – my first day at my new school! It was a disaster! There were two other boys in my class. They were horrible. On the first day they sent me to the wrong room for History. And then they hid my bag. But some of the other kids were really nice. They helped me to find it. I don't know what we had for lunch on my first day but I remember it tasted really strange. I still don't really like school food but my aunt says it won't kill me! Now school is OK. I've got some good friends and I'm on the cricket team.

1 Rizwan's story

a) *Read the text. Use your dictionary for any new words.*

b) *What are the pros[7] and cons[8] of life in England? Copy the grid and complete it.*

pros	cons
a friendly lady collected him from the flight ...	...

c) *Think. What would you like to ask Rizwan?*

[1]refugee [refjʊ'dʒi:] – *Flüchtling,* [2]Rizwan ['rɪzˌwɑ:n] – *Jungenname,* [3]Pakistan [ˌpɑ:kɪ'stɑ:n] – *Pakistan,* [4]earthquake ['ɜ:θkweɪk] – *Erdbeben,* [5]Wolverhampton ['wʊlvəˌhæmptən] – *Stadt in England,* [6]to adopt [ə'dɒpt] – *adoptieren,* [7]pro [prəʊ] – *Vorteil,* [8]con [kɒn] – *Nachteil*

5 Harbour Road[1]
Brighton (A)
BT5 8QU
(B) 22nd October

(C) Dear 'Cool' Magazine,

(D) This is my first letter to a magazine. I just wanted to say that I found your story about Rizwan very interesting. I felt a bit like him on my first trip to England. I wasn't a refugee of course. I was on a two-week exchange visit to Brighton with my school. (E)

(F) I am in England at the moment. It is my third visit here. This time I am visiting my exchange partner on my own[2].

I wasn't very happy in England the first time I was here. Like Rizwan I found everything strange and I didn't like the food. My English wasn't very good and I couldn't always understand my family. I only ate ham sandwiches and bananas for the first few days!! (G)

But at the weekend everything changed. I went windsurfing[3] in Cornwall with my partner and his older brother. We slept in tents and cooked our own meals. It was great fun!

It can be very hard at first in a new country but with good friends around it is a lot easier. I think sport is a good way to make friends. (H)

(I) Best wishes[4],
Martin (J)

WRITING 

Planning a letter

A Address with postcode[5]
B Date
C You start like this
D First word with capital letter
E Why you are writing
F A new paragraph[6] for each new idea
G Comments[7] about the article
H Closing[8] words
I Saying 'goodbye'
J Your name

2 Martin's letter

Read the letter which Martin wrote to 'Cool' magazine after he had read about Rizwan. Imagine you want to write a letter to a magazine. Check the parts in the skills box and put these parts in the right order.

Make comments. • Say 'goodbye'. • Your address • How you start • Capital letter at beginning • Use paragraphs. • The date • Say why you are writing. • Close the letter. • Sign the letter.

3 A letter to a magazine (→ p. 66/ex. 1)

a) *Now plan a letter. Check that you have put all the parts in the right order.*
b) *Use your plan and write a letter to 'Cool' Magazine.*
c) *Show it to your partner. Have you forgotten anything?*

[1]Harbour Road [ˌhɑːbə 'rəʊd] – *Straßenname,* [2]on my own [əʊn] – *auf eigene Faust,* [3]windsurfing ['wɪndˌsɜːfɪŋ] – *Windsurfen,* [4]Best wishes [best 'wɪʃɪz] – *schöne Grüße,* [5]postcode ['pəʊstkəʊd] – *Postleitzahl,* [6]paragraph ['pærəgrɑːf] – *Absatz,* [7]comment ['kɒment] – *Bemerkung,* [8]closing ['kləʊzɪŋ] – *abschließend*

KINGSDALE
Comprehensive School

Kingsdale Outdoor Centre

Many years ago Mr Clays was a pupil at Kingsdale School. When his father died last year, he was able[1] to give his old farmhouse in Wales to the school. The teachers wanted to use it as an outdoor centre. But they weren't able to use it without repairs[2] and they had little[3] time and less[4] money. They had to ask the head teacher[5] for some money for wood and paint. The school wasn't able to pay for them. But the teachers were allowed[6] to have a stall at the summer fair. Luckily[7] they were able to raise[8] enough money.
They weren't able to do all the work themselves. But they didn't have to work alone. Parents and other teachers were able to help them. Pupils were allowed to help, too, but they weren't allowed to miss lessons. So they had to help during the summer holidays. The head teacher was able to open the centre in September.

1 What did they say?

a) *Copy the grammar box on the right and make a grid. Find the negative forms from the text.*

	statements	negative statements
can	was/were able to	wasn't/ …
may	was/were allowed to	…
must	…	…

▶ can → was/were able to
may → was/were allowed to
must → had to
→ G19

b) *Read the text again. Match the people with the statements.*

▶ needn't → didn't have to
→ G19

Mr Clays
two Geography teachers
the head teacher
parents and other teachers
pupils

You needn't work alone.
We can't use it without repairs.
We must help during the school holidays.
Pupils may help, too, but they mustn't miss lessons.
I can give my father's farmhouse to the school.

2 Rules for the pupils

a) *Write the rules. Example:* 1. You **may pick** apples but you … .

1 may/mustn't

2 needn't/must

3 may/mustn't

4 needn't/may

5 may/mustn't

6 needn't/must

b) *Now write what the pupils reported. Example:* 1. We **were allowed to** … .

[1]to be able to ['eɪbl] – *können,* [2]repair [rɪ'peə] – *Reparatur,* [3]little ['lɪtl] – *hier: wenig,* [4]less [les] – *weniger,* [5]head teacher [hed 'ti:tʃə] – *Rektor/Rektorin,* [6]to be allowed to [ə'laʊd] – *dürfen,* [7]luckily ['lʌkɪli] – *glücklicherweise,* [8]to raise [reɪz] – *hier: sammeln*

3 Team work

At the end of the week, what were/weren't the teams able to do? Write sentence.

Example: Team A1 **was able to insulate**[1] … and paint … . But they **weren't able to** … .

Team A: In the house	
A1	insulate walls/paint doors + windows
A2	prepare + paper[2] walls/paint doors + windows
A3	insulate walls/prepare + paper walls
Team B: In the garden	
B1	clear[3] the garden/build a wall
B2	build a wall/plant[4] vegetables
B3	clear the garden/plant vegetables

4 Let's talk: We weren't allowed to do that!

What were/weren't you allowed/able to do on your last school trip? Talk to a partner.

A: Were you able to … on your last school trip?
B: No, we weren't allowed to do that! But we were able to … . What about you?
A: We weren't able to … because … . But we were allowed to … instead[5]. That was great fun!

go swimming/cycling/climbing/canoeing/ …
visit a castle/museum/zoo/ …
sleep in tents/stay at a youth hostel[6]/ …
work on a farm/on a school project/ …
learn to ski[7]/ride a horse/ …
do lots of shopping/eat ice-cream for lunch/
stay awake[8]/go out in the evenings/
listen to loud music all night/
take your own DVDs with you …

5 For my folder: A school project

Write about a project at your school (a concert, sports day, a play, a film project, …).
What were you able to do/(not) allowed to do? Was there anything you had to do?

Our film project

For the film project at our school we had to organize a lot: We were allowed to use our own cameras but we also had to borrow some. Of course, we weren't allowed to film when … ! Pupils who were able to write good stories, wrote the … . We had to … .

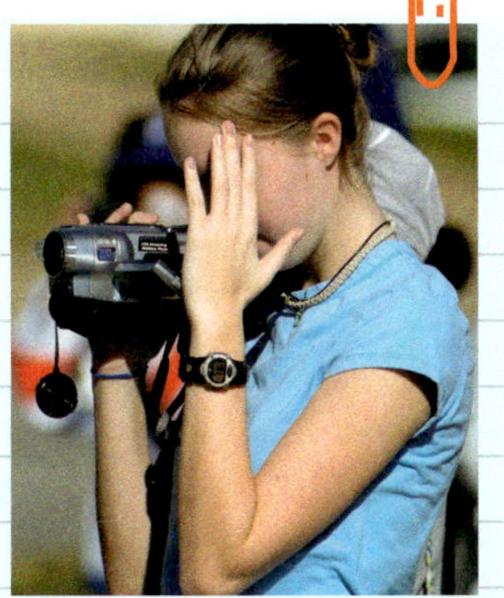

[1]to insulate ['ɪnsjəleɪt] – *isolieren*, [2]to paper ['peɪpə] – *tapezieren*, [3]to clear [klɪə] – *aufräumen*, [4]to plant [plɑ:nt] – *pflanzen*, [5]instead [ɪn'sted] – *stattdessen*, [6]youth hostel ['ju:θ ˌhɒstl] – *Jugendherberge*, [7]to ski [ski:] – *Ski fahren*, [8]awake [ə'weɪk] – *wach*

The legend[1] of King Arthur

Step 1: Get ready

a) *Look at the title. What do you think this story is about?*

b) *Look at the people in the story. What do you know about them?*

King Uther Lady Igraine Merlin Sir Ector Kay as a child/young man
The lords[2] A servant Arthur Arthur as a baby

Step 2: Look

a) *Look at the pictures on pages 102 to 109. Who can you see? What is happening in each picture? Use the skills box to help you.*

b) *Find a title for each picture.*

PICTURE SKILLS

Getting information from pictures

1. Who can you see? What do they look like? What are they wearing? How old are they? What are they doing/saying? How do you think they feel?
2. What else can you see in the picture?
3. Look at the pictures again and tell the story in your own words.

Step 3: Skim

a) *Look at the different paragraphs[3] A–F. Skim each paragraph and look out for key words. Write notes.*

b) *Answer these questions for each paragraph: When does the story happen? Where does it happen? Who are the people in the text? What happens? Why?*

READING SKILLS

Skimming

Skim the text. Don't read every word.
Just look out for key words.
Ask: When? Where? Who? What? Why?
Write notes.

[1]legend ['ledʒənd] – *Legende,* [2]lord [lɔ:d] – *Lord,* [3]paragraph ['pærəgrɑ:f] – *Paragraf, Abschnitt*

Step 4: Read

a) *Read the paragraphs. Look up the words which you don't know.*

b) *Find a title for each paragraph.*

c) *Write a summary for each paragraph.*

Step 5: Analyse[1]

a) *Look at the text. Who is in it?*

b) *Describe the people. Each group makes a poster for one of the people.*

c) *Present your poster to the class.*

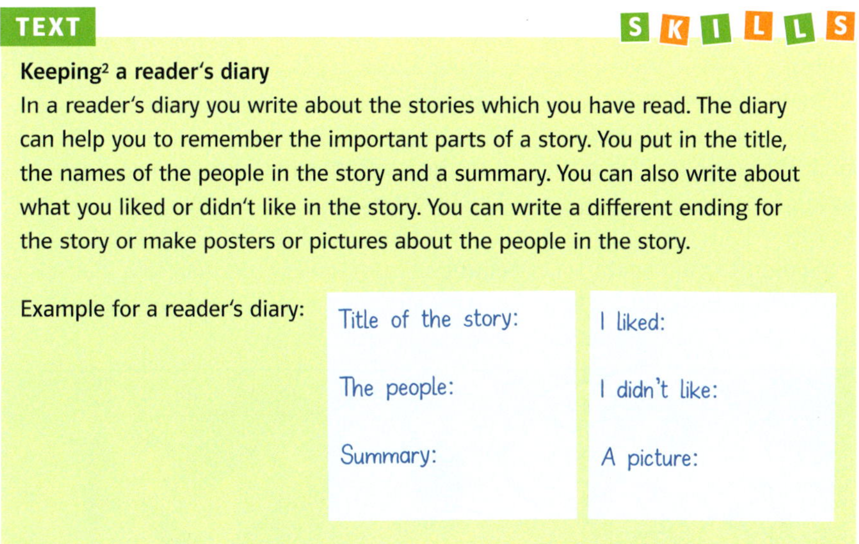

TEXT SKILLS

Keeping[2] a reader's diary

In a reader's diary you write about the stories which you have read. The diary can help you to remember the important parts of a story. You put in the title, the names of the people in the story and a summary. You can also write about what you liked or didn't like in the story. You can write a different ending for the story or make posters or pictures about the people in the story.

Example for a reader's diary:

Title of the story:	I liked:
The people:	I didn't like:
Summary:	A picture:

Step 6: Write

a) *There is a gap[3] in the story. It doesn't give you any information about Arthur when he was a boy. Find the gap.*

b) *Write a short text about what happened to Arthur when he was a boy. Use the words in the box.*

c) *Find a title for your text.*

d) *Read your text to the class.*

WRITING 

Spelling

When you have written a text, read it again and check your spelling.
Use the word list in your book. If you can't find a word in your book, use a dictionary.

lessons difficult • learn a lot of things • weather good • go fishing • ride • fall off • break arm • fight with sticks • hurt Kay

[1]to analyse ['ænlaɪz] – *analysieren*, [2]to keep [ki:p] – *hier: führen*, [3]gap [gæp] – *Lücke*

L2, 8–13 The legend of King Arthur: How Arthur became king

A *King Arthur is more famous than the kings and queens who you can find in history books. But no one really knows if he ever really lived.*
If King Arthur lived, it was over a thousand years ago when Britain was fighting Saxon[1] and Danish[2] invaders[3]. There are hundreds of different stories about how Arthur became King of Britain. This is just one of them …

It happened a long, long time ago, more than a thousand years have passed since then[4]. At that time, Britain was very different from today. There were forests[5] everywhere. Wolves and bears[6] lived there.
The most powerful[7] men were wizards and strange things happened where they walked. The King of Britain at that time was Uther. He had castles and land but he was unhappy because he had no wife.
"A king must have a queen," Uther said. "I need a son, who will wear my crown when I die." He loved the beautiful Lady Igraine but he wasn't able to marry her. She was already married to the Duke[8] of Cornwall. "How can I make Lady Igraine love me?" Uther asked himself. Uther was a fighter[9].
So he decided to fight against Lady Igraine's husband[10], the Duke of Cornwall, and he killed him.
"Now I can marry the beautiful Igraine!" he said. But Igraine was, of course, very angry with Uther.
'Maybe it wasn't such a good idea to kill her husband,' he thought. 'Now she'll never love me!'
One night love-sick[11] King Uther was having supper alone in his castle. "Oh, how can I get Igraine to marry me?" he asked himself. Suddenly a big, black bird flew into the room through an open window. The bird sat down on a chair.
As Uther looked at the bird, it slowly changed into[12] a very old man in a black cape[13]. He had a white beard, a long nose and angry red eyes.

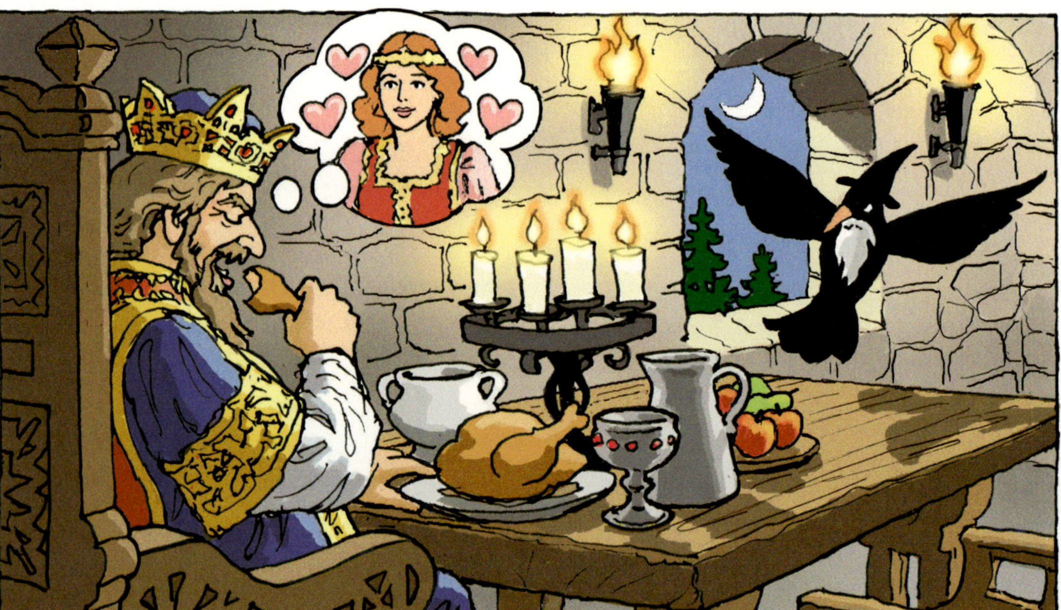

[1]Saxon ['sæksən] – *sächsisch,* [2]Danish ['deɪnɪʃ] – *dänisch,* [3]invader [ɪn'veɪdə] – *Invasor,* [4]then [ðen] – *damals,*
[5]forest ['fɒrɪst] – *Wald,* [6]bear [beə] – *Bär,* [7]powerful ['paʊəfl] – *mächtig,* [8]Duke [dju:k] – *Herzog,*
[9]fighter ['faɪtə] – *Kämpfer,* [10]husband ['hʌzbənd] – *Ehemann,* [11]love-sick ['lʌvsɪk] – *liebeskrank,*
[12]to change into [tʃeɪndʒ] – *sich verwandeln in,* [13]cape [keɪp] – *Umhang*

B Uther was scared. "Wh-who are you?" he asked. "What do you want?" "I am Merlin the Wizard and I want your son!"
"Son … ? I haven't got a son," said Uther.
"No, but you'll have one when you marry Igraine," said the wizard and he smiled.
"Marry Igraine?" whispered Uther. "But … can your magic[1] really make Igraine love me, Merlin?" "She will start to love you very soon, O King! And she will become your wife. She will give you a son. But you will not be able to[2] keep him. You must give him to me."
"To you, Merlin?" the king asked. "But I need a son. Every king needs a son who will wear his crown when he is dead."
"Your son will wear your crown, Uther. But Britain is a dangerous place. You must give him to me, so that he can be safe."
"Oh, yes, Merlin! You're right! You can have him. It's a deal[3]! I'll give you the baby when it is born[4]!" He shook the wizard's ice-cold[5] hand. And it happened just as Merlin the Wizard had said. Lady Igraine started to love Uther. Very soon they married and a year later a beautiful baby boy was born. Uther ran through the castle to see the new baby. When he opened the door of her bedroom, his wife was sleeping. But she was not alone. Someone was already standing beside the bed with the baby in his arms!

"Merlin! What are you doing here? Give me my son!" "Don't you remember our deal, Uther?" said Merlin. "You promised the child to me!" "But I need a son! One day he will be the next king!" "Don't worry, Uther! The child will be king, but … ." "Give him back," said Uther and he took out his sword[6]. He tried to grab the baby from the wizard's ice-cold hands. But the strange, old man changed into a big, black bird.
Uther watched him as he flew into the night sky with his little son. "Come back, Merlin!" he shouted. "Give me back my son!"

[1]magic ['mædʒɪk] – *Magie,* [2]to be able to [eɪbl] – *können,* [3]It's a deal! [di:l] – *Abgemacht!,*
[4]when it is born [bɔ:n] – *wenn es auf die Welt kommt,* [5]ice-cold ['aɪskəʊld] – *eiskalt,* [6]sword [sɔ:d] – *Schwert*

C That same night, in another castle in Britain, another baby was born. She was the daughter[1] of Sir Ector. But both the baby girl and the mother died a few hours later.

Sir Ector was very sad. "How can I tell my little boy, Kay, that he has lost his mother and his new baby sister?" Sir Ector sat in his castle and cried and cried. Suddenly a black bird flew into the room through an open window and landed on the table.

As Sir Ector looked at the bird, it changed into a very old man in a black cape. He had a white beard, a long nose and angry red eyes, and he was carrying a bundle[2].

Sir Ector was very scared.

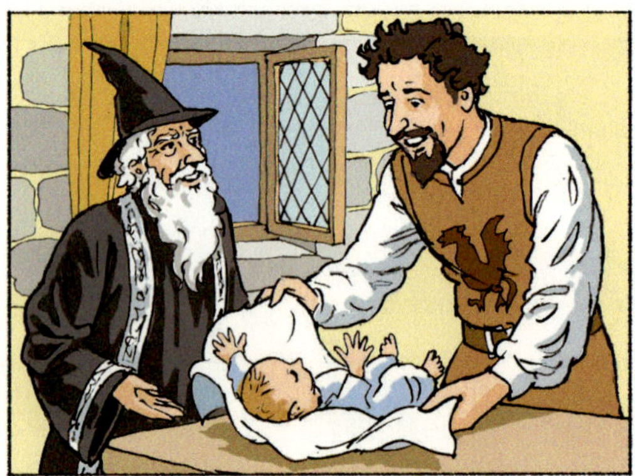

"Wh-who are you? Wh-where did you come from?" "I am Merlin the Wizard. I want you to look after this for me." Merlin put the bundle onto the table. Something in the blanket was moving. "It's a puppy[3] for little Kay to play with!" said Sir Ector. "Thank you Great Wizard!" "His name is Arthur."

"That's a funny name for a puppy," said Sir Ector.

"It isn't a puppy, stupid!" shouted Merlin. "Look inside!" Sir Ector looked inside the blanket. "It's a beautiful baby boy?!" he said. He was very surprised. "His name is Arthur. You must tell everyone that he is your son. One day he will be a very important man."

Sir Ector smiled at the child. "He can be a brother for Kay," he said happily. "Thank you, Merlin!"

"Remember," said the wizard, "don't tell anyone that I gave you little Arthur."

And with these words he changed into an huge, black bird again and flew out the window into the moonlight[4].

For the next 15 years people in Britain had a terrible time. King Uther died and the country had no king. All the lords fought against each other. They all wanted to be king. They attacked each other's castles. They burnt villages which belonged to other lords. The people who fought for them had no time to look after the farms, their animals and their families.

Thousands were hungry. Chaos[5] ruled[6] the land. There was no peace, only war[7].

[1]daughter ['dɔ:tə] – *Tochter*, [2]bundle ['bʌndl] – *Bündel*, [3]puppy ['pʌpi] – *junger Hund, Welpe*, [4]moonlight ['mu:nlaɪt] – *Mondlicht*, [5]chaos ['keɪɒs] – *Chaos*, [6]to rule [ru:l] – *beherrschen*, [7]war [wɔ:] – *Krieg*

D "There'll be no peace until one of us is King!" said one of the lords. They needed to decide who would be King of all Britain. So they had a big meeting in London. At first they talked but soon they were all shouting. One of the lords drew[1] his sword but suddenly they heard a terrible noise. There was lightning[2] and thunder[3], black clouds filled[4] the sky and heavy[5] rain fell. Suddenly they saw a big, black cloud. It was coming nearer and nearer! The cloud stopped and then it changed into an old man in a black cape, with a long nose and a white beard.

"Stop fighting!" said the old man.

"Wh-who are you?" asked the lord with the sword in his hand. This was an old man but he was very scared.

"I am Merlin the Wizard," Merlin said. "Our country needs peace!"

"We know that, Merlin!" said another lord. "But how?" "Tell us, which one of us shall be king, O Great Wizard!" shouted a third lord.

"None of you!" said Merlin. "The King of Britain is not here."

"How do we find him, Merlin?" a fourth lord asked.

"Follow me," said Merlin.

It was almost dark but the lords could see something. It was a large, white stone. In the middle of the stone was a sword. It was a beautiful sword with jewels on its handle[6]. On the white stone, the lords could see some gold letters:

Only the person who can take this sword from the stone is the true King of all Britain.

[1]to draw [drɔ:] – *ziehen*, [2]lightning ['laɪtnɪŋ] – *Blitz*, [3]thunder ['θʌndə] – Donner, [4]to fill [fɪl] – *füllen*, [5]heavy ['hevi] – *stark*, [6]handle ['hændl] – *Griff*

E One day a messenger[1] came to Sir Ector's castle with some important news.
Arthur was now 15 and Kay, who was older, was now a knight. He was very bossy[2] to young Arthur. He told him to brush[3] his horse and to clean the stables[4]. He even told him to prepare his bath[5]. "Hurry up, Arthur!" Kay shouted. "I haven't got all day!" Kay treated[6] Arthur like a servant.
Sir Ector and Kay were in the big hall in the castle when the messenger arrived.
"This isn't for you, Arthur," said Sir Ector. "Please leave the room!"
"But, Father," said Arthur. "I want to hear the messenger's news, too." "I'm sorry, Arthur, but you're too young," said Sir Ector.
"Yeah[7]," laughed Kay. "The news is only for knights. Go and play, little boy!"
Arthur was very sad. He went to the stables to sit with his favourite horse.
The messenger's servant was giving the messenger's horse some water.
"Why are you so sad?" asked the servant.
"I want to hear the messenger's news," said Arthur. "But my father and brother say it's only for knights." "I can tell you the news," said the servant. "There's going to be[8] a big tournament[9]." "A tournament?"
said Arthur. "With knights on horses?"
"That's right," said the servant. "In London. All the best knights in England will be there. There'll be sword fights, children's games, honey[10] cakes, and Merlin the Wizard will be there!"
"Merlin the Wizard," said Arthur. "Wow! They say he can do real magic!"
"That's right! And they're going to choose[11] the new King of Britain. You see, there's this stone with a sword … ."

But Arthur did not stay to hear the rest. He was so excited about the tournament, he ran into the house where Sir Ector and Kay were just coming out of the room with the messenger.
"Father, please can I come with you to the tournament? Please, please! There'll be knights on horses, sword fights, children's games and honey cakes and Merlin the Wizard will be there … ."

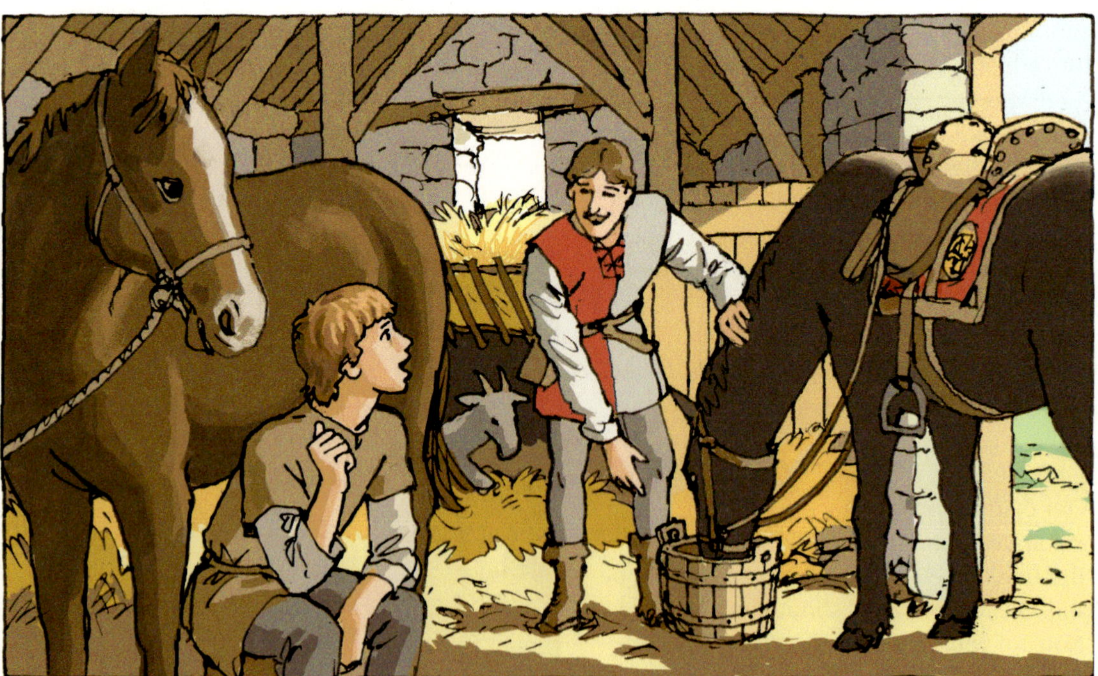

[1]messenger ['mesɪndʒə] – *Bote*, [2]bossy ['bɒsi] – *herrisch*, [3]to brush [brʌʃ] – *bürsten*, [4]stable ['steɪbl] – *Stall*, [5]bath [bɑːθ] – *Bad*, [6]to treat [triːt] – *behandeln*, [7]yeah [jeə] – *ja*, [8]going to be ['gəʊɪŋ ˌtə] – *wird sein*, [9]tournament ['tʊənəmənt] – *Turnier*, [10]honey ['hʌni] – *Honig*, [11]going to choose ['gəʊɪŋ ˌtə] – *werden wählen*

"How do you know about the tournament, Arthur? Were you listening outside the door?"

Arthur did not want to get the messenger's servant into trouble so he said, "Erm! Yes, Father, I'm sorry … . But please, can I come with you?"

Sir Ector was not too pleased with Arthur but he was a good, strong boy.

"OK. You can come. We need someone to carry our heavy bags. We leave at five o'clock tomorrow morning. London is a long way."

It took two days for the journey from the west of Britain to London on horseback[1]. Sir Ector and the boys spent the night at an inn[2].

Next morning they got up early and continued on their way to London. Suddenly Kay stopped his horse. He got off[3] and started to look for something in his bags. Sir Ector was ahead of[4] him on his horse.

"What are you looking for, Kay?" asked Arthur.

"Don't tell Father," Kay said. "But I think I've left my sword at the inn. I don't want Father to know. A knight shouldn't be so forgetful[5] …"

"I can get it," said Arthur. Maybe Kay would be nicer to him if he got his sword for him.

"Thanks, Arthur!" said Kay.

Arthur rode back to the inn as fast as he could. But when he got there, the place was empty.

An old man was sitting outside the inn. He had a long nose and a white beard.

"Where is the innkeeper[6]?" Arthur asked him. "They've all gone to the tournament," he said.

"That's strange," said Arthur. "I didn't pass them on the road. Which way did they go, old man?" The old man pointed with his long finger. "That way, my boy! Go past the old meeting place then turn left and right and left again. You can't miss it."

Arthur thanked the strange old man and rode away. Suddenly he saw the strangest thing – a large, white stone. And there was a sword in it. Arthur looked at it. It wasn't an ordinary[7] sword. It had beautiful jewels on its handle.

'Kay will be really angry with me if I don't find his sword,' thought Arthur. 'Maybe he'll like this one.'

He went up to the stone, took the handle and pulled. The sword came out as if the stone was butter. Then he rode his horse back to Kay as fast as he could.

[1]on horseback ['hɔːsbæk] – *zu Pferd,* [2]inn [ɪn] – *Herberge,* [3]to get off [get‿'ɒf] – *absteigen,* [4]ahead of [ə'hed‿əv] – *vor,* [5]forgetful [fə'getfl] – *vergesslich,* [6]innkeeper ['ɪnˌkiːpə] – *Wirt,* [7]ordinary ['ɔːdnri] – *gewöhnlich*

F "Here you are, Kay," he said, and he gave him the sword.

"B-but this isn't my sword," said Kay.

"I know," said Arthur. "I found it."

Kay was looking at the jewels on the sword's handle. He was thinking about the messenger. He had spoken about a sword with jewels on its handle in a stone.

"W-was this sword in a stone, Arthur?" Kay asked.

"Yes, how did you know?" Arthur replied[1].

Kay did not answer. "How did you get it out, Arthur?"

"I just pulled it," laughed Arthur. "And out it came, as if the stone was butter!"

Just then Sir Ector came back on his horse. He was very angry. "Come on, you two! We'll be late for the tournament!"

"Look what Arthur found!" said Kay and he showed him the sword. The jewels on its handle shone[2] in the sunlight[3].

Sir Ector was shocked! "I'm sorry, Father," said Arthur. "I can put it back … ."

"Take us to the place where you found it, Arthur," he said. They rode back.

"Put the sword back in the stone, Arthur," said Sir Ector.

"Yes, sir," said Arthur. "I'll never steal anything again." Arthur pushed the sword back into the stone. Sir Ector and Kay were very excited. "Now go and wait by the horses, Boy," said Sir Ector.

"But … how could Arthur pull it out?" said Kay. "He's only a stupid kid … he's not even a knight!" "I have no idea, Son. But I'm going to try[4] it." Sir Ector took the handle of the sword in his big hands and pulled. But nothing happened.

"You try, Kay!" he said.

Kay jumped onto the stone. He took the sword's handle in his hands and pulled until his face was red.

"Ouf! I c-can't move it an inch," he said.

Arthur was waiting with the horses. Suddenly he heard Sir Ector's voice.

"Arthur!" he called. "Come here!"

'Ohh no … ,' thought Arthur. He went back to the place where Sir Ector and Kay were standing. "Were you lying[5] about this sword?" "No," said Arthur. "I'm sorry. I'll never steal again."

A large group of knights came down the road from the tournament. With them were the innkeeper and the little old man with the long nose and white beard.

'My father won't tell me off[6] in front of all these people,' he thought. 'Everyone will know then that his son is a thief[7].'

"Pull the sword from the stone if you can Arthur," said Sir Ector.

All the knights laughed. "Ha ha! Get this boy out of our way," said one of the knights. "We have important business[8] to do here!"

"No, let him try," said Sir Ector.

[1]to reply [rɪ'plaɪ] – *antworten*, [2]to shine [ʃaɪn] – *glänzen*, [3]sunlight ['sʌnlaɪt] – *Sonnenlicht*, [4]going to try ['ɡəʊɪŋ ˌtə] – *werde versuchen*, [5]to lie [laɪ] – *lügen*, [6]to tell off [tel‿'ɒf] – *ausschimpfen*, [7]thief [θiːf] – *Dieb*, [8]business ['bɪznɪs] – *Geschäfte*

Everyone was silent[1] as young Arthur took the handle of the sword in both hands and pulled. The sword came out like a knife out of butter. "Ahhh!" said the knights.

They all knelt down[2] in front of Arthur. Sir Ector even pushed Kay onto his knees. Arthur didn't know what was happening.

"Kay, Father, get up, please! Why are you all kneeling in front of me?"

The only person who was not kneeling was the little old man.

"Hail[3], O Great King of all Britain!" he said.

"Hail, O King!" said all the knights.

The old man took off his old coat. Underneath[4] was a black cape.

"Wow! It's Merlin the Wizard!" said Arthur. "But how can I be king? Ha ha! I'm not even a knight yet."

"Read the words on the stone, King Arthur," said Merlin. "Only the person who can take this sword from the stone is the true King of all Britain."

"Father, what is all this about?" asked Arthur.

"I am not your father," said Sir Ector. "Merlin the Wizard brought you to me when you were a baby. One day this baby will be a very important man, he said."

"Arthur's the King of all Britain?" said Kay. "It's not fair!" But no one could hear him.

"Hail, O King!" said all the knights again.

"Wow!" said Arthur. "I'm King of all Britain! Does this mean I can go to the tournament?" All the knights laughed.

"The King can do whatever[5] he likes, my boy," said Merlin.

King Arthur was a very good king. He and his knights stopped the terrible wars and brought peace to Britain. They didn't fight real wars but the knights had fantastic tournaments every Saturday. Honey cakes were free[6] for all the children.

[1]silent ['saɪlənt] – *still*, [2]to kneel down [ˌniːl 'daʊn] – *niederknien*, [3]Hail! [heɪl] – *Heil!*, [4]underneath [ˌʌndə'niːθ] – *darunter*, [5]whatever [ˌwɒt'evə] – *was (auch) immer*, [6]free [friː] – *kostenlos*

The Canterville Ghost (a modern[1] version[2])

Step 1: Before you start

a) *Look quickly at pages 112 to 117. What kind of text do you think "The Canterville Ghost" is (a story, a legend, a poem, a play, …)?*

b) *Now read the skills box. Were you right?*

TEXT 

Recognizing[3] a play

1. A play is a sort of dialogue which you act.
2. There are different characters[4] in a play. Each actor has to learn a part and act it.
3. A play has different scenes. Each scene tells a different part of the story. There is often a new scene when there is a change of time or place in the story.
4. Stage directions[5] are in brackets[6]. They are important for the actors because they tell them what to do in a scene.
5. Additional[7] information can also come from a narrator[8] who can, for example, give an introduction to the story.

Example:

Scene 1 In the Great Hall of Canterville House

The Otises, an American family, have just bought a house from Lord Canterville. …

Lord Canterville: *(worried)* **Er, Mr Otis? – May I have a word with you?**

Mr Otis: **Sure, Lord Canterville, what is it?**

(He leads Mr Otis to one side. The kids and their mother talk quietly.)

Lord Canterville: *(softly)* **Well, Mr Otis, er ... I must warn you. …**

6. You can perform a play or you can make a film or radio play from it. A radio play is like a film without pictures. You must understand everything that happens from what you hear, from the way the actors speak and from the sound effects[9].

Step 2: Before you read

a) *Look at page 112 again. How many characters are there in the play? Who are they?*

b) *Look at pages 112 to 117. How many different scenes are there? Where or when do they happen?*

c) *Find all the stage directions. Check any new words.*

d) *What information do we get from the narrator?*

Step 3: The first reading

Look at each picture and read the scenes. What happens in each scene? Write 2–3 sentences.

[1]modern ['mɒdn] – *modern,* [2]version ['vɜːʃn] – *Version,* [3]to recognize ['rekəgnaɪz] – *erkennen,* [4]character ['kærəktə] – *Charakter, Figur,* [5]stage direction ['steɪdʒ dɪˌrekʃn] – *Regieanweisung,* [6]bracket ['brækɪt] – *Klammer,* [7]additional [ə'dɪʃnl] – *zusätzlich,* [8]narrator [nə'reɪtə] – *Erzähler/Erzählerin,* [9]sound effect ['saʊnd ɪˌfekt] – *Hintergrundgeräusch*

Step 4: Different jobs

Choose a director and assistant, actors and people who can do sound effects.

Step 5: Prepare the radio play

a) *Director and assistant: Plan the scenes. Use the skills box.*

GROUP SKILLS

Director/assistant

1. Make a plan for each scene.
2. Discuss your plan with the actors. Who can play two or more characters?

Scene 1: narrator, Lord Canterville, …

characters	people
narrator	Jenny
Lord Canterville	Andy
Mr Otis	…

3. Rehearse with the actors. Check that no lines are wrong or missing.

b) *Actors: Prepare your lines with the help of the skills box for actors.*

c) *People who do sound effects: Make a plan for all the sounds you need in the play. Use the skills box for sound effects to help you.*

GROUP SKILLS

The actors

1. Make a copy of the play and highlight[1] your lines. Look up the new words and practise the pronunciation[2] with other actors.
2. Imagine you are your character. Are you happy, sad, … ? Try to speak your lines with the right feeling. The stage directions can often help.
3. Read your lines, so that other people can understand and enjoy them. Practise on your own[3] and in your group.

Sound effects

1. Look for places in the play where you need sound effects or could use music.
2. Make a list of sounds and people who can do them.
3. Talk about how you can make the sounds and then practise them.

To rattle[4] chains:

To tap[5] on armour[6]:

Step 6: Record the radio play

The director and assistant should make sure that everyone knows what to do at what time.
The actors should follow the scenes and be ready to speak when it is their turn.
The people who do sound effects must have everything ready before each scene starts.
Record the play scene by scene.

[1]to highlight ['haɪlaɪt] – *markieren,* [2]pronunciation [prəˌnʌnsi'eɪʃn] – *Aussprache,* [3]on your own [ˌɒn jər‿'əʊn] – *allein,* [4]to rattle ['rætl] – *rasseln,* [5]to tap [tæp] – *klopfen,* [6]armour ['ɑ:mə] – *Rüstung*

L2, 14–19

The Canterville Ghost

Mr Otis

Mrs Otis

Virginia (their daughter[1])

The twins[2] (their sons)

Lord Canterville

The ghost of Sir Simon de Canterville

4 Children

Scene 1 In the Great Hall of Canterville House

The Otises, an American family, have just bought a house from Lord Canterville.

Lord Canterville: Here are the keys. Now Canterville House is yours. It's very old and the roof is not very good but I hope it's what you want.

Mr Otis: Oh, I'm sure it is, Lord Canterville. We love these fantastic old English houses, don't we[3]?

Mrs Otis: We sure do[4], dear. They have so much history. I mean, just look at this old suit of armour[5]! *(Taps suit.)* 1575!

Virginia: It's all so different from our old house in New York.

Twins: Yeah, the rooms are spooky and dark! / It's great for hide and seek[6]!

Lord Canterville: *(worried)* Er, Mr Otis? – May I have a word with you?

Mr Otis: Sure, Lord Canterville, what is it?
(He leads Mr Otis to one side. The kids and their mother talk quietly.)

Lord Canterville: *(softly)* Well, Mr Otis, er … I must warn[7] you. I don't think your family can live here at Canterville House because …

Mr Otis: Because what?

Lord Canterville: Because, well, … you see … there's a ghost.

Mr Otis: A ghost?

Lord Canterville: Shhh! *(whispers)* Don't tell your children, Mr Otis. They'll be so scared. It's the ghost of Sir Simon de Canterville, my great-great-great-great *(stops for breath)* great-great-grandfather[8]! He died in 1575. When he lived, he never worked. He was lazy[9] and just spent all the family's money. So now he walks around the house at night and rattles his chains!

Mr Otis: He walks around the house and rattles his chains? Ha ha! Do you hear that everyone? Lord Canterville says this old place has its own ghost! The ghost of Sir Simon de Canterville! *(The whole family laughs.)*

Twin 1: Great, Dad!

Twin 2: If there's a ghost, I want to be the first to see him!

Mr Otis: Lord Canterville says the ghost walks around the house at night and rattles his chains! *(The family laughs harder.)*

Lord Canterville: Hmph! Well, you can all laugh, but don't say I didn't tell you.

[1]daughter ['dɔ:tə] – *Tochter,* [2]twin [twɪn] – *Zwilling,* [3]don't we ['dəʊnt wi:] – *nicht wahr,* [4]we sure do [ˌwi: ʃɔ: 'du:] – *natürlich,* [5]suit of armour [ˌsu:t əv‿'ɑ:mə] – *Rüstung,* [6]hide and seek [ˌhaɪd‿ənd 'si:k] – *Verstecken,* [7]to warn [wɔ:n] – *warnen,* [8]great-grandfather [ˌgreɪt'grændˌfɑ:ðə] – *Urgroßvater,* [9]lazy ['leɪzi] – *faul*

Mr Otis: Goodbye, Lord Canterville. Don't worry about us. We're not frightened of some old ghost. (*Big, heavy door closes.*) These silly English lords[1] and their ghosts! Ha ha! (*There is suddenly the sound of thunder*[2] *and wind.*)

Mrs Otis: Oh! The weather! It has suddenly changed!

Virginia: Yeah, look, Mom, it's raining! The sun was out a minute ago!

Twins: It's so dark./It's a storm!

Mrs Otis: That's strange: The storm started when we were laughing at the ghost.

Mr Otis: Now dear, it's just the English weather! We must buy some umbrellas.

Virginia: You mean, we must buy some buckets[3], Dad. Look! The roof is so old, it's raining into the house! (*sound of rain drops*[4]) (*fade*[5])

Scene 2 Night time: Outside Mr and Mrs Otis' bedroom

(*Somebody is snoring*[6], *an owl hoots.*)

Ghost: (*angry*) What are they doing in my house? Americans! Hmph! Isn't their country big enough for them! Those terrible twins! 'If there's a ghost, I want to be the first to see him!' Yuk! What do they think this is, some joke? I have to frighten them away. Moo-ha-hahaa! Hmmm. They're sleeping now. Let's start with the father: I'll just go through this wall. (*Sound of chains along the wooden floor gets closer to the snoring sounds.*)

Ghost: He's sleeping. I'll rattle my chains. That always spooks[7] people!

Mr Otis: (*wakes up*) Huh? Dear, is that you? What's that terrible noise? Oh! It's you. Hey mister[8], let me give you some oil[9] for those chains.

They'll be much quieter, you know. Hmmm. Let's see, I always keep a bottle of 'Best American Oil' beside the bed here. Ah! Here it is. Let's put some on. There! Better? See? Now they don't rattle. What did I tell you! Your chains won't rattle with 'Best American'! Well, good night!

Ghost: Hmph! He wasn't scared! He just fell asleep again! And what has he done? My old chains don't rattle now! But I can go and frighten those twins. Ah! That's the door to their bedroom. OOF! (*sound of a pillow*[10] *as it hits the ghost's head*) My head! What's this? A pillow? Who threw it? (*giggles*[11], *footsteps as they run away*) Argh! Those twins! I'll get them! But how can I frighten them if my chains don't rattle? I know! My old suit of armour! That'll frighten them! Moo-ha-hahaa!

[1]lord [lɔ:d] – *Adliger*, [2]thunder ['θʌndə] – *Donner*, [3]bucket ['bʌkɪt] – *Eimer*, [4]drop [drɒp] – *Tropfen*, [5]to fade [feɪd] – *ausblenden*, [6]to snore [snɔ:] – *schnarchen*, [7]to spook [spu:k] – *Angst machen*, [8]mister ['mɪstə] – *hier: Sie (Anrede)*, [9]oil [ɔɪl] – *Öl*, [10]pillow ['pɪləʊ] – *Kopfkissen*, [11]giggle ['gɪgl] – *Kichern*

Scene 3 Second night: In the Great Hall

(An owl hoots.)

Ghost: Here's the suit of armour. I'll just put it on and … *(loud sound as armour falls)* Oops! I dropped it! Someone's coming!

Twin 1: Hey, it's a burglar! He's trying to steal the suit of armour!

Twin 2: Let's use our pea shooters[1] on him! *(sound as peas hit the armour)*

Ghost: Stop! Stop! You're hurting me!

Mr Otis: *(comes out of his room)* What's happening?

Twin 2: Dad! This burglar wanted to steal the old suit of armour!

Mr Otis: Well done, kids. I've got my gun! Put your hands up, burglar!

Ghost: *(terribly frightened)* D-Don't shoot[2], kind sire[3]!

Mr Otis: Oh, it's you again. We thought you were a burglar. We're really sorry, Sir Simon. Come on kids, let's go back to bed. Good night!

Twin 1: Awww! I thought it was a real burglar. It's only that stupid old ghost. Good night, Dad!

Ghost: *(alone now)* I c-can't believe it … all the other families were frightened of me. Maybe I'm not a very scary ghost now. Let's see, I'll try my ghost's laugh. That usually makes people hide under their beds! Moo-ha-hahaa! *(Nothing happens. He laughs louder.)* Moo-ha-hahaa! *(louder)* MOO-HA-HAHAA!

Mrs Otis: *(like she's talking to baby)* Awww! Have you got a tummy[4] ache[5]? You poor thing! Look, I've got a bottle of medicine[6] for tummy aches. It's called 'Tummy All Better'. See? Here … drink it aaall! *(Ghost drinks loudly.)*

Ghost: Yeetch!

Mrs Otis: Yes, I know it doesn't taste very good but remember: 'Tummy All Better' makes tummies all better! Good night, Sir Simon! *(She leaves.)*

Ghost: Argh! What sort of a ghost am I! I can't spook any of these people at all! Mrs Otis gave me a yukky tummy medicine. Mr Otis put oil on my chains so now they don't rattle. And those horrible twins shot me with their pea shooters! Grrr! I'll show them! Tomorrow night I'll stand beside their bed in the moonlight and put a cold hand on their shoulder[7]. Moohahhhah! *(fade)*

[1]pea shooter ['pi: ˌʃu:tə] – *Blasrohr,* [2]to shoot [ʃu:t] – *schießen,* [3]kind sire [ˌkaɪnd 'saɪə] – *edler Herr (Anrede),* [4]tummy ['tʌmi] – *Bauch,* [5]ache [eɪk] – *Schmerzen,* [6]medicine ['medsn] – *Medizin,* [7]shoulder ['ʃəʊldə] – *Schulter*

Scene 4 Third night: Upstairs outside the twins' bedroom

Ghost: Hmm. Which is their room? Ah, here it is! I'll just open the door … *(sound of squeaky[1] door; sound as bucket of water falls and wets[2] the ghost; giggles from the twins)* Argh! Who put that bucket of water on top of the door? I'm all wet!

Twins: BOO!

Ghost: Argh! Help! Help! I'm getting out of here!

Twin 1: *(laughing)* What a great idea to put that bucket of water on top of the door! Did you see him run?

Twin 2: Yeah! He looked just like he'd seen …

Twins: … a ghost! Hahaha!

Twin 1: Wait! I almost forgot about the string[3] at the top of the stairs.

Twin 2: The string?

Twin 1: You know, the special surprise[4] we made for him.

Twin 2: Oh yeah! The special surprise! He'll be at the top of the stairs just about …

Twins: … now! Have a good trip, Sir Simon! Ha ha! *(terrible noise as ghost falls down stairs) (fade)*

Scene 5 In the attic[5]

(sound of wind as it blows; the wooden floor creaks; sound of rain)

Ghost: I'm staying up here in the attic … far away from those horrible Americans. Brrr! That bucket of water was so cold! Why did I open their bedroom door? Why didn't I just go through the wall? I am a stupid ghost! When they said BOO!, I was so scared I ran away. *(door opens, footsteps)* Someone's coming into the attic! It's … the daughter!

Virginia: Oh, hello, it's you, Sir Simon. It's raining in my bedroom. I came up here to find the hole[6]. Ooh, Sir Simon! What have you done to your head?

Ghost: Ask your brothers!

[1]squeaky ['skwi:ki] – *quietschend,* [2]to wet [wet] – *nass machen,* [3]string [strɪŋ] – *Schnur,* [4]surprise [sə'praɪz] – *Überraschung,* [5]attic ['ætɪk] – *Dachboden,* [6]hole [həʊl] – *Loch*

Virginia: I'm sorry about the twins, they are a little … lively[1]. Well, but maybe you just shouldn't frighten people, then they'll leave you alone[2].

Ghost: What? I shouldn't frighten people! I'm a ghost: the Canterville Ghost! I rattle my chains, I have a scary laugh[3], and I put an ice-cold[4] hand on people's shoulders. It's my job! I've been doing it since 1575. And I was a very good ghost before your family arrived.

Virginia: You poor ghost. Isn't it lonely in this big house all alone all these years?

Ghost: Ghosts always live alone. I've frightened so many people away from Canterville House. I frightened Lord Canterville and his family away, too. Ha ha! I saw him: He gave your father the keys and he ran out the front door[5]! No one stays here. They all shout: There's a ghost! Ha ha! In more than 400 years I've frightened so many people. And people only come up here to the attic to leave their rubbish because it's where I live.

Virginia: That's why the roof hasn't been fixed for over 400 years. Look at the rain! It's coming in through there! One day Canterville House will fall down[6]. And we all won't have a home. This is your home, too, Sir Simon!

Ghost: I know. But I'm a ghost. Ghosts don't fix roofs …

Virginia: But people can! Can't you see, Sir Simon: If people live here, they can look after the house. You mustn't frighten people away … Where will you live, poor ghost, if the house falls down?

Ghost: *(sighs[7])* You're right. And it's getting harder to frighten people now. Even little kids aren't scared of me. I think they watch too many ghost films on that thing – er, what do you call it? Ah, yes: TV.

Virginia: And you must be bored and lonely here, Sir Simon.

Ghost: A ghost's life is boring when no one is scared of you. And I am lonely here and the house is falling down. But what can I do?

Virginia: Hmmm. I have an idea, my friend.

[1]lively ['laɪvli] – *lebhaft,* [2]to leave alone [ˌli:v‿ə'ləʊn] – *in Ruhe lassen,* [3]laugh [lɑ:f] – *Lachen,* [4]ice-cold ['aɪskəʊld] – *eiskalt,* [5]front door [frʌnt 'dɔ:] – *Haustür,* [6]to fall down [fɔ:l 'daʊn] – *einstürzen,* [7]to sigh [saɪ] – *seufzen*

Scene 6 Midnight: In the Great Hall

(clock strikes[1] midnight and sounds of small excited crowd)

Twin 2: Buy your tickets for the Tour[2] of Canterville House!

Twin 1: A tour of a different kind!

Child 1: It's not a normal tour with a boring guide[3]. It's a real Ghost Tour and the guide is a ghost! They say he goes through walls!

Child 2: He made the moon come out. There were heavy clouds just an hour ago.

Child 3: Yeah! And he sometimes wears a cool suit of armour! I saw him on TV.

Child 4: You can win something if you guess the weight of his chains. This is much better than the London Dungeon!

Other children: Yes, this is really exciting./Can we take photos?/I don't know, but can you see ghosts in photos?/Great, I think the tour is starting.

Mrs Otis: Welcome to Canterville House everyone! The Ghost Tour starts in the Great Hall. This way please! *(Crowd noise fades to background[4].)*

Mr Otis: Well, how do you like your new job, Sir Simon?

Ghost: I love it, Mr Otis! It's so much better than my old one! I meet more people. I haven't had so many friends since … 1575! I never knew people could be so nice. I don't want to frighten them at all[5].

Twin 1: Hey, hi, Sir Simon!

Twin 2: We've sold so many tickets for your Ghost Tour!

Ghost: Well done, boys!

Virginia: With the money we can fix the roof so the rain doesn't come in.

Ghost: I've never seen so many people here! And it's all thanks to your family … Your family has saved Canterville House! Oh, I must go. It's time for the Ghost Tour! *(talking to the crowd)* Good evening, ladies and gentlemen, boys and girls! Welcome to Canterville House! *(sound of excited crowd)*
I am the ghost of Sir Simon Canterville and I'll be your guide today … *(fade)*

[1]to strike [straɪk] – *schlagen,* [2]tour [tʊə] – *Tour, Rundgang,* [3]guide [gaɪd] – *Führer/Führerin,*
[4]background ['bækgraʊnd] – *Hintergrund,* [5]not … at all [ət‿'ɔːl] – *überhaupt nicht*

Mediation and communication

Unit 1

COMMUNICATION

SKILLS

Beim sinngemäßen Übertragen eines deutschen Textes ins Englische solltest du folgende Arbeitsschritte beachten:

1. Suche wichtige Informationen heraus und schreibe Stichpunkte auf Deutsch auf.
2. Überlege, ob du dafür die englischen Vokabeln kennst. Versuche nicht gleich zu übersetzen. Kannst du denselben Sachverhalt umschreiben? Wenn das nicht möglich ist, dann verwende ein Wörterbuch.
3. Beachte, dass die englische und die deutsche Satzstellung oft unterschiedlich sind.
4. Verwende einfache, kurze Sätze auf Englisch. Lass alles Unwichtige weg.

Situation: Handball ist ein deutsches Spiel, das in England nicht gespielt wird. Stell dir vor, du willst ein Handballspiel mit deinem englischen Austauschpartner besuchen. Lies die Informationen aus dem Internet und beantworte die Fragen deines Partners.

Handball

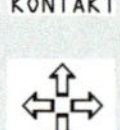

Das Spielfeld in der Halle ist 40 Meter lang und 20 Meter breit. Die Torhöhe beträgt zwei Meter, die Breite drei Meter. Innerhalb des Torraumes darf sich nur der Torhüter aufhalten. Die sechs Feldspieler dürfen über die Begrenzungslinie springen, müssen aber den Ball werfen, bevor sie Bodenkontakt haben.
Die Spielzeit beträgt 2x30 Minuten. Die Spieler müssen den Ball spätestens nach drei Sekunden abgegeben haben. Währenddessen dürfen sie nicht mehr als drei Schritte mit dem Ball in der Hand machen. Verstöße werden von den zwei Schiedsrichtern mit Freiwürfen, gelben Karten oder Zwei-Minuten-Strafen geahndet. Die dritte Zeitstrafe für einen Spieler bzw. die rote Karte zieht eine Disqualifikation nach sich.

1. How high and wide is the goal?
2. How many players are there in a team?
3. Can the players stand in the goal area?
4. How long do they usually play?
5. How long can a player keep the ball?
6. What happens if a player breaks a rule?

Unit 2

COMMUNICATION 

Aus Broschüren benötigst du oft nur bestimmte Informationen wie z. B. Preise, Öffnungszeiten usw. Mache dir einen Stichwortzettel mit den Fakten, nach denen du suchen willst, und schreibe danach gezielt die Informationen heraus.

Situation: Stell dir vor, deine Klasse plant einen Besuch in London. Ihr möchtet den „Tower" besichtigen. Ihr seid 25 Schüler und Schülerinnen, ein Lehrer und eine Lehrerin. Die Lehrerin bringt ihre Familie mit – ihren Mann und ihre beiden Söhne, die vier und zehn Jahre alt sind.

THE TOWER OF LONDON
Planning your visit
OPENING HOURS

1 MARCH - 31 OCTOBER	1 NOVEMBER - 29 FEBRUARY
Tues–Sat: 09:00–18:00	Tues–Sat: 09:00–17:00
Sun–Mon: 10:00–18:00	Sun–Mon: 10:00–17:00
Last admission: 17:00	Last admission: 16:00

ADMISSION CHARGES

Adults: £14.50
Students (with ID) and senior citizens (60+): £10.50
Children 5–16: £9.50 (Children under 5: Free)
Family ticket: £37.50 (up to 2 adults and 3 children)
Group discount: (15 or more): Adults £13.00, children £8.55

Groups should not join the main queue. There is a special group ticket office where you can collect your tickets. Then just follow the signs to the group entrance. All coach drivers and Blue Badge Guides bringing groups to the Tower are admitted free of charge.

1. *Lies den Prospekt und plane den Ausflug.*
2. *Finde einen günstigen Termin.*
3. *Errechne für jeden die Kosten.*
4. *Schreibe eine kurze Mail an den „Tower". Informiere sie über den geplanten Ausflug. Sage, wer kommt und wann, und frage, ob ihr richtig gerechnet habt.*

Unit 3

COMMUNICATION 

Auf Bahnhöfen oder Flughäfen werden wichtige Informationen häufig über Lautsprecher weitergegeben. Das ist für den ausländischen Besucher manchmal nicht ganz einfach.

1. Man muss unerwartet eine meist sehr schnell vorgetragene Ansage verstehen.
2. Manchmal sind Hintergrundgeräusche sehr störend.
3. Die Ansagen enthalten häufig auch unbekannte Wörter.
4. Man kann sie nur ein- bis zweimal hören.

Konzentriere dich deshalb auf wichtige Wörter wie Personen- und Ortsnamen, Zahlen- und Zeitangaben, Substantive und Verben als Schlüsselwörter. Versuche damit, den Sinn der Ansage zu erschließen.

2, 8 **Situation:** Höre nun die folgenden Ansagen auf dem Bahnhof.

1. Du stehst mit deiner Familie auf Bahnsteig 6 und willst nach Bristol. Wann geht dein Zug und was musst du beachten?
2. Wo muss Herr Hausmann hin?
3. Du willst eine Stunde in die Stadt gehen. Was kannst du mit deinem Gepäck machen?

Unit 4

COMMUNICATION

Besucher sind oft auf die freundliche Unterstützung anderer angewiesen. Wenn du einem Besucher helfen willst, musst du nicht wörtlich übersetzen, sondern nur die wichtigsten Informationen vermitteln.

Situation: Stell dir vor, ein Austauschschüler ist im Sekretariat. Die Schulsekretärin versucht, ihm einiges auf Deutsch zu erklären. Der Austauschschüler versteht sie leider nicht. Du hilfst ihm und sagst auf Englisch:

1. dass die Schule eine Fußballmannschaft hat und dass er dort mitmachen kann.
2. dass die Cafeteria von 11 bis 14 Uhr geöffnet ist. Füge hinzu, dass er gern mit dir mitkommen kann. Du gehst auch dorthin.
3. wenn er in den Computerraum muss, soll er die Treppe hochgehen. Es ist der Raum neben dem Musikraum.
4. wenn er seine Turnschuhe in der Turnhalle vergessen hat, kann der Hausmeister ihm helfen. Er hat sein Büro neben der Turnhalle.
5. dass er ein Schließfach hier im Sekretariat bekommen kann. Er möge einen Augenblick warten.

Unit 5

COMMUNICATION

SKILLS

Im Englischen gibt es viele Höflichkeitsformen, die du nicht vergessen darfst.

Excuse me, please, … .
I'm really sorry but … .
Please, can you … ?
Please, don't … .
Could you …, please?
Would you …, please?

Situation: Du bist mit deiner Familie in England unterwegs. Dabei erlebst du folgende Szenen:

1. Einige Leute fangen an, auf dem Kinderspielplatz neben eurem Haus Fußball zu spielen. Der nächste Fußballplatz ist nicht weit – nur fünf Minuten zu Fuß. Deine Mutter ist sehr verärgert und du übersetzt für sie.
2. Das Mobiltelefon deines Vaters klingelt im Museum und er muss dringend telefonieren. Er möchte sich wegen der Störung entschuldigen. Übersetze für ihn.
3. Eure Freunde wollen in ein Restaurant. Deine Schwester will zur Imbissbude. Sie wartet nicht gerne auf die Bedienung und sie möchte anschließend noch ins Kino. Versuche, deine Freunde zum Vorschlag deiner Schwester zu überreden.
4. Deine Mutter hat versehentlich einen Passanten mit ihrem Schirm gestoßen. Hilf ihr, sich zu entschuldigen.

Unit 5

COMMUNICATION SKILLS

Texte aus Filmprogrammen ins Englische zu übertragen, sieht auf den ersten Blick ziemlich kompliziert aus. Es ist aber ganz einfach, wenn du Folgendes beachtest:

1. Lies den gesamten deutschen Text sehr aufmerksam und überlege, welche Informationen darin besonders wichtig sind.
2. Beantworte die Fragen:
   Um was für einen Film handelt es sich und welchen Titel hat er?
   „Wer?" handelt/spielt „Wo?" und „Wann?"
   „Was?" geschieht?
   „Wie?" und „Warum?" geschieht es?
   Mache dir dazu Notizen.
3. Versuche nun, für die einzelnen Informationen englische Formulierungen zu finden. Beachte, dass es auf den Sinn ankommt, nicht auf die wörtliche Übersetzung.

Situation: Du willst mit deinem englischen Partner eine DVD auswählen. Gib deinem/r Freund/in einen groben Überblick auf Englisch über die Handlung, damit er/sie sich leichter entscheiden kann.

Komödie

Der Rosarote Panther (neu) (The Pink Panther)

Ein Fußballmanager wird ermordet. Er sitzt mitten in einem voll besetzten Stadion und ihm wird der berühmteste Ring der Welt geklaut: der Rosarote Panther. Inspektor Clouseau soll ermitteln. Sein Chef Dreyfus (Kevin Kline) verzweifelt an seinem Mitarbeiter und gibt ihm den Detektiv Ponton (Jean Reno) zur Seite. Als die Polizisten bei ihren Ermittlungen auf Xania (Beyoncé Knowles) stoßen, die schöne Freundin des Toten, beginnt die Arbeit Spaß zu machen.

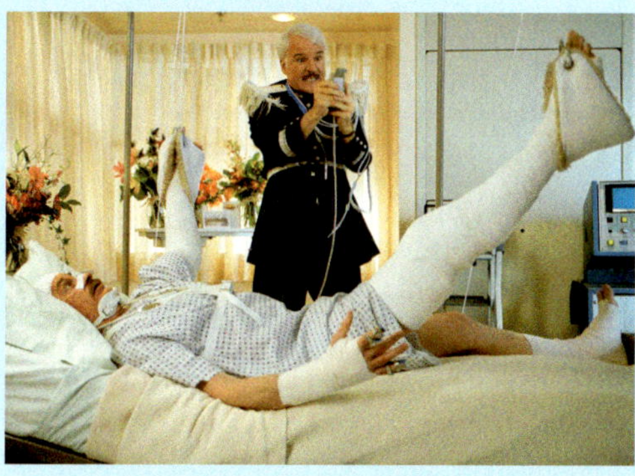

Zeichentrick

Bambi 2 – Der Herr der Wälder (Bambi and the Great Prince of the Forest)

Das Kinopublikum war weltweit zu Tränen gerührt, als am Ende des ersten Teils („Bambi", 1942) Bambis Mutter starb. Bambis Vater soll jetzt für seinen Sohn sorgen, aber als König des Waldes hat er kaum Zeit, sich um ihn zu kümmern. Bambi kommt deshalb zu einer Pflegemutter. Mit seinen Freunden, dem Hasen Klopfer und dem Stinktier Blume, macht Bambi den Wald unsicher. Gleichzeitig versucht er, seinen Vater zu beeindrucken.

Hallo! Hier fangen die Grammatikseiten deines Schülerbuchs an. Aber keine Angst, wir lassen dich nicht allein in diesem Dschungel. Wir, Jack und Jane, sind deine Begleiter. Komm einfach mit, wir zeigen dir den Weg! Unser Freund Nutty weist dich auf besondere Schwierigkeiten hin und hilft dir, die harten Nüsse zu knacken.

So arbeitest du mit dem Grammatikanhang:

GRAMMAR **SKILLS**

- Jeden Grammatikpunkt kannst du am besten verstehen, indem du ihn mit deinen eigenen Worten erklärst.

  1. Lege dir dazu in deinem *folder* ein Kapitel *My grammar* an oder arbeite weiter mit deinen *grammar cards*. Notiere darauf die Überschrift des Grammatikpunkts und schreibe einige Beispiele mit Übersetzung. Formuliere nun die Regel.
  2. Überprüfe alle Teile der Regel an Beispielen. Arbeite dabei mit verschiedenen Farben, Unterstreichungen usw.
  3. Du kannst oft eine kurze Bildungsformel entwickeln, z. B. ***be + ing*** für das *present progressive*. Zusammenhänge und Regeln lassen sich auch grafisch darstellen. Hierfür kannst du deine eigenen Symbole entwickeln oder diese verwenden:

     - - - - -➤ Dauer einer Handlung
     X Zeitpunkt
     └───↑ Wort/Satzglied wird an eine andere Stelle gesetzt
     - - - - -➤| Ende einer Handlung

  Du hast sicher selbst noch viele Einfälle.

- Reime und Eselsbrücken helfen beim Einprägen. Du kannst natürlich auch selber reimen!
- Zum Schluss kannst du an einer kleinen Aufgabe in *Test yourself* überprüfen, ob du alles verstanden hast.

G1 Die einfache Gegenwart — *The simple present*

Mit dem ***simple present*** drückst du aus, was **(nicht) regelmäßig passiert** oder was **jemand (nicht) regelmäßig tut.** Du kannst auch **Tatsachen und Fakten** beschreiben.
Signalwörter: *sometimes, always, often, every (day/month/year), on Mondays, never*

Aussagen
Our team always **plays** on Sundays. — *Unsere Mannschaft spielt immer sonntags.*
American football players **wear** helmets. — *American-Football-Spieler tragen Helme.*

Verneinung
Our team **doesn't play** on Mondays. — *Unser Team spielt montags nicht.*
German football players **don't wear** helmets. — *Deutsche Fußballspieler tragen keine Helme.*

Fragen
Does a rugby ball **look** like an egg? — *Sieht ein Rugby-Ball wie ein Ei aus?*
– **No,** it **doesn't./Yes,** it **does.** — *– Nein./Ja.*
When do the teams usually **play**? — *Wann spielen die Teams gewöhnlich?*
What does a rugby ball **look** like? — *Wie sieht ein Rugby-Ball aus?*

Be und *have got* sind Hilfsverben. D. h. kein *do/does* bei Frage und Verneinung.

My friends **aren't** on the team.
Have they **got** time?

Are your friends on the team?
– No, they **haven't got** time.

My grammar
1. Schreibe je zwei Beispielsätze für Aussagen, Verneinung und Fragen.
2. Erkläre deinem/r Partner/in, was du beim ***simple present*** beachten musst.

Test yourself
Tell an English-speaking friend something about your team.

Sage:
- was ihr spielt,
- wann ihr trainiert,
- wie oft ihr trainiert,
- wie viele Spieler in der Mannschaft sind,
- was ihr anhabt,
- wie euer Verein heißt.

G 2 Die Verlaufsform der Gegenwart *The present progressive*

Wenn du beobachten kannst oder ausdrücken möchtest, dass eine Handlung **in diesem Moment** verläuft oder dass jemand **gerade** etwas (im Moment des Sprechens) **tut**, verwendest du das ***present progressive***. Du bildest das ***present progressive*** mit einer Form von *be* ***(am/is/are)*** und der Endung **-ing** am Verb. Willst du den Satz **verneinen**, setzt du einfach ***not*** hinter die Form von *be* (Kurzform ***isn't/aren't***). Eine **Frage** beginnst du mit ***Am/Is/Are***. Wird ein **Fragewort** verwendet, steht dieses immer **ganz am Anfang** vor *am/is/are*.
Signalwörter: ***just, now, at the moment***

Aussagen
Marcia and her friends **are** play**ing** now. — *Marcia und ihre Freunde spielen jetzt.*

Verneinung
She **isn't** wear**ing** jeans at the moment. — *Sie trägt im Moment keine Jeans.*

Fragen
Are they winning? — *Gewinnen sie gerade?*
– **Yes,** they **are.**/**No,** they **aren't.** — *– Ja./Nein.*
What is the referee do**ing**? — *Was macht der Schiedsrichter gerade?*

sit + -ing = sitting
make + -ing = making

Kurzer Mitlaut wird verdoppelt, stummes -e wird abgekoppelt!

My grammar
1. Schreibe Beispielsätze für Aussagen, Verneinung und Fragen.
2. Erkläre dann deinem/r Partner/in, warum die Sätze im *present progressive* stehen müssen.
3. Finde eine Bildungsformel, die dir hilft, dich schnell zu erinnern.

Test yourself
Look at the picture and complete the sentences.

1. What … Nutty … (*do*)?
2. He … (*ride*) on a tiger.
3. … Jack … (*ride*), too?
4. No, he … . He … (*fall*) into the water.
5. And what … Jane … (*do*)?
6. She … (*play*) beach volleyball.
7. What … the elephant … (*wear*)?
8. It … (*wear*) a swimsuit.

G 3 Die Zeiten der Gegenwart — *The present tenses*

Simple present	**Present progressive**
Handlungen, die **normalerweise oder regelmäßig** passieren, stehen im ***simple present***. **Fakten** und **Tatsachen** werden immer durch das ***simple present*** ausgedrückt.	Handlungen, die nur einmal passieren und **gerade im Verlauf sind**, werden durch das ***present progressive*** hervorgehoben.

In the summer **I** usually **visit** my grandparents.
Im Sommer besuche ich normalerweise meine Großeltern.

But now **I'm visiting** friends.
Aber jetzt besuche ich gerade Freunde.

Often, always usually –
mit *simple present* stehen die.

Doch *at the moment* oder *now*,
steh'n mit *progressive*, ganz genau!

My grammar

1. Schreibe aus deinem Schülerbuch Seite 12 je drei Beispielsätze heraus, in denen solche zeitlichen Gegenüberstellungen ausgedrückt werden.
2. Markiere das, was üblicherweise passiert, mit einer Farbe und das, was gerade passiert, mit einer anderen. Kreise die Signalwörter ein.

Test yourself

What happens usually and what is happening now?

1. Jack usually plays football but today he's … .

1

play football / jump through the trees

2

go swimming / play volleyball

3

go shopping / climb a tree

4

sleep under a tree / catch her lunch

G 4 Die einfache Vergangenheit — *The simple past*

Du verwendest das ***simple past***, um über **Vergangenes** zu berichten. Dazu hängst du bei den regelmäßigen Verben die Endung ***-ed*** an die **Grundform** des Verbs an. Bei den unregelmäßigen Verben benutzt du die **zweite Form (Stammform)** (vgl. S. 210). Bei **Verneinungen** verwendet man ***didn't*** vor der Grundform des Verbs. **Fragen** beginnen mit ***Did*** bzw. mit **Fragewort** und ***did.*** Auch hier steht das Verb in der Grundform.
Signalwörter: ***yesterday, ago, last, in (2006)***

Aussagen

Yesterday a pickpocket **robbed** five people.	*Gestern hat ein Taschendieb fünf Leute bestohlen.*
He **stole** their wallets.	*Er stahl ihre Brieftaschen.*

Verneinung

He **didn't get** much money.	*Er hat nicht viel Geld bekommen.*

Fragen

Did they **catch** him?	*Haben sie ihn gefangen?*
– Yes, they **did.** / No, they **didn't.**	*– Ja. / Nein.*
How did he **do** it?	*Wie hat er es gemacht?*

Das *simple past* von *am / is / are* heißt ***was / were***. Hier braucht man bei Verneinungen und Fragen nicht mit *did* zu umschreiben.
The pickpocket **wasn't** very clever but the people **were** glad to get their things back. **What was** the name of the pickpocket?

My grammar
Vervollständige die folgenden Merksätze:

…, … und *last* stehen stets mit *simple past*!
Did in Fragen kein Problem, das Verb muss in der … steh'n!
Simple present – *am, is, are*, *simple past* – …, …, na klar!
… wird verdoppelt, … wird abgekoppelt!

Test yourself
Complete the sentences.

The police … *(stop)* a pickpocket in London. What … he … *(get)*? He … *(get)* five wallets but he … *(not get)* much money. Where … they … *(catch)* him? They … *(catch)* him at Monument.

G 5 Das Stützwort *one / ones* — *The prop word 'one / ones'*

Substantive, die sich in einem Text **wiederholen,** können durch ***one*** (Singular) und ***ones*** (Plural) ersetzt werden. Häufig stehen dabei noch ein Adjektiv (z. B. *young*), ein Demonstrativpronomen *(this / that)*, eine Präposition + Substantiv (z. B. *on the left*) oder *Which*?

mit einem Adjektiv
The black and white **one** is called Madonna. — *Der Schwarzweiße heißt Madonna.*

mit einem Demonstrativpronomen
This **one** has blue eyes and that **one** has broken his leg. — *Dieser hat blaue Augen und jener hat sich das Bein gebrochen.*

mit einer Präposition + Substantiv
The **ones** on the left are Madonna's children. — *Die beiden links sind Madonnas Kinder.*

mit *Which*?
Which **one** do you like best? — *Welcher gefällt dir am besten?*

My grammar

1. Suche dir aus den Beispielsätzen der Übungen 2 oder 3 auf der Seite 29 einige Sätze heraus und schreibe sie in deinen *folder*. Schreibe darüber das Wort, das durch *one / ones* ersetzt wird. Unterstreiche die Wörter, die das Wort weiter erklären in einer anderen Farbe.
2. Erkläre deinem/r Partner/in, warum hier *one* und *ones* steht.

Test yourself

Where can you use the prop word 'one / ones'? Write the correct sentences in your folder.

Nutty: Look. All these hats are in my shop.
Jane: Which hats are your favourites?
Nutty: The hat on the left is expensive. It's £15. The hat next to it is cheap. It's the cheapest hat. And the hat on my head is the most beautiful hat.

G 6 Die vollendete Vergangenheit *The past perfect*

Wenn du in einer Erzählung oder in einem Bericht mehrere Ereignisse der Reihe nach erwähnen möchtest, verwendest du das ***simple past***. Wenn du jedoch betonen möchtest, dass **ein Ereignis weiter in der Vergangenheit zurückliegt als ein anderes**, kannst du dies mit dem ***past perfect*** ausdrücken. Bei den regelmäßigen Verben bildest du diese Zeitform mit ***had*** und der ***Grundform*** des Verbs mit der Endung ***-ed***, bei den unregelmäßigen Verben mit ***had*** und der **dritten Form (Stammform).** **Signalwörter** für eine weiter zurückliegende Handlung sind häufig ***after*** und ***when.***

After Julia and David **had explained** their idea, the reporters wrote articles.	*Nachdem Julia und David ihre Idee erklärt hatten, schrieben die Reporter Artikel.*
When they **had completed** the wheel, they slowly lifted it.	*Als sie das Rad fertig gestellt hatten, zogen sie es langsam nach oben.*
After they **had built** the Eye, it became one of the most famous landmarks in the world.	*Nachdem sie das Eye gebaut hatten, wurde es eines der berühmtesten Wahrzeichen der Welt.*

When und *after* zeigen an – das *past perfect* folgt sodann!
Had mit Grundform + *-ed* – für die Bildung ist OK!
Bei unregelmäßigen Verben merke dir – 3. Stammform nehmen wir.

My grammar

1. Suche aus dem Text auf Seite 30 noch drei weitere Beispielsätze heraus. Stelle die zeitliche Reihenfolge grafisch dar.
2. Unterstreiche die weiter zurückliegende Handlung rot und kreise die Wörter ein, die dir das anzeigen.
3. Schreibe unter die Beispiele eine kurze Bildungsformel.

Test yourself

Complete the text.

Nutty's birthday

Yesterday Nutty woke up early. He was very excited because it was his birthday. After he … (*eat*) breakfast, he … (*make*) a big chocolate cake for his friends. When he … (*finish*) the cake, he … (*put*) it on the table. He waited. After he … (*wait*) for two hours, he … (*be*) very sad. No birthday cards, no text messages, no phone calls. He decided to go swimming. After he … (*pack*) his rucksack, he … (*go*) to the river. Two hours later he … (*go*) home and … (*open*) the front door. When he … (*open*) the door, he … (*hear*) his friends say, 'Happy Birthday!' He was really happy.

G 7 Die modalen Hilfsverben *The modal verbs 'can / can't, must / mustn't, needn't'*

Die Wörter *can/can't/must/mustn't* und *needn't* sind **Modalverben.** Du brauchst sie, wenn du von einer Fähigkeit, einer Erlaubnis, einem Verbot oder einer Verpflichtung sprechen willst. Sie sind **für alle Personen gleich** und können nur im ***simple present*** verwendet werden.
Das **Vollverb** dahinter steht immer in der **Grundform.** Wenn du Fragen bildest, setzt du wie bei anderen Hilfsverben auch das **modale Hilfsverb an den Anfang** der Frage bzw. hinter das Fragewort.

Aussagen und Verneinung

I **can swim** but I **can't dive.**	*Ich kann schwimmen, aber ich kann nicht tauchen.*
You **must be** careful but you **needn't worry.**	*Du musst vorsichtig sein, aber du musst dir keine Sorgen machen.*
You **mustn't swim** when the red flag is flying.	*Du darfst nicht schwimmen, wenn die rote Fahne weht.*

Fragen

Can you **swim** very fast?	*Kannst du sehr schnell schwimmen?*
Can't we **run** around in a swimsuit?	*Können wir nicht im Badeanzug herumlaufen?*
Who can't swim?	*Wer kann nicht schwimmen?*
Can (**May**) I **go** to the beach?	*Kann (Darf) ich zum Strand gehen?*

Can heißt können, *must* heißt müssen.
Und das musst du sonst noch wissen:
muss nicht *needn't* – darf nicht *mustn't*
dann sind alle *modals* passend.

My grammar

1. Lies dir noch einmal die Beispielsätze oben durch.
2. Schreibe zu den Modalverben *can / can't / must / mustn't* und *needn't* jeweils einen eigenen Beispielsatz. Übersetze deine Sätze ins Deutsche.

Test yourself

Complete the sentences. Use 'can / can't / must / mustn't' or 'needn't'.

We … escape! We … go through the trees. We … take the helicopter. We … get across the river but we … swim. We … take the boat. We … wait. We … hurry up!

G 8 Relativsätze *Relative clauses*

Relativsätze werden durch die Relativpronomen ***who, which*** oder ***that*** eingeleitet. Sie erklären ein Substantiv des Hauptsatzes näher. ***Who, which*** und ***that*** werden sowohl für den Singular als auch für den Plural gebraucht. ***Who*** bezieht sich nur auf Personen, ***which*** nur auf Dinge; **that** kann sich sowohl auf Personen als auch auf Dinge beziehen.

All the signs **which** you see around you are in English.	*Alle Schilder, **die** man um sich herum sieht, sind auf Englisch.*
Everyone **who** lives here can speak English.	*Jeder, **der** hier lebt, kann Englisch sprechen.*
Later they rebuilt Stonehenge with bigger stones **that** came from South Wales.	*Später baute man Stonehenge wieder auf mit Steinen, **die** aus Südwales kamen.*

Wenn du ausdrücken willst, dass (zu) **jemandem etwas gehört,** so verwendest du das Relativpronomen ***whose.*** Es bezieht sich hauptsächlich auf **Personen** oder **Tiere.** Es steht ebenfalls für Singular und Plural und wird mit ‚deren/dessen' übersetzt.

A passenger **whose** plane lands in Heathrow will see signs in English.	*Ein Flugreisender, **dessen** Flugzeug in Heathrow landet, wird die Schilder auf Englisch sehen.*
Teachers **whose** jobs are in the Irish Republic must learn Irish.	*Lehrer, **deren** Arbeitsplatz in der Republik Irland ist, müssen Irisch lernen.*

whose = dessen, deren
who's = *who is* = wer ist

My grammar

1. Relativpronomen heißen in der Grammatik auch bezügliche Fürwörter. Schreibe eigene Relativsätze und zeige mit Pfeilen an, worauf sich die Relativpronomen beziehen.
2. Erkläre deinem/r Partner/in, was du bei solchen Sätzen beachten musst.

Test yourself

Put in 'who'/'which' or 'whose' and find good German translations.

1. People … live in tree houses don't usually have windows.
2. A panther is an animal … can climb trees.
3. The panther … name is Pat likes to visit Jack in the tree house.
4. But other animals … are frightened always hide behind the cupboard.

G 9 Satzstellung von Adverbialbestimmungen der Zeit und des Ortes

Position of phrases of time and place in a sentence

Die Wortstellung im Aussagesatz ist Subjekt – Verb – Objekt **(S – V – O).** Dabei bilden Verb und Objekt (V + O) eine feste Einheit, man darf keine anderen Satzteile dazwischenstellen. **Zeitangaben** *(yesterday, in the morning, tomorrow, next week)* können am **Anfang** oder am **Ende** eines Satzes stehen.

	S	V	O	
	The people	rebuilt	the stone circle.	
Around 600 years later	the people	rebuilt	the stone circle.	
	The people	rebuilt	the stone circle	**around 600 years later.**

Orts- und Zeitangaben in Kombination stehen in der Regel am Ende des Satzes. Es gilt: **Ort vor Zeit.** Will man die **Zeitangaben stärker betonen,** stellt man sie an den **Satzanfang.**

Zeit		**Ort**	**Zeit**
	We took the bus	to Stonehenge	**last week.**
Last week	we took the bus	to Stonehenge.	

My grammar

1. Suche noch drei weitere Beispiele aus dem Text auf Seite 49 und erkläre daran die Stellung von Orts- und Zeitbestimmungen.
2. Vergleiche diese Sätze mit ihrer deutschen Übersetzung. Was ist anders?

Test yourself

Put the words in the right order.

1. swims / Jane / Every day / in the river
2. One morning / under the trees / a lion / sees / she
3. arrives / an elephant / at the river / Five minutes later
4. is / on the elephant / Two minutes later / Jane

G 10 Das *will*-Futur — *The 'will'-future*

Du verwendest das ***will-future***, wenn du etwas voraussagen willst (z. B. Wetter, Horoskop), wenn du dich spontan für etwas entscheidest oder wenn du etwas versprichst oder jemandem Hilfe anbietest. Du bildest das ***will-future*** mit ***will*** (Kurzform ***'ll***) und der Grundform des Verbs. Bei **Verneinungen** wird ***will not*** (Kurzform ***won't***) vor die **Grundform des Verbs** gesetzt. Wenn du eine **Frage** stellst, steht ***Will*** oder ein **Fragewort +** ***will*** am Anfang der Frage. In der **Kurzantwort** verwendest du ***will*** oder ***won't.***
Signalwörter: ***probably, maybe, I'm sure, I think, I promise, I hope, I know***

Aussagen

I'm sure we**'ll** live out of town.	*Ich bin sicher, wir werden außerhalb der Stadt wohnen.*
I think a garden **will mean** more work.	*Ich denke, ein Garten bedeutet mehr Arbeit.*

Verneinung

I promise I **won't be** late.	*Ich verspreche, dass ich nicht zu spät komme.*
I'm tired. – OK. We **won't walk.**	*Ich bin müde. – O. k. Wir laufen nicht.*

Fragen

What will happen?	*Was wird geschehen?*
Will we **live** out of town?	*Werden wir außerhalb der Stadt wohnen?*
– Yes, we **will.** / No, we **won't.**	*– Ja. / Nein.*

Beachte! Im Deutschen verwendest du oft die Gegenwart.
will = werden, *want to* = wollen

I think I'll feed the fish first.

I think, I promise, probably, mit *will-future* stehen die.

My grammar
Schreibe je drei Sätze mit ***will*** und mit ***want to*** und übersetze sie.

Test yourself
What can you say?

1. Du versprichst deiner Freundin, ihr zu helfen.
2. Du bist dir sicher, dass es morgen regnet.
3. Du denkst, dass deine Freundin auf dich warten wird.

G 11 Fragen mit dem modalen Hilfsverb *shall*

Questions with the modal verb 'shall'

Mit dem modalen Hilfsverb ***shall*** (sollen) kannst du **Wünsche erfragen** und **Vorschläge machen.** Es steht wie im Deutschen am Anfang der Frage. Es ist **für alle Personen gleich** und kann nur im ***simple present*** verwendet werden. Das **Vollverb** dazu steht immer in der **Grundform.**

Shall I help you with your room?	*Soll ich dir mit deinem Zimmer helfen?*
Shall we paint the walls green?	*Sollen wir die Wände grün streichen?*

G 12 Bedingungssätze

'if'-clauses

Wenn du eine **erfüllbare Bedingung** ausdrücken möchtest, kannst du das mit einem ***if*-Satz** tun. Bedingungssätze bestehen aus zwei Teilen: dem **Nebensatz mit *if*** (wenn), der die **Bedingung ausdrückt,** und dem **Hauptsatz**, der erklärt, **was passiert,** wenn diese Bedingung (nicht) erfüllt wird. Der ***if*-Satz** steht im ***simple present*** und im **Hauptsatz** wird das ***will-future*** verwendet. Der *if*-Satz kann am Anfang oder am Ende des Satzes stehen.

If-Satz	Hauptsatz	
If she **needs** a key for the locker,	she'**ll buy** one.	*Wenn sie einen Schlüssel für das Schließfach braucht, wird sie einen kaufen.*
If she **arrives** late,	she **won't know** where to go.	*Wenn sie zu spät kommt, weiß sie nicht, wohin sie gehen muss.*

My grammar

Erkläre deinem/r Partner/in an den beiden Beispielsätzen, welche erfüllbare Bedingung hier ausgedrückt wird und welche Folgen im Hauptsatz beschrieben werden.

Test yourself

Complete these sentences.

1. If my parents move to another place, I … .
2. If it rains tomorrow, I … .
3. If you're late for the lesson, you … .

G 13 Pronomen – Übersicht *Pronouns – a review*

Pronomen heißen auch **Fürwörter**. Sie stehen eigentlich **für** ein anderes Wort im Satz und **ersetzen** dieses. Du kennst schon mehrere Gruppen von Pronomen.

Personalpronomen		**Objektpronomen**		**Possessivpronomen**	
I	ich	**me**	mir/mich	**my**	mein
you	du/Sie	**you**	dir/dich/Ihnen/Sie	**your**	dein/Ihr
he	er	**him**	ihm/ihn	**his**	sein
she	sie	**her**	ihr/sie	**her**	ihr
it	es	**it**	ihm/es	**its**	sein
we	wir	**us**	uns	**our**	unser
you	ihr/Sie	**you**	euch/Ihnen/Sie	**your**	euer/Ihr
they	sie	**them**	ihnen/sie	**their**	ihr

G 14 Reflexivpronomen *Reflexive pronouns*

Mit dem **Reflexivpronomen** kannst du ausdrücken, dass jemand etwas **selbst oder für sich selbst** tut. Dann entspricht es den deutschen Pronomen mich/mir (selbst), dich/dir (selbst), sich (selbst) etc. Du kannst es auch benutzen, um zu betonen, dass du etwas selbst gemacht hast.

Singular
I – myself
you – yourself
he – himself
she – herself
it – itself

Plural
we – ourselves
you – yourselves
they – themselves

Verben, die im Deutschen mit „sich" gebildet werden, werden nicht automatisch im Englischen von den Reflexivpronomen *-self*/*-selves* begleitet.
Im Englischen kann „sich waschen" *to wash* oder *to wash yourself* und „sich anziehen" *to dress* oder *to dress yourself* heißen.

My grammar

1. Erkläre deinem/r Partner/in, wie sich *-self* im Plural verändert.
2. Welche anderen Wörter bilden die Pluralform wie *-self*? Finde drei Beispiele.
3. Welche Verben, die im Deutschen mit „sich" gebildet werden, brauchen im Englischen kein *-self/-selves*? Finde Beispiele in der Vokabelliste in deinem Buch.

Test yourself

Fill in the right reflexive pronoun.

1. You needn't help me. I can do this … .
2. She fell off her bike and hurt … .
3. Cats always clean … .
4. We can see … in the mirror.

G15 *some* und *any* — *'some' and 'any'*

Mit ***some*** oder ***any*** drückst du eine **unbestimmte Menge** oder Anzahl aus: „einige", „etwas", „ein paar". In Verneinungen: „kein/e", „nichts". In **Aussagen** verwendest du ***some,*** in **Fragen** und **Verneinungen** meist ***any.*** Im Deutschen werden *some* und *any* oft nicht übersetzt.

Aussagen

You'll see **some** great stars in this film.	*In diesem Film wirst du (einige) große Stars sehen.*
We'll have **some** fun.	*Wir werden Spaß haben.*

Verneinung und Fragen

Have you got **any** questions about pets?	*Haben Sie Fragen zu Haustieren?*
He could**n't** get **any** information.	*Er konnte keine Informationen bekommen.*

A
NEGATIVE
Y

S
POSITIVE
M
E

Bei Fragen mit *can* verwendest du immer *some*. *Can I have some information, please?*
Any kann auch in Aussagen vorkommen. Dann heißt es auf Deutsch „irgendein" oder „jeder/jede/jedes". *You can ask any questions you like.*

G16 Zusammensetzungen mit *some* und *any* — *Compounds of 'some' and 'any'*

Nach den gleichen Regeln wie *some* und *any* werden auch ihre Zusammensetzungen verwendet: **somebody/(not) anybody** (jemand/niemand), **somewhere/(not) anywhere** (irgendwo/nirgendwo), **something/(not) anything** (etwas/nichts).

Aussagen	Verneinung	Fragen
Somebody called just an hour ago.	Who can help? – I'm sorry. I ca**n't** think of **anybody.**	**Has anybody** seen this teenager?
He had **something** in a big bag.	I'm sure he has**n't** got **anything** to hide.	**Did** he have **anything** with him?
I think I saw the lad **somewhere.**	We ca**n't** find the boy **anywhere.**	**Have** you seen your brother **anywhere** today?

My grammar

Du kennst noch eine weitere Zusammensetzung mit *some* und *any*. Du findest sie im *Dictionary*. Nenne sie und erläutere jeweils an einem Beispielsatz die Regel.

Test yourself

1. There are … great films on TV tonight.
2. Are there … soaps on BBC 1?
3. Have you seen the TV magazine … ?
4. … has taken it.
5. You can't find … in this house!

G17 Die Verlaufsform der Vergangenheit *The past progressive*

Mit dem ***past progressive*** drückst du aus, wenn in der Vergangenheit etwas gerade passierte oder eine Handlung länger andauerte. Du bildest das ***past progressive*** mit einer Form von *be* ***(was/were)*** und der Endung ***-ing*** am Verb. Willst du den Satz verneinen, setzt du einfach ***not*** hinter ***was/were*** (Kurzform ***wasn't/weren't***). Eine Frage beginnst du mit ***Was/Were*** oder mit **Fragewort** + ***was/were***.

Aussagen

I **was walking** my dog in the park. — *Ich habe meinen Hund im Park spazieren geführt.*
They **were cleaning** the kitchen. — *Sie haben die Küche sauber gemacht.*

Verneinung

I **wasn't writing** an e-mail. — *Ich habe keine E-Mail geschrieben.*
We **weren't watching** TV. — *Wir haben nicht ferngesehen.*

Fragen

Was he **watching** TV? — *Schaute er fern?*
– Yes, he **was.**/No, he **wasn't.** — *– Ja./Nein.*
What were you **doing**? — *Was hast du gemacht?*

My grammar

1. Wie bildest du das *past progressive*? Erkläre es deinem/r Partner/in.
2. Vergleiche das *past progressive* mit dem *present progressive*. Was ist gleich? Was ist anders?

Test yourself

Look at the picture and complete the sentences.

1. What … they all … ? Nutty … his T-shirt.
2. Jane and Jack … their T-shirts, they … the drums.
3. The tiger … in the tree. He … a banana.

G18 Sätze mit *when* und *while* — *Sentences with 'when' and 'while'*

Simple past	**Past progressive**
Wenn du in einem Bericht mehrere Ereignisse der Reihe nach erwähnen möchtest, verwendest du das ***simple past.***	Wenn du betonen möchtest, dass eine Handlung in der Vergangenheit gerade passierte oder länger andauerte, verwendest du das ***past progressive.***

Wenn du ausdrücken möchtest, dass eine **Handlung noch andauert**, während eine neue, kurze Handlung eintritt, benutzt du das ***past progressive.*** Die **neu eintretende Handlung** wird mit dem ***simple past*** ausgedrückt. Das ***past progressive*** wird auch gebraucht, um **gleichzeitig verlaufende Handlungen** auszudrücken, die nicht beendet sind.
Signalwörter: *when, while*

Sätze mit ***when:*** 

When Polly passed the TV room, nobody was sitting there. — *Als Polly am Fernsehraum vorbeiging, saß niemand da.*

Two people were hiding in the tree, **when** Polly came into the garden. — *Zwei Leute versteckten sich gerade im Baum, als Polly in den Garten kam.*

Sätze mit ***while***: 

While the ambulance was taking Mr Mangold to the hospital, a guest was having breakfast. — *Während der Krankenwagen Herrn Mangold ins Krankenhaus brachte, frühstückte ein Gast.*

Lady Richstone was packing her things, **while** the policemen were looking under the beds. — *Lady Richstone packte ihre Sachen, während die Polizisten unter den Betten nachschauten.*

Im *while*-Satz ***past progressive,*** im *when*-Satz ***simple past.***
Achtung: *when* = als

My grammar
Suche dir je zwei Sätze mit *when* und *while* aus der Unit heraus und stelle sie grafisch dar.

Test yourself
Complete the sentences. Use the simple past or the past progressive.

1. When Jack … (*go*) to bed, Jane … (*think*) about a new tree house.
2. While Jack … (*sleep*), Jane … (*work*).
3. When Jack … (*wake up*), Jane … (*smile*).
4. While Jane and Jack … (*sit*) in their new tree house, Nutty … (*collect*) wood for his house.

G19 Die modalen Hilfsverben und ihre Ersatzformen

The modal verbs 'to be able to', 'to be allowed to' and 'to have to'

Can, may, must und *needn't* haben **Ersatzformen: *to be able to, to be allowed to*** und ***to have to***.
Diese kannst du in alle Zeiten setzen.

simple present	simple past	will-future
can	was/were able to	will be able to
may	was/were allowed to	will be allowed to
must	had to	will have to
needn't	didn't have to	won't have to

My grammar

1. Suche je einen Beispielsatz mit *to be able to, to be allowed to* und *to have to* aus dem Text auf Seite 98. Übersetze die Sätze ins Deutsche.
2. Setze deine Sätze ins *will-future*.

Test yourself

Say these sentences in English.

1. Gestern durfte ich Fernsehen schauen.
2. Gestern musste ich mit dem Hund spazieren gehen.
3. Letzte Woche musste ich nicht in die Schule gehen.
4. Am Sonntag konnte ich nicht Fußball spielen.

Grammatical terms

(Lateinisch) / Deutsch	Englisch	Englisches Beispiel
Adjektiv / Eigenschaftswort G5	adjective	quick, small, nice, old
Adverb / Umstandswort	adverb	always, often, quickly, loudly
Adverbialbestimmung des Ortes G9	adverbial phrase of place	to Stonehenge
Adverbialbestimmung der Zeit G9	adverbial phrase of time	last week, around 600 years later
Apostroph	apostrophe	I'm, you're, here's
Bedingungssätze G12	'if'-clauses	If it's sunny, we'll go swimming.
Demonstrativpronomen / hinweisendes Fürwort G5	demonstrative pronoun	this, that, these, those
Entscheidungsfrage	'yes/no'-question	Do you like computers?
Frage mit Fragewort	question with question word	What's your name?
Futur / Zukunft G10	'will'-future	It will be sunny at the weekend.
Häufigkeitsadverb	adverb of frequency	always, often, sometimes, never
Hauptsatz G12	main clause	She will buy a key.
Hilfsverb G1	auxiliary	be, have got, do

(Lateinisch) / Deutsch	Englisch	Englisches Beispiel
Imperativ / Befehlsform	imperative	Don't talk! Listen, please.
Infinitiv / Grundform des Verbs G10	infinitive	to do, to go, to see
Konsonant / Mitlaut	consonant	b, d, k, l, r, n
Kurzantwort	short answer	Yes, I did. No, he won't.
Kurzform	short form	I'm, we're, she's got, we won't
Langform	long form	I am, we are, she has got, we will not
Mengenangaben	expressions of quantity	some, any, a lot of, much, many
modales Hilfsverb / Modalverb G7, 19	modal verb	must, mustn't, need, needn't, should, shouldn't
Nebensatz G12	sub-clause	If she arrives late, ...
Objektpronomen G13	object pronoun	me, you, him, her, it, us, them
Perfekt	present perfect	Tom has painted the walls.
Personalpronomen / persönliches Fürwort G13	personal pronoun	I, you, she, he, it, we, you, they
Plural / Mehrzahl	plural	girls, children, babies
Plusquamperfekt / vollendete Vergangenheit	past perfect	After they had explained their idea, the reporters wrote articles.
Possessivbegleiter / besitzanzeigendes Fürwort G13	possessive pronoun	my, your, his, her, its, our, their
Präposition G5	preposition	in, on, at, about, over
Präsens / einfache Gegenwart G1	simple present	I live in Greenwich.
Präteritum / einfache Vergangenheit G4	simple past	I watched TV yesterday.
Reflexivpronomen / rückbezügliches Fürwort G13	reflexive pronoun	myself, ourselves
Relativpronomen G8	relative pronoun	Sam is the boy who I like.
Relativsatz G8	relative clause	Everyone who lives here can speak English.
Sätze mit *when* und *while* G18	sentences with 'when' and 'while'	When Polly passed the TV room, nobody was sitting there.
Signalwort G1, 2, 4, 6, 10, 17	signal word	last, ago, yesterday, ever, yet
Singular / Einzahl	singular	a girl, a boy, an apple
Steigerung von Adjektiven	comparison of adjectives	old – older – the oldest, good – better – the best
Stützwort *one/ones* G5	prop word 'one/ones'	Which one do you like best?
Substantiv / Hauptwort	noun	book, dog, sandwich
Verb / Tätigkeitswort	verb	to be, to go, to do, to write
Verlaufsform der Gegenwart G2	present progressive	We are having a party.
Verlaufsform der Vergangenheit G17	past progressive	I was walking my dog in the park.
Vokal / Selbstlaut	vowel	a, e, i, o, u
Vollverb G9	verb	to go, to do, to write
Wortstellung im Aussagesatz G9	word order in a sentence	S – V – O: The people rebuilt the stone circle.
Zusammensetzungen mit *some* und *any* G16	compounds of 'some' and 'any'	somebody, anybody, someone, anyone, something, anything, somewhere, anywhere

VOCABULARY

Diese Checkliste kann dir helfen, Fehler zu vermeiden und deine Rechtschreibung zu verbessern. Prüfe alle deine Texte damit.

- Schreibung:
  - ☐ ‚gh' wird meist nicht gesprochen. Vergiss es beim Schreiben nicht.
  - ☐ ‚k' kommt vor ‚t' so gut wie nie vor, z.B. action – Aktion, October – Oktober
- Gleiche Aussprache, unterschiedliche Schreibung:
  - ☐ [iː] z.B. teacher, meeting, media, magazine, people, field
  - ☐ [uː] z.B. food, route, to do, swimsuit, supermarket, true, crew
- Gleiche Aussprache, unterschiedliche Schreibung und Bedeutung:
  - ☐ [iː] z.B. see – sehen, sea – Meer; meet – treffen, meat – Fleisch
  - ☐ [uː] z.B. two – zwei, too – auch
- Verdoppelung der Endkonsonanten:
  - ☐ to stop – stopping, stopped
  - ☐ to plan – planning, planned
- ‚y' wird zu ‚ie':
  - ☐ in der 3. Person Singular: z.B. to carry – he carries; to cry – she cries; **aber**: to buy – she buys
  - ☐ im Plural: z.B. city – cities, party – parties; **aber**: boy – boys
  - ☐ bei der Steigerung von Adjektiven: z.B. happy – happier – (the) happiest; easy – easier – (the) easiest
- Ähnlich und doch anders:
  - ☐ Wortendung ‚le': z.B. *engl.* simple – *dt.* simpel; *engl.* title – *dt.* Titel; *engl.* middle – *dt.* Mittel
  - ☐ ‚ph' statt ‚f': z.B. *engl.* phone – *dt.* Telefon; *engl.* photo – *dt.* Foto
- Großschreibung:
  - ☐ Monatsnamen: z.B. January, July, December
  - ☐ Wochentage: z.B. Monday, Wednesday, Saturday
  - ☐ Eigennamen: z.B. Tom, Lisa, the Brooks, the London Eye, the Thames
  - ☐ geografische Namen: Bristol, Greenwich, Germany, Italy
- Plural:
  - ☐ Der Plural bekommt normalerweise ein -s: z.B. friend – friends, chair – chairs, film – films
  - ☐ Endet ein Wort auf s oder x, wird -es angehängt: z.B. bus – buses, box – boxes
  - ☐ Manche Wörter haben einen unregelmäßigen Plural: z.B. man – men, child – children, shelf – shelves, mouse – mice
- Apostroph:
  - ☐ bei Kurzformen: z.B. she is → she's; they are → they're
  - ☐ beim Genitiv-s: z.B. Sam's bike, Emma's family, the Jacksons' house, the children's games
- Wörterbuch:
  - ☐ Prüfe die Schreibung aller Wörter, bei denen du dir nicht ganz sicher bist, indem du sie im Wörterbuch nachschlägst.

Vocabulary

Auf den folgenden Seiten findest du alle neuen englischen Wörter und Ausdrücke. Sie stehen in der Reihenfolge, wie sie im Buch vorkommen. Diese Wortliste ist in drei Spalten aufgeteilt:

- Links stehen die englischen Wörter und Sätze.
- In der Mitte werden sie übersetzt.
- Rechts findest du Beispiele, Erklärungen und Tipps, die dir beim Lernen helfen.

Die fett gedruckten Wörter musst du lernen. Normal gedruckte Wörter solltest du wiedererkennen, wenn du sie hörst oder liest.

Gleich nach jedem neuen englischen Wort steht die Lautschrift in eckigen Klammern. Sie zeigt dir, wie das neue Wort ausgesprochen wird. Wie du diese Lautzeichen liest, siehst du unten.

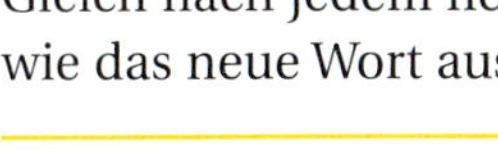

Englische Laute

Mitlaute

[b]	bed	[p]	picture
[d]	day	[r]	red
[ð]	the	[s]	six
[f]	family	[ʃ]	she
[g]	go	[t]	ten
[ŋ]	morning	[tʃ]	lunch
[h]	house	[v]	video
[j]	you	[w]	we, one
[k]	can, milk	[z]	easy
[l]	letter	[ʒ]	revision
[m]	man	[dʒ]	page
[n]	no	[θ]	thank you

Selbstlaute

[ɑː]	car
[æ]	apple
[e]	pen
[ə]	again
[ɜː]	girl
[ʌ]	but
[ɪ]	it
[i]	happy
[iː]	teacher
[ɒ]	dog
[ɔː]	ball
[ʊ]	book
[u]	January
[uː]	too, two

Doppellaute

[aɪ]	I, my
[aʊ]	now, mouse
[eɪ]	name, they
[eə]	there, pair
[ɪə]	here, idea
[əʊ]	hello
[ɔɪ]	boy
[ʊə]	sure

[ː] der vorangehende Laut ist lang, z. B. *you* [juː]

[ˈ] die folgende Silbe wird betont, z. B. *hello* [həˈləʊ]

In jeder *Unit* findest du Tipps zum Vokabellernen sowie einen Kasten mit *Useful phrases*, die dir helfen, dich auf Englisch zu verständigen.

Außerdem gibt es zu jeder *Unit* einen Kasten, in dem du Interessantes zur Landeskunde erfährst.

Am Ende der *Units* kannst du wieder nützliche Ausdrücke für deinen *Folder* sammeln.

Auf das *Vocabulary* folgt das *Dictionary*, eine alphabetische Wortliste aller englischen Wörter im Buch. Wenn du ein Wort nicht verstehst, kannst du es hier nachschlagen

Abkürzungen und Zeichen

pl	Plural, Mehrzahl	!	Achtung!
sing	Singular, Einzahl	↔	ist das Gegenteil von
10	Auf dieser Seite kommen die Wörter vor.	→	ist verwandt mit
		=	entspricht

! *Homework* hat keine Mehrzahl.
old ↔ new
teach → teacher
Dear Sam = Lieber Sam

Unit 1 What's your game?

Erinnerst du dich an die Tipps vom letzten Schuljahr?

In den ersten zwei Bänden hast du schon viele nützliche Tipps kennen gelernt, die dir das Vokabellernen erleichtern. Hier nochmals eine kleine Zusammenfassung zur Erinnerung:

- Lerne möglichst immer am gleichen Arbeitsplatz.
- Führe deine Vokabeldatei fort.
- Nimm dir mehrmals am Tag kleine Lernportionen vor, die du dann jeweils für eine kurze Zeit (10 Minuten) bearbeitest.
- Stelle für jedes neue Wort so viele Zusammenhänge wie möglich her.
- Gestalte das Lernen spannender, indem du mit anderen lernst oder Vokabellernspiele spielst.

Check-in

8	**home** [həʊm]	Heimat →	England is the Queen's *home*. One of her *homes* is Buckingham Palace. She is not *at home* today.
	rugby ['rʌgbi]	Rugby	
	century ['sentʃri]	Jahrhundert →	We're now in the 21st *century*.
	each [i:tʃ]	jede/jeder/jedes	
	its [ɪts]	sein, seine; ihr, ihre →	The school has *its* own rules.
	they [ðeɪ]	*hier:* man	
	grass [grɑ:s]	Gras	
	American football [əˌmerɪkən 'fʊtbɔ:l]	Football	
	player ['pleɪə]	Spieler/Spielerin, Mitspieler/Mitspielerin →	to play → *player*
	helmet ['helmət]	Helm →	American football players wear *helmets*.
	during *(+ noun)* ['djʊərɪŋ]	während *(+ Nomen)*	
	to **catch, caught, caught** [kætʃ, kɔ:t, kɔ:t]	fangen, erreichen →	to throw a ball ↔ to *catch* a ball
	stadium ['steɪdiəm]	Stadion →	Players play football in a football *stadium*.
	you [ju:; jə]	man →	*You* use a rugby ball for rugby.
	to **learn** [lɜ:n]	erfahren	
	to **bat** [bæt]	schlagen	
	bat [bæt]	Schläger	
	glove [glʌv]	Handschuh →	You wear shoes on your feet and *gloves* on your hands.
	rugby boot ['rʌgbɪ ˌbu:t]	Rugbyschuh, Stollenschuh	
	at the front [frʌnt]	vorne, im vorderen Teil	
	at the back [bæk]	hinten, im hinteren Teil	
9	**baseball** ['beɪsbɔ:l]	Baseball →	*Baseball* is an American ball game.
	batter ['bætə]	Schlagmann/Schlagfrau →	to bat → *batter*
	to **score** [skɔ:]	punkten, ein Tor schießen →	Just before the end of the match our team *scored* and we won 1-0.
	run [rʌn]	Run, Runde	
	action ['ækʃn]	Handlung, Aktion	

stand [stænd]	Tribüne →	Our seats are at the back of the *stand*.
souvenir [ˌsuːvəˈnɪə]	Souvenir, Andenken	
against [əˈgenst]	gegen	
competition [ˌkɒmpəˈtɪʃn]	Wettbewerb, Turnier →	In a *competition* the person or team who is the best wins.

Cricket

Auch wenn Fußball inzwischen die beliebteste Sportart in England ist – der Nationalsport ist Cricket. Ein Cricket-Feld besteht aus einem runden oder ovalen Stück Rasen. Ein Cricket-Team besteht aus elf Spielern. Sie spielen mit einem Ball, der etwas kleiner ist als ein Baseball, und einem Schläger, der wie ein Paddel geformt ist. Die Spielregeln sind sehr kompliziert und die Spieler tragen meistens weiße Spielkleidung. Die beiden Schiedsrichter tragen lange, weiße Kittel und sehen dabei oft aus wie der Milchmann um die Ecke. Sie genießen jedoch großen Respekt und es gilt als sehr unsportlich, die Entscheidung eines Schiedsrichters zu kritisieren. Cricket-Spiele dauern entweder einen Tag oder fünf Tage. Da jeder Spieltag durch eine Mittags- und durch eine Teepause unterbrochen wird, bringen die Zuschauer traditionell einen Picknickkorb zum Spiel mit.

Was ist der deutsche Nationalsport? Gibt es im deutschen Sport auch Traditionen, die jemand aus einem anderen Land komisch finden könnte?

Language

10	regular [ˈregjələ]	regelmäßig	
	pitch [pɪtʃ]	Spielfeld →	Let's go to the *pitch* and do some runs.
	national [ˈnæʃnl]	landesweit →	He plays for the *national* team.
	best [best]	am besten	
	beach [biːtʃ]	Strand →	The kids are playing on the *beach*.
	net [net]	Netz	
	across [əˈkrɒs]	über, hinüber, quer durch/ darüber →	They walked *across* the street.
	court [kɔːt]	Spielfeld →	They play tennis on a *court*.
	sand [sænd]	Sand →	You can make houses and castles with *sand* on the beach.
	goalkeeper [ˈgəʊlˌkiːpə]	Torwart	
	back line [ˌbæk ˈlain]	Grundlinie	
	to **kill** [kɪl]	töten; *hier:* tot machen	
	signal [ˈsɪgnl]	Zeichen	
11	**full (of)** [fʊl]	ganz, voll (von/mit)	
	birth [bɜːθ]	Geburt →	birthday → *birth*
	height [haɪt]	Höhe, Größe →	high → *height*
	weight [weɪt]	Gewicht →	His *weight* is 245 lb.
	foot, feet *(pl)* [fʊt; fiːt]	Fuß *(Längenmaß: 30,48 cm)* →	In British and American English, heights are often given in *feet*.
	inch [ɪnʃ]	Zoll *(Längenmaß: 2,54 cm)* →	There are 12 *inches* in 1 foot.

gramme (g) [græm]	Gramm	
stone [stəʊn]	*brit. Gewichtseinheit* (= 6,35 kg) →	There are 14 pounds in 1 *stone*.
profile ['prəʊfaɪl]	Steckbrief; Profil, Porträt	
union ['juːnjən]	Liga; Vereinigung, Union	
was/were born [bɔːn]	wurde(n) geboren →	I *was born* in Berlin in 1994.
about [ə'baʊt]	ungefähr, circa, etwa →	at *about* 12 = maybe a bit earlier or later
personal ['pɜːsnl]	persönlich →	person → *personal*
UK [juː'keɪ]	→	short for the United Kingdom
the **USA** [ˌjuːes'eɪ]	→	the United States of America
yourself [jɔː'self]	dich selbst	
future ['fjuːtʃə]	Zukunft	
12 present progressive [ˌpreznt prə'gresɪv]	Verlaufsform des Präsens/ der Gegenwart	
couch potato ['kaʊtʃ pəˌteɪtəʊ]	Stubenhocker	
couch [kaʊtʃ]	Couch, Sofa	
to **cycle** ['saɪkl]	Rad fahren →	to ride a bike
secretary ['sekrətri]	Sekretär/Sekretärin	
firm [fɜːm]	Firma →	Marcia works as a secretary in a *firm*.
racing ['reɪsɪŋ]	Renn-	
boss [bɒs]	Boss, Chef/Chefin	
could [kʊd]	könnte/könnten →	If you want to be polite, you can ask *'Could you …?'*
walk [wɔːk]	Spaziergang →	to walk → *a walk*
active ['æktɪv]	aktiv →	action → to act → *active*
enough [ɪ'nʌf]	genug, genügend →	Have we got *enough* milk for breakfast?
you see [jʊ 'siː]	weißt du	
to **imagine** [ɪ'mædʒɪn]	sich (etwas) vorstellen →	Can you *imagine* what it's like at an American school?
jersey ['dʒɜːzi]	Trikot	
pool [puːl]	Schwimmbecken	
swimsuit ['swɪmsuːt]	Badeanzug	
tennis ['tenɪs]	Tennis	
star [stɑː]	Star, Stern →	There are a lot of *stars* in this film.
umpire ['ʌmpaɪə]	Schiedsrichter/ Schiedsrichterin →	In cricket and tennis they have *umpires*.
half-time [ˌhɑːf'taɪm]	Halbzeit →	The break in the middle of a (football) game.
score [skɔː]	Punktestand, Spielstand →	What's the *score*? = Wie steht es?
referee [ˌrefr'iː]	Schiedsrichter/ Schiedsrichterin	
to **blow, blew, blown** [bləʊ, bluː, bləʊn]	blasen →	The wind *is blowing*.
whistle ['wɪsl]	Trillerpfeife	
It's a draw. [ˌɪts‿ə 'drɔː]	Es steht unentschieden.	
swimming pool ['swɪmɪŋ ˌpuːl]	Schwimmbecken; Schwimmbad →	There's a *swimming pool* in Greenwich.

13	**dance** [dɑːnts]	Tanz →	to dance → a *dance*
	snapshot ['snæpʃɒt]	Schnappschuss	
	someone else [ˌsʌmwʌn‿'els]	jemand anderes	
	to pretend [prɪ'tend]	vorgeben, tun als ob	

Signalwörter für *simple present* und *present progressive*

Wenn dich zwischen dem *simple present* und dem *present progressive* entscheiden musst, können dir die folgenden Signalwörter helfen:

Simple present	Present progressive
always	at the moment
every day/week/…	(right) now
never	today
often	
on Mondays/Tuesdays/…	
sometimes	
usually	

Get fit!

14	presentation [ˌprezn'teɪʃn]	Präsentation	
	to prepare [prɪ'peə]	vorbereiten, zubereiten →	to get something ready
	talk [tɔːk]	Vortrag, Rede →	to talk → *a talk*
	diagram ['daɪəgræm]	Diagramm →	A *diagram* can help to show how something works or to make facts clearer.
	special ['speʃl]	besonders, speziell	
	to give a talk [ˌgɪv‿ə 'tɔːk]	einen Vortrag/eine Rede halten	
	useful ['juːsfl]	nützlich →	You can often use that phrase. So it's a *useful* phrase.
	while [waɪl]	während	
	catcher ['kætʃə]	Fänger/Fängerin →	to catch → *catcher*
	base [beɪs]	Base	
	pitcher ['pɪtʃə]	Werfer/Werferin →	The *pitcher* throws the ball to the batter.
	home plate ['həʊm ˌpleɪt]	Home Plate	
	at the top [ət ðə 'tɒp]	oben, im oberen Teil	
	top [tɒp]	Spitze, oberer Teil →	the highest point of something
	at the bottom [ət ðə 'bɒtəm]	unten, im unteren Teil	
	bottom ['bɒtəm]	Boden, Grund, unterer Teil →	top ↔ *bottom*
	to discuss [dɪ'skʌs]	diskutieren	
	to **be missing** [biː 'mɪsɪŋ]	fehlen	
	suggestion [sə'dʒestʃn]	Vorschlag, Anregung	

Useful phrases: Discuss a talk

Die folgenden *phrases* helfen dir bei der Diskussion in der Klasse.

☺

The talk was good/interesting.	Der Vortrag war gut/interessant.
He/she spoke clearly.	Er/sie hat deutlich gesprochen.
He/she showed us good photos.	Er/sie hat gute Fotos gezeigt.
I learned some new facts about the topic.	Ich habe einige neue Fakten zu dem Thema gelernt.
He/she could answer all the questions.	Er/sie konnte alle Fragen beantworten.

☹

The talk wasn't good/was boring.	Der Vortrag war nicht gut/war langweilig.
He/she didn't speak clearly enough.	Er/sie hat nicht deutlich genug gesprochen.
The photos weren't good.	Die Fotos waren nicht gut.
The facts weren't interesting.	Die Fakten waren nicht interessant.
He/she couldn't answer all the questions.	Er/sie konnte nicht alle Fragen beantworten.

Overheard

15	overheard [ˌəʊvə'hɜ:d]	zufällig mitgehört	
	description [dɪ'skrɪpʃn]	Beschreibung →	to describe → *description*
	row [rəʊ]	Reihe	
	half-price [ˌhɑ:f'praɪs]	zum halben Preis →	The tickets are *half-price*.
	to **send off** [send‿'ɒf]	vom Platz verweisen →	The referee *sent off* a player from the pitch.
	British ['brɪtɪʃ]	britisch →	The Lehmanns are German, and the Taylors are *British*.
	figure ['fɪgə]	Zahl, Ziffer	
	cup [kʌp]	Tasse, Kelch; Pokal →	Would you like a *cup* of tea?
	BC (= before Christ) [bi:'si:]	vor Christus	
	goal post ['gəʊl pəʊst]	Torpfosten	
	post [pəʊst]	Pfosten, Mast	

Facts and fiction

16	fiction ['fɪkʃn]	Erfindung, Fiktion	
	practice ['præktɪs]	Training →	Football *practice* is on Fridays.
	nearly ['nɪəli]	fast, annähernd →	I must go home. It's *nearly* five o'clock.
	doorstep ['dɔ:step]	Türstufe	
	next door [ˌnekst 'dɔ:]	nebenan	
	ancient ['eɪnʃnt]	alt →	*ancient* = old
	to **moan** [məʊn]	(sich) (be)klagen →	Pupils always *moan* about their homework.
	to **dig up, dug up, dug up** [dɪg‿'ʌp, dʌg‿'ʌp, dʌg‿'ʌp]	ausgraben	
	lonely ['ləʊnli]	einsam	
	to **feel sorry for** [fi:l 'sɒri]	Mitleid haben mit, bedauern →	I *felt sorry* for him. = Er hat mir Leid getan.
	home-made [ˌhəʊm'meɪd]	selbst gemacht →	These biscuits are *home-made*.
	well [wel]	gut	

	fight [faɪt]	Kampf	
	thick [θɪk]	dick *(nicht für Personen)*; dumm →	There's a really *thick* fog.
	to **come down** [kʌm 'daʊn]	herunterkommen, sich legen	
	fair [feə]	gerecht, fair →	That was a *fair* game.
17	**not … either** [ˌnɒt … 'aɪðə]	auch nicht →	Terry doesn't live in Germany. Sam does*n't* live there *either*.
	to **substitute** ['sʌbstɪtjuːt]	auswechseln, ersetzen →	They *substituted* a player.
	instead of [ɪn'sted‿əv]	statt, anstatt →	They had twelve players *instead of* eleven.
	What a laugh! [ˌwɒt‿ə 'lɑːf]	Wie lustig!	
	to **run into** [rʌn‿'ɪntə]	laufen gegen, stoßen gegen →	Yesterday I *ran into* the classroom door.
	to **knock out** [nɒk‿'aʊt]	k.o. schlagen, umhauen	
	himself [hɪm'self]	sich (selbst) →	He knocked *himself* out.
	to **take off** [teɪk‿'ɒf]	wegbringen, fortschaffen	
	crowd [kraʊd]	Menschenmenge →	a lot of people all together in one place
	rest [rest]	Rest	
	to belong (to) [bɪ'lɒŋ]	gehören (zu)	
	to **change your mind** [ˌtʃeɪndʒ jə 'maɪnd]	deine Meinung ändern	

Wordwise

18	mind map ['maɪnd mæp]	Wörternetz *(eine Art Schaubild)*	
	noun [naʊn]	Nomen	
	the same [seɪm]	derselbe/dieselbe/ dasselbe; gleich	
19	preposition [ˌprepə'zɪʃn]	Präposition	

Check-out

21	mixed bag ['mɪkst bæg]	Vermischtes	

Prepositions with nouns

Je nachdem, mit welchem Wort Präpositionen zusammenstehen, können sie unterschiedliche Übersetzungen haben.

in		*on*		*at*	
in April	im April	*on Monday*	am Montag	*at 8 o'clock*	um 8 Uhr
in the afternoon	am Nachmittag	*on Mondays*	montags	*at night*	in der Nacht
in London	in London	*on June 6th*	am 6. Juni	*at the weekend*	am Wochenende
in the street	auf der Straße	*on the table*	auf dem Tisch	*at home*	zu Hause
in English	auf Englisch	*on holiday*	im Urlaub	*at the doctor's*	beim Arzt

For my folder: Sports

Nun kennst du schon viele verschiedene Sportarten. Schreibe sie in deinen *folder* und sammle die Wörter und Ausdrücke, die zu den einzelnen Sportarten gehören.

Beach volleyball:

sand, court, ball, back line, kill the ball, net …

Unit 2 Out and about in London

Lerntipp: Organisation beim Vokabellernen

- Warte nicht mit dem Lernen bis zum letzten Augenblick! Verteile die zu lernenden Vokabeln möglichst gleichmäßig auf die Zeit, die zur Verfügung steht.
- Überlege dir, wann du besonders gut lernen kannst. Bist du zu bestimmten Zeiten eher müde (z. B. nach dem Mittagessen)? Dann suche dir eine günstige Zeit aus, in der du „fit" bist. Nutze diese „Spitzenzeiten" aus.

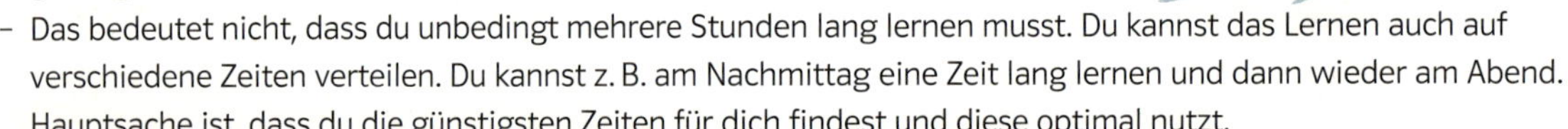

- Das bedeutet nicht, dass du unbedingt mehrere Stunden lang lernen musst. Du kannst das Lernen auch auf verschiedene Zeiten verteilen. Du kannst z. B. am Nachmittag eine Zeit lang lernen und dann wieder am Abend. Hauptsache ist, dass du die günstigsten Zeiten für dich findest und diese optimal nutzt.

Check-in

26	**capsule** ['kæpsju:l]	Kapsel	
	spectacular [spek'tækjələ]	spektakulär	
	view [vju:]	Aussicht, Sicht →	You can get a nice *view* from that tower.
	palace ['pælɪs]	Palast →	The Queen lives in Buckingham *Palace*.
	royal ['rɔɪəl]	königlich	
	to **relive** [ˌri:'lɪv]	wieder erleben →	You can *relive* some of the most terrible events.
	great [greɪt]	groß →	big
	queue [kju:]	(Warte-)Schlange →	People are waiting in a *queue* in front of the cinema.
	traffic jam ['træfɪk ˌdʒæm]	Stau	
	traffic ['træfɪk]	Verkehr →	all the cars, buses etc. that are moving on a road
	Tube [tju:b]	Londoner U-Bahn	
	to **go far** [gəʊ 'fɑ:]	weit kommen, es weit bringen	
	trendy ['trendi]	modisch	
	to **build, built, built** [bɪld, bɪlt, bɪlt]	bauen →	When did they *build* the Buckingham Palace?
	tower ['taʊə]	Turm →	The *Tower* of London
	building ['bɪldɪŋ]	Gebäude →	to build → *a building*
	valuable ['væljuəbl]	wertvoll	

Das London Dungeon

Mitten im Zentrum von London, direkt unter dem Kopfsteinpflaster des historischen Stadtteils Southwark, befindet sich das wohl gruseligste Museum der Welt: das London Dungeon. In dunklen Kellergewölben, die früher als Gefängnis für Schwerverbrecher dienten, werden die blutigsten und grausamsten Ereignisse in der Geschichte Englands erzählt. Foltermethoden, Krankheiten und grausame Morde werden mit Wachsfiguren nachgestellt, und überall lauern als Monster verkleidete Schauspieler und versuchen, die Besucher zu erschrecken.
Das Museum kann auch von Privatpersonen für gruselige Partys gemietet werden und jedes Jahr am 31. Oktober findet im Dungeon eine Furcht erregende Halloween-Party statt.

Wie denkst du über ein solches Museum? Würdest du das Dungeon besuchen? Gibt es etwas Ähnliches auch in Deutschland?

	jewel ['dʒu:əl]	Juwel	
	world [wɜ:ld]	Welt	
	crown [kraʊn]	Krone →	The Queen sometimes wears a *crown*.
	caption ['kæpʃn]	Untertitel; Bildunterschrift	
27	**underground** ['ʌndəgraʊnd]	U-Bahn →	A lot of cities have got an *underground*.

Language

28	simple past [ˌsɪmpl 'pɑ:st]	einfache Vergangenheit	
	tourist ['tʊərɪst]	Tourist/Touristin →	In summer there are many more *tourists* in London than in winter.
	pickpocket ['pɪkˌpɒkɪt]	Taschendieb/Taschendiebin	
	local ['ləʊkl]	lokal, örtlich	
	newspaper ['nju:sˌpeɪpə]	Zeitung →	Tim reads the *newspaper* every morning.
	route [ru:t; raʊt]	Route	
	to **change** [tʃeɪndʒ]	umsteigen →	He *changed* at Tower Hill.
	thanks to ['θæŋks tə]	dank (dir/ihnen), wegen →	*Thanks to* my dog it's never boring at home.
	to **rob** [rɒb]	rauben, ausrauben →	A pickpocket *robbed* my uncle.
	within [wɪ'ðɪn]	innerhalb	
	teenager ['ti:nˌeɪdʒə]	Teenager, Jugendliche/Jugendlicher	
	busy ['bɪzi]	belebt →	This street is very *busy*.
	handbag ['hænbæg]	Handtasche	
	businessman, businessmen *(pl)* ['bɪznɪsmən; 'bɪznɪsmen]	Geschäftsmann	
	rucksack ['rʌksæk]	Rucksack →	We need a bigger *rucksack* for our next trip.
	finally ['faɪnli]	endlich, schließlich	
	cathedral [kə'θi:drl]	Kathedrale, Dom	
	toy [tɔɪ]	Spielzeug →	something a child plays with
	fine [faɪn]	Geldbuße, Geldstrafe	
29	**rich** [rɪtʃ]	reich →	*Rich* people have a lot of money.

one(s) [wʌn(z)]	*(Platzhalter für ein Nomen)* →	! Beim Übersetzen dieses Wortes musst du aufpassen, wer oder was im Satz gemeint ist!
to **become, became, become** [bɪ'kʌm, bɪ'keɪm, bɪ'kʌm]	werden →	*to become* rich = reich werden
blond(e)-haired ['blɒnd,heəd]	blond →	a *blond-haired* boy – a *blonde-haired* girl
actress ['æktrəs]	Schauspielerin →	an actor – an *actress*
model ['mɒdl]	Model, Modell →	Naomi Campbell is a famous *model.*
sporty ['spɔ:ti]	sportlich →	sport → *sporty*
prince [prɪns]	Prinz	
souvenir [ˌsu:və'nɪə]	Souvenir, Andenken	
30 **millennium** [mɪ'leniəm]	Jahrtausend →	A thousand years; *here*: the year 2000.

Useful phrases: Getting around

Die folgenden *phrases* helfen dir dabei, dich im Großstadtdschungel zurechtzufinden.

Excuse me, how do I get to … ?	Entschuldigung, wie komme ich nach/zu … ?
Where are the nearest toilets, please?	Wo sind die nächsten Toiletten?
Turn left/right.	Biegen Sie links/rechts ab.
I'd like a ticket to … .	Ich hätte gerne eine Fahrkarte nach … .
Let's take the … Line to … .	Lasst uns die … Linie nach … nehmen.
We must change to the … Line there.	Wir müssen dort in die … Linie umsteigen.
We get off at … .	Wir steigen an der Haltestelle … aus.
Is there a post office near here?	Gibt es in der Nähe eine Post?
How much is a postcard/letter to Germany?	Wie viel kostet eine Postkarte/ein Brief nach Deutschland?

after ['ɑ:ftə]	nachdem →	*After* the show had finished, I went home.
to **enter** ['entə]	sich beteiligen an; eintreten, betreten →	They *entered* the competition.
landmark ['lændmɑ:k]	Wahrzeichen, Markstein →	The Tower is one of London's most famous *landmarks.*
to **give up** [gɪv‿'ʌp]	aufgeben →	They didn't *give up* their dream.
article ['ɑ:tɪkl]	Artikel	
to **come true** [kʌm 'tru:]	wahr werden →	Their dream *came true.*
architect ['ɑ:kɪtekt]	Architekt/Architektin	
rim [rɪm]	Radkranz	
piece [pi:s]	Stück →	Would you like a *piece* of cake?
to **complete** [kəm'pli:t]	vervollständigen	
wheel [wi:l]	Rad →	A bike has got two *wheels.*
to **lift** [lɪft]	hochziehen, hochheben →	They *lifted* the wheel.
to **add** [æd]	hinzufügen, addieren	
platform ['plætfɔ:m]	Plattform, Tribüne, Bahnsteig →	a *platform* for visitors
to **fix (to)** [fɪks]	befestigen, anbringen; reparieren →	They *fixed* capsules *to* the wheel.
huge [hju:dʒ]	riesig, gewaltig →	very, very big
to **design** [dɪ'zaɪn]	entwerfen; zeichnen	

	towards [tə'wɔ:dz]	in Richtung, auf … zu, darauf zu	
	to **construct** [kən'strʌkt]	bauen, konstruieren	
31	**fortress** ['fɔ:trəs]	Festung	
	prison ['prɪzn]	Gefängnis	
	menagerie [mə'nædʒri]	Menagerie →	A *menagerie* is a small zoo.
	past perfect [ˌpɑ:st 'pɜ:fɪkt]	Plusquamperfekt	
	conqueror ['kɒŋkrə]	Eroberer	
	king [kɪŋ]	König →	In Germany there are no *kings* or queens.
	to **die** [daɪ]	sterben	
	wild [waɪld]	wild →	pets – farm animals – *wild* animals
	to **marry** ['mæri]	heiraten	
	monastery ['mɒnəstri]	Kloster	
	university [ˌju:nɪ'vɜ:səti]	Universität	
	exhibition [ˌeksɪ'bɪʃn]	Ausstellung, Vorführung →	At an art *exhibition*, you can see a lot of different pictures.

Neue Adjektive in *Unit 2*

rich	*richer*	*the richest*	reich
sporty	*sportier*	*the sportiest*	sportlich
trendy	*trendier*	*the trendiest*	modisch
spectacular	*more spectacular*	*most spectacular*	spektakulär
valuable	*more valuable*	*most valuable*	wertvoll

Get fit!

32	skimming ['skɪmɪŋ]	Überfliegen	
	to skim [skɪm]	überfliegen	
	to look out (for) [lʊk‿'aʊt]	Ausschau halten (nach), suchen (nach)	
	to protect [prə'tekt]	(be)schützen	
	fifth [fɪfθ]	Fünftel	
	quarter ['kwɔ:tə]	Viertel	
	to **destroy** [dɪ'strɔɪ]	zerstören →	The fire *destroyed* a lot of buildings.
	wood [wʊd]	Holz	
	straw [strɔ:]	Stroh →	People built houses with wood and *straw*.
	baker ['beɪkə]	Bäcker/Bäckerin →	A *baker* makes bread.
	to **put out** [pʊt‿'aʊt]	ausmachen; löschen	
	fire [faɪə]	Feuerstelle, Kaminfeuer →	Please put out the *fire* when you leave.
	to **smell, smelt, smelt** [smel, smelt, smelt]	riechen →	He could *smell* smoke.
	smoke [sməʊk]	Rauch	
	spark [spɑ:k]	Funke(n) →	A *spark* can start a fire in seconds.
	flame [fleɪm]	Flamme	
	to **burn, burnt, burnt** [bɜ:n, bɜ:nt, bɜ:nt]	(ver)brennen →	The fire *burnt* for four days.
	for … [fɔ:; fə]	… lang →	*for* a week = eine Woche lang

fire brigade ['faɪə brɪˌgeɪd]	Feuerwehr	
to **damage** ['dæmɪdʒ]	beschädigen	
half [hɑ:f]	Hälfte	
boat [bəʊt]	Boot, Schiff →	A *boat* is a small ship.
to the country [tʊ ðə 'kʌntri]	aufs Land	

Neue unregelmäßige Verben in *Unit 2*

to build	*built*	*built*	bauen
to become	*became*	*become*	werden
to smell	*smelt*	*smelt*	riechen
to burn	*burnt*	*burnt*	brennen

Overheard

33	announcement [ə'naʊntsmənt]	Ankündigung, Durchsage	
	meaning ['mi:nɪŋ]	Bedeutung	
	dialogue ['daɪəlɒg]	Dialog, Gespräch →	Two people are talking. Listen to their *dialogue*.
	attention [ə'tentʃn]	Aufmerksamkeit	
	ladies and gentlemen [ˌleɪdiz‿n 'dʒentlmən]	meine Damen und Herren	
	customer ['kʌstəmə]	Kunde/Kundin →	A *customer* buys things in a shop.

Facts and fiction

34	to **train** [treɪn]	eine Ausbildung machen →	I'm *training* to be a teacher.
	gardener ['gɑ:dnə]	Gärtner/Gärtnerin →	garden → *gardener*
	courier ['kʊriə]	Kurier	
	pollution [pə'lu:ʃn]	(Umwelt-)Verschmutzung	
	to **argue** ['ɑ:gju:]	streiten, argumentieren →	You don't *argue* with a bus.
	to **carry** ['kæri]	befördern	
	tin [tɪn]	Dose, Büchse →	a *tin* of dog food
	sauerkraut ['saʊəkraʊt]	Sauerkraut	
	milkman, milkmen *(pl)* ['mɪlkmən; 'mɪlkmen]	Milchmann →	milk → *milkman*
	round [raʊnd]	Runde	
	tradition [trə'dɪʃn]	Tradition	
	dairy ['deəri]	Molkerei	
	company ['kʌmpəni]	Gesellschaft, Firma; Kompanie →	I work for a big *company*.
	to **deliver** [dɪ'lɪvə]	liefern	
	at the crack of dawn [ˌkræk‿əv 'dɔ:n]	im Morgengrauen →	very early in the morning
	customer ['kʌstəmə]	Kunde/Kundin →	A *customer* buys things in a shop.
	since [sɪnts]	seit, seitdem	
	taxi ['tæksi]	Taxi →	Most London *taxis* are black.

	learning ['lɜːnɪŋ]	um zu lernen	
	like the back of my hand [laɪk ðə 'bæk‿əv maɪ ˌhænd]	wie meine Westentasche →	very well
	kind [kaɪnd]	Art, Sorte →	What *kind* of music do you like?
	to **expect** [ɪk'spekt]	erwarten	
35	**punk** [pʌŋk]	Punk	
	style [staɪl]	Stil; *hier:* Frisur →	I like your new hair *style*!
	post office ['pəʊst‿ˌɒfɪs]	Postamt	
	regular ['regjələ]	Stammkunde/ Stammkundin	
	to **get interested in** [get 'ɪntrəstɪd]	sich interessieren für	
	mess [mes]	Durcheinander →	There's a terrible *mess* in my room.
	diary ['daɪəri]	Tagebuch; Terminkalender	
	entry ['entri]	Eintrag	

Lautschrifträtsel

In dieser Unit habt ihr viele Wörter kennen gelernt, die den entsprechenden deutschen Wörtern sehr ähnlich sind. Jedoch unterscheiden sich die englischen und deutschen Wörter oft in der Aussprache. Ihr könnt euch die Aussprache und Schreibweise dieser Wörter besser einprägen, wenn ihr das folgende Spiel macht.

['tæksi]	['ləʊkl]	['ʌndəgraʊnd]
['plætfɔːm]	['ɑːkɪtekt]	['beɪkə]
[spek'tækjələ]	[trə'dɪʃn]	[waɪld]

In dem Kasten findet ihr die Lautschrift einiger Wörter dieser Unit. Eure Aufgabe ist es:
- zu erkennen, um welches Wort es sich handelt,
- es richtig auszusprechen
- und es richtig aufzuschreiben.

Na, wer von euch schafft es am schnellsten ohne Fehler?

Dieses Spiel könnt ihr natürlich erweitern, indem ihr in eurem *Dictionary* noch andere Wörter sucht, die auf Deutsch und Englisch sehr ähnlich sind.

Check-out

39	tense [tens]	Zeit, Zeitform (*grammatisch*)

For my folder: A London sight

Nun hast du schon einige Sehenswürdigkeiten von London kennen gelernt. Natürlich gibt es dort noch viel mehr zu sehen. Suche dir eine Sehenswürdigkeit aus, die dich besonders interessiert. Dazu kannst du auch das Internet benutzen. Mache ein Poster mit Bild und schreibe alle Adjektive auf, die deine Sehenswürdigkeit näher beschreiben.

Unit 3 Here we come!

Lerntipp: Englisch im Alltag

Achte während des Tages auf alle englischen Wörter, die dir begegnen. Ob im Supermarkt, im Fernsehen, in Büchern, auf Werbeplakaten oder Schildern am Bahnhof, Flughafen etc: Du wirst erstaunt sein, wie oft man im Alltag auf die englische Sprache stößt. Das ist ein gutes Training, um auf noch unbekannte Vokabeln aufmerksam zu werden. Deinen Sprachschatz erweiterst du ganz leicht, indem du dir ein schönes Heft oder Notizbuch kaufst, das speziell für solche Vokabeln da ist. Nimm es so oft wie möglich mit, vor allem, wenn du verreist! Die noch unbekannten Wörter kannst du dann zu Hause in einem Wörterbuch nachschlagen. Da du mit jedem Wort eine kleine Geschichte oder bestimmte besondere Umstände verbindest (zum Beispiel: „Ach ja! Dieses Wort habe ich am Bahnhof gesehen, im Kino gehört" etc), wirst du es dir sehr leicht merken können!

Check-in

44	**coastline** ['kəʊstlaɪn]	Küstenlinie →	Germany has a *coastline* of 2,389 km.
	to **travel** ['trævl]	reisen →	We *travelled* to England last year.
45	**cliff** [klɪf]	Klippe	
	circle ['sɜ:kl]	Kreis →	Stand in the middle of the *circle*.
	almost ['ɔ:lməʊst]	fast, beinahe →	*almost* = nearly
	kilometre ['kɪləʊˌmi:tə; kɪ'lɒmɪtə]	Kilometer	
	officer ['ɒfɪsə]	Beamter/Beamtin →	A police *officer* is a man or woman in the police.
	smuggler ['smʌglə]	Schmuggler/Schmugglerin →	I'm reading an exciting adventure story about *smugglers* on the coast of Cornwall.

Schmuggler

Schmuggler gibt es in England seit dem 14. Jahrhundert, als die ersten Zölle eingeführt wurden. Zuerst wurde nur Wolle geschmuggelt, später vor allem Tee, Alkohol und Tabak. In manchen Regionen, wie z. B. in Cornwall, war das Schmuggeln die größte Einnahmequelle ganzer Dörfer und sogar wichtiger als Landwirtschaft und Fischerei. Im 18. Jahrhundert erreichte der Schmuggel in England seinen Höhepunkt. Die Zölle waren zu dieser Zeit so hoch, dass sich viele Menschen nur geschmuggelten Tee oder Alkohol leisten konnten. Die Schmuggelware kam auf kleinen Segelschiffen oder Fischerbooten vom europäischen Kontinent. Schmugglerschiffe waren meist schwarz angemalt und hatten schwarze Segel. Sie kamen nachts, damit die Küstenwächter sie nicht entdeckten. Als Verstecke wurden Höhlen an der Küste genutzt oder die Ware wurde im Sand vergraben. Mitte des 19. Jahrhunderts ging der Schmuggel allmählich zurück, da die Zölle gesenkt wurden und die Küstenwache verstärkt wurde. Trotzdem gibt es auch heute noch Schmuggler, die vor allem Menschen, Waffen und Drogen illegal nach Großbritannien bringen.

Wie war das früher in Deutschland? Gab es auch Schmuggler? Schmuggeln kann man Tee und Tabak, aber auch Menschen, Waffen und Drogen. Ist beides gleich schlimm?

	to **take** [teɪk]	dauern, *(Zeit)* brauchen →	It *takes* more than 1 1/2 hours to get to London by train.
	anywhere ['eniweə]	überall, irgendwo →	You can get to the coast from *anywhere* very quickly.
	channel ['tʃænl]	Kanal; Programm →	The *Channel* is the sea between the south coast of England and the north coast of France.
	ferry ['feri]	Fähre	
	to **land** [lænd]	landen →	We *landed* in Dover.
	international [ˌɪntə'næʃnl]	international →	Heathrow is an *international* airport.
	passenger ['pæsndʒə]	Passagier/Passagierin, Beifahrer/Beifahrerin →	A person who is travelling by plane, train, bus, car, etc.
	port [pɔ:t]	Hafen	
	cruise [kru:z]	Kreuzfahrt	
	ocean liner ['əʊʃn ˌlaɪnə]	Ozeandampfer →	The Titanic was an *ocean liner.*
	ocean ['əʊʃn]	Ozean	
	to **sail** [seɪl]	segeln, fahren *(Schiff)* →	The ship *sailed* across the ocean.
	speaker ['spi:kə]	Sprecher/Sprecherin →	to speak → *speaker*
	swimmer ['swɪmə]	Schwimmer/Schwimmerin →	to swim → *swimmer*

Language

46	modal auxiliary verb [ˌməʊdl ɔ:g'zɪljəri 'vɜ:b]	modales Hilfsverb	
	possible ['pɒsəbl]	möglich	
	lifeguard ['laɪfˌgɑ:d]	Rettungsschwimmer/ Rettungsschwimmerin	
	to **fly** [flaɪ]	wehen →	When the red flag is *flying*, you can't go into the sea.
	sun [sʌn]	Sonne →	The *sun* is out, so it's nice in the garden.
	paradise ['pærəˌdaɪs]	Paradies	
	on record [ɒn 'rekɔ:d]	verzeichnet, dokumentiert	
	clean [kli:n]	sauber →	If you clean something, it becomes *clean.*
	sandy ['sændɪ]	sandig →	A *sandy* beach is nice for a holiday.
	sensible ['sensɪbl]	vernünftig	
	safe [seɪf]	sicher →	*safe* ↔ dangerous; *safe* [f] → to save [v]
	to **windsurf** ['wɪndsɜ:f]	windsurfen	
	to **canoe** [kə'nu:]	Kanu fahren	
	age [eɪdʒ]	Alter, Zeitalter →	What *age* is Lester? = How old is Lester?
	bin [bɪn]	Mülleimer, Mülltonne	
	to **be lost** [bi: 'lɒst]	sich verirrt haben	
47	speech bubble ['spi:tʃ ˌbʌbl]	Sprechblase	
	to **dive** [daɪv]	tauchen	
	Well done! [ˌwel 'dʌn]	Gut gemacht!	
	stranger ['streɪndʒə]	Fremder/Fremde →	I don't know that man – he's a *stranger.*
	rubber ring [ˌrʌbə 'rɪŋ]	Schwimmreifen	
	rubber ['rʌbə]	Gummi; Kautschuk	
	ring [rɪŋ]	Ring	
	alone [ə'ləʊn]	alleine →	together ↔ *alone*

	stamp [stæmp]	Briefmarke →	Do you have a *stamp* for a letter or a postcard?
	p.m. [ˌpiːˈem]	nachmittags *(Uhrzeit)* →	My dad finishes work at 6 *p.m.*
48	relative pronoun [ˌrelətɪv ˈprəʊnaʊn]	Relativpronomen	
	yard [jɑːd]	Elle *(Längenmaß: 0,914 m)*	
	metre [ˈmiːtə]	Meter	
	centimetre [ˈsentɪˌmiːtə]	Zentimeter	
	to **notice** [ˈnəʊtɪs]	bemerken →	Did you *notice* her new hair style?
	everyone [ˈevriwʌn]	jeder	
	for example [ˌfər‿ɪgˈzɑːmpl]	zum Beispiel	
	below [bɪˈləʊ]	unterhalb, unten	
	Gaelic [ˈgeɪlɪk]	gälisch →	*Gaelic* is a language from Scotland or Ireland.
	Welsh [welʃ]	walisisch; Waliser/Waliserin →	*Welsh* people are from Wales.
	Cornish [ˈkɔːnɪʃ]	kornisch; aus Cornwall →	*Cornish* people are from Cornwall.
	official [əˈfɪʃl]	offiziell	
	news *(sg.)* [njuːz]	Nachricht(en), Neuigkeit(en) →	That'**s** good *news*. = Das **sind** gute Nachrichten.
	to **signal** [ˈsɪgnl]	signalisieren, ein Zeichen geben	
	whose [huːz]	dessen, deren *(Relativpronomen)* →	That's the boy *whose* family lives next door.
	to define [dɪˈfaɪn]	definieren	
49	**mystery** [ˈmɪstri]	Geheimnis, Rätsel	
	beginning [bɪˈgɪnɪŋ]	Anfang, Beginn →	*beginning* ↔ end
	around [əˈraʊnd]	ungefähr, zirka, etwa →	*around* 12 = at about 12
	wooden [ˈwʊdn]	hölzern →	wood → *wooden*
	to **rebuild**, **rebuilt**, **rebuilt** [ˌriːˈbɪld, ˌriːˈbɪlt, ˌriːˈbɪlt]	wieder aufbauen; wiederherstellen →	to build → *to rebuild*
	ton [tʌn]	Tonne *(Gewicht)*	
	to **replace** [rɪˈpleɪs]	ersetzen →	If you break a window, you must *replace* it.
	up to [ˈʌp tə]	bis zu	
	way [weɪ]	Art, Weise	
	to **stand**, **stood**, **stood** [stænd, stʊd, stʊd]	stehen	
	position [pəˈzɪʃn]	Position	
	exactly [ɪgˈzæktli]	genau	
	exact [ɪgˈzækt]	genau	
	attraction [əˈtrækʃn]	Attraktion, Sehenswürdigkeit →	Stonehenge is a big tourist *attraction*.
	all over [ˌɔːl‿ˈəʊvə]	überall →	*all over* the world = auf der ganzen Welt
	summary [ˈsʌmri]	Zusammenfassung	
	a.m. [ˌeɪˈem]	vormittags *(Uhrzeit)*	

Useful phrases: Travelling

Wenn du einmal auf Reisen bist, können die folgenden *phrases* sehr nützlich sein.

Questions about trains/buses

Could you tell me the time of the next train/bus to …, please?	Könnten Sie mir die Abfahrtszeit des nächsten Zuges/Busses nach … sagen?
Do I have to change trains?	Muss ich umsteigen?
What platform does it leave from?	An welchem Bahnsteig fährt er ab?
What time does it arrive ?	Wann kommt er an?
How long is the journey?	Wie lange dauert die Reise?

Questions about flying

Is there a flight to …, please?	Gibt es einen Flug nach … ?
Do I have to change planes?	Muss ich umsteigen?
Is there a bus to the airport?	Gibt es einen Bus zum Flughafen?
How long is the flight?	Wie lange dauert der Flug?

Get fit!

50	to let [let]	lassen	
	to bother ['bɒðə]	stören, belästigen	
	to **match** [mætʃ]	passen zu; zuordnen, zusammenfügen	
	meat [mi:t]	Fleisch →	I don't eat *meat*, only fruit and vegetables.
	passports *(pl)* ['pɑ:spɔ:ts]	Passkontrolle	
	passport ['pɑ:spɔ:t]	Pass, Reisepass →	You need a *passport* to go to the USA.
	friendly ['frendli]	freundlich, nett	
	situation [ˌsɪtju'eɪʃn]	Situation	
	trolley ['trɒli]	Gepäckwagen, Einkaufswagen, Handkarren →	Could you get us a *trolley* for the luggage, please?
	phone box ['fəʊn ˌbɒks]	Telefonzelle →	Is there a *phone box* near here?

Overheard

51	cigarette [ˌsɪgr'et]	Zigarette	
	conversation [ˌkɒnvə'seɪʃn]	Unterhaltung	
	son [sʌn]	Sohn	
	to **ring, rang, rung** [rɪŋ, ræŋ, rʌŋ]	anrufen	

Facts and fiction

52	**announcement** [ə'naʊntsmənt]	Ankündigung, Durchsage	
	to **trust** [trʌst]	vertrauen →	Of course I *trust* you!
	whom [hu:m]	wem, wen	
	mother ['mʌðə]	Mutter	
	father ['fɑ:ðə]	Vater →	mother ↔ *father*

	English	German	Example
	tug [tʌg]	Ziehen, Zupfen	
	side [saɪd]	Seite →	Do you sleep on your back or on your *side*?
	to **take off** [teɪk‿'ɒf]	ausziehen →	to wear ↔ *to take off*
	to **rest** [rest]	sich entspannen, sich ausruhen	
	this evening [ðɪs 'i:vnɪŋ]	heute Abend →	There's a great film on TV *this evening*.
	basement ['beɪsmənt]	Kellergeschoss, Untergeschoss	
	blind [blaɪnd]	blind →	Achtung Aussprache!
	although [ɔ:l'ðəʊ]	obwohl	
	helpless ['helpləs]	hilflos →	If you can't walk, you are *helpless*.
	independent [ˌɪndɪ'pendənt]	unabhängig	
	to **lie down** [laɪ 'daʊn]	(sich) hinlegen, niederlegen	
	to **lie, lay, lain** [laɪ, leɪ, leɪn]	liegen →	The book is *lying* on the table.
	to **feel for** ['fi:l fə]	tasten nach	
	no idea [ˌnəʊ‿aɪ'dɪə]	keine Ahnung →	I have *no idea* where he can be.
	stairs *(pl)* [steəz]	Treppe →	The *stairs* **are** wet. = Die Treppe **ist** nass.
	footstep ['fʊtstep]	Schritt →	foot → *footstep*
	both [bəʊθ]	beide →	Robert and David *both* like football.
	aftershave ['ɑ:ftəʃeɪv]	Aftershave, Rasierwasser	
53	to **get out** [get‿'aʊt]	entkommen	
	to **touch** [tʌtʃ]	berühren; antippen	
	fuse-box ['fju:zbɒks]	Sicherungskasten →	If you know where the *fuse-box* is, you can turn off all the lights in the house there.
	furious ['fjʊəriəs]	wütend →	very, very angry
	to **crawl** [krɔ:l]	kriechen, krabbeln, schleichen	
	to **grab** [græb]	greifen, schnappen	
	Crash! [kræʃ]	Bumm!, Krach!	
	to **take your chance** [ˌteɪk jɔ: 'tʃɑ:ns]	etwas wagen, etwas riskieren →	*Take your chance* and try it!
	to **run upstairs** [ˌrʌn‿ʌp'steəz]	die Treppe hinaufrennen	
	to **lock** [lɒk]	abschließen →	to close with a key
	icon ['aɪkɒn]	Ikone	
	would [wʊd]	würde(n)	
	to **be wrong** [bi: 'rɒŋ]	Unrecht haben →	Sorry, but you *are wrong*.
	to **understand, understood, understood** [ˌʌndə'stænd, ˌʌndə'stʊd, ˌʌndə'stʊd]	verstehen →	Sorry, I can't *understand* you. I don't speak French.
	hint [hɪnt]	Hinweis, Spur, Anspielung	
	whole [həʊl]	ganz	

Wordwise

	English	German	Example
55	measurement ['meʒəmənt]	Maß, Maßeinheit	
	European [ˌjʊərə'pi:ən]	europäisch →	Germany and England are *European* countries.

Check-out

56 **engine** ['endʒɪn] — Maschine, Motor
to remind [rɪ'maɪnd] — erinnern
57 **loch** [lɒx] — See *(schottisch)*
lake [leɪk] — See →

You can swim in a *lake*.

Prepositions

B is **above** D. B is **between** A and C.

A is **next** to B. *A B C* C comes **after** B.
A comes **before** B.
D is **under** B. *D*

House A is **above** house B.
House B is **below** house A.

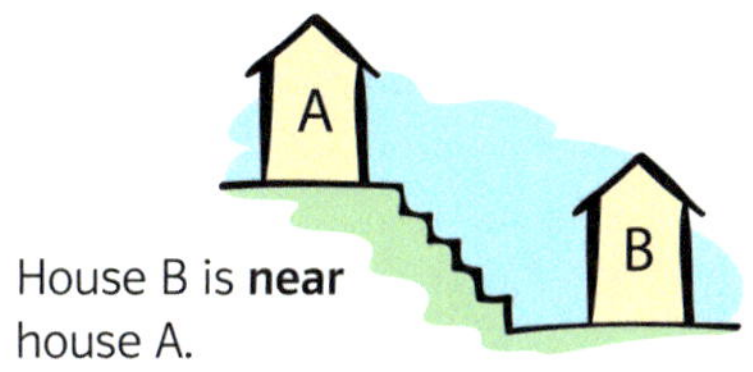

House B is **near** house A.

The ball was **on** the box before it fell **off** it.

Circle A is **inside** circle B.
Circle C is **outside** circles A and B.

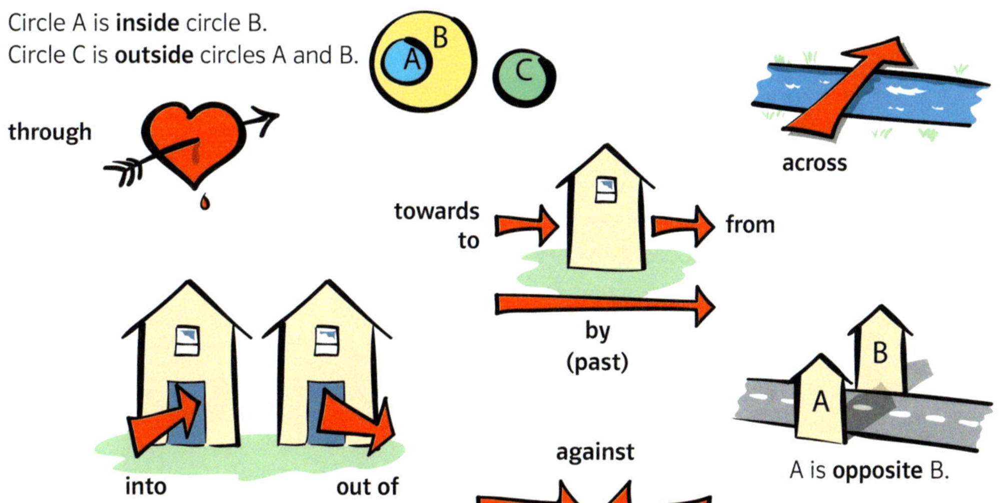

A is **opposite** B.

For my folder: People from different countries

In dieser Unit hast du gelernt, dass es auf den britischen Inseln verschiedene Länder gibt, in denen unterschiedliche Sprachen gesprochen werden. Zeichne oder kopiere dir eine Umrisskarte der britischen Inseln. Zeichne die verschiedenen Länder ein und schreibe dazu, welche Sprachen dort gesprochen werden. Kannst du mit Hilfe des Internets für jede Sprache ein Beispielwort finden?

Unit 4 Let it out!

Lerntipp: Die richtige Lernmethode

Ich lerne am besten Vokabeln, wenn ich
- sie aufschreibe,
- sie auf Band aufnehme und anhöre,
- meine eigenen Beispielsätze mache,
- Reime mit ihnen mache,
- sie in Listen oder *mind maps* gruppiere,
- Bilder dazu male,
- Gegensatzpaare oder Wörter mit gleicher oder ähnlicher Bedeutung notiere,
- schwierige Stellen und häufige Fehlerquellen farbig markiere.

Check-in

62	to **let**, **let**, **let** [let, let, let]	lassen	
	reason ['riːzn]	Grund	
	tattoo [tæt'uː]	Tätowierung	
	disappointed [ˌdɪsə'pɔɪntɪd]	enttäuscht	
	frustrated [frʌs'treɪtɪd]	frustriert	
	strict [strɪkt]	Grund →	The rules at our school are very *strict*.
	to **have an argument** ['ɑːgjəmənt]	sich streiten	
	argument ['ɑːgjəmənt]	Argument, Streit →	Tom had an *argument* with his girlfriend.
	unfair [ʌn'feə]	ungerecht, unfair	
	similar ['sɪmɪlə]	ähnlich	
	I want my ... pierced. [aɪ 'wɒnt maɪ ... 'pɪəst]	Ich möchte mein ... piercen lassen.	
	to **want sb to do sth** [wɒnt]	wollen, dass jemand etwas tut →	Sandra *wants her friend to go out* with her.
	eyebrow ['aɪbraʊ]	Augenbraue	
	tongue [tʌŋ]	Zunge	
63	**direct** [dɪ'rekt]	direkt	
	respect [rɪ'spekt]	Respekt →	Do you have *respect* for your teachers?
	poetry slam ['pəʊətri ˌslæm]	Poetry Slam *(Gedichtwettbewerb)*	
	poetry ['pəʊətri]	Lyrik	
	year-old [ˌjɪər‿'əʊld]	-jährig; -Jähriger/-Jährige →	a 15-*year-old* boy
	winner ['wɪnə]	Gewinner/Gewinnerin, Sieger/Siegerin →	to win → *winner*
	to **take part in** [teɪk 'pɑːt‿ɪn]	teilnehmen an →	You can *take part in* a lot of activities at our school.
	workshop ['wɜːkʃɒp]	Workshop, Werkstatt →	to work → *workshop*
	hip hop ['hɪp hɒp]	Hip-Hop	
	performance [pə'fɔːməns]	Aufführung, Vorstellung	
	to **take place** [teɪk 'pleɪs]	stattfinden →	*to take place* = stattfinden to sit down = Platz nehmen

poet ['pəʊɪt]	Dichter/Dichterin, Poet/Poetin	
to **invent** [ɪn'vent]	erfinden →	If you *invent* something, you are the first person who thinks of it or makes it.
live [laɪv]	live →	Achtung Aussprache! life [laɪf] – *live* [laɪv].
teenage ['ti:neɪdʒ]	jugendlich →	Your *teenage* years are the time from the age of 13 to the age of 19.
poem ['pəʊɪm]	Gedicht	
wish [wɪʃ]	Wunsch	
boyfriend ['bɔɪfrend]	Freund *(in einer Paarbeziehung)* →	Robert is a friend, but he isn't Anna's *boyfriend*.
special ['speʃl]	besonders, speziell →	It's a *special* day for Robert today, it's his birthday.
to **perform** [pə'fɔ:m]	aufführen, auftreten →	*to perform* → performance
in all [ɪn‿'ɔ:l]	insgesamt, im Ganzen	
organizer ['ɔ:gənaɪzə]	Organisator/Organisatorin, Veranstalter/Veranstalterin →	to organize → *organizer*
audience ['ɔ:diəns]	Publikum →	Achte auf die Betonung: ['–]
slamster ['slæmstə]	Teilnehmer/Teilnehmerin an einem Poetry Slam	
each [i:tʃ]	je, jeweils →	The T-shirts are £5 *each*.
content ['kɒntent]	Inhalt	
response [rɪ'spɒns]	Reaktion, Antwort	

Hip-Hop in Großbritannien

In Großbritannien gibt es eine Hip-Hop-Szene, die seit den 1990ern immer bekannter und erfolgreicher wird. Wie in den USA entwickelte sich der Hip-Hop aus der Graffiti- und Breakdance-Szene. Zunächst kopierten die britischen Rapper von US-amerikanischen Künstlern, aber schon bald begann man zu experimentieren und der britische Hip-Hop entwickelte sich in verschiedene Richtungen. Da viele der britischen Rapper aus Familien mit karibischer Herkunft stammen, ist ihre Musik auch vom Reggae beeinflusst. Großstädte wie London, Birmingham, Manchester und Bristol sind die Zentren des britischen Hip-Hops. Die meisten Rapper kommen aus armen Familien und singen über die Probleme in ihrem Umfeld: Arbeitslosigkeit, Armut, Gewalt und Drogen. Die britischen Rapper tragen aber weniger teuren Schmuck, da sie nicht so reich sind wie die amerikanischen Künstler. Einige britische Rapper sind aber sehr erfolgreich und auch in Deutschland bekannt, wie z. B. Mattafix und die Gorillaz.

Was weißt du über die deutsche Hip-Hop-Szene? Welche deutschen Rapper kennst du?

Language

64 **diary** ['daɪəri]	Tagebuch; Terminkalender	
disaster [dɪ'zɑ:stə]	Desaster, Katastrophe →	a terrible event
village ['vɪlɪdʒ]	Dorf	
cottage ['kɒtɪdʒ]	kleines Landhaus, Ferienhaus	
middle ['mɪdl]	Mitte; Mittel- →	*middle* = centre

	nowhere ['nəʊweə]	nirgendwo, nirgendwohin	
	not even [nɒt‿'i:vn]	nicht einmal	
	to **hang out, hung out, hung out** [hæŋ‿'aʊt, hʌŋ‿'aʊt, hʌŋ‿'aʊt]	sich herumtreiben →	If you *hang out* with somebody, you spend time with them.
	steel band [ˌsti:l 'bænd]	Steelband *(Band, deren Instrumente aus leeren Ölfässern bestehen)*	
	to **upset, upset, upset** [ʌp'set, ʌp'set, ʌp'set]	erschrecken, durcheinander bringen; umstoßen	
	feeling ['fi:lɪŋ]	Gefühl →	to feel → *feeling*
	useless ['ju:sləs]	nutzlos →	useful ↔ *useless*
	to **text** [tekst]	Textnachricht (SMS) schicken, simsen →	Lauren is *texting* a message to Nyla.
	worry ['wʌri]	Sorge	
65	to **put out** [pʊt‿'aʊt]	hinausstellen	
	suggestion [sə'dʒestʃn]	Vorschlag, Anregung →	to suggest → *suggestion*
	sis [sɪs]	Schwesterchen	
	shall [ʃæl; ʃəl]	sollen →	*Shall* I help you?
	to **get off** [get‿'ɒf]	wegräumen von, abräumen von	
	change of place [ˌtʃeɪndʒ‿əv 'pleɪs]	Ortswechsel	
66	**comprehensive school** [kɒmprɪ'hensɪv ˌsku:l]	Gesamtschule	
	survival [sə'vaɪvl]	Überleben	
	notice board ['nəʊtɪs bɔ:d]	schwarzes Brett →	Look at the *notice board* for more information.
	notice ['nəʊtɪs]	Anschlag, Notiz	
	vending machine ['vendɪŋ məˌʃi:n]	Warenautomat →	Are there any sweets in the *vending machine*?
	machine [mə'ʃi:n]	Maschine, Apparat	
	leaflet ['li:flət]	Flugblatt, Prospekt	
	to **guess** [ges]	raten, vermuten →	*Guess* who called me!
	yukky ['jʌki]	ekelhaft	
	session ['seʃn]	Veranstaltung	
	as soon as [əz 'su:n‿əz]	sobald →	soon → *as soon as*
	shy [ʃaɪ]	schüchtern →	When he was a child, he was very *shy*.
67	to say out loud [ˌseɪ‿aʊt 'laʊd]	laut sagen	
	pronoun ['prəʊnaʊn]	Pronomen	
	reflexive pronoun [rɪ'fleksɪv ˌprəʊnaʊn]	Reflexivpronomen	
	mirror ['mɪrə]	Spiegel →	If you look at yourself in a *mirror*, you see a true 'picture' of yourself.
	to **scare** ['skeə]	erschrecken, einen Schrecken einjagen, Angst machen →	to *scare* → scared
	abroad [ə'brɔ:d]	im/ins Ausland →	They live *abroad* (= im Ausland). They went *abroad* (= ins Ausland).

Welcome to … ['welkəm tə]	Willkommen in …	
to **compare** [kəm'peə]	vergleichen	
system ['sɪstəm]	System	
compulsory [kəm'pʌlsri]	obligatorisch, zwingend	
of age [əv‿'eɪdʒ]	im Alter von →	At 5 years *of age* you start school.
state [steɪt]	Staat, Land; staatlich; Zustand →	country or part of a country
as well as [əz 'wel‿əz]	sowohl … als auch	
private ['praɪvɪt]	privat	
following ['fɒləʊɪŋ]	folgend/folgender/folgende/folgendes →	Let's look at the *following* example.
grid [grɪd]	Gitter, Tabelle	
primary school ['praɪməri ˌsku:l]	Grundschule →	My little sister goes to *primary school*.
grammar school ['græmə ˌsku:l]	Gymnasium	
exam [ɪg'zæm]	Examen, Prüfung	
GCSE [ˌdʒi:si:es'i:]	Prüfung zum Abschluss der Sekundarstufe →	General Certificate of Secondary Education
A-levels *(pl)* ['eɪlevlz]	brit. Abitur	
possible ['pɒsəbl]	möglich	
college ['kɒlɪdʒ]	College; Institut →	A lot of young people go to a *college* after they leave school.
advanced [əd'vɑ:nst]	fortgeschritten	
level ['levl]	Ebene, Niveau →	Lisa is taking her *A-levels*.

Pronomen

Personalpronomen	Objektpronomen	Possessivpronomen	Reflexivpronomen
I	me	my	myself
you	you	your	yourself
he/she/it	him/her/it	its	himself/herself/itself
we	us	our	ourselves
you	you	your	yourselves
they	them	their	themselves

Get fit!

68 writing ['raɪtɪŋ]	Schreiben	
code [kəʊd]	Code, Verschlüsselung	
secret ['si:krət]	geheim →	Don't tell the others, it's *secret*.
simple ['sɪmpl]	einfach, simpel	
sort [sɔ:t]	Art, Sorte	
glad [glæd]	froh →	happy – pleased – *glad*
to **put in** [pʊt‿'ɪn]	einschieben	
extra ['ekstrə]	zusätzlich; Zusatz	
training ['treɪnɪŋ]	Training, Ausbildung →	We'll have extra *training* at the weekend.
lots of love [ˌlɒts‿əv 'lʌv]	viele Grüße *(am Briefende)*	

	English	German	Example
	Ha! [hɑː]	Ha!	
	to **wish** [wɪʃ]	wünschen	
	proud of ['praʊd‿əv]	stolz auf →	My parents are *proud of* me.
	to **make it** ['meɪk‿ɪt]	es schaffen	
	to **jump about** [ˌdʒʌmp‿ə'baʊt]	herumspringen	
	info ['ɪnfəʊ]	Info	
	winning goal ['wɪnɪŋ gəʊl]	Siegtreffer	

Overheard

	English	German	Example
69	helpline ['helplaɪn]	telefonischer Beratungsdienst, Notruf	
	caller ['kɔːlə]	Anrufer/Anruferin	
	to **fight, fought, fought** [faɪt, fɔːt, fɔːt]	streiten, kämpfen →	Don't *fight* about the new CD, please.
	to **stay out** [steɪ‿'aʊt]	wegbleiben →	How long can you *stay out* at night?
	to **advise** [əd'vaɪz]	raten	
	answerphone ['ɑːnsəfəʊn]	Anrufbeantworter →	Please leave a message on my *answerphone*.
	to **suggest** [sə'dʒest]	vorschlagen	
	It's ... speaking. [ɪts ... 'spiːkɪŋ]	Hier spricht	

Useful phrases: A project

Wenn du mit anderen ein Projekt vorbereitest, könnt ihr die folgenden Sätze verwenden.

Let's work together.	Lasst uns zusammenarbeiten.
Why don't we talk about ... ?	Warum sprechen wir nicht über ... ?
I think it's interesting because	Ich finde es interessant, weil ... .
I've got a book/magazine/film about	Ich habe ein Buch/eine Zeitschrift/einen Film über ... .
We can look for more information on the Internet.	Wir können im Internet mehr Informationen suchen.
What have you found/written?	Was hast du/habt ihr gefunden?
Have you found any interesting information?	Hast du/Habt ihr interessante Informationen gefunden?
Let's make a poster.	Lasst uns ein Poster machen.

Facts and fiction

	English	German	Example
70	**choice** [tʃɔɪs]	Wahl, Auswahl →	to choose → *choice*
	fuss [fʌs]	Aufregung, Wirbel	
	you'd better [jʊd 'betə]	du solltest lieber	
	sudden ['sʌdn]	plötzlich →	There was a *sudden* noise.
	glare [gleə]	blendender Glanz, grelles Licht	

What the heck … ? [ˌwɒt ðə ˈhek]	Was zum Teufel … ?	
such [sʌtʃ]	solch →	It was *such* a good party that nobody wanted to go home.
wreck [rek]	Wrack →	Achtung Aussprache: *wreck*, *write*, *wrong*.
to **try hard** [traɪ‿ˈhɑːd]	sich stark bemühen	
lead [led]	Blei	
stroke [strəʊk]	Schlag(anfall) →	My grandad had a *stroke* last week.
harm [hɑːm]	Schaden, Verletzung	
dear [dɪə]	Schatz *(Anrede)*	
to **have a fit** [ˌhæv‿ə ˈfɪt]	einen Anfall bekommen, Zustände kriegen	
to **care** [keə]	sich kümmern, sich interessieren, wichtig nehmen →	If you *care about* something, it's important to you.
to **get into such a state** [get‿ɪntə ˈsʌtʃ‿ə ˈsteɪt]	durchdrehen, (sich) verrückt machen	
to the brink [tə ðə ˈbrɪŋk]	an den Rand, bis zur Oberkante	
to **swerve** [swɜːv]	ausweichen, ausscheren →	The car *swerved* because there was a dog in the street.
curve [kɜːv]	Kurve	
alive [əˈlaɪv]	lebendig →	live → *alive*
to **shake, shook, shaken** [ʃeɪk, ʃʊk, ˈʃeɪkn]	schütteln, zittern	
leaf, leaves *(pl)* [liːf; liːvz]	Blatt	
wave [weɪv]	Welle →	In a storm the *waves* are very big.
to **go weak** [gəʊ ˈwiːk]	schwach werden	
weak [wiːk]	schwach	
to **choke** [tʃəʊk]	ersticken	
glee [gliː]	Entzücken →	She choked with *glee*.

For my folder: My own poem

In dieser Unit hast du einige Gedichte gelesen und selbst gereimt. Nun kannst du versuchen, selbst ein Gedicht zu schreiben. Mache dir eine Liste von Wörtern, die sich reimen. Benutze die Wörter und schreibe Sätze, die sich reimen. Nun kannst du versuchen, ein Gedicht daraus zu bilden. Suche zum Schluss einen Titel für dein Gedicht.

race – face: I washed my face. I went to the race.
fast – past: I ran very fast. All the others ran past.
around – ground: There were stones all around. I fell to the ground.
red – bed: My leg hurt and was red. I went to bed.

The race

I washed my face
before I went to the race.
I ran very fast
but all the others ran past.
There were stones all around
and I fell to the ground.
My leg hurt and was red
so I went to bed.

Unit 5 Screen shots

Lerntipp: Themen-Wortketten

Mit den Wörtern aus einem Themenbereich (z. B. *TV*) könnt ihr gut eine Wortkette bilden, in der die Wörter durch ihre Anfangs- und Endbuchstaben verbunden sind, z. B.

SCRIPTHRILLEREALITYSHOW oder CARTOONEWSCRIPT

Ihr könnt euch diese Ketten entweder einzeln oder in Gruppen ausdenken und aufschreiben. Anschließend tauscht ihr eure Wortkettenrätsel aus und versucht alle Wörter herauszuschreiben, die ihr entdecken könnt. Dabei ist es natürlich am besten, wenn die Kette so lang wie möglich ist, damit die andere Gruppe lange zu tun hat. Denn: Wer zuerst fertig ist, hat gewonnen!

Check-in

80	**screen shot** ['skri:n ˌʃɒt]	Screenshot	
	screen [skri:n]	Bildschirm, Leinwand →	TVs and computers have a *screen*.
	shot [ʃɒt]	Schuss, Schlag →	When you hit the ball at tennis, you play a *shot*.
	programme ['prəʊgræm]	Programm, Sendung →	There's an interesting *programme* about animals on TV tonight.
	tough [tʌf]	hart, rau, zäh →	A *tough* job is a hard one.
	fair [feə]	blond, hell	
	heroine ['herəʊɪn]	Heldin →	hero – *heroine*
	average ['ævrɪdʒ]	durchschnittlich →	an *average* teenager = a normal teenager
	daily ['deɪli]	täglich →	! Achtung Schreibung: da**y** → *daily*
	talk show ['tɔ:k ˌʃəʊ]	Talkshow	
	reality show [ri'æləti ˌʃəʊ]	Realityshow	
	viewer ['vju:ə]	Zuschauer/Zuschauerin →	a view → *viewer*
	per [pɜ:]	pro	
	industry ['ɪndəstri]	Industrie →	Achte auf die Betonung!
	twice [twaɪs]	zweimal →	two times
	musical ['mju:zɪkl]	Musical →	music → *musical*
	success [sək'ses]	Erfolg	
	catchy ['kætʃi]	eingängig →	a *catchy* song = ein Ohrwurm
	colourful ['kʌləfəl]	bunt, farbig →	colour → *colourful*
	dramatic [drə'mætɪk]	dramatisch →	A *dramatic* film is a very exciting film.
	scene [si:n]	Szene, Schauplatz →	This is a very quiet *scene* in the play, nothing is happening.
	in contrast to [ɪn 'kɒntrɑ:st tə]	im Gegensatz zu	
	contrast ['kɒntrɑ:st]	Kontrast, Gegensatz →	Achte auf die Betonung!
	seldom ['seldəm]	selten →	not very often
	to **kiss** [kɪs]	küssen →	In love stories people often *kiss*.
	cartoon [kɑ:'tu:n]	Cartoon, Zeichentrickfilm →	'Tom and Jerry' is a *cartoon*.
	comedy ['kɒmədi]	Komödie	
	detective story [dɪ'tektɪv ˌstɔ:ri]	Krimi →	*Detective stories* are often exciting.

	documentary [ˌdɒkjəˈmentri]	Dokumentarfilm
	docu soap [ˈdɒkjʊ səʊp]	Dokusoap
	science fiction [ˌsaɪəns ˈfɪkʃn]	Sciencefiction
	fiction [ˈfɪkʃn]	Erfindung, Fiktion
	thriller [ˈθrɪlə]	Thriller
81	**myth** [mɪθ]	Mythos
	grave [greɪv]	Grab → Do you know Gelert's *grave*?
	script [skrɪpt]	Drehbuch
	bit [bɪt]	Auszug, Teil, Stückchen
	to **go (together) with** [ˈgəʊ wɪð]	passen zu → Which colour *goes with* blue?
	to convince [kənˈvɪnts]	überzeugen

Sherlock Holmes

Der Privatdetektiv Sherlock Holmes wurde von dem britischen Autor Sir Arthur Conan Doyle im späten 19. Jahrhundert erfunden. Mit seinem Begleiter Dr. Watson löst er Kriminalfälle durch eine Arbeitsmethode, die ausschließlich auf detailgenauer Beobachtung und nüchterner Schlussfolgerung beruht. Holmes trägt meistens einen karierten Mantel mit passender Mütze und hat immer einen Spazierstock dabei. Er raucht gerne Pfeife und empfängt seine Klienten in seinem berühmten, aber fiktiven Wohnsitz, Baker Street 221b, London. Diese Adresse gibt es gar nicht, weil der Häuserblock mit den Nummern von 201 bis 241 abgerissen wurde. Auf der gegenüberliegenden Straßenseite hat deshalb ein Haus die Nummer 221b bekommen. Dort befindet sich heute ein Sherlock-Holmes-Museum. Es gibt ca. 56 Kurzgeschichten und vier Romane über Sherlock Holmes, u. a. *Die Abenteuer des Sherlock Holmes*, *Eine Studie in Scharlachrot* und *Der Hund von Baskerville*, von denen auch viele verfilmt wurden.

Hast du in deiner Freizeit schon mal eine Sherlock-Holmes-Geschichte gelesen oder einen Film gesehen? Gibt es auch einen berühmten deutschen Detektiv?

Useful phrases: A discussion about films

Wenn du mit anderen über Filme diskutierst, können dir die folgenden *phrases* helfen.

I'd like to watch ….	Ich würde gerne … sehen.
No, I'd rather watch ….	Nein, ich würde lieber … sehen.
I have already seen this film.	Ich habe diesen Film schon gesehen.
This film is boring/interesting/scary/funny ….	Dieser Film ist langweilig/interessant/gruselig/lustig ….
I like this actor/actress.	Mir gefällt dieser Schauspieler/diese Schauspielerin.
I don't like thrillers/love stories ….	Ich mag keine Thriller/Liebesgeschichten ….
There are a lot of exciting/dramatic scenes in this film.	In diesem Film gibt es viele spannende/dramatische Szenen.

Language

82	negative statement [ˌnegətɪv ˈsteɪtmənt]	Verneinung
	negative [ˈnegətɪv]	negativ, verneint → 'Isn't' is a *negative* form of 'to be'.
	statement [ˈsteɪtmənt]	Aussage, Behauptung

	pet [pet]	Haustier, Liebling →	You can have a cat or a dog as a *pet*.
	final ['faɪnl]	letzte/letzter/letztes	
	seaside ['si:saɪd]	Küste, Meeresküste →	It's nice to spend a week at the *seaside*.
	rescue ['reskju:]	Rettung →	to rescue → *rescue*
	cook [kʊk]	Koch/Köchin →	cooking → *cook*
	link [lɪŋk]	Verbindung, Bindeglied	
	host [həʊst]	Gastgeber, Talkmaster →	The *host* at a party is the man who has invited the people.
	charts *(pl)* [tʃɑ:ts]	Charts, Hitparade	
	hit [hɪt]	Hit →	a very popular song
	series, series *(pl)* ['sɪəri:z]	Serie →	A TV *series* is a number of programmes with the same title, all about the same topic, family, etc.
	hound [haʊnd]	Jagdhund →	'The *Hound* of the Baskervilles' is a famous book.
	sitcom ['sɪtkɒm]	Situationskomödie	
	alien ['eɪliən]	Fremder/Fremde, Außerirdischer/ Außerirdische →	The film 'ET' is about an *alien*.
	diamond ['daɪəmənd]	Diamant	
	jewellery ['dʒu:əlri]	Schmuck	
	countdown ['kaʊntdaʊn]	Countdown	
	emergency [ɪ'mɜ:dʒnsi]	Notfall, Notlage →	In an *emergency*, call the doctor or the police.
	patient ['peɪʃnt]	Patient/Patientin →	There are a lot of *patients* in this hospital.
	travel ['trævl]	Reise	
	on the job [ˌɒn ðə 'dʒɒb]	bei der Arbeit	
83	**runaway** ['rʌnəˌweɪ]	Ausreißer/Ausreißerin →	to run away → *a runaway*
	PC [ˌpi:'si:]	Polizeibeamter/ Polizeibeamtin →	*PC* is short for *Police Constable*.
	anybody ['eniˌbɒdi]	irgendjemand, jeder (beliebige) →	any – *anybody* - anyone – anything – anywhere some – somebody – someone – something – somewhere
	lad [læd]	Junge	
	somebody ['sʌmbədi]	jemand →	*somebody* = someone
	He had something on his mind. [maɪnd]	Ihn beschäftigte etwas. →	If you *have something on your mind*, you are worried about something.
	mind [maɪnd]	Geist, Verstand	
	perhaps [pə'hæps]	vielleicht →	another word for 'maybe'
84	**hotel** [həʊ'tel]	Hotel	
	safe [seɪf]	Safe, Tresor →	Can you really keep your money safe in a *safe?*
	to **attack** [ə'tæk]	angreifen →	Let's play "Robin Hood". We can *attack* Nottingham Castle.
	inspector [ɪn'spektə]	Inspektor	
	crime [kraɪm]	Verbrechen; Kriminalität	
	suspect ['sʌspekt]	Verdächtigter/Verdächtigte	
	to **smoke** [sməʊk]	rauchen	

pipe [paɪp]	Pfeife →	He is smoking *a pipe*.
reception [rɪ'sepʃn]	Rezeption, Empfang →	Every hotel has a *reception*.
85 heading ['hedɪŋ]	Überschrift	
downstairs [daʊn'steəz]	(die Treppe) hinunter/ herunter	
upstairs [ʌp'steəz]	(die Treppe) hinauf/herauf	
receptionist [rɪ'sepʃnɪst]	Empfangschef/ Empfangschefin →	reception → *receptionist*
to **pass** [pɑ:s]	vorbeigehen an	
nobody ['nəʊbədi]	niemand	
guard [gɑ:d]	Wache; Wächter/Wächerin →	A *guard* watches and protects a person or a place (often a building).
ladder ['lædə]	Leiter →	He used *a ladder* to reach the top shelf.
while [waɪl]	während	
to **pay, paid, paid** [peɪ, peɪd, peɪd]	(be)zahlen	
guest [gest]	Gast →	Someone who you invite to your house or to a party.

Get fit!

86 expressive [ɪk'spresɪv]	ausdrucksstark	
reading ['ri:dɪŋ]	Lesen	
intonation [ˌɪntə'neɪʃn]	Satzmelodie	
to stress [stres]	betonen	
to relax [rɪ'læks]	sich entspannen, sich ausruhen	
to take a deep breath [ˌteɪk‿ə 'di:p ˌbreθ]	tief Luft holen	
deep [di:p]	tief	
breath [breθ]	Atem, Atemzug	
copy ['kɒpi]	Kopie →	to copy → a *copy*
phonetic [fə'netɪk]	phonetisch	
pause [pɔ:z]	Pause	
son [sʌn]	Sohn →	Terry is Mr and Mrs Jackson's *son*.
mistake [mɪ'steɪk]	Fehler	
called [kɔ:ld]	genannt	
brave [breɪv]	tapfer, mutig →	If you do something dangerous, that's silly or *brave*.
wife, wives *(pl)* [waɪf; waɪvz]	Ehefrau →	Mrs Taylor is Mr Taylor's *wife*.
hunting ['hʌntɪŋ]	Jagen	
to **get on** [get‿'ɒn]	aufsteigen	
to **open** ['əʊpn]	sich öffnen, aufgehen	
to **turn** [tɜ:n]	drehen, sich umdrehen →	Please *turn* and look at me.
strong [strɒŋ]	stark	
wolf, wolves *(pl)* [wʊlf; wʊlvz]	Wolf →	Achtung Aussprache!
tooth, teeth *(pl)* [tu:θ; ti:θ]	Zahn →	Achte auf den Plural!
blood [blʌd]	Blut	

	cry [kraɪ]	Schrei →	to cry → a *cry*
	hurt [hɜːt]	verletzt	
	dead [ded]	tot →	*dead* ↔ alive
	shocked [ʃɒkt]	geschockt, schockiert	
	to **bury** ['beri]	begraben, beerdigen	
	gravestone ['greɪvstəʊn]	Grabstein	
	to sound [saʊnd]	klingen, sich anhören	

Overheard

87	to **walk up to** [wɔːk‿'ʌp tə]	hingehen, zugehen auf →	to go to somebody
	director [dɪ'rektə]	Direktor/Direktorin, Regisseur/Regisseurin →	When you make a film, the *director* tells everyone what to do.
	assistant [ə'sɪstnt]	Assistent/Assistentin →	An *assistant* is someone who helps you.
	to **film** [fɪlm]	filmen →	a film → *to film*
	secret ['siːkrət]	Geheimnis	
	Sir [sɜː]	Sir *(Anrede für einen Ritter)*	

Facts and fiction

88	to **murder** ['mɜːdə]	ermorden →	to kill somebody
	to **glow** [gləʊ]	leuchten	
	dark [dɑːk]	Dunkelheit →	dark → *the dark*
	only ['əʊnli]	einzige/einziger/einziges →	! the *only* way = der einzige Weg *only* five pounds = nur fünf Pfund
	inheritor [ɪn'herɪtə]	Erbe/Erbin	
	nephew ['nefjuː]	Neffe →	your sister's or brother's son
	What's the matter? [ˌwɒts ðə 'mætə]	Was ist los? →	You look terrible. *What's the matter?*
	to **solve** [sɒlv]	lösen →	Holmes *solved* a lot of a mysteries.
	trust [trʌst]	Vertrauen →	to trust → *trust*
	to **agree** [ə'griː]	zustimmen, einer Meinung sein →	I *agree* with you. = I think what you say is right.
	poor [pɔː; pʊə]	arm →	*poor* ↔ rich
	boot [buːt]	Stiefel →	When you ride a horse, you wear *boots*, not shoes.
	beard [bɪəd]	Bart	
	servant ['sɜːvnt]	Diener/Dienerin →	service → *servant*
	barking ['bɑːkɪŋ]	Bellen →	to bark → *barking*
	sense [sens]	Sinn, Bedeutung	
	smell [smel]	Geruch, Gestank →	Pooh, what a terrible *smell*!
	to **go for a walk** [ˌgəʊ fər‿ə 'wɔːk]	spazieren gehen	
	to **sound** [saʊnd]	klingen, sich anhören	
	absolutely [ˌæbsə'luːtli]	absolut, völlig	
89	**grey** [greɪ]	grau →	I like *grey* eyes.
	scientist ['saɪəntɪst]	Wissenschaftler/ Wissenschaftlerin	
	painting ['peɪntɪŋ]	Gemälde	

	fireplace ['faɪəpleɪs]	Kamin →	In my dream house there's a *fireplace* in the living room.
	powder ['paʊdə]	Puder, Pulver	
90	to **knock** [nɒk]	klopfen; stoßen, schlagen →	Achtung Aussprache!
	close [kləʊs]	nahe	
	to **share** [ʃeə]	teilen	
	size [saɪz]	Größe, Kleidergröße →	These jeans are the wrong *size*.
	to **sniff** [snɪf]	schnüffeln, schnuppern →	The dog *was sniffing* around.
	enormous [ɪ'nɔ:məs]	enorm, riesig	
	body ['bɒdi]	Körper	
	towards [tə'wɔ:dz]	in Richtung, auf … zu, darauf zu →	He was scared when three men came *towards* him.
	gunshot ['gʌnʃɒt]	Schuss	
	to **echo** ['ekəʊ]	widerhallen	
	gun [gʌn]	Schusswaffe →	A man with a *gun* went into a shop and said, "Give me the money!"
	Her Majesty [hə 'mædʒəsti]	Ihre Majestät	
	to **arrest** [ə'rest]	festnehmen, verhaften →	The police caught Mr Stapleton and *arrested* him.
91	report [rɪ'pɔ:t]	Bericht, Meldung	
	reader ['ri:də]	Leser/Leserin	

Wordwise

93	unit ['ju:nɪt]	Kapitel, Einheit	

Unbekannte Wörter umschreiben

Beim Englischsprechen kann es vorkommen, dass du ein bestimmtes Wort nicht kennst oder dass du ein Wort benutzt, das dein Gesprächspartner nicht versteht. Solche Wörter musst du entsprechend umschreiben oder erklären können. Dazu kannst du Sätze mit den Wörtern *who, which* oder *where* bilden:

- eine Person: **A doctor** is a man/woman/someone **who** works in a hospital.
- eine Sache: **A film** is something **which** you can watch on TV, on DVD or in the cinema.
- ein Ort: **A shop** is a place **where** you can buy something.
- eine Eigenschaft: **When** you are sad, you are not happy.

For my folder: My favourite programme

Du hast bestimmt auch einen Lieblingsfilm oder eine Lieblingsserie. Mach dir dazu dein eigenes Plakat. Schreibe darauf, um welche Art von Programm es sich handelt (Comedy, Thriller etc.) und suche passende Nomen und Adjektive dazu.

dramatic	detective story
exciting	docu soap
funny	thriller
…	…

Dictionary

In dieser alphabetischen Liste ist das Vokabular von *Orange Line 1* und *2* enthalten. Namen werden in einer gesonderten Liste am Ende des Vokabulars aufgelistet.
Das Zeichen ° bei einem Eintrag weist darauf hin, dass das Wort zum rezeptiven Wortschatz zählt.
Die mit * gekennzeichneten Verben sind unregelmäßig.
Wendungen, die aus mehreren Wörtern bestehen, werden meist unter mehreren Stichwörtern aufgeführt.
So ist z. B. *at home* unter *at* und *home* zu finden.
Die Fundstellen verweisen auf das erstmalige Vorkommen der Wörter, z. B.
actress ['æktrəs] Schauspielerin **III U2,** 29 kommt zum ersten Mal vor in Band III, Unit 2, Seite 29.
colour ['kʌlə] Farbe **I LUA,** 24 kommt zum ersten Mal vor in Band I, Link-up A, Seite 24.
U = Unit, LU = Link-up, FA = Fakultativer Anhang (nur Namen)

A

a, an [ə; ən] ein/eine **I U1,** 10
a bit [ə 'bɪt] ein bisschen **I U2,** 35
a few [ə 'fju:] einige, ein paar **II U4,** 52
a lot [ə 'lɒt] viel **II U1,** 15
a lot of [ə 'lɒt‿əv] viel/viele, eine Menge **I U2,** 30
a week [ə 'wi:k] pro Woche, in der Woche **II U4,** 52
about [ə'baʊt] über **I U3,** 40; ungefähr, circa, etwa **III U1,** 11
out and about ['aʊt‿nd‿ə'baʊt] unterwegs °**I U4,** 54
to jump about [ˌdʒʌmp‿ə'baʊt] herumspringen **III U4,** 68
What about ...? [wɒt‿ə'baʊt] Was ist mit ...?; Wie wäre es mit ...? **I U2,** 30
What's the film about? [wɒts ðə 'fɪlm‿əˌbaʊt] Wovon handelt der Film? °**II U3,** 43
above [ə'bʌv] oben, über, oberhalb **II U5,** 70
abroad [ə'brɔ:d] im/ins Ausland **III U4,** 67
absolutely [ˌæbsə'lu:tli] absolut, völlig **III U5,** 88
accent ['æksnt] Akzent **II U3,** 36
accident ['æksɪdnt] Unfall **II U3,** 41
across [ə'krɒs] waagerecht *(im Kreuzworträtsel)* °**II U3,** 42; über, hinüber, quer durch/darüber **III U1,** 10
to **act** [ækt] spielen *(Theater)* **I U7,** 90
action ['ækʃn] Handlung, Aktion **III U1,** 9
active ['æktɪv] aktiv **III U1,** 12
activity [æk'tɪvəti] Aktivität °**I U7,** 91
actor ['æktə] Schauspieler **I U7,** 96
actress ['æktrəs] Schauspielerin **III U2,** 29
to **add** [æd] hinzufügen, addieren **III U2,** 30
address [ə'dres] Adresse **I U5,** 70
adjective ['ædʒəktɪv] Adjektiv, Eigenschaftswort °**I U1,** 22
advanced [əd'vɑ:nst] fortgeschritten **III U4,** 67
adventure [əd'ventʃə] Abenteuer **II U6,** 80
adverb ['ædvɜ:b] Adverb °**II U7,** 90
adverb of manner [ˌædvɜ:b‿əv 'mænə] Adverb der Art und Weise °**II U7,** 90
advice [əd'vaɪs] Rat, Ratschlag °**II U4,** 52
to **advise** [əd'vaɪz] raten **III U4,** 69
after ['ɑ:ftə] nach **I LUB,** 39; nachdem **III U2,** 30
afternoon [ˌɑ:ftə'nu:n] Nachmittag **I U2,** 34
afternoon tea [ˌɑ:ftənu:n 'ti:] Nachmittagstee **I U7,** 94
in the afternoon [ˌɪn ði: ˌɑ:ftə'nu:n] nachmittags, am Nachmittag **I U3,** 47
aftershave ['ɑ:ftəʃeɪv] Aftershave, Rasierwasser **III U3,** 52
again [ə'gen] wieder **I U3,** 48
against [ə'genst] gegen **III U1,** 9
age [eɪdʒ] Alter, Zeitalter **III U3,** 46
of age [əv‿'eɪdʒ] im Alter von **III U4,** 67
ago [ə'gəʊ] vor *(zeitlich)* **II U2,** 26
to **agree** [ə'gri:] zustimmen, einer Meinung sein **III U5,** 88
air [eə] Luft **II U4,** 55
on the air [ˌɒn ði‿'eə] auf Sendung **II U4,** 55
airport ['eəpɔ:t] Flughafen **II U7,** 89
alarm [ə'lɑ:m] Alarm **II U7,** 90
alarm clock [ə'lɑ:m ˌklɒk] Wecker **I U5,** 75
A-levels *(pl)* ['eɪlevlz] brit. Abitur **III U4,** 67
alien ['eɪliən] Fremder/Fremde, Außerirdischer/Außerirdische **III U5,** 82
alive [ə'laɪv] lebendig **III U4,** 70
all [ɔ:l] alle/alles; ganz **I U3,** 50
all over [ˌɔ:l‿'əʊvə] überall **III U3,** 49
in all [ɪn‿'ɔ:l] insgesamt, im Ganzen **III U4,** 63
almost ['ɔ:lməʊst] fast, beinahe **III U3,** 45
alone [ə'ləʊn] alleine **III U3,** 47
along [ə'lɒŋ] entlang **I U7,** 91
alphabet ['ælfəbet] Alphabet, Abc **I U1,** 15
alphabetical [ˌælfə'betɪkl] alphabetisch **I U6,** 88
already [ɔ:l'redi] schon **I U2,** 34
also ['ɔ:lsəʊ] auch **I U5,** 68
although [ɔ:l'ðəʊ] obwohl **III U3,** 52
always ['ɔ:lweɪz] immer, ständig **I U1,** 16
a.m. [ˌeɪ'em] vormittags *(Uhrzeit)* **III U3,** 49
ambulance ['æmbjələnts] Krankenwagen **II U4,** 55
American [ə'merɪkən] amerikanisch; Amerikaner/Amerikanerin **II U4,** 50
American football [əˌmerɪkən 'fʊtbɔ:l] Football **III U1,** 8
ancient ['eɪnʃnt] alt **III U1,** 16
and [ænd] und **I U1,** 11

angry ['æŋgri] verärgert, böse **II U1,** 18
to be angry with [bi: 'æŋgri wɪð] böse sein auf **II U2,** 26
animal ['ænɪml] Tier **I U6,** 82
announcement [ə'naʊntsmənt] Ankündigung, Durchsage **III U3,** 52
anorak ['ænəræk] Anorak **II U6,** 82
another [ə'nʌðə] noch ein/eine, ein anderer/eine andere/ein anderes **II U3,** 44
answer ['ɑ:nsə] Antwort **I U4,** 58
to **answer** ['ɑ:nsə] antworten, beantworten **°I LUA,** 24
answerphone ['ɑ:nsəfəʊn] Anrufbeantworter **III U4,** 69
any ['enɪ] einige; etwas **II U4,** 54
anybody ['eni,bɒdi] irgendjemand, jeder (beliebige) **III U5,** 83
anyone ['eniwʌn] irgendjemand, jeder (beliebige) **III U5,** 83
anything ['eniθɪŋ] etwas, irgendetwas **I U5,** 66
anywhere ['eniweə] überall, irgendwo **III U3,** 45
apple ['æpl] Apfel **I U1,** 14
April ['eɪprl] April **I U5,** 70
architect ['ɑ:kɪtekt] Architekt/Architektin **III U2,** 30
area ['eəriə] Gebiet; Fläche **II U7,** 94
arena [ə'ri:nə] Arena, Stadion **II U2,** 22
to **argue** ['ɑ:gju:] streiten, argumentieren **III U2,** 34
argument ['ɑ:gjəmənt] Streit; Argument **III U4,** 62
to have an argument [,hæv‿ən‿'ɑ:gjəmənt] sich streiten **III U4,** 62
arm [ɑ:m] Arm **II U3,** 40
around [ə'raʊnd] um … herum, umher **II U6,** 78; ungefähr, zirka, etwa **III U3,** 49
to **arrest** [ə'rest] festnehmen, verhaften **III U5,** 90
to **arrive** [ə'raɪv] ankommen **I U6,** 86
Art [ɑ:t] Kunst **II U1,** 10
article ['ɑ:tɪkl] Artikel **III U2,** 30
as [æz; əz] als, wie **II U4,** 52
as … as [æz … æz; əz … əz] so … wie … **II U4,** 52
as long as [əz 'lɒŋ‿əz] solange **I U7,** 94
as soon as [əz 'su:n‿əz] sobald **III U4,** 66
as well as [əz 'wel‿əz] sowohl … als auch **III U4,** 67
to **ask** [ɑ:sk] fragen **I U3,** 44
to ask (for) ['ɑ:sk fə] fragen (nach), bitten (um) **I U4,** 60
*to be **asleep** [,bi:‿ə'sli:p] schlafen **II U7,** 94
assembly [ə'sembli] Versammlung, Morgenappell **II U1,** 10
assistant [ə'sɪstnt] Assistent/Assistentin **III U5,** 87
shop assistant ['ʃɒp‿ə,sɪstnt] Verkäufer/Verkäuferin **II U5,** 67
at [æt; ət] auf **I U1,** 10
at first [ət 'fɜ:st] zuerst, zunächst **II U6,** 80
at home [ət 'həʊm] zu Hause **I U2,** 26
at least [ət 'li:st] wenigstens, mindestens **I U6,** 87
at night [ət 'naɪt] nachts **II U3,** 47
at once [ət 'wʌnts] sofort, plötzlich **II U7,** 94
at the back [ət ðə 'bæk] im hinteren Teil, hinten **III U1,** 8
at the bottom [ət ðə 'bɒtəm] unten, im unteren Teil **III U1,** 14
at the front [ət ðə 'frʌnt] im vorderen Teil, vorne **III U1,** 8
at the moment [æt ðə 'məʊmənt] im Augenblick, momentan **I U7,** 90
at the top [ət ðə 'tɒp] oben, im oberen Teil **III U1,** 14
to **attack** [ə'tæk] angreifen **III U5,** 84
attention [ə'tentʃn] Aufmerksamkeit **°III U2,** 33
attraction [ə'trækʃn] Attraktion, Sehenswürdigkeit **III U3,** 49
audience ['ɔ:diəns] Publikum **III U4,** 63
audition [ɔ:'dɪʃn] Vorsprechen, Vorsingen, Vortanzen **II U5,** 64
August ['ɔ:gəst] August **I U5,** 70
aunt [ɑ:nt] Tante **I U2,** 28
Australian [ɒs'treɪliən] australisch; Australier/Australierin **II U4,** 50
autograph ['ɔ:təgrɑ:f] Autogramm **I U7,** 96
autumn ['ɔ:təm] Herbst **I U6,** 79
average ['ævrɪdʒ] durchschnittlich **III U5,** 80
away [ə'weɪ] weg **I U3,** 48
to run away [rʌn‿ə'weɪ] wegrennen **I U3,** 48

B

baby ['beɪbi] Baby, Säugling **I U6,** 82
back [bæk] Rücken **II U3,** 41
at the back [ət ðə 'bæk] im hinteren Teil, hinten **III U1,** 8
back [bæk] zurück **I U3,** 42; Hinter-, rückwärtig **II U4,** 56
back line [,bæk'laɪn] Grundlinie **III U1,** 10
bad [bæd] schlecht **I U5,** 74
bad luck [,bæd 'lʌk] Pech **I U4,** 63
badminton ['bædmɪntən] Badminton, Federball **I U3,** 40
bag [bæg] Tasche, Tüte **I U1,** 14
mixed bag ['mɪkst bæg] Vermischtes **°III U1,** 21
school bag ['sku:l bæg] Schultasche, Schulranzen **I U1,** 14
sleeping bag ['sli:pɪŋ ,bæg] Schlafsack **I U6,** 84
baker ['beɪkə] Bäcker/Bäckerin **III U2,** 32
ball [bɔ:l] Ball **I U1,** 20
balloon [bə'lu:n] Luftballon **°I U5,** 71
banana [bə'nɑ:nə] Banane **II U1,** 15
to go bananas [,gəʊ bə'nɑ:nəz] verrückt werden, durchdrehen **II U5,** 66
steel **band** [,sti:l 'bænd] Steelband *(Band, deren Instrumente aus leeren Ölfässern bestehen)* **III U4,** 64
to **bang** [bæŋ] fest klopfen **II U7,** 94
piggy **bank** ['pɪgi bæŋk] Sparschwein **II U2,** 23
burger **bar** ['bɜ:gə ,bɑ:] Fastfood-Restaurant **I U5,** 68
to **bark** [bɑ:k] bellen **I U3,** 48
barking ['bɑ:kɪŋ] Bellen **III U5,** 88
barn [bɑ:n] Scheune **II U7,** 88
barn owl ['bɑ:n‿əʊl] Schleiereule **II U7,** 94
base [beɪs] Base **III U1,** 14
baseball ['beɪsbɔ:l] Baseball **III U1,** 9
basement ['beɪsmənt] Kellergeschoss, Untergeschoss **III U3,** 52
basketball ['bɑ:skɪtbɔ:l] Basketball **I U3,** 40
bat [bæt] Schläger **III U1,** 8
to **bat** [bæt] schlagen **III U1,** 8
bathroom ['bɑ:θrʊm] Bad, Badezimmer **I LUA,** 24
batter ['bætə] Schlagmann/Schlagfrau **III U1,** 9
battery ['bætri] Batterie, Akku **II U7,** 95
BC (= before Christ) [bi:'si:] vor Christus **III U1,** 15
*to **be** [bi:] sein **I U1,** 23
to be angry with [bi: 'æŋgri wɪð] böse sein auf **II U2,** 26
to be asleep [,bi:‿ə'sli:p] schlafen **II U7,** 94

English – German

to be cold [bi: 'kəʊld] frieren **II U2,** 24
to be fed up [bi: ˌfed‿'ʌp] die Nase voll haben **I U2,** 34
to be frightened (of) [bi: 'fraɪtnd] Angst haben (vor) **II U6,** 83
to be fun [bi: 'fʌn] Spaß machen **I U3,** 43
to be good with … [bi: 'gʊd wɪð] gut mit … umgehen können **I U2,** 34
to be in a hurry [bi:‿ɪn‿ə 'hʌri] es eilig haben **I U2,** 30
to be lost [bi: 'lɒst] sich verirrt haben **III U3,** 46
to be missing [bi: 'mɪsɪŋ] fehlen **III U1,** 14
to be nuts about [bi: ˌnʌts‿ə'baʊt] verrückt nach … sein **II U1,** 18
to be on [bi:‿'ɒn] an der Reihe sein; im Gange sein, laufen **II U5,** 70; an sein, brennen *(Licht)* **II U7,** 94
to be pleased with [bi: 'pli:zd wɪð] zufrieden sein mit **I U6,** 87
to be right [bi: 'raɪt] Recht haben **II U4,** 56
to be trapped [bi: 'træpt] in der Falle sitzen **II U6,** 83
to be upset [bi: ʌp'set] aufgeregt sein, bestürzt sein **II U3,** 44
to be worried [bi: 'wʌrid] besorgt sein, beunruhigt sein **I U6,** 87
to be wrong [bi: 'rɒŋ] Unrecht haben **III U3,** 53
beach [bi:tʃ] Strand **III U1,** 10
bean [bi:n] Bohne **II U4,** 54
beard [bɪəd] Bart **III U5,** 88
beautiful ['bju:tɪfl] schön, wunderschön **I U6,** 78
because [bɪ'kɒz] weil **I U2,** 30
*to **become** [bɪ'kʌm] werden **III U2,** 29
bed [bed] Bett **I LUA,** 25
to get out of bed [ˌget‿aʊt‿əv 'bed] aufstehen **II U7,** 94
bedroom ['bedrʊm] Schlafzimmer **I LUA,** 24
before [bɪ'fɔ:] vor, bevor **I LUB,** 39
*to **begin** [bɪ'gɪn] beginnen, anfangen **II U3,** 47
beginning [bɪ'gɪnɪŋ] Anfang, Beginn **III U3,** 49
behind [bɪ'haɪnd] hinter **I U1,** 18
to **believe** [bɪ'li:v] glauben **II U1,** 18
bell [bel] Glocke, Klingel **II U2,** 24
The bell rings. [ðə 'bel rɪŋz] Es klingelt. **II U4,** 50
to **belong (to)** [bɪ'lɒŋ] gehören (zu) **III U5,** 90
below [bɪ'ləʊ] unterhalb, unten **III U3,** 48
beside [bɪ'saɪd] neben, außer **II U1,** 18
best [best] beste/bester/bestes **II U1,** 14; am besten **III U1,** 10
*to **bet** [bet] wetten **II U1,** 14
better ['betə] besser **II U4,** 50
you'd better [jʊd 'betə] du solltest lieber **III U4,** 70
between [bɪ'twi:n] zwischen **I U7,** 90
big [bɪg] groß **I U1,** 12
bike [baɪk] Fahrrad **I LUB,** 38
by bike [baɪ 'baɪk] mit dem Fahrrad **I U4,** 57
bin [bɪn] Mülleimer, Mülltonne **III U3,** 46
bird [bɜ:d] Vogel **II U4,** 59
birth [bɜ:θ] Geburt **III U1,** 11
birthday ['bɜ:θdeɪ] Geburtstag **I U5,** 68
biscuit ['bɪskɪt] Keks **I U5,** 68
bit [bɪt] Auszug, Teil, Stückchen °**III U5,** 81
a bit [ə 'bɪt] ein bisschen **I U2,** 35
black [blæk] schwarz **I LUA,** 24
blanket ['blæŋkɪt] (Woll-)Decke **II U6,** 74
wet blanket [wet 'blæŋkɪt] Miesmacher/Miesmacherin **II U6,** 74
blind [blaɪnd] blind **III U3,** 52
bloke [bləʊk] Typ, Kerl **I U7,** 96
blond [blɒnd] blond **II U2,** 28
blond(e)-haired ['blɒndˌheəd] blond **III U2,** 29
blood [blʌd] Blut **III U5,** 86
*to **blow** [bləʊ] blasen **III U1,** 12
to blow up [bləʊ‿'ʌp] aufblasen °**I U5,** 71
blue [blu:] blau **I LUA,** 24
board [bɔ:d] Tafel, Wandtafel **I U1,** 18
notice board ['nəʊtɪs bɔ:d] schwarzes Brett **III U4,** 66
boat [bəʊt] Boot, Schiff **III U2,** 32
body ['bɒdi] Körper **III U5,** 90
book [bʊk] Buch **I U1,** 14
exercise book ['eksəsaɪz ˌbʊk] Heft, Übungsheft **I U1,** 14
boot [bu:t] Stiefel **III U5,** 88
rugby boot ['rʌgbi bu:t] Rugbyschuh, Stollenschuh **III U1,** 8
rubber boots *(pl)* [ˌrʌbə 'bu:ts] Gummistiefel **II U6,** 74
bored [bɔ:d] gelangweilt **II U2,** 24
boring ['bɔ:rɪŋ] langweilig **I U1,** 20
*was/were **born** [bɔ:n] wurde(n) geboren **III U1,** 11
to **borrow** ['bɒrəʊ] borgen, leihen **I U2,** 34
boss [bɒs] Boss, Chef/Chefin **III U1,** 12
both [bəʊθ] beide **III U3,** 52
to **bother** ['bɒðə] stören, belästigen °**III U3,** 50
bottle ['bɒtl] Flasche **I U5,** 68
bottom ['bɒtəm] Boden, Grund, unterer Teil **III U1,** 14
at the bottom [ət ðə 'bɒtəm] unten, im unteren Teil **III U1,** 14
bowl [bəʊl] Schüssel **II U4,** 50
box [bɒks] Kiste, Schachtel, Kasten **I U5,** 68
phone box ['fəʊn ˌbɒks] Telefonzelle **III U3,** 50
boy [bɔɪ] Junge **I U1,** 16
boyfriend ['bɔɪfrend] Freund *(in einer Paarbeziehung)* **III U4,** 63
brave [breɪv] tapfer, mutig **III U5,** 86
bread [bred] Brot **II U4,** 49
break [breɪk] Pause **II U1,** 12
*to **break** [breɪk] (zer)brechen, kaputtmachen **II U5,** 68
to **break-dance** ['breɪkdɑ:nts] Breakdance tanzen **I LUB,** 38
breakfast ['brekfəst] Frühstück **I U3,** 44
breath [breθ] Atem, Atemzug °**III U5,** 86
to take a deep breath [ˌteɪk‿ə 'di:p ˌbreθ] tief Luft holen °**III U5,** 86
bridge [brɪdʒ] Brücke **I LUC,** 52
fire **brigade** ['faɪə brɪˌgeɪd] Feuerwehr **III U2,** 32
brilliant ['brɪljənt] toll, prima; leuchtend **II U5,** 70
*to **bring** [brɪŋ] bringen, mitbringen **I U3,** 43
to bring in [brɪŋ‿'ɪn] hereinbringen, mitbringen °**I U7,** 93
to the **brink** [tə ðə 'brɪŋk] an den Rand, bis zur Oberkante **III U4,** 70
British ['brɪtɪʃ] britisch **III U1,** 15
broken ['brəʊkn] kaputt, zerbrochen, gebrochen **I U6,** 84
brother ['brʌðə] Bruder **I LUA,** 25
brown [braʊn] braun **I LUA,** 24
speech **bubble** ['spi:tʃ ˌbʌbl] Sprechblase °**III U3,** 47
*to **build** [bɪld] bauen **III U2,** 26
building ['bɪldɪŋ] Gebäude **III U2,** 26
bully ['bʊli] jemand, der andere tyrannisiert **II U3,** 36
to **bully** ['bʊli] tyrannisieren **II U3,** 36
*to go **bump** [gəʊ 'bʌmp] rumsen °**II U7,** 94
burger ['bɜ:gə] Hamburger **I U5,** 68
burger bar ['bɜ:gə ˌbɑ:] Fastfood-Restaurant **I U5,** 68

burglar ['bɜ:glə] Finbrecher/ Einbrecherin **II U7,** 90
*to **burn** [bɜ:n] (ver)brennen **III U2,** 32
to **bury** ['beri] begraben, beerdigen **III U5,** 86
bus [bʌs] Bus **I LUC,** 52
bus stop ['bʌs ˌstɒp] Bushaltestelle **I LUC,** 52
on the bus [ˌɒn ðə 'bʌs] im Bus **II U1,** 18
bush [bʊʃ] Busch, Strauch **I U6,** 86
businessman, businessmen *(pl)* ['bɪznɪsmən; 'bɪznɪsmen] Geschäftsmann **III U2,** 28
busy ['bɪzi] beschäftigt, ausgefüllt **I U2,** 34; belebt **III U2,** 28
but [bʌt] aber **I U2,** 26
butter ['bʌtə] Butter **I U7,** 94
button ['bʌtn] Auslöser; Knopf **II U7,** 95
*to **buy** [baɪ] kaufen **I U5,** 66
by [baɪ] bis **II U6,** 78
by bike [baɪ 'baɪk] mit dem Fahrrad **I U4,** 57
bye [baɪ] tschüss **I U1,** 16

C

café ['kæfeɪ] Café **I U3,** 48
cafeteria [ˌkæfə'tɪəriə] Cafeteria **I U1,** 20
cake [keɪk] Kuchen **I U5,** 68
calendar ['kæləndə] Kalender **I U5,** 71
call [kɔ:l] Anruf °**I U6,** 83
phone call ['fəʊn ˌkɔ:l] (Telefon-)Anruf °**II U4,** 57
to **call** [kɔ:l] rufen, anrufen, nennen **I U3,** 48
called [kɔ:ld] genannt **III U5,** 86
That's what I call .... [ˌðæts wɒt‿'aɪ ˌkɔ:l] Das nenne ich .... **II U1,** 14
caller ['kɔ:lə] Anrufer/Anruferin °**III U4,** 69
calm [kɑ:m] ruhig **II U6,** 80
camera ['kæmrə] Kamera, Fotoapparat **II U5,** 62
camping ['kæmpɪŋ] Camping, Zelten **I U6,** 84
***can** [kæn] können, dürfen **I U1,** 19
to **canoe** [kə'nu:] Kanu fahren **III U3,** 46
cap [kæp] Kappe, Mütze **I U5,** 66
capital letter [ˌkæpɪtl 'letə] Großbuchstabe °**II U3,** 37
capsule ['kæpsju:l] Kapsel **III U2,** 26
caption ['kæpʃn] Untertitel; Bildunterschrift °**III U2,** 26
car [kɑ:] Auto **I U3,** 49
card [kɑ:d] Karte **I LUB,** 38
to **care** [keə] sich kümmern, sich interessieren, wichtig nehmen **III U4,** 70
I don't care. [aɪ dəʊnt 'keə] Es ist mir egal. **II U4,** 58
careful ['keəfl] vorsichtig; sorgfältig **II U6,** 80
caretaker ['keəˌteɪkə] Hausmeister/ Hausmeisterin **I U1,** 12
carrot ['kærət] Karotte, Mohrrübe **II U1,** 15
to **carry** ['kæri] tragen **I U6,** 80; befördern **III U2,** 34
cartoon [kɑ:'tu:n] Cartoon, Zeichentrickfilm **III U5,** 80
pencil **case** ['pensl ˌkeɪs] Mäppchen **I U1,** 14
castle ['kɑ:sl] Schloss, Burg **II U7,** 88
cat [kæt] Katze **I U2,** 26
*to **catch** [kætʃ, kɔ:t] fangen, erreichen **III U1,** 8
catcher ['kætʃə] Fänger/Fängerin **III U1,** 14
catchy ['kætʃi] eingängig **III U5,** 80
cathedral [kə'θi:drl] Kathedrale, Dom **III U2,** 28
CD [ˌsi:'di:] CD **I U5,** 69
CD player [ˌsi:'di: ˌpleɪə] CD-Player **II U4,** 56
Celsius (C) ['selsiəs] Celsius **II U6,** 78
centimetre ['sentɪˌmi:tə] Zentimeter **III U3,** 48
centre ['sentə] Zentrum, Mittelpunkt **I LUC,** 52
information centre [ɪnfə'meɪʃn ˌsentə] Informationszentrum **I LUC,** 52
century ['sentʃri] Jahrhundert **III U1,** 8
chain [tʃeɪn] Kette **II U3,** 40
chair [tʃeə] Stuhl **I U1,** 18
to take your **chance** [ˌteɪk jɔ: 'tʃɑ:ns] etwas wagen, etwas riskieren **III U3,** 53
change [tʃeɪndʒ] Wechselgeld; Änderung **II U4,** 55
change of place [ˌtʃeɪndʒ‿əv 'pleɪs] Ortswechsel °**III U4,** 65
to **change** [tʃeɪndʒ] (ver)ändern, tauschen, wechseln **II U3,** 42; umsteigen **III U2,** 28
to change your mind [ˌtʃeɪndʒ jə 'maɪnd] deine Meinung ändern **III U1,** 17
channel ['tʃænl] Kanal; Programm **III U3,** 45
charity ['tʃærɪti] Wohltätigkeit, Wohltätigkeitsverein **I U7,** 90
chart [tʃɑ:t] Schaubild, Diagramm °**II U4,** 51
charts *(pl)* [tʃɑ:ts] Charts, Hitparade **III U5,** 82
chat [tʃæt] Geplauder, Unterhaltung **I U2,** 33
to **chat** [tʃæt] sich unterhalten **I U2,** 33
cheap [tʃi:p] billig **I U5,** 68
to **check** [tʃek] überprüfen **I U6,** 82
cheese [tʃi:z] Käse **I U5,** 68
chicken ['tʃɪkɪn] Huhn, Hähnchen **II U4,** 49
child, children *(pl)* [tʃaɪld; 'tʃɪldrɪn] Kind **I U2,** 26
only child ['əʊnli ˌtʃaɪld] Einzelkind **I U2,** 26
Chinese [tʃaɪ'ni:z] chinesisch **II U4,** 49
chips *(pl)* [tʃɪps] Pommes frites **II U1,** 14
chocolate ['tʃɒklət] Schokolade **I U1,** 18
choice [tʃɔɪs] Wahl, Auswahl **III U4,** 70
to **choke** [tʃəʊk] ersticken **III U4,** 70
*to **choose** [tʃu:z] wählen, auswählen **I U4,** 54
church [tʃɜ:tʃ] Kirche **I LUC,** 52
cigarette [ˌsɪgr'et] Zigarette °**III U3,** 51
cinema ['sɪnəmə] Kino **II U1,** 18
circle ['sɜ:kl] Kreis **III U3,** 45
city ['sɪti] Stadt, Großstadt **II U7,** 89
to **clap** [klæp] klatschen **I U1,** 15
class [klɑ:s] Schulklasse, Klasse **I U1,** 16; Kurs, Unterricht **II U1,** 18
classroom ['klɑ:srʊm] Klassenzimmer **I U1,** 16
to **clean** [kli:n] säubern, reinigen **II U3,** 40
clean [kli:n] sauber **III U3,** 46
clear [klɪə] klar **II U7,** 90
to **click** [klɪk] klicken **II U5,** 64
cliff [klɪf] Klippe **II U7,** 93;
to **climb** ['klaɪm] klettern, steigen, besteigen **II U2,** 30
clock [klɒk] Uhr **I U4,** 54
alarm clock [ə'lɑ:m ˌklɒk] Wecker **I U5,** 75
o'clock [ə'klɒk] Uhr *(Zeitangabe)* **I U3,** 40
close [kləʊs] nahe **III U5,** 90
to **close** [kləʊz] schließen, zumachen **I LUC,** 53
closed [kləʊzd] zu, geschlossen °**I U2,** 32
clothes *(pl)* [kləʊθs] Kleider, Kleidung **II U2,** 23
cloud [klaʊd] Wolke **II U7,** 94

English – German

cloudy ['klaʊdi] wolkig **II U6,** 78
club [klʌb] Klub, Verein, Arbeitsgemeinschaft **I LUB,** 39
clue [klu:] Hinweis **II U1,** 13
coast [kəʊst] Küste **II U7,** 88
coastline ['kəʊstlaɪn] Küstenlinie **III U3,** 44
coat [kəʊt] Mantel **II U7,** 90
code [kəʊd] Code, Verschlüsselung °**III U4,** 68
coke [kəʊk] Cola **II U4,** 49
cold [kəʊld] kalt **I U4,** 62
to be cold [bi: 'kəʊld] frieren **II U2,** 24
to **collect** [kə'lekt] sammeln **I LUB,** 38; abholen **II U5,** 71
college ['kɒlɪdʒ] College; Institut **III U4,** 67
colour ['kʌlə] Farbe **I LUA,** 24
colourful ['kʌləfl] bunt, farbig **III U5,** 80
*to **come** [kʌm] kommen **I U2,** 33
Come on. [kʌm‿'ɒn] Komm./Kommt. **I U2,** 35
to come down [kʌm 'daʊn] herunterkommen, sich legen **III U1,** 16
to come in [kʌm‿'ɪn] hereinkommen **I U3,** 48
to come over [kʌm‿'əʊvə] herüberkommen **I U2,** 27
to come true [kʌm 'tru:] wahr werden **III U2,** 30
comedy ['kɒmədi] Komödie **III U5,** 80
comic ['kɒmɪk] **I LUB,** 38
company ['kʌmpəni] Gesellschaft, Firma; Kompanie **III U2,** 34
comparative [kəm'pærətɪv] Komparativ **II U4,** 50
to **compare** [kəm'peə] vergleichen **III U4,** 67
competition [ˌkɒmpə'tɪʃn] Wettbewerb, Turnier **III U1,** 9
to **complete** [kəm'pli:t] vervollständigen **III U2,** 30
comprehensive school [kɒmprɪ'hensɪv ˌsku:l] Gesamtschule **III U4,** 66
compulsory [kəm'pʌlsri] obligatorisch, zwingend **III U4,** 67
computer [ˌkəm'pju:tə] Computer **I LUA,** 25
concert ['kɒnsət] Konzert **II U2,** 23
conqueror ['kɒŋkrə] Eroberer °**III U2,** 31
to **construct** [kən'strʌkt] bauen, konstruieren **III U2,** 30
content ['kɒntent] Inhalt **III U4,** 63
to **continue** [kən'tɪnju:] weitergehen, weitermachen °**II U2,** 27
contrast ['kɒntrɑ:st] Kontrast, Gegensatz **III U5,** 80
in contrast to [ɪn 'kɒntrɑ:st tə] im Gegensatz zu **III U5,** 80
conversation [ˌkɒnvə'seɪʃn] Unterhaltung °**III U3,** 51
to **convince** [kən'vɪnts] überzeugen °**III U5,** 81
cook [kʊk] Koch/Köchin **III U5,** 82
cooking ['kʊkɪŋ] Kochen, Koch- **I U3,** 40
cool [ku:l] cool, prima **I U1,** 20
copy ['kɒpi] Kopie °**III U5,** 86
to **copy** ['kɒpi] abschreiben, kopieren **II U5,** 63
cornflakes ['kɔ:nfleɪks] Cornflakes **I U5,** 68
Cornish ['kɔ:nɪʃ] kornisch; aus Cornwall **III U3,** 48
to **correct** [kə'rekt] korrigieren, verbessern °**I LUB,** 38
correct [kə'rekt] richtig, korrekt **II U1,** 10
corridor ['kɒrɪdɔ:] Gang, Flur, Korridor **I U7,** 96
cottage ['kɒtɪdʒ] kleines Landhaus, Ferienhaus **III U4,** 64
couch [kaʊtʃ] Couch, Sofa **III U1,** 12
couch potato ['kaʊtʃ pəˌteɪtəʊ] Stubenhocker **III U1,** 12
*__could__ [kʊd] konnte/konnten **II U4,** 52; könnte/könnten **III U1,** 12
countdown ['kaʊntdaʊn] Countdown **III U5,** 82
country ['kʌntri] Land **I U2,** 29
in the country [ˌɪn ðə 'kʌntri] auf dem Land **I U6,** 78
to the country [tʊ ðə 'kʌntri] aufs Land **III U2,** 32
courier ['kʊriə] Kurier **III U2,** 34
course [kɔ:s] Gang *(Menü)* **II U4,** 49
of course [əv 'kɔ:s] natürlich, selbstverständlich **I U1,** 19
court [kɔ:t] Spielfeld **III U1,** 10
cousin ['kʌzn] Cousin/Cousine **I U2,** 28
cover ['kʌvə] Einband, Titelseite **II U5,** 64
cow [kaʊ] Kuh **I U6,** 82
at the **crack** of dawn [ˌkræk‿əv 'dɔ:n] im Morgengrauen **III U2,** 34
Crash! [kræʃ] Bumm!, Krach! **III U3,** 53
to **crawl** [krɔ:l] kriechen, krabbeln, schleichen **III U3,** 53
crazy ['kreɪzi] verrückt **I U7,** 96
to drive crazy [draɪv 'kreɪzi] verrückt machen **II U5,** 71
to **creak** [kri:k] knarren, quietschen **II U7,** 94
ice-**cream** [aɪs 'kri:m] Eiscreme **I U7,** 92
cricket ['krɪkɪt] Kricket **I U7,** 92
crime [kraɪm] Verbrechen; Kriminalität **III U5,** 84
crisp [krɪsp] Kartoffelchip **I U1,** 18
crossword (puzzle) ['krɒswɜ:d 'pʌzl] Kreuzworträtsel °**I U5,** 71
crowd [kraʊd] Menschenmenge **III U1,** 17
crown [kraʊn] Krone **III U2,** 26
cruise [kru:z] Kreuzfahrt **III U3,** 45
cry [kraɪ] Schrei **III U5,** 86
to **cry** [kraɪ] weinen; schreien, rufen **II U3,** 36
cup [kʌp] Tasse, Kelch; Pokal **III U1,** 15
cupboard ['kʌbəd] Küchenschrank, Schrank **I U1,** 18
curry ['kʌri] Curry *(Gewürz oder Gericht)* **II U4,** 49
curve [kɜ:v] Kurve **III U4,** 70
customer ['kʌstəmə] Kunde/Kundin **III U2,** 34
customs *(pl)* ['kʌstəmz] Zoll **II U7,** 90
to **cycle** ['saɪkl] Rad fahren **III U1,** 12

D

dad [dæd] Papa, Vati **I LUA,** 25
daily ['deɪli] täglich **III U5,** 80
dairy ['deəri] Molkerei **III U2,** 34
to **damage** ['dæmɪdʒ] beschädigen **III U2,** 32
dance [dɑ:nts] Tanz **III U1,** 13
to **dance** [dɑ:nts] tanzen **I U3,** 40
dangerous ['deɪndʒrəs] gefährlich **II U4,** 56
dark [dɑ:k] Dunkelheit **III U5,** 88
dark [dɑ:k] dunkel **I U2,** 34
date [deɪt] Datum **I U5,** 70
at the crack of **dawn** [ˌkræk‿əv 'dɔ:n] im Morgengrauen **III U2,** 34
day [deɪ] Tag **I LUB,** 39
Have a nice day. [ˌhæv‿ə naɪs 'deɪ] Einen schönen Tag (noch). **II U4,** 55
one day [wʌn 'deɪ] eines Tages **II U3,** 36
sports day ['spɔ:ts deɪ] Sportfest **I U7,** 90
dead [ded] tot **III U5,** 86
dear [dɪə] Schatz *(Anrede)* **III U4,** 70
dear [dɪə] lieb **I U3,** 44
Dear [dɪə] Lieber …, Liebe … *(Anrede in Briefen)* **II U3,** 36

December [dɪ'sembə] Dezember **I U5,** 70
to **decide** [dɪ'saɪd] entscheiden **II U5,** 64
deep [di:p] tief °**III U5,** 86
to **define** [dɪ'faɪn] definieren °**III U3,** 48
definition [ˌdefɪ'nɪʃn] Definition **II U1,** 20
degree (°) [dɪ'gri:] Grad **II U6,** 78
to **delete** [dɪ'li:t] löschen *(Text)* **II U5,** 63
to **deliver** [dɪ'lɪvə] liefern **III U2,** 34
department store [dɪ'pɑ:tmənt stɔ:] Kaufhaus **I LUC,** 52
departure [dɪ'pɑ:tʃə] Abflug, Abreise **II U7,** 90
to **describe** [dɪ'skraɪb] beschreiben °**I U7,** 92
description [dɪ'skrɪpʃn] Beschreibung °**III U1,** 15
to **design** [dɪ'zaɪn] entwerfen; zeichnen **III U2,** 30
desk [desk] Schreibtisch **I U1,** 18; Schalter **II U7,** 90
dessert [dɪ'zɜ:t] Dessert, Nachtisch **II U4,** 49
to **destroy** [dɪ'strɔɪ] zerstören **III U2,** 32
detective [dɪ'tektɪv] Detektiv/ Detektivin **II U2,** 30
  detective story [dɪ'tektɪv ˌstɔ:ri] Krimi **III U5,** 80
  store detective ['stɔ: dɪˌtektɪv] Kaufhausdetektiv/ Kaufhausdetektivin **II U2,** 30
diagram ['daɪəgræm] Diagramm °**III U1,** 14
dialogue ['daɪəlɒg] Dialog, Gespräch **III U2,** 33
diamond ['daɪəmənd] Diamant **III U5,** 82
diary ['daɪəri] Tagebuch; Terminkalender **III U4,** 64
dictionary ['dɪkʃnri] Wörterbuch °**II U3,** 46
to **die** [daɪ] sterben **III U2,** 31
diet [daɪət] Diät **II U4,** 52
  to go on a diet [ˌgəʊ‿ɒn‿ə 'daɪət] eine Diät machen **II U4,** 52
different ['dɪfrnt] anders, verschieden **I U6,** 78
difficult ['dɪfɪklt] schwierig **II U1,** 13
*to **dig up** [dɪg‿'ʌp] ausgraben **III U1,** 16
digital ['dɪdʒɪtl] digital **II U5,** 62
dining room ['daɪnɪŋ rʊm] Esszimmer, Speisesaal **I LUA,** 24
direct [dɪ'rekt] direkt **III U4,** 63
director [dɪ'rektə] Direktor/Direktorin, Regisseur/Regisseurin **III U5,** 87
dirty ['dɜ:ti] schmutzig **II U1,** 10
to **disappear** [ˌdɪsə'pɪə] verschwinden **II U6,** 83
disappointed [ˌdɪsə'pɔɪntɪd] enttäuscht **III U4,** 62
disaster [dɪ'zɑ:stə] Desaster, Katastrophe **III U4,** 64
disco ['dɪskəʊ] Disko **I U5,** 74
to **discuss** [dɪ'skʌs] diskutieren °**III U1,** 14
to **dive** [daɪv] tauchen **III U3,** 47
divorced from [dɪ'vɔ:st frəm] geschieden von **I U2,** 28
DJ [ˌdi:'dʒeɪ] DJ **I U2,** 33
*to **do** [du:] machen, tun **I U1,** 15
  to do sports [du: 'spɔ:ts] Sport treiben **I U7,** 92
doctor ['dɒktə] Arzt/Ärztin **II U3,** 40
  to see a doctor [si: ə 'dɒktə] zum Arzt gehen **II U4,** 52
docu soap ['dɒkju ˌsəʊp] Dokusoap **III U5,** 80
documentary [ˌdɒkjə'mentri] Dokumentarfilm **III U5,** 80
dog [dɒg] Hund **I U2,** 27
  dog-tired [ˌdɒg'taɪəd] hundemüde **I U3,** 49
  to walk the dog [wɔ:k ðə 'dɒg] mit dem Hund spazieren gehen **I U3,** 42
domino ['dɒmɪnəʊ] Dominospiel °**II U2,** 26
door [dɔ:] Tür **I U1,** 18
  next door [ˌnekst 'dɔ:] nebenan **III U1,** 16
doorbell ['dɔ:bel] Türklingel **II U5,** 66
doorstep ['dɔ:step] Türstufe **III U1,** 16
double ['dʌbl] Doppelgänger, das Doppelte **I U7,** 97
down [daʊn] nach unten, herunter, hinunter, nieder **II U2,** 30; senkrecht *(im Kreuzworträtsel)* °**II U3,** 42
  Go down .... ['gəʊ daʊn] Geh ... entlang. **I LUC,** 53
  to come down [kʌm 'daʊn] herunterkommen, sich legen **III U1,** 16
  to go down [gəʊ 'daʊn] hinuntergehen, entlanggehen **II U2,** 30
  to lie down [laɪ 'daʊn] (sich) hinlegen, niederlegen **III U3,** 52
  to sit down [sɪt 'daʊn] sich setzen, sich hinsetzen **I U1,** 19
down under [daʊn‿'ʌndə] in Australien °**II U1,** 17
to **download** [ˌdaʊn'ləʊd] herunterladen **II U5,** 63
downstairs [ˌdaʊn'steəz] unten, im unteren Stock **I U2,** 27; (die Treppe) hinunter/herunter **III U5,** 85
drama ['drɑ:mə] Theater, Drama **I U3,** 40
dramatic [drə'mætɪk] dramatisch **III U5,** 80
It's a **draw.** [ˌɪts‿ə 'drɔ:] Es steht unentschieden. **III U1,** 12
*to **draw** [drɔ:] zeichnen **I LUB,** 38
dream [dri:m] Traum **I LUA,** 25
to **dress** [dres] sich anziehen **I U3,** 44
drink [drɪŋk] Getränk **I U7,** 95
*to **drink** [drɪŋk] trinken **I U5,** 75
*to **drive** [draɪv] fahren **I U6,** 86
  to drive crazy [draɪv 'kreɪzi] verrückt machen **II U5,** 71
driver ['draɪvə] Fahrer/Fahrerin **I U4,** 54
to **drop** [drɒp] fallen, fallen lassen **II U1,** 18
drums *(pl)* [drʌmz] Schlagzeug **I U2,** 26
dump [dʌmp] Dreckloch, Müllkippe **II U7,** 88
during *(+ noun)* ['djʊərɪŋ] während *(+ Nomen)* **III U1,** 8
DVD [di:vi:'di:] DVD **II U5,** 62
  DVD player [di:vi:'di: 'pleɪə] DVD-Player **II U5,** 62
to **dye** [daɪ] färben **II U2,** 28

E

each [i:tʃ] jede/jeder/jedes **III U1,** 8; je, jeweils **III U4,** 63
  each other [ˌi:tʃ‿'ʌðə] sich gegenseitig **II U1,** 19
ear [ɪə] Ohr **II U3,** 40
early ['ɜ:li] früh **I U3,** 46
east [i:st] Osten **I U4,** 54
easy ['i:zi] einfach, leicht **I U1,** 20
*to **eat** [i:t] essen, fressen **I U3,** 44
to **echo** ['ekəʊ] widerhallen **III U5,** 90
education [edʒʊ'keɪʃn] Erziehung, Bildung **II U1,** 10
  Physical Education (PE) [ˌfɪzɪkl‿edʒʊ'keɪʃn] Sport *(Schulfach)* **II U1,** 10
  Religious Education (RE) [rɪˌlɪdʒəs‿edʒʊ'keɪʃn] Religionsunterricht **II U1,** 12
egg [eg] Ei **I U5,** 68
not ... **either** [ˌnɒt ... 'aɪðə] auch nicht **III U1,** 17
elbow ['elbəʊ] Ellbogen **II U3,** 41

English – German

elephant ['elɪfənt] Elefant **I U7,** 96
else [els] sonst, noch **I U5,** 66
someone else [ˌsʌmwʌn‿'els] jemand anderes °**III U1,** 13
e-mail ['i:meɪl] E-Mail **I U3,** 44
embarrassing [ɪm'bærəsɪŋ] peinlich **II U2,** 26
emergency [ɪ'mɜ:dʒnsi] Notfall, Notlage **III U5,** 82
empty ['empti] leer **II U1,** 18
end [end] Ende, Schluss **II U6,** 84
in the end [ɪn ði:‿'end] schließlich, zum Schluss **II U6,** 80
to **end** [end] enden **I U5,** 76
to end in ['end‿ɪn] enden auf °**II U7,** 90
ending ['endɪŋ] Ende, Schluss (*einer Geschichte*) °**II U1,** 19
enemy ['enəmi] Feind/Feindin **II U3,** 43
engine ['endʒɪn] Maschine, Motor **III U3,** 56
English ['ɪŋglɪʃ] englisch **I U1,** 11
to **enjoy** [ɪn'dʒɔɪ] sich erfreuen, genießen **II U6,** 80
enormous [ɪ'nɔ:məs] enorm, riesig **III U5,** 90
enough [ɪ'nʌf] genug, genügend **III U1,** 12
to **enter** ['entə] sich beteiligen an; eintreten, betreten **III U2,** 30
entry ['entri] Eintrag °**III U2,** 35
envelope ['envələʊp] Briefumschlag, Umschlag **II U7,** 90
environment [ɪn'vaɪərnmənt] Umwelt, Umgebung **II U6,** 74
er [ɜ:] äh °**I U1,** 12
erm [ɜ:m] äh °**II U3,** 38
to **escape** [ɪ'skeɪp] flüchten, entkommen **II U6,** 78
etc. [ɪt'setrə] usw., et cetera **II U1,** 10
euro ['jʊərəʊ] Euro *(Währung)* **I U5,** 73
European [ˌjʊərə'pi:ən] europäisch **III U3,** 55
even ['i:vn] selbst, sogar **I U7,** 90
not even [nɒt‿'i:vn] nicht einmal **III U4,** 64
evening ['i:vnɪŋ] Abend **I U3,** 47
in the evening [ˌɪn ði: 'i:vnɪŋ] abends, am Abend **I U3,** 47
that evening [ˌdæt‿'i:vnɪŋ] an diesem Abend **II U1,** 19
this evening [ðɪs 'i:vnɪŋ] heute Abend **III U3,** 52
event [ɪ'vent] Veranstaltung, Ereignis **I U7,** 90
ever ['evə] jemals **II U5,** 66
every ['evri] jede/jeder/jedes **I U3,** 40
everyone ['evriwʌn] jeder **III U3,** 48
everything ['evriθɪŋ] alles **II U4,** 50
everywhere ['evriweə] überall **II U5,** 71
evidence ['evɪdnts] Beweis °**II U6,** 83
exact [ɪg'zækt] genau **III U3,** 49
exactly [ɪg'zæktli] genau **III U3,** 49
exam [ɪg'zæm] Examen, Prüfung **III U4,** 67
example [ɪg'zɑ:mpl] Beispiel °**I U1,** 13
for example [ˌfər‿ɪg'zɑ:mpl] zum Beispiel **III U3,** 48
exchange [ɪks'tʃeɪndʒ] Austausch, Tausch **I U7,** 94
excited [ɪk'saɪtɪd] aufgeregt **I U5,** 74
exciting [ɪk'saɪtɪŋ] spannend, aufregend **II U4,** 51
Excuse me! [ɪk'skju:z mi:] Entschuldigung! **I U3,** 42
exercise ['eksəsaɪz] Übung, Aufgabe **I U1,** 19
exercise book ['eksəsaɪz ˌbʊk] Heft, Übungsheft **I U1,** 14
to **exercise** ['eksəsaɪz] üben, Sport machen **II U4,** 52
exhibition [ˌeksɪ'bɪʃn] Ausstellung, Vorführung **III U2,** 31
to **expect** [ɪk'spekt] erwarten **III U2,** 34
expensive [ɪk'spentsɪv] teuer **I U5,** 68
experiment [ɪk'sperɪmənt] Experiment, Versuch **II U1,** 13
to **explain** [ɪk'spleɪn] erklären, erläutern **II U5,** 64
expressive [ɪk'spresɪv] ausdrucksstark °**III U5,** 86
extra ['ekstrə] zusätzlich; Zusatz **III U4,** 68
eye [aɪ] Auge **I U2,** 35
eyebrow ['aɪbraʊ] Augenbraue **III U4,** 62

F

face [feɪs] Gesicht **I U3,** 48
fact [fækt] Fakt, Tatsache **II U2,** 32
fact-file on ['fækt,faɪl] Datei mit Informationen über °**II U2,** 32
in fact [ɪn 'fækt] in der Tat, genau genommen **II U7,** 94
fair [feə] Messe, Jahrmarkt **I U7,** 90
summer fair ['sʌmə ˌfeə] Sommerfest **I U7,** 90
fair [feə] gerecht, fair **III U1,** 16; blond, hell **III U5,** 80
*to **fall** [fɔ:l] fallen, herunterfallen, hinfallen **II U2,** 26
to fall off [fɔ:l‿'ɒf] herunterfallen **II U3,** 40
family ['fæmli] Familie **I LUA,** 25
family tree ['fæmli tri:] Familienstammbaum °**I U2,** 28
famous ['feɪməs] berühmt **I U4,** 54
fan [fæn] Fan **II U5,** 66
fantastic [fæn'tæstɪk] fantastisch, großartig **I U7,** 94
far [fɑ:] weit **II U6,** 78
to go far [gəʊ 'fɑ:] weit kommen, es weit bringen **III U2,** 26
farm [fɑ:m] Bauernhof, Farm **I U6,** 78
farmer ['fɑ:mə] Bauer/Bäuerin, Landwirt/Landwirtin **I U6,** 82
farmhouse ['fɑ:mhaʊs] Bauernhaus **II U7,** 88
fashion ['fæʃn] Mode **II U6,** 82
fast [fɑ:st] schnell **II U4,** 50
fast food [ˌfɑ:st 'fu:d] Schnellimbiss °**II U4,** 50
father ['fɑ:ðə] Vater **III U3,** 52
favourite ['feɪvrɪt] Lieblings- **I U1,** 12
February ['februəri] Februar **I U5,** 70
*to **feed** [fi:d] füttern **I U6,** 80
to be fed up [bi: ˌfed‿'ʌp] die Nase voll haben **I U2,** 34
*to **feel** [fi:l] fühlen, sich fühlen **II U3,** 40
to feel for ['fi:l fə] tasten nach **III U3,** 52
to feel sick [fi:l 'sɪk] Übelkeit verspüren **II U3,** 46
to feel sorry for [fi:l 'sɒri] Mitleid haben mit, bedauern **III U1,** 16
feeling ['fi:lɪŋ] Gefühl **III U4,** 64
ferry ['feri] Fähre **III U3,** 45
few [fju:] wenige **II U5,** 71
a few [ə 'fju:] einige, ein paar **II U4,** 52
fiction ['fɪkʃn] Erfindung, Fiktion **III U5,** 80
science fiction [ˌsaɪəns 'fɪkʃn] Sciencefiction **III U5,** 80
field [fi:ld] Feld, Acker **I U6,** 88
sports field ['spɔ:ts fi:ld] Sportplatz **I U7,** 92
fierce [fɪəs] bösartig **II U5,** 70
fifth [fɪfθ] Fünftel **III U2,** 32
fight [faɪt] Kampf **III U1,** 16
*to **fight** [faɪt] streiten, kämpfen **III U4,** 69
figure ['fɪgə] Figur, Gestalt **II U7,** 94; Zahl, Ziffer °**III U1,** 15
to **fill** in [fɪl‿'ɪn] ausfüllen, einsetzen **II U5,** 64
film [fɪlm] Film **II U3,** 43
to **film** [fɪlm] filmen **III U5,** 87

final ['faɪnl] letzte/letzter/letztes **III U5,** 82
finally ['faɪnli] endlich, schließlich **III U2,** 28
*to **find** [faɪnd] finden **I U3,** 48
to find out [faɪnd‿'aʊt] herausfinden **I U4,** 62
fine [faɪn] Geldbuße, Geldstrafe **III U2,** 28
fine [faɪn] gut, in Ordnung, fein, schön **I U7,** 94
finger ['fɪŋgə] Finger **II U3,** 41
to **finish** ['fɪnɪʃ] beenden, erledigen, aufhören **I U2,** 34
fire [faɪə] Feuer, Brand **I U7,** 96; Feuerstelle, Kaminfeuer **III U2,** 32
fire brigade ['faɪə brɪ,geɪd] Feuerwehr **III U2,** 32
Where's the fire? [,weəz ðə 'faɪə] Wo brennt's denn? **I U7,** 96
fireplace ['faɪəpleɪs] Kamin **III U5,** 89
firm [fɜ:m] Firma **III U1,** 12
first [fɜ:st] zuerst; erste/erster/erstes **I U4,** 54
at first [ət 'fɜ:st] zuerst, zunächst **II U6,** 80
fish, fish *(pl)* [fɪʃ] Fisch **I U6,** 78
to **fish** [fɪʃ] fischen, angeln **I U6,** 82
fishing ['fɪʃɪŋ] Angeln, Fischen **I U6,** 78
*to have a **fit** [,hæv‿ə 'fɪt] einen Anfall bekommen, Zustände kriegen **III U4,** 70
to **fit** [fɪt] passen **II U6,** 76
fit [fɪt] fit **II U4,** 52
to **fix (to)** [fɪks] befestigen, anbringen; reparieren **III U2,** 30
flag [flæg] Flagge, Fahne **I U2,** 29
flame [fleɪm] Flamme **III U2,** 32
flash [flæʃ] Aufblinken, Blitzen **II U7,** 95
flash flood ['flæʃ ,flʌd] flutartige Überschwemmung, Sintflut **II U6,** 74
flat [flæt] Wohnung **I U2,** 26
flight [flaɪt] Flug **II U2,** 23
flood [flʌd] Überschwemmung, Hochwasser **II U6,** 74
flash flood ['flæʃ ,flʌd] flutartige Überschwemmung, Sintflut **II U6,** 74
floor [flɔ:] Fußboden **II U5,** 71
flower ['flaʊə] Blume **I U6,** 78
*to **fly** [flaɪ] fliegen **II U7,** 88; wehen **III U3,** 46
fog [fɒg] Nebel **II U6,** 78
foggy ['fɒgi] neblig **I U6,** 79
folder ['fəʊldə] Ordner, Mappe **I U4,** 60
to **follow** ['fɒləʊ] hinterhergehen, folgen, befolgen **I U7,** 96
following ['fɒləʊɪŋ] folgende/folgender/folgendes **III U4,** 67
food [fu:d] Essen, Nahrung, Lebensmittel **I U7,** 95
fast food [,fɑ:st 'fu:d] Schnellimbiss °**II U4,** 50
foot, feet *(pl)* [fʊt; fi:t] Fuß **I U4,** 54; Fuß *(Längenmaß: 30,48 cm)* **III U1,** 11
on foot [ɒn 'fʊt] zu Fuß **I U4,** 57
football ['fʊtbɔ:l] Fußball **I U1,** 12
American football [ə,merɪkən 'fʊtbɔ:l] Football **III U1,** 8
footstep ['fʊtstep] Schritt **III U3,** 52
for [fɔ:; fə] für **I U1,** 11; seit **II U5,** 69
for ... [fɔ:; fə] ... lang **III U2,** 32
for example [,fər‿ɪg'zɑ:mpl] zum Beispiel **III U3,** 48
for hours [fər‿'aʊəz] stundenlang **II U4,** 52
for supper [fə 'sʌpə] zum Abendessen **II U3,** 38
forecast ['fɔ:kɑ:st] Vorhersage *(Wetter)* **II U6,** 78
to **forecast** ['fɔ:kɑ:st] vorhersagen *(Wetter)* °**II U6,** 79
foreign ['fɒrɪn] fremd, ausländisch **II U1,** 10
*to **forget** [fə'get] vergessen **I U4,** 60
fork [fɔ:k] Gabel **II U4,** 50
form [fɔ:m] Formular, Form **II U5,** 64
long form ['lɒŋ fɔ:m] Langform °**I U1,** 16
fortress ['fɔ:trəs] Festung **III U2,** 31
free [fri:] frei **I U3,** 40
French [frentʃ] französisch **II U1,** 18
fresh [freʃ] frisch **II U4,** 54
Friday ['fraɪdeɪ] Freitag **I LUB,** 39
friend [frend] Freund/Freundin **I U1,** 16
friendly ['frendli] freundlich, nett °**III U3,** 50
to **frighten away** [,fraɪtn‿ə'weɪ] abschrecken **II U7,** 88
*to be **frightened** (of) [bi: 'fraɪtnd] Angst haben (vor) **II U6,** 83
frightening ['fraɪtnɪŋ] schrecklich, furchtbar, beängstigend **II U6,** 80
from [frɒm] aus, von **I U1,** 10
divorced from [dɪ'vɔ:st frəm] geschieden von **I U2,** 28
Where are you from? [,weər‿ə jə 'frɒm] Woher kommst du? **I U1,** 11
at the **front** [ət ðə 'frʌnt] im vorderen Teil, vorne **III U1,** 8
in **front of** [ɪn 'frʌnt‿əv] vor **I U3,** 49
fruit [fru:t] Obst, Frucht **II U1,** 15
frustrated [frʌs'treɪtɪd] frustriert **III U4,** 62
full (of) [fʊl] ganz, voll (von/mit) **III U1,** 11
fun [fʌn] Spaß **I U3,** 41
Have fun! [,hæv 'fʌn] Viel Spaß! **I U6,** 82
to be fun [bi: 'fʌn] Spaß machen **I U3,** 43
to have fun [,hæv 'fʌn] Spaß haben, sich amüsieren **I U6,** 82
funeral ['fju:nrəl] Beerdigung **II U6,** 76
funny ['fʌni] komisch, lustig **I LUA,** 25
furious ['fjʊəriəs] wütend **III U3,** 53
furniture ['fɜ:nɪtʃə] Möbel **I LUA,** 25
fuse-box ['fju:zbɒks] Sicherungskasten **III U3,** 53
fuss [fʌs] Aufregung, Wirbel **III U4,** 70
future ['fju:tʃə] Zukunft °**III U1,** 11

G

Gaelic ['geɪlɪk] gälisch **III U3,** 48
game [geɪm] Spiel **I U2,** 26
miming game ['maɪmɪŋ geɪm] Pantomime °**I U6,** 81
garden ['gɑ:dn] Garten **I U2,** 26
gardener ['gɑ:dnə] Gärtner/Gärtnerin **III U2,** 34
gate [geɪt] Tor, Pforte; Gate **II U7,** 90
GCSE [,dʒi:si:es'i:] Prüfung zum Abschluss der Sekundarstufe **III U4,** 67
g'day [gə'deɪ] Tag, hallo *(australische Begrüßung)* °**II U1,** 14
ladies and **gentlemen** [,leɪdiz‿n 'dʒentlmən] meine Damen und Herren °**III U2,** 33
Geography [dʒi'ɒgrəfi] Geografie, Erdkunde **II U1,** 10
German ['dʒɜ:mən] deutsch; Deutscher/Deutsche **I U1,** 17
*to **get** [get] kommen, bekommen, besorgen **I U3,** 44; holen **II U2,** 26; werden **II U6,** 83
to get hungry [get 'hʌŋgri] Hunger bekommen **II U4,** 56
to get interested in [get 'ɪntrəstɪd] sich interessieren für **III U2,** 35
to get into [get‿'ɪntə] einsteigen in *(Auto)* **I U5,** 75
to get into such a state [get‿,ɪntə 'sʌtʃ‿ə 'steɪt] durchdrehen, (sich) verrückt machen **III U4,** 70

English – German

to get lost [get 'lɒst] verloren gehen, sich verirren **I U3, 48**
to get off [get ͜ 'ɒf] aussteigen aus **I U4, 59**; wegräumen von, abräumen von **III U4, 65**
to get on [get ͜ 'ɒn] aufsteigen; einsteigen *(in Zug, Bus …)* **III U5, 86**
to get onto [get ͜ 'ɒntə] einsteigen *(Bus)* **II U1, 19**
to get out [get ͜ 'aʊt] aussteigen **I U6, 86**; entkommen **III U3, 53**
to get out of bed [ˌget ͜ aʊt ͜ əv 'bed] aufstehen **II U7, 94**
to get ready [get 'redi] sich vorbereiten **II U5, 68**
to get … right [get … 'raɪt] richtig machen **II U3, 44**
to get up [get ͜ 'ʌp] aufstehen **I U3, 44**
to get … wrong [get … 'rɒŋ] falsch machen **II U3, 44**; falsch verstehen **°II U3, 47**
ghost [gəʊst] Geist, Gespenst **I U2, 34**
girl [gɜːl] Mädchen **I U1, 16**
girlfriend ['gɜːlfrend] Freundin *(in einer Paarbeziehung)* **II U3, 39**
*to **give** [gɪv] geben, schenken **I U4, 60**
to give … a dirty look [ˌgɪv ͜ ə dɜːti 'lʊk] einen vernichtenden Blick zuwerfen **II U1, 10**
to give a talk [ˌgɪv ͜ ə 'tɔːk] einen Vortrag/eine Rede halten **°III U1, 14**
to give up [gɪv ͜ 'ʌp] aufgeben **III U2, 30**
glad [glæd] froh **III U4, 68**
glare [gleə] blendender Glanz, grelles Licht **III U4, 70**
glass [glɑːs] Glas **II U4, 50**
glee [gliː] Entzücken **III U4, 70**
glove [glʌv] Handschuh **III U1, 8**
to **glow** [gləʊ] leuchten **III U5, 88**
*to **go** [gəʊ] gehen **I U1, 19**
Go down … . ['gəʊ daʊn] Geh … entlang. **I LUC, 53**
Go left. [gəʊ 'left] Biege nach links ab. **I LUC, 52**
Go right. [gəʊ 'raɪt] Biege nach rechts ab. **I LUC, 52**
to go bananas [ˌgəʊ bə'nɑːnəz] verrückt werden, durchdrehen **II U5, 66**
to go bump [gəʊ 'bʌmp] rumsen **°II U7, 94**
to go down [gəʊ 'daʊn] hinuntergehen, entlanggehen **II U2, 30**
to go far [gəʊ 'fɑː] weit kommen, es weit bringen **III U2, 26**
to go for a walk [ˌgəʊ fər ͜ ə 'wɔːk] spazieren gehen **III U5, 88**
to go in [gəʊ 'ɪn] hineingehen **II U2, 26**
to go + -ing [gəʊ] … gehen **II U4, 52**
to go off [gəʊ ͜ 'ɒf] losgehen *(Alarm)* **II U7, 95**
to go on a diet [ˌgəʊ ͜ ɒn ə 'daɪət] eine Diät machen **II U4, 52**
to go out [gəʊ ͜ 'aʊt] (hin)ausgehen, erlöschen **II U3, 38**
to go over [gəʊ ͜ 'əʊvə] hinübergehen **II U3, 38**
to go red [gəʊ 'red] rot werden **II U1, 11**
to go up [gəʊ ͜ 'ʌp] hinaufgehen **°I U4, 61**
to go weak [gəʊ 'wiːk] schwach werden **III U4, 70**
to go (together) with ['gəʊ wɪð] passen zu **III U5, 81**
to go without [ˌgəʊ wɪ'ðaʊt] ohne … auskommen **II U4, 52**
to go wrong [gəʊ 'rɒŋ] schief gehen **II U6, 85**
goal [gəʊl] Tor, Ziel **I U1, 12**
goal post ['gəʊl pəʊst] Torpfosten **III U1, 15**
winning goal ['wɪnɪŋ gəʊl] Siegtreffer **III U4, 68**
goalkeeper ['gəʊlˌkiːpə] Torwart **III U1, 10**
goblin ['gɒblɪn] Kobold **II U7, 90**
My **God!** [maɪ 'gɒd] Mein Gott! **II U6, 82**
gold [gəʊld] Gold **II U7, 90**
good [gʊd] gut **I U1, 16**
Good grief! [gʊd 'griːf] Du liebe Zeit! **II U2, 28**
Good luck! [ˌgʊd 'lʌk] Viel Glück! **I U4, 63**
Good morning! [ˌgʊd 'mɔːnɪŋ] Guten Morgen! **I U1, 16**
I'm good at … [aɪm 'gʊd ͜ ət] ich bin gut in … **I U1, 20**
to be good with … [biː 'gʊd wɪð] gut mit … umgehen können **I U2, 34**
to have a good time [ˌhæv ͜ ə gʊd 'taɪm] sich amüsieren **I U5, 75**
goodbye [gʊd'baɪ] auf Wiedersehen **I U1, 19**
to **grab** [græb] greifen, schnappen **III U3, 53**
grammar ['græmə] Grammatik **°II U1, 16**
grammar school ['græmə ˌskuːl] Gymnasium **III U4, 67**
gramme [græm] Gramm **III U1, 11**
grandad ['grændæd] Opa **I LUA, 25**
grandma ['grændmɑː] Oma **I LUA, 25**
grass [grɑːs] Gras **III U1, 8**
grave [greɪv] Grab **III U5, 81**
gravestone ['greɪvstəʊn] Grabstein **III U5, 86**
great [greɪt] großartig, toll **I U2, 26**; groß **III U2, 26**
Greek [griːk] griechisch; Grieche/Griechin **I U2, 29**
green [griːn] grün **I LUA, 24**
greenhouse ['griːnhaʊs] Gewächshaus **II U6, 81**
grey [greɪ] grau **III U5, 89**
grid [grɪd] Gitter, Tabelle **III U4, 67**
Good **grief!** [gʊd 'griːf] Du liebe Zeit! **II U2, 28**
ground [graʊnd] Boden **II U2, 26**
group [gruːp] Gruppe **I U4, 54**
guard [gɑːd] Wache; Wächter/Wächerin **III U5, 85**
to **guard** [gɑːd] bewachen **II U7, 90**
to **guess** [ges] raten, vermuten **III U4, 66**
guest [gest] Gast **III U5, 85**
gun [gʌn] Schusswaffe **III U5, 90**
gunshot ['gʌnʃɒt] Schuss **III U5, 90**
gym [dʒɪm] Turnhalle **I U3, 40**

H

Ha! [hɑː] Ha! **°III U4, 68**
hair [heə] Haar, Haare **II U2, 28**
hairdresser ['heəˌdresə] Friseur/Friseurin **II U2, 28**
half [hɑːf] Hälfte **III U2, 32**
half [hɑːf] halb **II U6, 83**
half an hour [ˌhɑːf ͜ ən ͜ 'aʊə] eine halbe Stunde **II U2, 26**
half past (two) ['hɑːf pɑːst] halb (drei) **I U3, 40**
half-price [ˌhɑːf'praɪs] zum halben Preis **III U1, 15**
half-sister ['hɑːfˌsɪstə] Halbschwester **I U2, 26**
half-time [ˌhɑːf'taɪm] Halbzeit **III U1, 12**
hall [hɔːl] Halle, Saal, Flur **I U3, 40**
ham [hæm] Schinken **II U4, 49**
hand [hænd] Hand **II U3, 41**
Hands off! [hændz ͜ 'ɒf] Hände weg! **II U4, 50**
handbag ['hænbæg] Handtasche **III U2, 28**
*to **hang** out [hæŋ ͜ 'aʊt] sich herumtreiben **III U4, 64**

Hang on! [ˈhæŋ‿ɒn] Moment mal! Warte mal! **I U6,** 82
to **happen** [ˈhæpn] geschehen, passieren **I U6,** 86
happy [ˈhæpi] glücklich, froh **I U2,** 33
hard [hɑːd] hart, schwierig, stark **II U6,** 82
to try hard [traɪ‿ˈhɑːd] sich stark bemühen **III U4,** 70
harm [hɑːm] Schaden, Verletzung **III U4,** 70
hat [hæt] Hut **II U2,** 26
hate [heɪt] Hass **II U1,** 10
to **hate** [heɪt] hassen **II U1,** 10
*to **have** [hæv] haben **I U5,** 68
Have a nice day. [ˌhæv‿ə naɪs ˈdeɪ] Einen schönen Tag (noch). **II U4,** 55
Have fun! [ˌhæv ˈfʌn] Viel Spaß! **I U6,** 82
to have a fit [ˌhæv‿ə ˈfɪt] einen Anfall bekommen, Zustände kriegen **III U4,** 70
to have a good time [ˌhæv‿ə gʊd ˈtaɪm] sich amüsieren **I U5,** 75
to have an argument [ˌhæv‿ən‿ˈɑːgjəmənt] sich streiten **III U4,** 62
to have a party [ˌhæv‿ə ˈpɑːti] eine Party feiern **I U5,** 68
to have fun [ˌhæv ˈfʌn] Spaß haben, sich amüsieren **I U6,** 82
to have got [hæv ˈgɒt] besitzen, haben **I U2,** 30
to have supper [hæv ˈsʌpə] zu Abend essen **I U3,** 44
to have to [ˈhæv tə] müssen **II U5,** 64
he [hiː] er **I U1,** 12
head [hed] Kopf **II U3,** 36
heading [ˈhedɪŋ] Überschrift °**III U5,** 85
headphones *(pl)* [ˈhedfəʊnz] Kopfhörer **II U4,** 56
healthy [ˈhelθi] gesund **II U4,** 50
*to **hear** [hɪə] hören **I U6,** 78
heating [ˈhiːtɪŋ] Heizung **II U6,** 78
heavy [ˈhevi] schwer **II U4,** 51
height [haɪt] Höhe, Größe **III U1,** 11
helicopter [ˈhelɪˌkɒptə] Helikopter, Hubschrauber **II U6,** 83
Hello! [heˈləʊ] Hallo! **I U1,** 10
helmet [ˈhelmət] Helm **III U1,** 8
help [help] Hilfe **I U2,** 34
to **help** [help] helfen **I U2,** 34
helpful [ˈhelpfəl] hilfreich **II U5,** 71
helpless [ˈhelpləs] hilflos **III U3,** 52
helpline [ˈhelplaɪn] telefonischer Beratungsdienst, Notruf °**III U4,** 69
her [hɜː] ihr/ihre; sie **I U2,** 26
Her Majesty [hə ˈmædʒəsti] Ihre Majestät °**III U5,** 90
here [hɪə] hier **I U1,** 12
Here you are! [ˈhɪə juː‿ɑː] Bitte schön! **I U1,** 20
hero, heroes *(pl)* [ˈhɪərəʊ; ˈhɪərəʊz] Held **II U3,** 43
heroine [ˈherəʊɪn] Heldin **III U5,** 80
hey [heɪ] he °**I U1,** 16
Hi! [haɪ] Hi! **I U1,** 10
*to **hide** [haɪd] verstecken, sich verstecken **I U6,** 86
high [haɪ] hoch, groß **II U2,** 30
him [hɪm] ihn, ihm **I U4,** 60
himself [hɪmˈself] sich (selbst) **III U1,** 17
hint [hɪnt] Hinweis, Spur, Anspielung °**III U3,** 53
hip hop [ˈhɪp hɒp] Hip-Hop °**III U4,** 63
his [hɪz] sein/seine **I LUA,** 25
History [ˈhɪstəri] Geschichte **II U1,** 10
hit [hɪt] Hit **III U5,** 82
*to **hit** [hɪt] schlagen, treffen **II U3,** 36
hobby [ˈhɒbi] Hobby **I LUB,** 38
hockey [ˈhɒki] Hockey **II U1,** 16
ice hockey [ˈaɪs ˌhɒki] Eishockey **II U2,** 23
holiday(s) [ˈhɒlədeɪ(z)] Urlaub, Ferien **II U7,** 88
home [həʊm] Zuhause, Heim; nach Hause **I U1,** 11; Heimat **III U1,** 8
home-made [ˌhəʊmˈmeɪd] selbst gemacht **III U1,** 16
at home [ət ˈhəʊm] zu Hause **I U2,** 26
home plate [ˈhəʊm ˌpleɪt] Home Plate **III U1,** 14
to take home [ˌteɪk ˈhəʊm] nach Hause bringen **I U2,** 35
homework [ˈhəʊmwɜːk] Hausaufgabe/ Hausaufgaben **I U1,** 19
to **hoot** [huːt] schreien, rufen *(Eule)* **II U7,** 94
to **hope** [həʊp] hoffen **I U5,** 72
horoscope [ˈhɒrəskəʊp] Horoskop **II U6,** 80
horrible [ˈhɒrəbl] schrecklich, furchtbar **II U2,** 24
horse [hɔːs] Pferd **I LUB,** 38
hospital [ˈhɒspɪtl] Krankenhaus **II U3,** 36
host [həʊst] Gastgeber, Talkmaster **III U5,** 82
hot [hɒt] heiß **I U6,** 79
hotel [həʊˈtel] Hotel **III U5,** 84
hound [haʊnd] Jagdhund **III U5,** 82
hour [ˈaʊə] Stunde **I U2,** 34
hours [ˈaʊəz] Öffnungszeiten **I U4,** 62
for hours [fər‿ˈaʊəz] stundenlang **II U4,** 52
half an hour [ˌhɑːf‿ən‿ˈaʊə] eine halbe Stunde **II U2,** 26
house [haʊs] Haus **I LUA,** 25
how [haʊ] wie **I U1,** 11
How are you? [ˌhaʊ‿ˈɑː juː] Wie geht es dir/Ihnen/euch? **I U6,** 83
how many [haʊ ˈmeni] wie viele **I U5,** 68
How much are … ? [ˌhaʊ ˈmʌtʃ‿ɑː] Wie viel kosten … ? **I U5,** 66
How much is … ? [ˌhaʊ ˈmʌtʃ‿ɪz] Wie viel kostet … ? **I U5,** 66
How old are you? [haʊ‿ˈəʊld‿ɑː juː] Wie alt bist du? **I U1,** 11
how to … [ˈhaʊ tə] wie man … °**II U3,** 37
huge [hjuːdʒ] riesig, gewaltig **III U2,** 30
hundred [ˈhʌndrəd] hundert **II U2,** 23
hungry [ˈhʌŋgri] hungrig **II U1,** 14
to get hungry [get ˈhʌŋgri] Hunger bekommen **II U4,** 56
hunting [ˈhʌntɪŋ] Jagen **III U5,** 86
*to be in a **hurry** [biː‿ɪn‿ə ˈhʌri] es eilig haben **I U2,** 30
Hurry up! [ˌhʌri‿ˈʌp] Beeil dich! **I U2,** 30
*to **hurt** [hɜːt] verletzen, weh tun **II U3,** 40
hurt [hɜːt] verletzt **III U5,** 86

I

I [aɪ] ich **I U1,** 10
I'd like to [ˌaɪd ˈlaɪk tə] ich würde gern **II U2,** 22
I don't care. [aɪ dəʊnt ˈkeə] Es ist mir egal. **II U4,** 58
I'd rather [aɪd ˈrɑːðə] ich würde lieber **II U2,** 22
I'm having … . [aɪm ˈhævɪŋ] Ich nehme … . **II U1,** 14
I'm scared. [aɪm ˈskeəd] Ich habe Angst. **II U3,** 44
I want my … pierced. [aɪ ˈwɒnt maɪ … ˈpɪəst] Ich möchte mein … piercen lassen. **III U4,** 62
ice [aɪs] Eis **II U2,** 23
ice-cream [aɪsˈkriːm] Eis, Eiscreme **I U7,** 92
ice hockey [ˈaɪs ˌhɒki] Eishockey **II U2,** 23
ice rink [ˈaɪs rɪŋk] **II U2,** 23
icon [ˈaɪkɒn] Ikone **III U3,** 53

English – German

idea [aɪ'dɪə] Idee, Einfall **I LUB, 38**
no idea [ˌnəʊ‿aɪ'dɪə] keine Ahnung **III U3, 52**
idiot ['ɪdɪət] Idiot, Dummkopf **I U1, 21**
if [ɪf] wenn, falls; ob **II U7, 90**
to **imagine** [ɪ'mædʒɪn] sich (etwas) vorstellen **III U1, 12**
important [ɪm'pɔ:tnt] wichtig; einflussreich **II U6, 74**
impression [ɪm'preʃn] Eindruck **°II U4, 57**
in [ɪn] in, auf; herein **I U1, 10**
in all [ɪn‿'ɔ:l] insgesamt, im Ganzen **III U4, 63**
in fact [ɪn 'fækt] in der Tat, genau genommen **II U7, 94**
in front of [ɪn 'frʌnt‿əv] vor **I U3, 49**
in the end [ɪn ði:‿'end] schließlich, zum Schluss **II U6, 80**
inch [ɪnʃ] Zoll *(Längenmaß: 2,54 cm)* **III U1, 11**
independent [ˌɪndɪ'pendənt] unabhängig **III U3, 52**
Indian ['ɪndiən] indisch **II U4, 49**
industry ['ɪndəstri] Industrie **III U5, 80**
info ['ɪnfəʊ] Info **°III U4, 68**
information [ˌɪnfə'meɪʃn] Information/Informationen **I LUC, 52**
information centre [ɪnfə'meɪʃn ˌsentə] Informationszentrum **I LUC, 52**
inheritor [ɪn'herɪtə] Erbe/Erbin **III U5, 88**
inside [ɪn'saɪd] innen, drin, nach drinnen **I U5, 75**
inspector [ɪn'spektə] Inspektor **III U5, 84**
instead of [ɪn'sted‿əv] statt, anstatt **III U1, 17**
instruction [ɪn'strʌkʃn] Instruktion, Anweisung **°II U4, 59**
interested ['ɪntrəstɪd] interessiert **II U1, 18**
to get interested in [get 'ɪntrəstɪd] sich interessieren für **III U2, 35**
interesting ['ɪntrəstɪŋ] interessant **II U4, 51**
international [ˌɪntə'næʃnl] international **III U3, 45**
Internet ['ɪntənet] Internet **II U1, 14**
to surf the Internet [ˌsɜ:f ði‿'ɪntənet] im Internet surfen **II U1, 14**
interview ['ɪntəvju:] Interview **II U1, 17**
to **interview** ['ɪntəvju:] interviewen **II U1, 17**
into ['ɪntə] in; in … hinein **I U3, 44**
to get into [get‿'ɪntə] einsteigen in *(Auto)* **I U5, 75**
to run into [rʌn‿'ɪntə] laufen gegen, stoßen gegen **III U1, 17**
intonation [ˌɪntə'neɪʃn] Satzmelodie **°III U5, 86**
introduction [ˌɪntrə'dʌkʃn] Einleitung **°II U4, 55**
to **invent** [ɪn'vent] erfinden **III U4, 63**
invitation [ˌɪnvɪ'teɪʃn] Einladung **I U5, 70**
to **invite** [ɪn'vaɪt] einladen **I U5, 68**
Irish ['aɪrɪʃ] irisch **II U7, 90**
to **iron** [aɪən] bügeln **II U7, 90**
irregular [ɪ'regjələ] unregelmäßig **°II U2, 26**
island ['aɪlənd] Insel **II U6, 82**
it [ɪt] es **I U1, 12**
It said … . [ɪt 'sed] Es lautete … . **II U2, 30**
Italian [ɪ'tæliən] italienisch; Italiener/Italienerin **I U2, 29**
its [ɪts] sein/seine; ihr/ihre **III U1, 8**

J

jacket ['dʒækɪt] Jacke **I U6, 86**
jam [dʒæm] Marmelade **I U7, 94**
traffic jam ['træfɪk ˌdʒæm] Stau **III U2, 26**
January ['dʒænjuəri] Januar **I U5, 70**
jazz [dʒæz] Jazz **II U3, 45**
jealous (of) ['dʒeləs] eifersüchtig, neidisch (auf) **II U3, 45**
jersey ['dʒɜ:zi] Trikot **III U1, 12**
jewel ['dʒu:əl] Juwel **III U2, 26**
jewellery ['dʒu:əlri] Schmuck **III U5, 82**
job [dʒɒb] Arbeitsstelle, Job **II U6, 80**
on the job [ˌɒn ðə 'dʒɒb] bei der Arbeit **III U5, 82**
to **jog** [dʒɒg] joggen **II U4, 52**
joke [dʒəʊk] Witz **I U1, 20**
to **joke** [dʒəʊk] scherzen, Witze machen **I U6, 82**
journey ['dʒɜ:ni] Reise, Fahrt **II U7, 90**
judge [dʒʌdʒ] Richter, Kampfrichter **II U5, 70**
July [dʒʊ'laɪ] Juli **I U5, 70**
long **jump** ['lɒŋ ˌdʒʌmp] Weitsprung **I U7, 90**
to **jump** [dʒʌmp] springen **II U2, 30**
to jump about [ˌdʒʌmp‿ə'baʊt] herumspringen **III U4, 68**
to jump up [dʒʌmp‿'ʌp] hochspringen, aufspringen **II U6, 82**
June [dʒu:n] Juni **I U5, 70**
just [dʒʌst] nur, gerade, einfach **I U2, 30**

K

kangaroo [ˌkæŋgər'u:] Känguru **°II U3, 46**
*to **keep** [ki:p] (be)halten **II U4, 55**
Keep out! [ki:p‿'aʊt] Eintritt verboten! **I U2, 26**
key [ki:] Schlüssel **II U5, 67**
kick [kɪk] Kick **III U1, 18**
to **kick** [kɪk] treten **I U5, 74**
kid [kɪd] Kind **I U3, 44**
to **kill** [kɪl] töten; tot machen **III U1, 10**
kilo (kg) ['kɪləʊ] Kilo(gramm) **II U4, 54**
kilometre ['kɪləʊˌmi:tə; kɪ'lɒmɪtə] Kilometer **III U3, 45**
kind [kaɪnd] Art, Sorte **III U2, 34**
king [kɪŋ] König **III U2, 31**
to **kiss** [kɪs] küssen **III U5, 80**
PE **kit** [ˌpi:‿'i: kɪt] Sportzeug **II U1, 10**
kitchen ['kɪtʃɪn] Küche **I LUA, 24**
knee [ni:] Knie **II U3, 41**
knife, knives *(pl)* [naɪf; naɪvz] Messer **II U4, 50**
knight [naɪt] Ritter **II U2, 22**
knock [nɒk] Klopfen, Schlag **I U2, 34**
to **knock** [nɒk] klopfen; stoßen, schlagen **III U5, 90**
to knock out [nɒk‿'aʊt] k.o. schlagen, umhauen **III U1, 17**
*to **know** [nəʊ] wissen, kennen **I U4, 58**

L

lab(oratory) [læb; lə'bɒrətri] Labor **II U2, 23**
lad [læd] Junge **III U5, 83**
ladder ['lædə] Leiter **III U5, 85**
ladies and gentlemen [ˌleɪdiz‿n 'dʒentlmən] meine Damen und Herren **°III U2, 33**
lake [leɪk] See **III U3, 57**
lamb [læm] Lamm, Lammfleisch **II U4, 49**
land [lænd] Land **I LUB, 38**
to **land** [lænd] landen **III U3, 45**
landmark ['lændmɑ:k] Wahrzeichen, Markstein **III U2, 30**
language ['læŋgwɪdʒ] Sprache **I U2, 29**
lantern ['læntən] Laterne **I U7, 90**
laptop ['læptɒp] Laptop **I U2, 34**
large [lɑ:dʒ] groß, riesig **I U5, 66**

lassi ['lasɪ] Lassi *(Jogurtgetränk)* **II U4,** 49
last [lɑ:st] letzte/letzter/letztes **I U7,** 90
last night [lɑ:st 'naɪt] gestern Abend/Nacht **II U3,** 37
late [leɪt] spät, zu spät, verspätet **I U1,** 16
later ['leɪtə] später **I U2,** 30
to **laugh** [lɑ:f] lachen **I U5,** 74
to laugh at ['lɑ:f‿ət] auslachen, sich lustig machen über **II U3,** 36
lead [led] Blei **III U4,** 70
leader ['li:də] Führer/Führerin, Anführer/Anführerin **II U6,** 80
leaf, leaves *(pl)* [li:f; li:vz] Blatt **III U4,** 70
leaflet ['li:flət] Flugblatt, Prospekt **III U4,** 66
to **lean out** [li:n‿'aʊt] (sich) hinauslehnen **II U7,** 94
*to **learn** [lɜ:n] lernen **I U3,** 40; erfahren **III U1,** 8
at **least** [ət 'li:st] wenigstens, mindestens **I U6,** 87
*to **leave** [li:v] lassen, verlassen, abfahren **I U3,** 43; (weg)gehen **II U1,** 18
left [left] linke/linker/linkes; links **I U4,** 55
Go left. [gəʊ 'left] Biege nach links ab. **I LUC,** 52
on the left [ɒn ðə 'left] links **I U2,** 28
to turn left [tɜ:n 'left] links abbiegen **II U7,** 97
left [left] übrig **II U4,** 54
leg [leg] Bein **II U3,** 41
lemonade [ˌlemə'neɪd] Limonade **I U5,** 68
*to **lend** [lend] leihen **II U7,** 90
leprechaun ['leprəkɔ:n] Gnom, Kobold °**II U7,** 90
lesson ['lesn] Unterrichtsstunde **I U1,** 15
*to **let** [let] lassen **III U4,** 62
Let's .... [lets] Lasst uns .... **I U1,** 10
letter ['letə] Buchstabe, Brief **I U1,** 15
capital letter [ˌkæpɪtl 'letə] Großbuchstabe °**II U3,** 37
lettuce ['letɪs] Kopfsalat **II U4,** 54
level ['levl] Ebene, Niveau **III U4,** 67
*to **lie** [laɪ] liegen **III U3,** 52
to lie down [laɪ 'daʊn] (sich) hinlegen, niederlegen **III U3,** 52
life, lives *(pl)* [laɪf; laɪvz] Leben **II U3,** 42
lifeguard ['laɪfˌgɑ:d] Rettungs-schwimmer/Rettungsschwimmerin **III U3,** 46
to **lift** [lɪft] hochziehen, hochheben **III U2,** 30
light [laɪt] Licht **II U7,** 94
to **like** [laɪk] mögen, gern haben **I U3,** 44
I'd like to [ˌaɪd 'laɪk tə] ich würde gern **II U2,** 22
would like [wʊd 'laɪk] hätte gern, möchte gern **II U4,** 52
like [laɪk] wie *(Vergleich)* **I U6,** 86
line [laɪn] Zeile, Text, Linie **I U3,** 43
back line [ˌbæk'lain] Grundlinie **III U1,** 10
ocean **liner** ['əʊʃn ˌlaɪnə] Ozeandampfer **III U3,** 45
link [lɪŋk] Verbindung, Bindeglied **III U5,** 82
lion ['laɪən] Löwe **II U5,** 68
lip balm ['lɪp bɑ:m] Lippenpflegestift **II U6,** 82
list [lɪst] Liste **I U5,** 68
to **listen** ['lɪsn] zuhören, anhören **I U1,** 11
little [lɪtl] klein **I U6,** 82
to **live** [lɪv] wohnen, leben **I U3,** 45
live [laɪv] live **III U4,** 63
living room ['lɪvɪŋ rʊm] Wohnzimmer **I LUA,** 24
local ['ləʊkl] lokal, örtlich **III U2,** 28
loch [lɒx] See *(schottisch)* °**III U3,** 57
to **lock** [lɒk] abschließen **III U3,** 53
locker ['lɒkə] Schließfach **II U1,** 10
lonely ['ləʊnli] einsam **III U1,** 16
long [lɒŋ] lang **I U3,** 44
long form ['lɒŋ fɔ:m] Langform °**I U1,** 16
long jump ['lɒŋ ˌdʒʌmp] Weitsprung **I U7,** 90
as long as [əz 'lɒŋ‿əz] solange **I U7,** 94
look [lʊk] Blick, Aussehen **II U1,** 10
to give ... a dirty look [ˌgɪv‿ə dɜ:ti 'lʊk] einen vernichtenden Blick zuwerfen **II U1,** 10
to **look** [lʊk] sehen, schauen, aussehen **I U1,** 12
to look after [lʊk‿'ɑ:ftə] sich kümmern um, aufpassen auf **II U1,** 14
to look at ['lʊk‿ət] ansehen **I U6,** 82
to look for ['lʊk fə] suchen **I U6,** 81
to look out (for) [lʊk‿'aʊt] Ausschau halten (nach), suchen (nach) °**III U2,** 32
to look round [lʊk 'raʊnd] sich umsehen **II U1,** 18
to look up [lʊk‿'ʌp] (hin)aufschauen; nachschlagen **II U2,** 30
*to **lose** [lu:z] verlieren **II U4,** 52
*to be lost [bi: 'lɒst] sich verirrt haben **III U3,** 46
to get lost [get 'lɒst] verloren gehen, sich verirren **I U3,** 48
a **lot** [ə 'lɒt] viel **II U1,** 15
a lot of [ə 'lɒt‿əv] viel/viele, eine Menge **I U2,** 30
lots (of) ['lɒts‿əv] viel/viele **II U7,** 88
lots of love [ˌlɒts‿əv 'lʌv] viele Grüße *(am Briefende)* **III U4,** 68
loud [laʊd] laut **II U7,** 91
to say out loud [ˌseɪ‿aʊt 'laʊd] laut sagen °**III U4,** 67
love [lʌv] Herzliche Grüße *(am Briefende)*; Liebe **I U6,** 78
lots of love [ˌlɒts‿əv 'lʌv] viele Grüße *(am Briefende)* **III U4,** 68
to **love** [lʌv] gern mögen, lieben **I U3,** 44
luck [lʌk] Glück **I U4,** 63
bad luck [ˌbæd 'lʌk] Pech **I U4,** 63
Good luck! [ˌgʊd 'lʌk] Viel Glück! **I U4,** 63
lucky ['lʌki] glücklich **I U1,** 16
you're lucky [ˌjʊə 'lʌki] du hast Glück **I U1,** 16
luggage ['lʌgɪdʒ] Gepäck **II U7,** 90
lunch [lʌntʃ] Mittagessen **I U1,** 18
lunchtime ['lʌntʃtaɪm] Mittag, Mittagszeit **I U1,** 19

M

machine [mə'ʃi:n] Maschine, Apparat **III U4,** 66
vending machine ['vendɪŋ məˌʃi:n] Warenautomat **III U4,** 66
mad [mæd] verrückt; wütend **II U1,** 18
magazine [mægə'zi:n] Zeitschrift, Magazin **I U2,** 33
main [meɪn] Haupt- **II U4,** 49
Her **Majesty** [hə 'mædʒəsti] Ihre Majestät °**III U5,** 90
*to **make** [meɪk] machen, tun **I U1,** 11
to make it ['meɪk‿ɪt] es schaffen **III U4,** 68
to make sure [meɪk 'ʃʊə] sichergehen **II U6,** 82
to make up [meɪk‿'ʌp] erfinden, sich ausdenken **I U4,** 62

English – German

make-up ['meɪkʌp] Make-up, Schminke **I U7,** 90
man, men *(pl)* [mæn; men] Mann **I U4,** 62
manager ['mænɪdʒə] Manager/Managerin **I U2,** 26
adverb of **manner** [ˌædvɜ:b‿əv 'mænə] Adverb der Art und Weise °**II U7,** 90
many ['meni] viele **I U5,** 68
how many [haʊ 'meni] wie viele **I U5,** 68
map [mæp] Stadtplan, Landkarte **I LUC,** 52
mind map ['maɪnd mæp] Wörternetz *(eine Art Schaubild)* °**III U1,** 18
March [mɑ:tʃ] März **I U5,** 70
mark [mɑ:k] Fleck **I U2,** 30; Note *(in der Schule)* **II U3,** 44
to **mark** [mɑ:k] markieren °**II U2,** 29
market ['mɑ:kɪt] Markt **II U2,** 22
married to ['mærid tə] verheiratet mit **I U2,** 28
to **marry** ['mæri] heiraten **III U2,** 31
match [mætʃ] Spiel, Wettkampf **II U2,** 24
to **match** [mætʃ] passen zu; zuordnen, zusammenfügen **III U3,** 50
to match up ['mætʃ‿ʌp] zusammenfügen °**II U4,** 52
Maths [mæθs] Mathematik **II U1,** 10
What's the **matter**? [ˌwɒts ðə 'mætə] Was ist los? **III U5,** 88
***may** [meɪ] kann/könnte(n) vielleicht **II U4,** 55
May [meɪ] Mai **I U5,** 70
maybe ['meɪbi] vielleicht **I U7,** 96
me [mi:] mich, mir **I LUB,** 38
meal [mi:l] Mahlzeit **II U4,** 52
*to **mean** [mi:n] bedeuten, meinen **I U4,** 55
meaning ['mi:nɪŋ] Bedeutung **III U2,** 33
measurement ['meʒəmənt] Maß, Maßeinheit °**III U3,** 55
meat [mi:t] Fleisch **III U3,** 50
media *(pl)* ['mi:diə] Medien °**II U5,** 62
medium ['mi:diəm] mittel **I U5,** 66
*to **meet** [mi:t] treffen, sich treffen **I U3,** 45
meeting ['mi:tɪŋ] Treffen, Besprechung **II U1,** 12
menagerie [mə'nædʒri] Menagerie **III U2,** 31
menu ['menju:] Speisekarte, Menü **II U1,** 14
Meow! [mi:'aʊ] Miau! °**I U2,** 35
mess [mes] Durcheinander **III U2,** 35
message ['mesɪdʒ] Nachricht **II U3,** 38
text message ['tekst ˌmesɪdʒ] SMS **I U6,** 80
metre ['mi:tə] Meter **III U3,** 48
mice *(pl)* [maɪs] Mäuse **I U3,** 45
microphone ['maɪkrəfəʊn] Mikrofon **II U5,** 71
middle ['mɪdl] Mitte; Mittel- **III U4,** 64
midnight ['mɪdnaɪt] Mitternacht **II U6,** 78
mile [maɪl] Meile *(brit. Längenmaß)* **II U6,** 74
milk [mɪlk] Milch **I U5,** 68
milkman, milkmen *(pl)* ['mɪlkmən; 'mɪlkmen] Milchmann **III U2,** 34
millennium [mɪ'leniəm] Jahrtausend **III U2,** 30
million ['mɪlɪən] Million **II U2,** 23
to **mime** [maɪm] pantomimisch darstellen °**I U6,** 81
miming game ['maɪmɪŋ geɪm] Pantomime °**I U6,** 81
mind [maɪnd] Geist, Verstand **III U5,** 83
He had something on his mind. [maɪnd] Ihn beschäftigte etwas. **III U5,** 83
mind map ['maɪnd mæp] Wörternetz *(eine Art Schaubild)* °**III U1,** 18
to change your mind [ˌtʃeɪndʒ jə 'maɪnd] deine Meinung ändern **III U1,** 17
mineral ['mɪnərəl] Mineral- **II U4,** 49
minute ['mɪnɪt] Minute **I U4,** 64
mirror ['mɪrə] Spiegel **III U4,** 67
to **miss** [mɪs] vermissen, fehlen; verpassen **II U6,** 76
to miss a turn [ˌmɪs‿ə 'tɜ:n] einmal aussetzen °**II U6,** 79
Miss [mɪs] Frau *(Anrede)* **I U7,** 94
missing ['mɪsɪŋ] fehlend °**I U4,** 64
to be missing [bi: 'mɪsɪŋ] fehlen **III U1,** 14
mistake [mɪ'steɪk] Fehler **III U5,** 86
mixed bag ['mɪkst bæg] Vermischtes °**III U1,** 21
to **moan** [məʊn] (sich) (be)klagen **III U1,** 16
mobile ['məʊbaɪl] Handy, Mobiltelefon **I U1,** 11
modal auxiliary verb [ˌməʊdl‿ɔ:g'zɪljəri 'vɜ:b] modales Hilfsverb °**III U3,** 46
model ['mɒdl] Model, Modell **III U2,** 29
moment ['məʊmənt] Moment, Augenblick **I U7,** 90
at the moment [æt ðə 'məʊmənt] im Augenblick, momentan **I U7,** 90
monastery ['mɒnəstri] Kloster **III U2,** 31
Monday ['mʌndeɪ] Montag **I LUB,** 39
on Mondays [ɒn 'mʌndeɪz] montags **I LUB,** 39
money ['mʌni] Geld **I U5,** 67
pocket money ['pɒkɪt ˌmʌni] Taschengeld **II U2,** 22
month [mʌnθ] Monat **I U5,** 70
moon [mu:n] Mond **II U7,** 94
moor [mɔ:] Hochmoor **II U6,** 74
more [mɔ:] mehr **I U2,** 29
morning ['mɔ:nɪŋ] Morgen, Vormittag **I U1,** 16
Good morning! ['gʊd 'mɔ:nɪŋ] Guten Morgen! **I U1,** 16
in the morning [ˌɪn ðə 'mɔ:nɪŋ] morgens, am Morgen, vormittags **I U3,** 47
the next morning [ðə ˌnekst 'mɔ:nɪŋ] am nächsten Morgen **II U1,** 18
most [məʊst] das meiste, die meisten **I U3,** 44
mother ['mʌðə] Mutter **III U3,** 52
mouse [maʊs] Maus **I U1,** 10
mouth [maʊθ] Mund **II U3,** 41
to **move** [mu:v] (sich) bewegen; umziehen **II U6,** 78
MP3 [ˌempi:'θri:] MP3 **II U5,** 62
MP3 player [ˌempi:'θri: ˌpleɪə] MP3-Player **II U5,** 62
Mr ['mɪstə] Herr *(Anrede)* **I U1,** 12
Mrs ['mɪsɪz] Frau *(Anrede)* **I U1,** 12
much [mʌtʃ] viel **I U5,** 66
How much are … ? [ˌhaʊ 'mʌtʃ‿ɑ:] Wie viel kosten … ? **I U5,** 66
How much is … ? [ˌhaʊ 'mʌtʃ‿ɪz] Wie viel kostet … ? **I U5,** 66
mum [mʌm] Mama, Mutti **I LUA,** 25
to **murder** ['mɜ:də] ermorden **III U5,** 88
museum [mju:'zi:əm] Museum **I LUC,** 52
music ['mju:zɪk] Musik **I U2,** 34
musical ['mju:zɪkl] Musical **III U5,** 80
***must** [mʌst] müssen **I U7,** 94
my [maɪ] mein/meine **I U1,** 10
My God! [maɪ 'gɒd] Mein Gott! **II U6,** 82
My name is … . [maɪ 'neɪm‿ɪz] Ich heiße … . **I U1,** 10
mystery ['mɪstri] Geheimnis, Rätsel **III U3,** 49
myth [mɪθ] Mythos **III U5,** 81

N

name [neɪm] Name **I U1,** 10
My name is … . [maɪ 'neɪm‿ɪz] Ich heiße … . **I U1,** 10
What's your name? [ˌwɒts jə 'neɪm] Wie heißt du? **I U1,** 11
national ['næʃnl] national **II U6,** 82; landesweit **III U1,** 10
near [nɪə] in der Nähe von, nahe **I LUC,** 53
nearly ['nɪəli] fast, annähernd **III U1,** 16
to **need** [ni:d] brauchen, benötigen, müssen **II U1,** 21
negative ['negətɪv] negativ, verneint °**III U5,** 82
negative statement [ˌnegətɪv 'steɪtmənt] Verneinung °**III U5,** 82
neighbour ['neɪbə] Nachbar/Nachbarin **II U7,** 90
nephew ['nefju:] Neffe **III U5,** 88
nervous ['nɜ:vəs] nervös, aufgeregt **II U5,** 71
net [net] Netz **III U1,** 10
never ['nevə] nie, niemals **I U3,** 44
new [nju:] neu **I U1,** 10
news *(sg.)* [nju:z] Nachricht(en), Neuigkeit(en) **III U3,** 48
newsagent ['nju:sˌeɪdʒənt] Zeitschriftenhändler/ Zeitschriftenhändlerin **I LUC,** 52
newspaper ['nju:sˌpeɪpə] Zeitung **III U2,** 28
next [nekst] nächste/nächster/ nächstes **I U5,** 69; als Nächstes °**II U1,** 19
next door [ˌnekst 'dɔ:] nebenan **III U1,** 16
next to ['nekst tə] neben **I U2,** 28
the next morning [ðə ˌnekst 'mɔ:nɪŋ] am nächsten Morgen **II U1,** 18
nice [naɪs] nett **I U1,** 12; schön **II U4,** 54
night [naɪt] Nacht **I U3,** 44
at night [ət 'naɪt] nachts **II U3,** 47
last night [lɑ:st 'naɪt] gestern Abend/Nacht **II U3,** 37
night nurse ['naɪt nɜ:s] Nachtschwester **I U3,** 47
no [nəʊ] nein, nicht; kein/keine **I U1,** 12
no idea [ˌnəʊ‿aɪ'dɪə] keine Ahnung **III U3,** 52
no one ['nəʊwʌn] niemand **II U2,** 30
nobody ['nəʊbədi] niemand **III U5,** 85
noise [nɔɪz] Geräusch, Lärm **I U2,** 35
none [nʌn] keiner/keine **II U7,** 88
normal ['nɔ:ml] normal **I U3,** 44
north [nɔ:θ] Norden **I U4,** 55
nose [nəʊz] Nase **II U3,** 41
not [nɒt] nicht **I U1,** 16
not … yet [jet] noch nicht **II U5,** 66
not … either [ˌnɒt 'aɪðə] auch nicht **III U1,** 17
not even [nɒt‿'i:vn] nicht einmal **III U4,** 64
note [nəʊt] Notiz, Anmerkung **II U1,** 11
sick note ['sɪk ˌnəʊt] Krankmeldung **II U2,** 28
to take notes [teɪk 'nəʊts] sich Notizen machen °**II U4,** 55
nothing ['nʌθɪŋ] nichts **II U4,** 50
notice ['nəʊtɪs] Anschlag, Notiz **III U4,** 66
notice board ['nəʊtɪs bɔ:d] schwarzes Brett **III U4,** 66
to **notice** ['nəʊtɪs] bemerken **III U3,** 48
noun [naʊn] Nomen °**III U1,** 18
November [nəʊ'vembə] November **I U5,** 70
now [naʊ] jetzt, nun **I U1,** 20
right now [ˌraɪt 'naʊ] jetzt gleich, in diesem Augenblick **I U7,** 92
nowhere ['nəʊweə] nirgendwo, nirgendwohin **III U4,** 64
number ['nʌmbə] Nummer, Zahl **I U1,** 11
phone number ['fəʊn ˌnʌmbə] Telefonnummer **I U1,** 11
nurse [nɜ:s] Krankenschwester, Krankenpfleger **I U3,** 47
night nurse ['naɪt nɜ:s] Nachtschwester **I U3,** 47
*to be **nuts** about [bi: ˌnʌts‿ə'baʊt] verrückt nach … sein **II U1,** 18

O

observatory [əb'zɜ:vətri] Observatorium, Sternwarte **I U5,** 73
ocean ['əʊʃn] Ozean **III U3,** 45
ocean liner ['əʊʃn ˌlaɪnə] Ozeandampfer **III U3,** 45
October [ɒk'təʊbə] Oktober **I U5,** 70
odd one out [ɒd wʌn‿'aʊt] das nicht dazu passende (Wort) **II U5,** 72
of [ɒv; əv] von **I U2,** 26
of course [əv 'kɔ:s] natürlich, selbstverständlich **I U1,** 19
off [ɒf] herunter, ab, weg von **II U3,** 36
to get off [get‿'ɒf] aussteigen aus **I U4,** 59; wegräumen von, abräumen von **III U4,** 65
to send off [send‿'ɒf] vom Platz verweisen **III U1,** 15
to take off [teɪk‿'ɒf] ausziehen **III U3,** 52
to **offer** ['ɒfə] anbieten °**II U6,** 77
office ['ɒfɪs] Büro **II U2,** 31
post office ['pəʊst‿ˌɒfɪs] Postamt **III U2,** 35
officer ['ɒfɪsə] Beamter/Beamtin **III U3,** 45
official [ə'fɪʃl] offiziell **III U3,** 48
often ['ɒfn] oft **I U3,** 44
oh [əʊ] oh °**I U1,** 12
OK [əʊ'keɪ] o.k. **I U1,** 12
is OK with us [ɪz‿əʊ'keɪ wɪð‿ʌs] ist uns recht **I U6,** 78
We're OK. [ˌwɪər‿əʊ'keɪ] Es geht uns gut. **I U6,** 83
old [əʊld] alt **I U1,** 11
How old are you? [haʊ‿'əʊld‿ɑ: ju:] Wie alt bist du? **I U1,** 11
on [ɒn] auf, an **I U1,** 14
on foot [ɒn 'fʊt] zu Fuß **I U4,** 57
on Mondays [ɒn 'mʌndeɪz] montags **I LUB,** 39
on record [ɒn 'rekɔ:d] verzeichnet, dokumentiert **III U3,** 46
on the air [ˌɒn ði‿'eə] auf Sendung **II U4,** 55
on the bus [ˌɒn ðə 'bʌs] im Bus **II U1,** 18
on the job [ˌɒn ðə 'dʒɒb] bei der Arbeit **III U5,** 82
on the left [ɒn ðə 'left] links **I U2,** 28
on the right [ɒn ðə 'raɪt] rechts **I U2,** 28
to be on [bi:‿'ɒn] an der Reihe sein; im Gange sein, laufen **II U5,** 70; an sein, brennen *(Licht)* **II U7,** 94
once [wʌnts] einmal, einst **II U3,** 36
at once [ət 'wʌnts] sofort, plötzlich **II U7,** 94
one day [wʌn 'deɪ] eines Tages **II U3,** 36
one(s) [wʌn(z)] *(Platzhalter für ein Nomen)* **III U2,** 29
only ['əʊnli] nur, bloß, erst **I U2,** 26; einzige/einziger/einziges **III U5,** 88
only child ['əʊnli ˌtʃaɪld] Einzelkind **I U2,** 26
onto ['ɒntu:; 'ɒntə] (auf …) hinauf, auf **II U1,** 19
Oops! [u:ps] Hoppla! Huch! °**I U1,** 20
to **open** ['əʊpn] öffnen, aufmachen **I U1,** 19; sich öffnen, aufgehen **III U5,** 86
open ['əʊpn] offen; geöffnet **II U2,** 23

opinion [ə'pɪnjən] Meinung °**II U4, 51**
opposite ['ɒpəzɪt] gegenüber °**II U4, 49**
or [ɔ:] oder **I U1, 11**
orange ['ɒrɪndʒ] Orange **II U4, 54**
order ['ɔ:də] Reihenfolge, Ordnung °**I U1, 21**
to **order** ['ɔ:də] bestellen **II U4, 49**
to **organize** ['ɔ:gənaɪz] organisieren **I U7, 90**
organizer ['ɔ:gənaɪzə] Organisator/Organisatorin, Veranstalter/Veranstalterin **III U4, 63**
other ['ʌðə] andere/anderer/anderes **I U7, 91**
each other [ˌi:tʃ‿'ʌðə] sich gegenseitig **II U1, 19**
our ['aʊə] unser/unsere **I U2, 26**
out [aʊt] heraus, draußen, außerhalb **I U3, 42**
Keep out! [ki:p‿'aʊt] Eintritt verboten! **I U2, 26**
out and about ['aʊt‿nd‿ə'baʊt] unterwegs °**I U4, 54**
out of ['aʊt‿əv] aus … heraus **I U3, 49**
to get out [get‿'aʊt] aussteigen **I U6, 86**; entkommen **III U3, 53**
to hang out [hæŋ‿'aʊt] sich herumtreiben **III U4, 64**
to put out [pʊt‿'aʊt] hinausstellen **III U4, 65**
to sort out [sɔ:t‿'aʊt] klären, regeln *(ein Problem)* **I U2, 30**
to take out [teɪk‿'aʊt] herausnehmen **I U3, 42**
outside [aʊt'saɪd] außerhalb, draußen, nach draußen **I U2, 30**
oven ['ʌvn] Backofen **I U3, 42**
over ['əʊvə] über **I U2, 26**; vorbei, vorüber **II U5, 70**
all over [ˌɔ:l‿'əʊvə] überall **III U3, 49**
over ['əʊvə] über **I U2, 26**
over there [ˌəʊvə 'ðeə] da drüben **I U5, 66**
to come over [kʌm‿'əʊvə] herüberkommen **I U2, 27**
overheard [ˌəʊvə'hɜ:d] zufällig mitgehört °**III U1, 15**
barn **owl** ['bɑ:n‿əʊl] Schleiereule **II U7, 94**
own [əʊn] eigener/eigene/eigenes **II U6, 76**
owner ['əʊnə] Besitzer/Besitzerin **II U5, 71**

P

to **pack** [pæk] packen **I U6, 80**
packet ['pækɪt] Päckchen, Paket **I U5, 68**
page [peɪdʒ] Seite **I U1, 19**
paint [peɪnt] Farbe **II U3, 40**
to **paint** [peɪnt] malen, anmalen **I U7, 90**
painting ['peɪntɪŋ] Gemälde **III U5, 89**
pair [peə] Paar °**I U1, 22**
palace ['pælɪs] Palast **III U2, 26**
to **panic** ['pænɪk] sich aufregen **II U5, 70**
panther ['pæntθə] Panter **II U2, 25**
paradise ['pærəˌdaɪs] Paradies **III U3, 46**
parents ['peərənts] Eltern **I U2, 26**
park [pɑ:k] Park **I U3, 40**
part [pɑ:t] Teil **II U3, 47**; Rolle **II U5, 70**
to take part in [teɪk 'pɑ:t‿ɪn] teilnehmen an **III U4, 63**
partner ['pɑ:tnə] Partner/Partnerin **I U1, 15**
party ['pɑ:ti] Party, Feier **I U5, 68**
to have a party [ˌhæv‿ə 'pɑ:ti] eine Party feiern **I U5, 68**
to **pass** [pɑ:s] weitergeben, herüberreichen **II U1, 18**; vorbeigehen an **III U5, 85**
passenger ['pæsndʒə] Passagier/Passagierin, Beifahrer/Beifahrerin **III U3, 45**
passport ['pɑ:spɔ:t] Pass, Reisepass **III U3, 50**
passports *(pl)* ['pɑ:spɔ:ts] Passkontrolle **III U3, 50**
past [pɑ:st] Vergangenheit **II U1, 13**
past perfect [ˌpɑ:st 'pɜ:fɪkt] Plusquamperfekt °**III U2, 31**
simple past [ˌsɪmpl 'pɑ:st] einfache Vergangenheit °**III U2, 28**
past [pɑ:st] vorbei, vorüber **I U7, 97**; nach *(Uhrzeit)* **II U1, 12**
half past (two) ['hɑ:f pɑ:st] halb (drei) **I U3, 40**
path [pɑ:θ] Pfad, Weg **II U4, 56**
patient ['peɪʃnt] Patient/Patientin **III U5, 82**
pause [pɔ:z] Pause °**III U5, 86**
to **pay** [peɪ] (be)zahlen **III U5, 85**
PC [ˌpi:'si:] PC **II U5, 63**
PC [ˌpi:'si:] Polizeibeamter/Polizeibeamtin °**III U5, 83**
pea [pi:] Erbse **II U4, 54**
peace [pi:s] Friede **II U7, 88**
pear [peə] Birne **II U4, 54**
pen [pen] Füller **I U1, 14**
pence *(pl)* [pents] Pence *(Währung)* **I U5, 67**
pencil ['pensl] Bleistift **I U1, 14**
pencil case ['pensl ˌkeɪs] Mäppchen **I U1, 14**
penknife, penknives *(pl)* ['pennaɪf; 'pennaɪvz] Taschenmesser **I U6, 84**
people ['pi:pl] Leute, Menschen **I U2, 29**
per [pɜ:] pro **III U5, 80**
past **perfect** [ˌpɑ:st 'pɜ:fɪkt] Plusquamperfekt °**III U2, 31**
to **perform** [pə'fɔ:m] aufführen, auftreten **III U4, 63**
performance [pə'fɔ:məns] Aufführung, Vorstellung **III U4, 63**
perhaps [pə'hæps] vielleicht **III U5, 83**
person ['pɜ:sn] Person **II U3, 42**
personal ['pɜ:snl] persönlich °**III U1, 11**
pet [pet] Haustier, Liebling **III U5, 82**
phone [fəʊn] Telefon **I U1, 11**
phone box ['fəʊn ˌbɒks] Telefonzelle **III U3, 50**
phone call ['fəʊn ˌkɔ:l] (Telefon-)Anruf °**II U4, 57**
phone number ['fəʊn ˌnʌmbə] Telefonnummer **I U1, 11**
to **phone** [fəʊn] anrufen, telefonieren **I U2, 33**
phonetic [fə'netɪk] phonetisch °**III U5, 86**
photo ['fəʊtəʊ] Foto, Fotografie **II U5, 64**
phrase [freɪz] Redewendung, Ausdruck °**I U1, 19**
physical ['fɪzɪkl] physisch, körperlich **II U1, 10**
Physical Education (PE) [ˌfɪzɪkl‿edʒʊ'keɪʃn] Sport *(Schulfach)* **II U1, 10**
to **pick** [pɪk] pflücken, auswählen **I U6, 78**
to pick up [pɪk‿'ʌp] aufheben, abholen **II U1, 18**
pickpocket ['pɪkˌpɒkɪt] Taschendieb/Taschendiebin **III U2, 28**
picture ['pɪktʃə] Bild **I U1, 14**
to take pictures [teɪk 'pɪktʃəz] fotografieren, Fotos machen **II U5, 62**
piece [pi:s] Stück **III U2, 30**
I want my … **pierced.** [aɪ 'wɒnt maɪ … 'pɪəst] Ich möchte mein … piercen lassen. **III U4, 62**
pig [pɪg] Schwein **I U6, 82**
piggy bank ['pɪgi bæŋk] Sparschwein **II U2, 23**
pink [pɪŋk] pink, rosa **I LUA, 24**

pipe [paɪp] Pfeife **III U5,** 84
pitch [pɪtʃ] Spielfeld **III U1,** 10
pitcher ['pɪtʃə] Werfer/Werferin **III U1,** 14
pizza ['piːtsə] Pizza **I U5,** 68
place [pleɪs] Platz, Stelle, Ort **I U2,** 26
change of place [ˌtʃeɪndʒ‿əv 'pleɪs] Ortswechsel °**III U4,** 65
to take place [teɪk 'pleɪs] stattfinden **III U4,** 63
plan [plæn] Plan **II U5,** 66
to **plan** [plæn] planen **II U4,** 52
plane [pleɪn] Flugzeug **II U2,** 23
plant [plɑːnt] Pflanze **II U6,** 74
plate [pleɪt] Teller **II U4,** 50
home plate ['həʊm ˌpleɪt] Home Plate **III U1,** 14
platform ['plætfɔːm] Plattform, Tribüne, Bahnsteig **III U2,** 30
play [pleɪ] Theaterstück, Spiel **I U7,** 90
to **play** [pleɪ] spielen **I U1,** 14
player ['pleɪə] Spieler/Spielerin, Mitspieler/Mitspielerin **III U1,** 8
CD player [ˌsiː'diː ˌpleɪə] CD-Player **II U4,** 56
DVD player [ˌdiːviː'diː 'pleɪə] DVD-Player **II U5,** 62
playground ['pleɪgraʊnd] Schulhof, Spielplatz **I U1,** 18
please [pliːz] bitte **I U1,** 19
*to be **pleased** with [biː 'pliːzd wɪð] zufrieden sein mit **I U6,** 87
plural ['plʊərəl] Plural, Mehrzahl **I U6,** 88
p.m. [ˌpiː'em] nachmittags *(Uhrzeit)* **III U3,** 47
pocket ['pɒkɪt] Hosen-/Jackentasche **II U2,** 22
pocket money ['pɒkɪt ˌmʌni] Taschengeld **II U2,** 22
poem ['pəʊɪm] Gedicht **III U4,** 63
poet ['pəʊɪt] Dichter/Dichterin, Poet/Poetin **III U4,** 63
poetry ['pəʊətri] Lyrik **III U4,** 63
poetry slam ['pəʊətri ˌslæm] Poetry Slam *(Gedichtwettbewerb)* **III U4,** 63
point [pɔɪnt] Punkt **II U4,** 53
to **point** [pɔɪnt] zeigen °**I U1,** 18
police [pə'liːs] Polizei **I U6,** 87
policeman, policemen *(pl)* [pə'liːsmən; pə'liːsmen] Polizist **II U2,** 31
Polish ['pəʊlɪʃ] polnisch **I U2,** 29
polite [pə'laɪt] höflich **II U3,** 39
pollution [pə'luːʃn] (Umwelt-)Verschmutzung **III U2,** 34
pony ['pəʊni] Pony **II U6,** 74

pool [puːl] Schwimmbecken **III U1,** 12
swimming pool ['swɪmɪŋ ˌpuːl] Schwimmbecken; Schwimmbad **III U1,** 12
poor [pɔː; pʊə] arm **III U5,** 88
popular ['pɒpjələ] populär, beliebt **II U2,** 23
pork [pɔːk] Schweinefleisch **II U4,** 49
port [pɔːt] Hafen **III U3,** 45
position [pə'zɪʃn] Position **III U3,** 49
possible ['pɒsəbl] möglich **III U4,** 67
post [pəʊst] Pfosten, Mast **III U1,** 15
goal post ['gəʊl pəʊst] Torpfosten **III U1,** 15
post office ['pəʊst‿ɒfɪs] Postamt **III U2,** 35
postcard ['pəʊstkɑːd] Postkarte **I U6,** 78
poster ['pəʊstə] Poster, Plakat **I U1,** 11
pot [pɒt] Topf **II U7,** 90
potato, potatoes *(pl)* [pə'teɪtəʊ] Kartoffel **II U4,** 54
couch potato ['kaʊtʃ pəˌteɪtəʊ] Stubenhocker **III U1,** 12
pound (£) [paʊnd] Pfund *(Währung)* **I U5,** 66
pound (lb) [paʊnd] Pfund *(Gewicht)* **II U4,** 52
powder ['paʊdə] Puder, Pulver **III U5,** 89
power ['paʊə] Kraft, Stärke, Macht **II U6,** 74
practice ['præktɪs] Training **III U1,** 16
to **practise** ['præktɪs] üben, proben, praktizieren **II U5,** 66
to **prepare** [prɪ'peə] vorbereiten, zubereiten °**III U1,** 14
preposition [ˌprepə'zɪʃn] Präposition °**III U1,** 19
present ['preznt] Geschenk **I U5,** 69; Gegenwart, Präsens °**II U2,** 26
present progressive [ˌpreznt prə'gresɪv] Verlaufsform des Präsens/der Gegenwart °**III U1,** 12
to **present** [prɪ'zent] präsentieren °**II U6,** 79
presentation [ˌprezn'teɪʃn] Präsentation °**III U1,** 14
president ['prezɪdnt] Präsident/Präsidentin °**II U3,** 42
to **press** [pres] drücken, pressen **II U7,** 95
to **pretend** [prɪ'tend] vorgeben, tun als ob °**III U1,** 13
price [praɪs] Preis **I U7,** 95
half-price [ˌhɑːf'praɪs] zum halben Preis **III U1,** 15

primary school ['praɪməri ˌskuːl] Grundschule **III U4,** 67
prince [prɪns] Prinz **III U2,** 29
to **print** [prɪnt] drucken **II U5,** 64
prison ['prɪzn] Gefängnis **III U2,** 31
private ['praɪvɪt] privat **III U4,** 67
probably ['prɒbəbli] wahrscheinlich **II U7,** 88
problem ['prɒbləm] Problem, Schwierigkeit **I U1,** 20
profile ['prəʊfaɪl] Steckbrief; Profil, Porträt °**III U1,** 11
programme ['prəʊgræm] Programm, Sendung **III U5,** 80
project ['prɒdʒekt] Projekt **I U2,** 34
promise ['prɒmɪs] Versprechen °**II U6,** 77
to **promise** ['prɒmɪs] versprechen **II U6,** 77
pronoun ['prəʊnaʊn] Pronomen °**III U4,** 67
reflexive pronoun [rɪ'fleksɪv ˌprəʊnaʊn] Reflexivpronomen °**III U4,** 67
relative pronoun [ˌrelətɪv 'preʊnaʊn] Relativpronomen °**III U3,** 48
to **protect** [prə'tekt] (be)schützen °**III U2,** 32
proud of ['praʊd‿əv] stolz auf **III U4,** 68
pudding ['pʊdɪŋ] Pudding; Nachtisch **II U4,** 49
to **pull** [pʊl] ziehen **II U4,** 57
punk [pʌŋk] Punk **III U2,** 35
pupil ['pjuːpl] Schüler/Schülerin **I U1,** 10
purple ['pɜːpl] lila, violett **I LUA,** 24
to **push** [pʊʃ] stoßen, schieben, drücken **II U3,** 36
*to **put** [pʊt] setzen, stellen, legen **I U3,** 42
to put down [pʊt 'daʊn] auflegen *(Telefon)*; hinlegen, hinstellen °**II U7,** 89
to put in [pʊt‿'ɪn] einsetzen **II U7,** 95; einschieben **III U4,** 68
to put on [pʊt‿'ɒn] anziehen, aufsetzen; einsetzen **I U6,** 81; auftragen *(Make-up)* **II U5,** 71
to put out [pʊt‿'aʊt] ausmachen; löschen **III U2,** 32; hinausstellen **III U4,** 65
to put up [pʊt‿'ʌp] aufstellen, aufbauen **I U6,** 84
puzzle ['pʌzl] Rätsel, Puzzle °**I U1,** 15
crossword (puzzle) ['krɒswɜːd 'pʌzl] Kreuzworträtsel °**I U5,** 71

English – German

Q

quarter ['kwɔːtə] Viertel **III U2,** 32
quarter past ['kwɔːtə pɑːst] Viertel nach **I U3,** 42
quarter to ['kwɔːtə tə] Viertel vor **I U3,** 42
queen [kwiːn] Königin **II U5,** 62
question ['kwestʃn] Frage **I U2,** 31
questionnaire [ˌkwestʃə'neə] Fragebogen °**II U4,** 53
queue [kjuː] (Warte-)Schlange **III U2,** 26
quick [kwɪk] schnell **I U6,** 86
quiet [kwaɪət] Ruhe, Stille **II U7,** 88
quiet ['kwaɪət] ruhig, still, leise **I U6,** 78
quiz [kwɪz] Quiz, Rätsel °**I U1,** 13

R

race [reɪs] Wettlauf, Rennen **I U7,** 92
to run a race [ˌrʌn‿ə 'reɪs] einen Wettlauf machen **I U7,** 92
racing ['reɪsɪŋ] Renn- **III U1,** 12
radio ['reɪdiəʊ] Radio **I U2,** 33
radio show ['reɪdiəʊ ˌʃəʊ] Radiosendung **I U2,** 33
rain [reɪn] Regen **II U6,** 78
to **rain** [reɪn] regnen **I U4,** 62
rainy ['reɪni] regnerisch, verregnet **I U6,** 79
rap [ræp] Rap **I U1,** 15
to **rap** [ræp] rappen **I U3,** 40
I'd **rather** [aɪd 'rɑːðə] ich würde lieber **II U2,** 22
to **reach** [riːtʃ] erreichen **II U6,** 78
*to **read** [riːd] lesen **I LUB,** 38
reader ['riːdə] Leser/Leserin °**III U5,** 91
reading ['riːdɪŋ] Lesen °**III U5,** 86
ready ['redi] fertig, bereit **II U4,** 50
to get ready [get 'redi] sich vorbereiten **II U5,** 68
real [rɪəl] echt, richtig, wirklich **II U3,** 38
reality show [ri'æləti ˌʃəʊ] Realityshow **III U5,** 80
really ['rɪəli] wirklich **I U2,** 34
reason ['riːzn] Grund °**III U4,** 62
*to **rebuild** [ˌriː'bɪld] wieder aufbauen; wiederherstellen **III U3,** 49
reception [rɪ'sepʃn] Rezeption, Empfang **III U5,** 84
receptionist [rɪ'sepʃnɪst] Empfangschef/Empfangschefin **III U5,** 85
recipe ['resɪpiː] Rezept **I U7,** 94
on **record** [ɒn 'rekɔːd] verzeichnet, dokumentiert **III U3,** 46
to **record** [rɪ'kɔːd] aufnehmen, aufzeichnen **II U5,** 63
red [red] rot **I LUA,** 24
to go red [gəʊ 'red] rot werden **II U1,** 11
referee [ˌrefr'iː] Schiedsrichter/Schiedsrichterin **III U1,** 12
reflexive pronoun [rɪ'fleksɪv ˌprəʊnaʊn] Reflexivpronomen °**III U4,** 67
registration [ˌredʒɪ'streɪʃn] **II U1,** 10
regular ['regjələ] Stammkunde/Stammkundin **III U2,** 35
regular ['regjələ] regelmäßig °**III U1,** 10
to **rehearse** [rɪ'hɜːs] proben *(ein Theaterstück)* **I U7,** 90
relative pronoun [ˌrelətɪv 'preʊnaʊn] Relativpronomen °**III U3,** 48
to **relax** [rɪ'læks] sich entspannen, sich ausruhen °**III U5,** 86
religious [rɪ'lɪdʒəs] religiös **II U1,** 12
Religious Education (RE) [rɪˌlɪdʒəs‿edʒʊ'keɪʃn] Religionsunterricht **II U1,** 12
to **relive** [ˌriː'lɪv] wieder erleben **III U2,** 26
to **remember** [rɪ'membə] sich erinnern (an), sich merken **I U3,** 49
to **remind** [rɪ'maɪnd] erinnern °**III U3,** 56
to **replace** [rɪ'pleɪs] ersetzen **III U3,** 49
report [rɪ'pɔːt] Bericht, Meldung °**III U5,** 91
to **report** [rɪ'pɔːt] berichten °**II U4,** 51
reporter [rɪ'pɔːtə] Reporter/Reporterin **I U7,** 92
rescue ['reskjuː] Rettung **III U5,** 82
to **rescue** ['reskjuː] retten **II U6,** 83
respect [rɪ'spekt] Respekt **III U4,** 63
response [rɪ'spɒns] Reaktion, Antwort **III U4,** 63
rest [rest] Rest **III U1,** 17
to **rest** [rest] sich entspannen, sich ausruhen **III U3,** 52
restaurant ['restrɒnt] Restaurant **II U4,** 55
revision [rɪ'vɪʒn] Wiederholung °**I U2,** 32
*to **rewrite** [ˌriː'raɪt] noch einmal schreiben °**II U4,** 58
rhyme [raɪm] Reim °**I LUA,** 25
rhyming ['raɪmɪŋ] (sich) reimend °**II U4,** 58
rice [raɪs] Reis **II U4,** 49
rich [rɪtʃ] reich **III U2,** 29
*to **ride** [raɪd] fahren, reiten **I LUB,** 38
rider [raɪdə] Fahrer/Fahrerin, Reiter/Reiterin **III U1,** 18
right [raɪt] richtig, korrekt **I U1,** 13; rechter/rechte/rechtes; rechts **I U4,** 55
Go right. [gəʊ 'raɪt] Biege nach rechts ab. **I LUC,** 52
on the right [ɒn ðə 'raɪt] rechts **I U2,** 28
right away [raɪt‿ə'weɪ] sofort, gleich **II U4,** 57
right now [ˌraɪt 'naʊ] jetzt gleich, in diesem Augenblick **I U7,** 92
to be right [biː 'raɪt] Recht haben **II U4,** 56
to get … right [get … 'raɪt] richtig machen **II U3,** 44
to turn right [tɜːn 'raɪt] rechts abbiegen **II U7,** 97
rim [rɪm] Radkranz **III U2,** 30
ring [rɪŋ] Ring **III U3,** 47
rubber ring [ˌrʌbə 'rɪŋ] Schwimmreifen **III U3,** 47
*to **ring** [rɪŋ] klingeln **I U5,** 75; anrufen **III U3,** 51
The bell rings. [ðə 'bel rɪŋz] Es klingelt. **II U4,** 50
ice **rink** ['aɪs rɪŋk] **II U2,** 23
*to **rise** [raɪz] steigen, wachsen, zunehmen **II U6,** 78
river ['rɪvə] Fluss **I LUC,** 52
road [rəʊd] Straße, Landstraße **I LUC,** 52
to **rob** [rɒb] rauben, ausrauben **III U2,** 28
role [rəʊl] Rolle **II U1,** 10
roof [ruːf] Dach **I U2,** 26
room [ruːm; rʊm] Zimmer, Raum; Platz **I U1,** 16
dining room ['daɪnɪŋ rʊm] Esszimmer, Speisesaal **I LUA,** 24
living room ['lɪvɪŋ rʊm] Wohnzimmer **I LUA,** 24
round [raʊnd] Runde **III U2,** 34
route [ruːt; raʊt] Route °**III U2,** 28
row [rəʊ] Reihe **III U1,** 15
royal ['rɔɪəl] königlich **III U2,** 26
RSVP [ˌɑːr‿es viː 'piː] um Antwort wird gebeten °**I U5,** 70
rubber ['rʌbə] Radiergummi **I U1,** 14; Gummi; Kautschuk **III U3,** 47
rubber boots *(pl)* [ˌrʌbə 'buːts] Gummistiefel **II U6,** 74
rubber ring [ˌrʌbə 'rɪŋ] Schwimmreifen **III U3,** 47
rubbish ['rʌbɪʃ] Abfall, Abfälle, Müll **I U6,** 84; Unsinn **II U7,** 94

rucksack ['rʌksæk] Rucksack **III U2,** 28
rugby ['rʌgbi] Rugby **III U1,** 8
rugby boot ['rʌgbi bu:t] Rugbyschuh, Stollenschuh **III U1,** 8
rule [ru:l] Regel, Vorschrift **I U3,** 43
ruler ['ru:lə] Lineal **I U1,** 14
run [rʌn] Lauf **II U4,** 57; Run, Runde **III U1,** 9
*to **run** [rʌn] rennen, laufen **I U3,** 48
to run a race [ˌrʌn‿ə 'reɪs] einen Wettlauf machen **I U7,** 92
to run away [rʌn‿ə'weɪ] wegrennen **I U3,** 48
to run into [rʌn‿'ɪntə] laufen gegen, stoßen gegen **III U1,** 17
to run upstairs [ˌrʌn‿ʌp'steəz] die Treppe hinaufrennen **III U3,** 53
runaway ['rʌnəˌweɪ] Ausreißer/Ausreißerin **III U5,** 83
runner ['rʌnə] Läufer/Läuferin **I U7,** 92
Russian ['rʌʃn] russisch; Russe/Russin **I U2,** 29

S

sad [sæd] traurig, bedauerlich **II U1,** 19
safe [seɪf] Safe, Tresor **III U5,** 84
safe [seɪf] sicher **III U3,** 46
to **sail** [seɪl] segeln, fahren *(Schiff)* **III U3,** 45
salad ['sæləd] Salat **II U4,** 49
same [seɪm] derselbe/dieselbe/dasselbe °**II U1,** 11
the same [seɪm] derselbe/dieselbe/dasselbe; gleich **III U1,** 18
sand [sænd] Sand **III U1,** 10
sandwich ['sænwɪdʒ] Sandwich, belegtes Brot **I U1,** 14
sandy ['sændɪ] sandig **III U3,** 46
Saturday ['sætədeɪ] Samstag **I U2,** 34
sauerkraut ['saʊəkraʊt] Sauerkraut **III U2,** 34
sausage ['sɒsɪdʒ] Wurst, Würstchen **II U4,** 49
to **save** [seɪv] retten; sparen **II U6,** 80
*to **say** [seɪ] sagen, sprechen **I U1,** 11
It said .... [ɪt 'sed] Es lautete .... **II U2,** 30
What does it say? [ˌwɒt dʌz‿ɪt 'seɪ] Was steht da? **II U3,** 44
to say out loud [ˌseɪ‿aʊt 'laʊd] laut sagen °**III U4,** 67
to **scare** ['skeə] erschrecken, einen Schrecken einjagen, Angst machen **III U4,** 67
scared [skeəd] verängstigt **I U2,** 35
I'm scared. [aɪm 'skeəd] Ich habe Angst. **II U3,** 44
scary ['skeəri] unheimlich, gruselig **II U7,** 95
scene [si:n] Szene, Schauplatz **III U5,** 80
school [sku:l] Schule **I U1,** 10
school bag ['sku:l bæg] Schultasche, Schulranzen **I U1,** 14
comprehensive school [kɒmprɪ'hensɪv ˌsku:l] Gesamtschule **III U4,** 66
grammar school ['græmə ˌsku:l] Gymnasium **III U4,** 67
primary school ['praɪməri ˌsku:l] Grundschule **III U4,** 67
Science ['saɪəns] Wissenschaft, Naturwissenschaft **II U1,** 10
science fiction [ˌsaɪəns 'fɪkʃn] Sciencefiction **III U5,** 80
scientist ['saɪəntɪst] Wissenschaftler/Wissenschaftlerin **III U5,** 89
scone [skɒn] Scone *(Gebäck)* **I U7,** 94
score [skɔ:] Punktestand, Spielstand **III U1,** 12
to **score** [skɔ:] punkten, ein Tor schießen **III U1,** 9
Scottish ['skɒtɪʃ] schottisch **II U3,** 36
screen [skri:n] Bildschirm, Leinwand **III U5,** 80
screen shot ['skri:n ˌʃɒt] Screenshot **III U5,** 80
script [skrɪpt] Drehbuch **III U5,** 81
sea [si:] Meer **II U7,** 88
seaside ['si:saɪd] Küste, Meeresküste **III U5,** 82
season ['si:zn] Jahreszeit, Saison **I U6,** 79
seat [si:t] Sitz, Sitzplatz **II U2,** 23
second ['seknd] Sekunde **I U2,** 30
secret ['si:krət] geheim °**III U4,** 68; Geheimnis **III U5,** 87
secretary ['sekrətri] Sekretär/Sekretärin **III U1,** 12
*to **see** [si:] sehen **I U2,** 33; besuchen **II U1,** 19
See you! ['si: jə] Bis dann! Bis .... **I U5,** 70
to see a doctor [si: ə 'dɒktə] zum Arzt gehen **II U4,** 52
you see [jʊ 'si:] weißt du **III U1,** 12
seldom ['seldəm] selten **III U5,** 80
*to **sell** [sel] verkaufen **I U7,** 90
*to **send** [send] schicken **I U6,** 80
to send in [send‿'ɪn] einschicken **II U5,** 64
to send off [send‿'ɒf] vom Platz verweisen **III U1,** 15
sense [sens] Sinn, Bedeutung **III U5,** 88
sensible ['sensɪbl] vernünftig **III U3,** 46
sentence ['sentənts] Satz °**I U1,** 13
September [sep'tembə] September **I U5,** 70
series, series *(pl)* ['sɪəri:z] Serie **III U5,** 82
servant ['sɜ:vnt] Diener/Dienerin **III U5,** 88
service ['sɜ:vɪs] Service, Dienst **II U6,** 83
session ['seʃn] Veranstaltung **III U4,** 66
*to **set** [set] stellen, einstellen **II U7,** 90
to set off [set‿'ɒf] auslösen *(Alarm)* **II U7,** 95
to set the table [ˌset ðə 'teɪbl] den Tisch decken **II U4,** 50
*to **shake** [ʃeɪk] schütteln, zittern **III U4,** 70
***shall** [ʃæl; ʃəl] sollen **III U4,** 65
to **share** [ʃeə] teilen **III U5,** 90
she [ʃi:] sie **I U1,** 12
shed [ʃed] Schuppen **I U2,** 26
sheep, sheep *(pl)* [ʃi:p] Schaf **I U6,** 78
shelf, shelves *(pl)* [ʃelf; ʃelvz] Regal, Regalbrett **I U2,** 30
ship [ʃɪp] Schiff **I U4,** 54
shirt [ʃɜ:t] Hemd **I U3,** 44
shocked [ʃɒkt] geschockt, schockiert **III U5,** 86
shoe [ʃu:] Schuh **I U1,** 12
shop [ʃɒp] Laden, Geschäft **I U2,** 26
shop assistant ['ʃɒp‿əˌsɪstnt] Verkäufer/Verkäuferin **II U5,** 67
sports shop ['spɔ:ts ʃɒp] Sportgeschäft **I U5,** 66
shopping ['ʃɒpɪŋ] Einkaufen, Einkauf **I U5,** 66
short [ʃɔ:t] kurz **I U4,** 55
shorts *(pl)* [ʃɔ:ts] Shorts, kurze Hose **II U1,** 10
shot [ʃɒt] Schuss, Schlag **III U5,** 80
screen shot ['skri:n ˌʃɒt] Screenshot **III U5,** 80
***should** [ʃʊd] sollte/sollten **II U4,** 52
to **shout** [ʃaʊt] schreien, rufen **I U1,** 15
show [ʃəʊ] Show, Sendung, Schau **I U2,** 33
radio show ['reɪdiəʊ ˌʃəʊ] Radiosendung **I U2,** 33
reality show [ri'æləti ˌʃəʊ] Realityshow **III U5,** 80
talk show ['tɔ:k ˌʃəʊ] Talkshow **III U5,** 80
*to **show** [ʃəʊ] zeigen **I U4,** 65

English – German

shower [ˈʃaʊə] Regenguss; Dusche **II U6, 74**
to **shuffle** [ˈʃʌfl] mischen **°II U6, 79**
shy [ʃaɪ] schüchtern **III U4, 66**
sick [sɪk] krank **II U3, 46**
sick note [ˈsɪk ˌnəʊt] Krankmeldung **II U2, 28**
to feel sick [fiːl ˈsɪk] Übelkeit verspüren **II U3, 46**
side [saɪd] Seite **III U3, 52**
sign [saɪn] Schild, Zeichen **I U2, 26**
to **sign** [saɪn] unterschreiben **II U5, 66**
signal [ˈsɪgnl] Signal **II U2, 26**; Zeichen **III U1, 10**
to **signal** [ˈsɪgnl] signalisieren, ein Zeichen geben **III U3, 48**
silly [ˈsɪli] dumm; Dummkopf **II U1, 11**
similar [ˈsɪmɪlə] ähnlich **°III U4, 62**
simple [ˈsɪmpl] einfach, simpel **°III U4, 68**
simple past [ˌsɪmpl ˈpɑːst] einfache Vergangenheit **°III U2, 28**
since [sɪnts] seit, seitdem **III U2, 34**
*to **sing** [sɪŋ] singen **I U2, 33**
singer [ˈsɪŋə] Sänger/Sängerin **II U1, 14**
Sir [sɜː] Sir *(Anrede für einen Ritter)* **°III U5, 87**
sis [sɪs] Schwesterchen **°III U4, 65**
sister [ˈsɪstə] Schwester **I LUA, 25**
half-sister [ˈhɑːfˌsɪstə] Halbschwester **I U2, 26**
*to **sit** [sɪt] sitzen **I U3, 48**
to sit down [sɪt ˈdaʊn] sich setzen, sich hinsetzen **I U1, 19**
to sit with [ˈsɪt wɪθ] sich setzen zu **I U5, 74**
sitcom [ˈsɪtkɒm] Situationskomödie **III U5, 82**
situation [ˌsɪtjuˈeɪʃn] Situation **°III U3, 50**
size [saɪz] Größe, Kleidergröße **III U5, 90**
to **skate** [skeɪt] Inlineskates fahren, skaten **I LUB, 38**
skateboard [ˈskeɪtbɔːd] Skateboard **I U4, 54**
skates *(pl)* [skeɪts] Inlineskates **I U4, 54**
skill [skɪl] Fertigkeit; Geschick **°II U1, 11**
to **skim** [skɪm] überfliegen **°III U2, 32**
skimming [ˈskɪmɪŋ] Überfliegen **°III U2, 32**
skirt [skɜːt] Rock **II U1, 10**
sky [skaɪ] Himmel **II U7, 94**
poetry **slam** [ˈpəʊətri ˌslæm] Poetry Slam *(Gedichtwettbewerb)* **III U4, 63**
slamster [ˈslæmstə] Teilnehmer/Teilnehmerin an einem Poetry Slam **III U4, 63**
*to **sleep** [sliːp] schlafen **I U3, 46**
sleeping bag [ˈsliːpɪŋ ˌbæg] Schlafsack **I U6, 84**
sleepy [ˈsliːpi] schläfrig, verschlafen **II U7, 94**
slow [sləʊ] langsam **I U2, 34**
small [smɔːl] klein **I U2, 26**
smell [smel] Geruch, Gestank **III U5, 88**
*to **smell** [smel] riechen **III U2, 32**
to **smile** [smaɪl] lächeln **I U3, 43**
smoke [sməʊk] Rauch **III U2, 32**
to **smoke** [sməʊk] rauchen **III U5, 84**
smuggler [ˈsmʌglə] Schmuggler/Schmugglerin **III U3, 45**
snack [snæk] Imbiss, Snack **II U4, 55**
snapshot [ˈsnæpʃɒt] Schnappschuss **°III U1, 13**
to **sniff** [snɪf] schnüffeln, schnuppern **III U5, 90**
snow [snəʊ] Schnee **II U6, 79**
to **snow** [snəʊ] schneien **II U6, 79**
snowy [ˈsnəʊi] verschneit **I U6, 79**
so [səʊ] so, also, deshalb **I U2, 26**
soap [səʊp] Seifenoper, Seife **I U7, 97**
docu soap [ˈdɒkju ˌsəʊp] Dokusoap **III U5, 80**
sofa [ˈsəʊfə] Sofa, Couch **I LUA, 25**
soft [sɒft] leise; weich, sanft **II U7, 94**
to **solve** [sɒlv] lösen **III U5, 88**
some [sʌm] einige; etwas **II U1, 13**
somebody [ˈsʌmbədi] jemand **III U5, 83**
someone [ˈsʌmwʌn] jemand **II U5, 70**
someone else [ˌsʌmwʌn‿ˈels] jemand anderes **°III U1, 13**
something [ˈsʌmθɪŋ] etwas **II U4, 56**
sometimes [ˈsʌmtaɪmz] manchmal **I U3, 44**
somewhere [ˈsʌmweə] irgendwo **II U4, 57**
son [sʌn] Sohn **III U5, 86**
song [sɒŋ] Lied **I U2, 33**
soon [suːn] bald **I U6, 78**
as soon as [əz ˈsuːn‿əz] sobald **III U4, 66**
sorry [ˈsɒri] Tut mir Leid. Entschuldigung. **I U1, 12**
I'm sorry about .... [aɪm ˈsɒri‿əˌbaʊt] Es tut mir Leid wegen .... **°II U3, 39**
to feel sorry for [fiːl ˈsɒri] Mitleid haben mit, bedauern **III U1, 16**
sort [sɔːt] Art, Sorte **°III U4, 68**
to **sort** [sɔːt] sortieren **°I U1, 21**
to sort out [sɔːt‿ˈaʊt] klären, regeln *(ein Problem)* **I U2, 30**
sound [saʊnd] Ton, Geräusch, Klang **I U6, 85**
to **sound** [saʊnd] klingen, sich anhören **III U5, 88**
soup [suːp] Suppe **II U1, 15**
sour [ˈsaʊə] sauer **II U4, 49**
south [saʊθ] Süden **I U4, 55**
southwest [ˌsaʊθˈwest] Südwesten **II U6, 78**
souvenir [ˌsuːvəˈnɪə] Souvenir, Andenken **III U2, 29**
spaghetti [spəˈgeti] Spaghetti **II U1, 13**
spark [spɑːk] Funke(n) **III U2, 32**
*to **speak** [spiːk] sprechen **I U4, 62**
It's ... speaking. [ɪts ... ˈspiːkɪŋ] Hier spricht .... **III U4, 69**
speaker [ˈspiːkə] Sprecher/Sprecherin **III U3, 45**
special [ˈspeʃl] besonders, speziell **III U4, 63**
spectacular [spekˈtækjələ] spektakulär **III U2, 26**
speech bubble [ˈspiːtʃ ˌbʌbl] Sprechblase **°III U3, 47**
to **spell** [spel] buchstabieren **I U4, 60**
spelling [ˈspelɪŋ] Orthographie, Rechtschreibung **°II U3, 43**
*to **spend** [spend] verbringen; ausgeben **I U6, 83**
spicy [ˈspaɪsi] würzig, pikant **II U4, 49**
sponge [spʌndʒ] Schwamm **I U7, 90**
spooky [ˈspuːki] unheimlich **I U2, 35**
spoon [spuːn] Löffel **II U4, 50**
sport [spɔːt] Sport **I U1, 12**
sports day [ˈspɔːts deɪ] Sportfest **I U7, 90**
sports field [ˈspɔːts fiːld] Sportplatz **I U7, 92**
sports shop [ˈspɔːts ʃɒp] Sportgeschäft **I U5, 66**
to do sports [duː ˈspɔːts] Sport treiben **I U7, 92**
sporty [ˈspɔːti] sportlich **III U2, 29**
spring [sprɪŋ] Frühling **I U6, 78**
stadium [ˈsteɪdiəm] Stadion **III U1, 8**
stairs *(pl)* [steəz] Treppe **III U3, 52**
stall [stɔːl] Stand, Bude **I U7, 90**
stall holder [ˈstɔːl ˌhəʊldə] Standbesitzer/Standbesitzerin **II U4, 54**
white elephant stall [ˌwaɪt ˈelɪfənt stɔːl] Trödelstand **I U7, 96**
stamp [stæmp] Briefmarke **III U3, 47**
stand [stænd] Tribüne **III U1, 9**
*to **stand** [stænd] stehen **III U3, 49**
star [stɑː] Star, Stern **III U1, 12**

word star ['wɜ:d stɑ:] Wortstern °**I U1,** 22
start [stɑ:t] Anfang, Beginn, Start **II U1,** 10
to **start** [stɑ:t] anfangen, starten **I U3,** 44
starter ['stɑ:tə] Vorspeise **II U4,** 49
state [steɪt] Staat, Land; staatlich; Zustand **III U4,** 67
to get into such a state [get‿ɪntə 'sʌtʃ‿ə 'steɪt] durchdrehen, (sich) verrückt machen **III U4,** 70
statement ['steɪtmənt] Aussage, Behauptung °**III U5,** 82
negative statement [ˌnegətɪv 'steɪtmənt] Verneinung °**III U5,** 82
station ['steɪʃn] Wache, Station, Bahnhof **I U6,** 87
to **stay** [steɪ] bleiben **I U4,** 60
to stay out [steɪ‿'aʊt] wegbleiben **III U4,** 69
to stay with ['steɪ wɪð] wohnen bei **I U6,** 78
*to **steal** [sti:l] stehlen **II U4,** 57
steel band [ˌsti:l 'bænd] Steelband *(Band, deren Instrumente aus leeren Ölfässern bestehen)* **III U4,** 64
stepdad ['stepdæd] Stiefvater **I U2,** 26
stick [stɪk] Stock **II U2,** 26
still [stɪl] noch, immer noch **II U1,** 21
stomach ['stʌmək] Magen, Bauch **II U3,** 41
stone [stəʊn] Stein **II U6,** 82; *brit. Gewichtseinheit* (= 6,35 kg) **III U1,** 11
stop [stɒp] Halt, Haltestelle **I LUC,** 52
bus stop ['bʌs ˌstɒp] Bushaltestelle **I LUC,** 52
to **stop** [stɒp] aufhören (mit), anhalten **I U3,** 42
to stop + -ing [stɒp] aufhören etw. zu tun **II U4,** 52
store [stɔ:] Kaufhaus, Geschäft, Laden **II U2,** 30
department store [dɪ'pɑ:tmənt stɔ:] Kaufhaus **I LUC,** 52
store detective ['stɔ: dɪˌtektɪv] Kaufhausdetektiv/ Kaufhausdetektivin **II U2,** 30
storm [stɔ:m] Sturm **II U6,** 81
stormy ['stɔ:mi] stürmisch **II U6,** 78
story ['stɔ:ri] Geschichte, Erzählung **I U1,** 21
detective story [dɪ'tektɪv ˌstɔ:ri] Krimi **III U5,** 80
strange [streɪndʒ] merkwürdig, seltsam **I U2,** 35
stranger ['streɪndʒə] Fremder/Fremde **III U3,** 47
straw [strɔ:] Stroh **III U2,** 32
stream [stri:m] Bach **II U6,** 82
street [stri:t] Straße **I LUC,** 52
to **stress** [stres] betonen °**III U5,** 86
strict [strɪkt] streng, strikt **III U4,** 62
stroke [strəʊk] Schlag(anfall) **III U4,** 70
strong [strɒŋ] stark **III U5,** 86
studio ['stju:diəʊ] Studio **I U2,** 33
to **study** ['stʌdi] studieren; lernen **II U6,** 74
stupid ['stju:pɪd] dumm, blöd **I U2,** 35
style [staɪl] Stil; Frisur **III U2,** 35
subject ['sʌbdʒɪkt] Schulfach; Thema **II U1,** 13
to **substitute** ['sʌbstɪtju:t] auswechseln, ersetzen **III U1,** 17
success [sək'ses] Erfolg **III U5,** 80
such [sʌtʃ] solch **III U4,** 70
sudden ['sʌdn] plötzlich **III U4,** 70
suddenly ['sʌdnli] plötzlich, auf einmal **I U2,** 35
to **suggest** [sə'dʒest] vorschlagen **III U4,** 69
suggestion [sə'dʒestʃn] Vorschlag, Anregung **III U4,** 65
summary ['sʌmri] Zusammenfassung °**III U3,** 49
summer ['sʌmə] Sommer **I U6,** 79
summer fair ['sʌmə ˌfeə] Sommerfest **I U7,** 90
sun [sʌn] Sonne **III U3,** 46
Sunday ['sʌndeɪ] Sonntag **I LUB,** 39
sunny ['sʌni] sonnig **I U6,** 79
suntan ['sʌntæn] Sonnenbräune **II U1,** 14
superlative [su:'pɜ:lətɪv] Superlativ **II U4,** 50
supermarket ['su:pəˌmɑ:kɪt] Supermarkt **I LUC,** 52
supper ['sʌpə] Abendessen **I U3,** 44
for supper [fə 'sʌpə] zum Abendessen **II U3,** 38
to have supper [hæv 'sʌpə] zu Abend essen **I U3,** 44
sure [ʃʊə] sicher **I U1,** 16
to make sure [meɪk 'ʃʊə] sichergehen **II U6,** 82
to **surf** [sɜ:f] (wind)surfen **II U1,** 14
to surf the Internet [ˌsɜ:f ði‿'ɪntənet] im Internet surfen **II U1,** 14
surfing ['sɜ:fɪŋ] Wellenreiten, Surfen **II U1,** 14
surprised [sə'praɪzd] überrascht, erstaunt **II U1,** 18
surprising [sə'praɪzɪŋ] überraschend **II U7,** 96
survey ['sɜ:veɪ] Umfrage **I U4,** 56
survival [sə'vaɪvl] Überleben **III U4,** 66
suspect ['sʌspekt] Verdächtigter/ Verdächtigte **III U5,** 84
swap [swɒp] Tausch **II U7,** 88
to **swap** [swɒp] tauschen **I LUB,** 38
sweatshirt ['swetʃɜ:t] Sweatshirt **II U1,** 10
sweet [swi:t] Bonbon, Süßigkeit **II U4,** 53
sweet [swi:t] süß **I LUA,** 24
to **swerve** [swɜ:v] ausweichen, ausscheren **III U4,** 70
*to **swim** [swɪm] schwimmen **I LUB,** 38
swimmer ['swɪmə] Schwimmer/ Schwimmerin **III U3,** 45
swimming pool ['swɪmɪŋ ˌpu:l] Schwimmbecken; Schwimmbad **III U1,** 12
swimsuit ['swɪmsu:t] Badeanzug **III U1,** 12
symbol ['sɪmbl] Symbol °**II U6,** 78
system ['sɪstəm] System **III U4,** 67

T

table ['teɪbl] Tisch **I U1,** 18
table-tennis ['teɪblˌtenɪs] Tischtennis **II U7,** 88
to set the table [ˌset ðə 'teɪbl] den Tisch decken **II U4,** 50
*to **take** [teɪk] nehmen, mitnehmen, wegnehmen, bringen **I U3,** 42; dauern, *(Zeit)* brauchen **III U3,** 45
to take a deep breath [ˌteɪk‿ə 'di:p ˌbreθ] tief Luft holen °**III U5,** 86
to take home [ˌteɪk 'həʊm] nach Hause bringen **I U2,** 35
to take notes [teɪk 'nəʊts] sich Notizen machen °**II U4,** 55
to take off [teɪk‿'ɒf] wegbringen, fortschaffen **III U1,** 17; ausziehen **III U3,** 52
to take out [teɪk‿'aʊt] herausnehmen **I U3,** 42
to take part in [teɪk 'pɑ:t‿ɪn] teilnehmen an **III U4,** 63
to take pictures [teɪk 'pɪktʃəz] fotografieren, Fotos machen **II U5,** 62
to take place [teɪk 'pleɪs] stattfinden **III U4,** 63
to take your chance [ˌteɪk jɔ: 'tʃɑ:ns] etwas wagen, etwas riskieren **III U3,** 53

English – German

takeaway ['teɪkəweɪ] Restaurant mit Straßenverkauf; Essen zum Mitnehmen **II U4,** 48
talk [tɔ:k] Vortrag, Rede **III U1,** 14
talk show ['tɔ:k ˌʃəʊ] Talkshow **III U5,** 80
to give a talk [ˌgɪv‿ə 'tɔ:k] einen Vortrag/eine Rede halten °**III U1,** 14
to **talk** [tɔ:k] sprechen, reden **I U1,** 10
to talk to ['tɔ:k tə] sprechen mit, reden mit **II U2,** 28
tall [tɔ:l] groß, hoch **II U3,** 36
to **taste** [teɪst] schmecken **I U7,** 94
tasty ['teɪsti] schmackhaft **II U4,** 50
Pizza is tastier. ['pi:tsə ɪz ˌteɪstɪə] Pizza schmeckt besser. **II U4,** 50
tattoo [tæt'u:] Tätowierung **III U4,** 62
taxi ['tæksi] Taxi **III U2,** 34
tea [ti:] Tee, Abendessen **I U7,** 94
afternoon tea [ˌɑ:ftənu:n 'ti:] Nachmittagstee **I U7,** 94
*to **teach** [ti:tʃ] unterrichten, lehren **I LUB,** 38
teacher ['ti:tʃə] Lehrer/Lehrerin **I U1,** 12
team [ti:m] Mannschaft, Team **II U2,** 23
technical ['teknɪkl] technisch °**II U7,** 96
Technology [tek'nɒlədʒi] Technik **II U1,** 10
teen [ti:n] Jugendlicher/Jugendliche **II U6,** 80
teenage ['ti:neɪdʒ] jugendlich **III U4,** 63
teenager ['ti:nˌeɪdʒə] Teenager, Jugendliche/Jugendlicher **III U2,** 28
*to **tell** [tel] erzählen, sagen **I U3,** 49
temperature ['temprətʃə] Temperatur **II U6,** 78
tennis ['tenɪs] Tennis **III U1,** 12
table-tennis ['teɪblˌtenɪs] Tischtennis **II U7,** 88
tense [tens] Zeit, Zeitform *(grammatisch)* °**III U2,** 39
tent [tent] Zelt **I U6,** 84
term [tɜ:m] Trimester *(Einteilung des englischen Schuljahrs)* °**II U1,** 10
terrible ['terəbl] schrecklich, furchtbar **I U2,** 35
test [test] Test, Klassenarbeit **II U3,** 44
to **test** [test] testen, prüfen °**I U2,** 31
text [tekst] Text °**I U2,** 27
text message ['tekst ˌmesɪdʒ] SMS **I U6,** 80
to **text** [tekst] Textnachricht (SMS) schicken, simsen **III U4,** 64
than [ðæn] als **I U4,** 55
to **thank** [θæŋk] danken **I U4,** 60
thank you ['θæŋk ju:] danke **I U1,** 12
thanks [θæŋks] danke **II U2,** 26
thanks to ['θæŋks tə] dank (dir/ihnen), wegen **III U2,** 28
that [ðæt] das, jenes **I U1,** 12
that (bad) ['ðæt bæd] so (schlimm) **II U2,** 24
that evening [ˌdæt‿'i:vnɪŋ] an diesem Abend **II U1,** 19
That's what I call .... [ˌðæts wɒt‿'aɪ ˌkɔ:l] Das nenne ich .... **II U1,** 14
that's why ['ðæts ˌwaɪ] deshalb **II U1,** 18
the [ðə; ði] der/die/das **I U1,** 11
their [ðeə] ihr/ihre **I U2,** 30
them [ðem] sie, ihnen **I U4,** 60
then [ðen] dann **I LUB,** 38
there [ðeə] dort, da **I U2,** 26
over there [ˌəʊvə 'ðeə] da drüben **I U5,** 66
there are [ðeər‿'ɑ:] da sind, es gibt **I U2,** 32
there is [ðeər‿'ɪz] da ist, es gibt **I U2,** 32
these [ði:z] diese, diese hier **I U6,** 84
they [ðeɪ] sie *(Mehrzahl)* **I U1,** 16; man **III U1,** 8
thick [θɪk] dick *(nicht für Personen)*; dumm **III U1,** 16
thing [θɪŋ] Sache, Ding **I U3,** 40
*to **think** [θɪŋk] denken **I U3,** 49; glauben **II U4,** 50
to think about ['θɪŋk‿əˌbaʊt] nachdenken über, denken an °**II U7,** 95
to think of ['θɪŋk‿əv] denken an °**II U3,** 39
third [θɜ:d] dritte/dritter/drittes **I U5,** 70
this [ðɪs] dies; diese/dieser/dieses **I U1,** 12
this evening [ðɪs 'i:vnɪŋ] heute Abend **III U3,** 52
those [ðəʊz] diese dort, jene **I U6,** 84
thousand ['θaʊznd] tausend **II U2,** 23
thriller ['θrɪlə] Thriller **III U5,** 80
through [θru:] durch **II U4,** 57
throw [θrəʊ] Wurf **III U1,** 18
*to **throw** [θrəʊ] werfen **I U3,** 49
Thursday ['θɜ:zdeɪ] Donnerstag **I LUB,** 39
to **tick** [tɪk] abhaken °**II U5,** 65
ticket ['tɪkɪt] Ticket, Fahrschein, Eintrittskarte **I U7,** 90
tiger ['taɪgə] Tiger **I U2,** 26
time [taɪm] Zeit **I U2,** 30; Mal **II U1,** 18
to have a good time [ˌhæv‿ə gʊd 'taɪm] sich amüsieren **I U5,** 75
What's the time, please? [ˌwɔts ðə 'taɪm ˌpli:z] Wie viel Uhr ist es, bitte?; Wie spät ist es, bitte? **I U3,** 42
to **time** [taɪm] stoppen, die Zeit nehmen **I U7,** 92
timeline ['taɪmlaɪn] Zeitleiste °**I U4,** 63
timetable ['taɪmteɪbl] Stundenplan, Fahrplan **II U1,** 12
tin [tɪn] Dose, Büchse **III U2,** 34
tiny ['taɪni] winzig **I LUA,** 25
tip [tɪp] Tipp **II U4,** 52
tired ['taɪəd] müde **II U3,** 38
dog-tired [ˌdɒg'taɪəd] hundemüde **I U3,** 49
title ['taɪtl] Titel, Überschrift **II U3,** 42
to [tʊ; tə] zu, nach, bis **I U1,** 19
today [tə'deɪ] heute **I U2,** 29
toe [təʊ] Zeh **II U3,** 41
together [tə'geðə] zusammen, miteinander **I LUB,** 38
toilet ['tɔɪlɪt] Toilette **I U1,** 19
tomato, tomatoes *(pl)* [tə'mɑ:təʊ; tə'mɑ:təʊz] Tomate **I U5,** 68
tomorrow [tə'mɒrəʊ] morgen **II U1,** 18
ton [tʌn] Tonne *(Gewicht)* **III U3,** 49
tongue [tʌŋ] Zunge **III U4,** 62
tongue twister ['tʌŋ ˌtwɪstə] Zungenbrecher °**II U4,** 55
tonight [tə'naɪt] heute Abend, heute Nacht **I U6,** 84
too [tu:] auch **I U1,** 10; zu **I U5,** 66
tooth, teeth *(pl)* [tu:θ; ti:θ] Zahn **III U5,** 86
top [tɒp] Spitze, oberer Teil **III U1,** 14
at the top [ət ðə 'tɒp] oben, im oberen Teil **III U1,** 14
topic ['tɒpɪk] Thema **I U2,** 33
torch [tɔ:tʃ] Taschenlampe, Fackel **I U6,** 84
to **touch** [tʌtʃ] berühren, antippen **III U3,** 53
tough [tʌf] hart, rau, zäh **III U5,** 80
tourist ['tʊərɪst] Tourist/Touristin **III U2,** 28
towards [tə'wɔ:dz] in Richtung, auf ... zu, darauf zu **III U5,** 90
tower ['taʊə] Turm **III U2,** 26
town [taʊn] Stadt **I U3,** 41
toy [tɔɪ] Spielzeug **III U2,** 28
tradition [trə'dɪʃn] Tradition **III U2,** 34
traffic ['træfɪk] Verkehr **III U2,** 26
traffic jam ['træfɪk ˌdʒæm] Stau **III U2,** 26
train [treɪn] Zug **I U4,** 54

to **train** [treɪn] eine Ausbildung machen **III U2,** 34
training ['treɪnɪŋ] Training, Ausbildung **III U4,** 68
transport ['træntspɔ:t] Transport **I U4,** 57
*to be **trapped** [bi: 'træpt] in der Falle sitzen **II U6,** 83
travel ['trævl] Reise **III U5,** 82
to **travel** ['trævl] reisen **III U3,** 44
tree [tri:] Baum **I U1,** 20
family tree ['fæmli tri:] Familienstammbaum °**I U2,** 28
trendy ['trendi] modisch **III U2,** 26
trick [trɪk] Trick, Streich **I U3,** 40
trip [trɪp] Ausflug, Reise **I U6,** 80
trolley ['trɒli] Gepäckwagen, Einkaufswagen, Handkarren **III U3,** 50
trouble ['trʌbl] Schwierigkeiten, Ärger **I U2,** 30
trousers *(pl)* ['traʊzəz] Hose **II U1,** 10
true [tru:] wahr **II U1,** 18
to come true [kʌm 'tru:] wahr werden **III U2,** 30
trust [trʌst] Vertrauen **III U5,** 88
to **trust** [trʌst] vertrauen **III U3,** 52
to **try** [traɪ] versuchen, probieren **II U1,** 10
to try hard [traɪ‿'hɑ:d] sich stark bemühen **III U4,** 70
T-shirt ['ti:ʃɜ:t] T-Shirt **I U2,** 30
tucker ['tʌkə] Essen *(australischer Ausdruck)* °**II U1,** 14
Tuesday ['tju:zdeɪ] Dienstag **I LUB,** 39
tug [tʌg] Ziehen, Zupfen **III U3,** 52
tunnel ['tʌnl] Tunnel, Unterführung **I U4,** 54
Turkish ['tɜ:kɪʃ] türkisch **I U2,** 29
It's your **turn.** [ɪts jɔ: 'tɜ:n] Du bist dran. **II U1,** 13
to **turn** [tɜ:n] drehen, sich umdrehen **III U5,** 86
to turn back [tɜ:n 'bæk] umkehren, zurückgehen **II U1,** 19
to turn left/right [tɜ:n 'left/'raɪt] links/rechts abbiegen **II U7,** 97
to turn off [tɜ:n‿'ɒf] abschalten, ausschalten **I U5,** 75
to turn over [ˌtɜ:n‿'əʊvə] (sich) umdrehen **II U7,** 94
to turn round [tɜ:n 'raʊnd] (sich) umdrehen **II U1,** 18
TV [ˌti:'vi:] Fernsehen, Fernseher **I LUA,** 25
twice [twaɪs] zweimal **III U5,** 80

U

umbrella [ʌm'brelə] Regenschirm **II U6,** 81
umpire ['ʌmpaɪə] Schiedsrichter/Schiedsrichterin **III U1,** 12
uncle ['ʌŋkl] Onkel **I U2,** 28
under ['ʌndə] unter **I U1,** 18
underground ['ʌndəgraʊnd] U-Bahn **III U2,** 27
to **underline** [ˌʌndə'laɪn] unterstreichen **II U1,** 18
underlined [ˌʌndə'laɪnd] unterstrichen °**I U7,** 98
*to **understand** [ˌʌndə'stænd] verstehen **III U3,** 53
unfair [ʌn'feə] ungerecht, unfair °**III U4,** 62
unhappy [ʌn'hæpi] unglücklich **I U2,** 33
unhealthy [ʌn'helθi] ungesund **II U4,** 53
uniform ['ju:nɪfɔ:m] Uniform **I U3,** 44
union ['ju:njən] Liga; Vereinigung, Union **III U1,** 11
unit ['ju:nɪt] Kapitel, Einheit °**III U5,** 93
university [ˌju:nɪ'vɜ:səti] Universität **III U2,** 31
until [ʌn'tɪl; n'tɪl] bis **II U4,** 56
up [ʌp] auf, hinauf, oben **II U2,** 30
Hurry up! [ˌhʌri‿'ʌp] Beeil dich! **I U2,** 30
What's up? [ˌwɒts‿'ʌp] Was ist los? **I U1,** 16
to get up [get‿'ʌp] aufstehen **I U3,** 44
to give up [gɪv‿'ʌp] aufgeben **III U2,** 30
to go up [gəʊ‿'ʌp] hinaufgehen °**I U4,** 61
to wake up [weɪk‿'ʌp] aufwecken, aufwachen **I U3,** 48
to walk up to [wɔ:k‿'ʌp tə] hingehen, zugehen auf **III U5,** 87
up to ['ʌp tə] bis zu **III U3,** 49
to **update** [ʌp'deɪt] aktualisieren °**II U5,** 62
to **upset** [ʌp'set] erschrecken, durcheinander bringen, umstoßen **III U4,** 64
to be **upset** [bi: ʌp'set] aufgeregt sein, bestürzt sein **II U3,** 44
upstairs [ʌp'steəz] oben, im oberen Stock **I U2,** 27; (die Treppe) hinauf/herauf **III U5,** 85
to run upstairs [ˌrʌn‿ʌp'steəz] die Treppe hinaufrennen **III U3,** 53
us [ʌs] uns **I U4,** 60
use [ju:s] Verwendung, Nutzung °**II U5,** 63
to **use** [ju:z] benutzen, verwenden **I U4,** 54
useful ['ju:sfl] nützlich °**III U1,** 14
useless ['ju:sləs] nutzlos **III U4,** 64
usually ['ju:ʒli] normalerweise, gewöhnlich **II U4,** 53

V

valuable ['væljuəbl] wertvoll **III U2,** 26
van [væn] Lieferwagen **I U6,** 86
vegetable ['vedʒtəbl] Gemüse **II U1,** 15
vending machine ['vendɪŋ məˌʃi:n] Warenautomat **III U4,** 66
verb [vɜ:b] Verb °**II U1,** 20
modal auxiliary verb [ˌməʊdl‿ɔ:g'zɪljəri 'vɜ:b] modales Hilfsverb °**III U3,** 46
very ['veri] sehr **I U1,** 20
video ['vɪdiəʊ] Video **I LUB,** 38
view [vju:] Aussicht, Sicht **III U2,** 26
viewer ['vju:ə] Zuschauer/Zuschauerin **III U5,** 80
village ['vɪlɪdʒ] Dorf **III U4,** 64
visit ['vɪzɪt] Besuch **I U7,** 94
to **visit** ['vɪzɪt] besuchen, besichtigen **I U4,** 54
visitor ['vɪzɪtə] Besucher/Besucherin **I U4,** 55
vocabulary [vəʊ'kæbjəlri] Wortschatz, Vokabular °**II U1,** 20
voice [vɔɪs] Stimme **II U2,** 31
volleyball ['vɒlibɔ:l] Volleyball **I U3,** 40

W

to **wait** [weɪt] warten **I U5,** 69
to wait for ['weɪt fɔ:] warten auf **I U6,** 86
waiter ['weɪtə] Kellner, Bedienung **II U4,** 55
*to **wake** [weɪk] (auf)wecken **II U7,** 94
to wake up [weɪk‿'ʌp] aufwecken, aufwachen **I U3,** 48
walk [wɔ:k] Spaziergang **III U1,** 12
to go for a walk [ˌgəʊ fər‿ə 'wɔ:k] spazieren gehen **III U5,** 88
to **walk** [wɔ:k] gehen, laufen **I U4,** 54
to walk the dog [wɔ:k ðə 'dɒg] mit dem Hund spazieren gehen **I U3,** 42
to walk up to [wɔ:k‿'ʌp tə] hingehen, zugehen auf **III U5,** 87

English – German

wall [wɔ:l] Wand, Mauer **I U1,** 18
wallet ['wɒlɪt] Brieftasche, Geldbeutel **II U4,** 56
to **want** (to) ['wɒnt tə] wollen, mögen **I U4,** 54
to want sb to do sth [wɒnt] wollen, dass jemand etwas tut **III U4,** 62
wardrobe ['wɔ:drəʊb] Kleiderschrank, Garderobe **I U2,** 30
warm [wɔ:m] warm **II U2,** 25
to **wash** [wɒʃ] waschen, sich waschen **I U3,** 44
to **watch** [wɒtʃ] ansehen, beobachten **I LUB,** 38; achten auf **II U2,** 31
water ['wɔ:tə] Wasser **I U5,** 68
wave [weɪv] Welle **III U4,** 70
to **wave** [weɪv] winken, schwenken **II U6,** 83
way [weɪ] Weg **I U3,** 42; Art, Weise **III U3,** 49
He is on his way to .... [ˌhi:ˌɪz‿ɒn hɪz 'weɪ tə] Er ist auf dem Weg zu .... **I U3,** 42
we [wi:] wir **I U1,** 16
weak [wi:k] schwach **III U4,** 70
to go weak [gəʊ 'wi:k] schwach werden **III U4,** 70
*to **wear** [weə] anhaben, tragen **I U3,** 45
weather ['weðə] Wetter **II U1,** 14
weatherman, weathermen *(pl)* ['weðəmən; 'weðəmen] Meteorologe °**II U6,** 78
webcam ['webkæm] Webcam °**II U5,** 63
website ['websaɪt] Website, Internetauftritt **II U5,** 64
Wednesday ['wenzdeɪ] Mittwoch **I LUB,** 39
week [wi:k] Woche **I LUB,** 39
a week [ə 'wi:k] pro Woche, in der Woche **II U4,** 52
weekend [ˌwi:k'end] Wochenende **I U3,** 45
weight [weɪt] Gewicht **III U1,** 11
Welcome to ... ['welkəm tə] Willkommen in ... **III U4,** 67
to **welcome** ['welkəm] willkommen heißen **I U7,** 90
You're **welcome.** [jʊə 'welkəm] Bitte sehr!, Gern geschehen! **I U1,** 19
well [wel] gut **III U1,** 16
as well as [əz 'wel‿əz] sowohl ... als auch **III U4,** 67
Well done! [ˌwel 'dʌn] Gut gemacht! **III U3,** 47
well [wel] also, na ja, nun gut **I U2,** 29
Welsh [welʃ] walisisch; Waliser/Waliserin **III U3,** 48
west [west] Westen **I U4,** 54
wet [wet] nass **II U6,** 74
wet blanket [wet 'blæŋkɪt] Miesmacher/Miesmacherin **II U6,** 74
what [wɒt] welche/welcher/welches **I LUA,** 25; was **I U1,** 11
What about ... ? [wɒt‿ə'baʊt] Was ist mit ... ? Wie wäre es mit ... ? **I U2,** 30
What a laugh! [ˌwɒt‿ə 'lɑ:f] Wie lustig! **III U1,** 17
What a week! [ˌwɒt‿ə 'wi:k] Was für eine Woche! **II U2,** 22
What does it say? [ˌwɒt dʌz‿ɪt 'seɪ] Was steht da? **II U3,** 44
What's the film about? [wɒts ðə 'fɪlm‿əˌbaʊt] Wovon handelt der Film? °**II U3,** 43
What's the matter? [ˌwɒts ðə 'mætə] Was ist los? **III U5,** 88
What's the time, please? [ˌwɔts ðə 'taɪm ˌpli:z] Wie viel Uhr ist es, bitte?; Wie spät ist es, bitte? **I U3,** 42
What's up? [ˌwɒts‿'ʌp] Was ist los? **I U1,** 16
What's your name? [ˌwɒts jə 'neɪm] Wie heißt du? **I U1,** 11
What the heck ... ? [ˌwɒt ðə 'hek] Was zum Teufel ... ? **III U4,** 70
wheel [wi:l] Rad **III U2,** 30
when [wen] wenn, als; wann **I U2,** 33
where [weə] wo, wohin **I U1,** 11
Where are you from? [ˌweər‿ə jə 'frɒm] Woher kommst du? **I U1,** 11
Where's the fire? [ˌweəz ðə 'faɪə] Wo brennt's denn? **I U7,** 96
which [wɪtʃ] welche/welcher/welches **II U1,** 14; der/dem/den/die/das *(Relativpronomen)* **II U3,** 42
while [waɪl] während **III U5,** 85
to **whisper** ['wɪspə] flüstern, zuflüstern **II U1,** 18
whistle ['wɪsl] Trillerpfeife **III U1,** 12
white [waɪt] weiß **I LUA,** 24
white elephant stall [ˌwaɪt 'elɪfənt stɔ:l] Trödelstand **I U7,** 96
who [hu:] wer, wem, wen **I U5,** 70; der/dem/den/die *(Relativpronomen)* **II U3,** 42
whole [həʊl] ganz °**III U3,** 53
whom [hu:m] wem, wen **III U3,** 52
whose [hu:z] wessen **II U5,** 68; dessen, deren *(Relativpronomen)* **III U3,** 48
why [waɪ] warum **I U5,** 70
wicked ['wɪkɪd] großartig **II U5,** 70
wife, wives *(pl)* [waɪf; waɪvz] Ehefrau **III U5,** 86
wig [wɪg] Perücke **II U2,** 28
wild [waɪld] wild **III U2,** 31
***will ('ll), won't** [wɪl; wəʊnt] werden, werden nicht *(futurisch)* **II U6,** 76
*to **win** [wɪn] gewinnen, siegen **II U7,** 91
wind [wɪnd] Wind **I U2,** 35
window ['wɪndəʊ] Fenster **I U1,** 18
to **windsurf** ['wɪndsɜ:f] windsurfen **III U3,** 46
windy ['wɪndi] windig **I U6,** 79
winner ['wɪnə] Gewinner/Gewinnerin, Sieger/Siegerin **III U4,** 63
winter ['wɪntə] Winter **I U6,** 79
wish [wɪʃ] Wunsch **III U4,** 63
to **wish** [wɪʃ] wünschen **III U4,** 68
with [wɪð] mit **I U1,** 14; bei **II U1,** 11
to go (together) with ['gəʊ wɪð] passen zu **III U5,** 80
within [wɪ'ðɪn] innerhalb **III U2,** 28
without [wɪ'ðaʊt] ohne **I U4,** 54
to go without [ˌgəʊ wɪ'ðaʊt] ohne ... auskommen **II U4,** 52
wizard ['wɪzəd] Zauberer **II U5,** 69
wolf, wolves *(pl)* [wʊlf; wʊlvz] Wolf **III U5,** 86
woman, women *(pl)* ['wʊmən; 'wɪmɪn] Frau **I U4,** 62
wood [wʊd] Holz **III U2,** 32
wooden ['wʊdn] hölzern **III U3,** 49
Woof! [wʊf] Wau! °**I U2,** 27
word [wɜ:d] Wort **I U1,** 15
word star ['wɜ:d stɑ:] Wortstern °**I U1,** 22
work [wɜ:k] Arbeit **I U3,** 47
to **work** [wɜ:k] arbeiten, funktionieren **I U3,** 48
worksheet ['wɜ:kʃi:t] Arbeitsblatt **I U4,** 58
workshop ['wɜ:kʃɒp] Workshop, Werkstatt **III U4,** 63
world [wɜ:ld] Erde, Welt **III U2,** 26
*to be **worried** [bi: 'wʌrid] besorgt sein, beunruhigt sein **I U6,** 87
worry ['wʌri] Sorge °**III U4,** 64
to **worry** ['wʌri] sich Sorgen machen **I U6,** 82; ängstigen, beunruhigen **II U3,** 45
worse [wɜ:s] schlimmer, schlechter **II U4,** 50
worst [wɜ:st] schlimmste/schlimmster/schlimmstes, schlechteste/schlechtester/schlechtestes **II U4,** 50
***would** [wʊd] würde(n) **III U3,** 53
would like [wʊd 'laɪk] hätte gern, möchte gern **II U4,** 52

wow [waʊ] wow °I U1, 12
wreck [rek] Wrack III U4, 70
*to **write** [raɪt] schreiben I U3, 43
to write down ['raɪt ˌdaʊn] aufschreiben °I LUB, 38
writing ['raɪtɪŋ] Schreiben °III U4, 68
wrong [rɒŋ] falsch I U1, 16
to be wrong [bi: 'rɒŋ] Unrecht haben III U3, 53
to get … wrong [get … 'rɒŋ] falsch machen II U3, 44; falsch verstehen °II U3, 47
to go wrong [gəʊ 'rɒŋ] schief gehen II U6, 85

Y

yard [jɑ:d] Elle *(Längenmaß: 0,914 m)* III U3, 48
year [jɪə] Jahr, Jahrgangsstufe I U1, 10
year-old [ˌjɪər‿'əʊld] -jährig; -Jähriger/-Jährige III U4, 63
yellow ['jeləʊ] gelb I LUA, 24
yes [jes] ja I U1, 12
yesterday ['jestədeɪ] gestern II U2, 26
not … **yet** [jet] noch nicht II U5, 66
you [ju:; jə] du, ihr, Sie I U1, 11; dich, dir, Ihnen, euch I LUB, 38; man III U1, 8
Here you are! ['hɪə ju:‿ˌɑ:] Bitte schön! I U1, 20
thank you ['θæŋk‿ju:] danke I U1, 12
you'd better [jʊd 'betə] du solltest lieber III U4, 70
you're lucky [ˌjʊə 'lʌki] du hast Glück I U1, 16
You're welcome. [jʊə 'welkəm] Bitte sehr!, Gern geschehen! I U1, 19
you see [jʊ 'si:] weißt du III U1, 12
young [jʌŋ] jung I U3, 45
your [jɔ:] dein/deine, euer/eure, Ihr/Ihre I U1, 11
Yours [jɔ:z] Dein …/Deine …/Euer …/Eure … *(in Briefen)* II U3, 36
yourself [jɔ:'self] dich selbst °III U1, 11
youth [ju:θ] Jugend II U3, 38
yukky ['jʌki] ekelhaft III U4, 66

Z

zoo [zu:] Zoo, Tierpark II U2, 22
zookeeper ['zu:ˌki:pə] Tierpfleger/Tierpflegerin, Wärter/Wärterin II U2, 26

Boys' names

Andy ['ændi] III U4, 69
Angus ['æŋgəs] II FA, 103
Arthur ['ɑ:θə] III FA, 100
Ben [ben] I U2, 27
Bob [bɒb] I U6, 78
Burt [bɜ:t] II U4, 55
Chandler ['tʃændlə] II U3, 37
Charles [tʃɑ:lz] III U5, 88
Charlie ['tʃɑ:li] I U2, 33
Daniel ['dænjəl] II U4, 51
Dave [deɪv] III U1, 9
David ['deɪvɪd] I U2, 28
Derek ['derɪk] II U4, 51
Dicken ['dɪkn] II FA, 110
Douglas ['dʌgləs] II FA, 102
Ector ['ektə] III FA, 100
Eric ['erɪk] I FA, 102
Fred [fred] III U3, 47
Henry ['henri] II FA, 114
Ian ['i:ən] III U5, 87
Jack [dʒæk] I FA, 102
Jake [dʒeɪk] II U1, 14
Jamal [dʒə'mɑ:l] III U4, 65
James [dʒeɪmz] I U2, 28
Jamie ['dʒeɪmi] III U1, 12
Jim [dʒɪm] I U5, 73
Jo [dʒəʊ] I FA, 105
Joey ['dʒəʊi] II U3, 37
John [dʒɒn] I U4, 57
Kay [keɪ] III FA, 100
Leo ['lɪ:əʊ] III U1, 16
Leon ['li:ɒn] III U1, 11
Leroy ['li:rɔɪ] III U4, 70
Llywelyn [lə'welɪn] III U5, 86
Marc [mɑ:k] III U4, 63
Mark [mɑ:k] I U4, 61
Matt [mæt] II U2, 31
Mike [maɪk] III U4, 72
Nelson ['nelsn] I U1, 13
Patrick ['pætrɪk] II U7, 88
Paul [pɔ:l] I U6, 85
Pete [pi:t] II U1, 11
Peter ['pi:tə] I U4, 61
Phil [fɪl] I U2, 28
Ray [reɪ] III U4, 68
Reece [ri:s] III U4, 69
Reg [redʒ] III U2, 34
Richard ['rɪtʃəd] I U2, 27
Rob [rɒb] I U2, 26
Robert ['rɒbət] II U4, 51
Rodger ['rɒdʒə] III U5, 89
Roger ['rɒdʒə] II U3, 36
Ross [rɒs] II U3, 37
Sam [sæm] I U1, 16
Steve [sti:v] I U1, 23
Ted [ted] I U2, 26
Terry ['teri] I U1, 10
Thomas ['tɒməs] I LUA, 25
Tim [tɪm] I LUA, 25
Todd [tɒd] II U3, 36
Tom [tɒm] I U1, 10
Tony ['təʊni] I LUA, 25
Uther ['ju:θə] III FA, 100

Girls' names

Alison ['ælɪsən] II U5, 67
Amanda [ə'mændə] III U5, 87
Anna ['ænə] I U3, 47
Barbara ['bɑ:brə] III U1, 12
Carrie ['kæri] III U4, 64
Daisy ['deɪzi] III U4, 64
Debbie ['debi] II U3, 36
Dorothy ['dɒrəθi] II U5, 68
Elena ['elɪnə] I U2, 28
Elizabeth [ɪ'lɪzəbəθ] III U2, 29
Em [em] II FA, 114
Emma ['emə] I U1, 12
Farah ['fɑ:rə] I U2, 26
Fiona [fi'əʊnə] I U1, 23
Glinda ['glɪndə] II FA, 114
Grace [greɪs] I U2, 26
Helen ['helən] II U7, 88
Igraine [ɪ'greɪn] III FA, 100
Jade [dʒeɪd] I U2, 27
Jane [dʒeɪn] III U2, 33
Jenna ['dʒenə] III U4, 69
Jenny ['dʒeni] I U4, 57
Julia ['dʒu:liə] III U2, 30
Julie ['dʒu:li] III U4, 72
Kate [keɪt] I U4, 57
Kath [kæθ] I U6, 78
Laura ['lɔ:rə] II U1, 11
Lauren ['lɔ:rən] III U4, 64
Lisa ['li:sə] I U1, 10
Marcia ['mɑ:siə] III U1, 12
Marg [mɑ:dʒ] III U5, 85
Maria [mə'ri:ə] I U2, 28
Mary ['meəri] I U4, 57
Monika ['mɒnɪkə] II U3, 37
Nadine [neɪ'di:n] I U1, 13
Nancy ['nænsi] III U1, 9
Nasreen [nʌs'ri:n] I U2, 26
Nicola ['nɪklə] I FA, 100
Nicole [nɪ'kəʊl] II U3, 36
Nyla ['naɪlə] III U4, 64
Pat [pæt] II U1, 16
Paula ['pɔ:lə] III U1, 11
Phoebe ['fi:bi] II U3, 37

Polly ['pɒli] **III U5,** 85
Pru [pru:] **III U2,** 35
Rachel ['reɪtʃl] **II U3,** 37
Ruby ['ru:bi] **III U4,** 65
Sally ['sæli] **I U6,** 85
Sarah ['seərə] **I U2,** 28
Sheila ['ʃi:lə] **III U1,** 15
Stella ['stelə] **II FA,** 104
Sue [su:] **I U2,** 27
Susan ['su:zn] **I U2,** 28
Suzanne [su:'zæn] **I U1,** 11
Tamara [tə'mɑ:rə] **I LUA,** 25
Tess [tes] **I U6,** 85
Tilly ['tɪli] **I LUA,** 25
Tina ['ti:nə] **I LUA,** 25
Tracy ['treɪsi] **I U2,** 28
Trina ['tri:nə] **III U1,** 15
Virginia [və'dʒɪnjə] **III FA,** 112

Surnames

Akodu [ə'kəʊdʊ] **III U4,** 68
Barnes ['bɑ:nz] **III U1,** 16
Barnfield ['bɑ:nfi:ld] **III U2,** 30
Barrymore ['bærimɔ:] **III U5,** 88
Baskerville ['bæskəvɪl] **III U5,** 82
Bell [bel] **II U4,** 52
Berry [beri] **III U1,** 9
Black [blæk] **II U1,** 11
Bland [blænd] **II FA,** 108
Brook [brʊk] **I U1,** 12
Brown [braʊn] **II U1,** 11
Burns [bɜ:nz] **III U5,** 83
Cage [keɪdʒ] **III U1,** 9
Canterville ['kæntəvɪl] **III FA,** 110
Carter ['kɑ:tə] **I U1,** 12
Cartwright ['kɑ:traɪt] **III U2,** 34
Clarke [klɑ:k] **III U3,** 52
George [dʒɔ:dʒ] **III U1,** 11
Glenn [glen] **III U4,** 70
Gruntle ['grʌntl] **II FA,** 108
Gulch [gʌltʃ] **II FA,** 114
Hall [hɔ:l] **III U5,** 87
Howard ['haʊəd] **II U1,** 14
Hunter ['hʌntə] **I U6,** 82
Jackson ['dʒæksn] **I U1,** 10
Jones [dʒəʊnz] **III U4,** 70
Lean [li:n] **I FA,** 104
Mangold ['mæŋgəʊld] **III U5,** 85
Marco ['mɑ:kəʊ] **II U1,** 11
Marks [mɑ:ks] **III U2,** 30
Martin ['mɑ:tɪn] **I FA,** 106
McArthur [mək'ɑ:θə] **II FA,** 102
Monte ['mɒnteɪ] **I U2,** 28
Morley ['mɔ:li] **III U4,** 64
Muir [mjʊə] **II FA,** 103
Newitt ['nju:ɪt] **III U5,** 84
Newman ['nju:mən] **I U1,** 12
O'Brien [əʊ'braɪən] **II U7,** 88
Otis ['əʊtɪs] **III FA,** 110
Pilch [pɪltʃ] **I U2,** 28
Richards ['rɪtʃədz] **II U3,** 45
Robbins ['rɒbɪnz] **III U3,** 51
Rose [rəʊz] **I U4,** 60
Simpson ['sɪmpsən] **III U5,** 82
Smith [smɪθ] **III U4,** 63
Spencer ['spentsə] **I U2,** 28
Stapleton ['steɪpltən] **III U5,** 89
Stavros ['stʌvrəs] **I U2,** 28
Taylor ['teɪlə] **I U1,** 10
Tiny ['taɪni] **I LUA,** 25
Watson ['wɒtsn] **III U5,** 81
White [waɪt] **III U2,** 33
Wilkins ['wɪlkɪnz] **III U4,** 70
Willis ['wɪlɪs] **III U5,** 87

Place names

Abergavenny [ˌæbəgə'veni] **III U1,** 11
Acton ['æktən] **III U2,** 34
America [ə'merɪkə] **II U3,** 36
Australia [ɒs'treɪliə] Australien **II ZI,** 8
Avondale ['eɪvndeɪl] **III U5,** 81
Baker Street ['beɪkə ˌstri:t] **III U5,** 88
Barcelona [ˌbɑ:sl'əʊnə] **III U1,** 15
Bath [bɑ:θ] **I U6,** 79
Bollywood ['bɒliwʊd] **III U5,** 80
Boston ['bɒstn] **III U1,** 15
Bow Church [ˌbəʊ 'tʃɜ:tʃ] **I FA,** 108
Brighton ['braɪtn] **III U3,** 44
Bristol ['brɪstl] **I U1,** 12
Britain ['brɪtn] **II FA,** 102
British Isles [ˌbrɪtɪʃ 'aɪlz] Britische Inseln **II ZI,** 8
California [ˌkælɪ'fɔ:niə] **III U1,** 11
Camden ['kæmdən] **II U2,** 22
Canada ['kænədə] Kanada **III U5,** 88
Chicago [ʃɪ'kɑ:gəʊ] **III U1,** 9
China ['tʃaɪnə] China **III U1,** 15
Cornwall ['kɔ:nwɔ:l] **II U6,** 78
Covent Garden [ˌkɒvnt 'gɑ:dn] **III U2,** 28
Dartmoor ['dɑ:tmɔ:] **III U5,** 88
Devon ['devn] **II U6,** 78
Dover ['dəʊvə] **III U3,** 44
Dublin ['dʌblɪn] **II U7,** 88
Eastbourne ['i:stbɔ:n] **III U3,** 44
England ['ɪŋglənd] England **I U2,** 29
Exmoor ['eksmɔ:] **II ZI,** 8
Folkestone ['fəʊkstən] **III U3,** 44
Germany ['dʒɜ:məni] Deutschland **I U2,** 29
Glasgow ['glɑ:zgəʊ] **II FA,** 102
Greece [gri:s] Griechenland **I U2,** 29
Greenwich ['grenɪdʒ] **I U1,** 10
Hastings ['heɪstɪŋz] **III U3,** 44
Heathrow [ˌhi:θ'rəʊ] **III U3,** 45
Hither Farm Road [ˌhɪðə fɑ:m 'rəʊd] **I U2,** 26
Holburne Road [ˌhɒlbɜ:n 'rəʊd] **I U2,** 26
Hollyoaks ['hɒliəʊks] **III U5,** 82
Hollywood ['hɒliwʊd] **III U5,** 80
India ['ɪndiə] **III U1,** 13
Ireland ['aɪələnd] Irland **II U6,** 85
Irish Sea [ˌaɪrɪʃ 'si:] **III U3,** 44
Isle of Dogs [ˌaɪl‿əv 'dɒgz] **I U4,** 54
Isle of Wight [ˌaɪl‿əv 'waɪt] **III U3,** 44
Istanbul [ˌɪstæn'bʊl] **I U1,** 13
Italy ['ɪtəli] Italien **I U2,** 29
Kansas ['kænzəs] **II FA,** 114
Kent [kent] **III U3,** 57
Kilkenny [kɪl'keni] **II U7,** 93
King's Road ['kɪŋz ˌrəʊd] **III U2,** 26
Limerick ['lɪmrɪk] **II ZI,** 8
Loch Ness [ˌlɒx 'nes] **II ZI,** 8
London ['lʌndən] **I U1,** 10
Madrid [mə'drɪd] **I U1,** 13
Manchester ['mæntʃɪstə] **III U2,** 39
Marble Arch ['mɑ:bl ˌɑ:tʃ] **III U2,** 28
Moher ['məʊhə] **II U7,** 93
Moscow ['mɒskəʊ] **III U3,** 52
Nairobi [naɪ'rəʊbi] **I U1,** 13
Neston ['nestn] **I U6,** 78
New York [ˌnju: 'jɔ:k] **I U4,** 55
Northern Ireland [ˌnɔ:ðn‿'aɪələnd] **II U7,** 89
Nottingham ['nɒtɪŋəm] **II U2,** 25
Paris ['pærɪs] **I U1,** 13
Park Row [ˌpɑ:k 'rəʊ] **I U4,** 60
Perth [pɜ:θ] **II ZI,** 8
Piccadilly Circus [ˌpɪkədɪli 'sɜ:kəs] **III U2,** 28
Poland ['pəʊlənd] Polen **I U2,** 29
Pond Road [ˌpɒnd 'rəʊd] **I U2,** 27
Pudding Lane [ˌpʊdɪŋ 'leɪn] **III U2,** 32
Republic of Ireland [rɪˌpʌblɪk‿əv‿'aɪələnd] Republik Irland **II U7,** 88
Russia ['rʌʃə] Russland **I U2,** 29
Sacramento [ˌsækrə'mentəʊ] **III U1,** 11
Salisbury ['sɔ:lzbri] **III U3,** 44
Scilly Isles ['sɪli ˌaɪlz] **II U6,** 78
Scotland ['skɒtlənd] Schottland **II ZI,** 8
Shannon ['ʃænən] **II U7,** 93
Sherwood Forest [ˌʃɜ:wʊd 'fɒrɪst] **II FA,** 110

Shoreditch [ʃɔ:'dɪtʃ] **III U2,** 35
Southampton [saʊ'θæmtən] **III U3,** 44
South England [ˌsaʊθ 'ɪŋglənd] Südengland **III U3,** 44
Spain [speɪn] Spanien **III U1,** 15
Stonehenge [stəʊn'hendʒ] **III U3,** 45
Tarr Steps [tɑ: 'steps] **II U6,** 82
the **Thames** [temz] **I U4,** 54
Tokyo ['təʊkiəʊ] **I U1,** 13
Turkey ['tɜ:ki] Türkei **I U2,** 29
Twickenham ['twiknəm] **III U1,** 8
UK [ju:'keɪ] **III U1,** 11
the **USA** [ˌju:es'eɪ] **III U1,** 11
Wales [weɪlz] Wales **II ZI,** 8
Wendover Road [ˌwendəʊvə 'rəʊd] **I U5,** 70
Western Australia [ˌwestən ɒs'treɪliə] **II U1,** 14
White Hart Lane [ˌwaɪt hɑ:t 'leɪn] **III U1,** 16
Wildcroft ['waɪldkrɒft] **I FA,** 100
Wiltshire ['wɪltʃə] **I U6,** 78
Wimbledon ['wɪmbldn] **III U1,** 15
North Sea [ˌnɔ:θ 'si:] Nordsee **III U3,** 44
Spain [speɪn] Spanien **III U1,** 15
United Kingdom [ju:ˌnaɪtɪd 'kɪŋdəm] Vereinigtes Königreich von Großbritannien und Nordirland **III U3,** 44

Other names

Accent ['æksnt] **III U2,** 35
Alice Fitzwarren ['ælis ˌfɪts'wɒrn] **I FA,** 108
Angelina Jolie [ˌændʒ'li:nə 'dʒəʊli] **III U2,** 29
Aquarius [ə'kweəriəs] Wassermann **II U6,** 80
Arena [ə'ri:nə] **II U2,** 22
Arsenal ['ɑ:snl] **III U1,** 16
Arthur Conan Doyle [ˌɑ:θə ˌkəʊnən 'dɔɪl] **III U5,** 87
Bakerloo Line [ˌbeɪkəl'u: ˌlaɪn] **III U2,** 28
Barker ['bɑ:kə] **I U2,** 27
Baskerville Hall [ˌbæskəvɪl 'hɔ:l] **III U5,** 88
Batman ['bætmæn] **III U5,** 87
BBC [ˌbi:bi:'si:] **III U5,** 82
Big Ben [ˌbɪg 'ben] **III U2,** 26
Birdy ['bɜ:di] **III U5,** 95
Blacky ['blæki] **I FA,** 108
Boxing Day ['bɒksɪŋ ˌdeɪ] **I FA,** 114
British Airways (BA) [ˌbrɪtɪʃ 'eəweɪz] **III U2,** 30
Buckingham Bridge [ˌbʌkɪŋəm 'brɪdʒ] **III U2,** 33
Buckingham Palace [ˌbʌkɪŋəm 'pælɪs] **II U3,** 47
Burger Bonanza [ˌbɜ:gə bə'nænzə] **II U3,** 44
Chalte Chalte ['tʃʌlte ˌtʃʌlte] **III U5,** 82
Charlie Chaplin [ˌtʃɑ:li 'tʃæplɪn] **III U4,** 72
Charlie Smart [ˌtʃɑ:li 'smɑ:t] **I FA,** 108
Chicago Cubs [ˌʃɪ'kɑ:gəʊ 'kʌbz] **III U1,** 9
Chicago Hope [ʃɪˌkɑ:geʊ 'həʊp] **III U5,** 87
Ching Ming [ˌtʃɪŋ 'mɪŋ] **II U4,** 48
Chunnel ['tʃʌnl] Tunnel durch den Ärmelkanal **III U3,** 45
Cincinnati Reds [ˌsɪntsɪnæti 'redz] **III U1,** 9
Circle Line ['sɜ:kl ˌlaɪn] **III U2,** 28
Concorde ['kɒŋkɔ:d] **III U2,** 38
Countdown ['kaʊntdaʊn] **III U5,** 82
Crawford Park [ˌkrɔ:fəd 'pɑ:k] **III U4,** 63
Cutty Sark [ˌkʌti 'sɑ:k] **I U4,** 54
Cutty Sark Gardens [kʌti ˌsɑ:k 'gɑ:dnz] **I U4,** 54
Derrek Lee [ˌderɪk 'li:] **III U1,** 9
Diamond Hotel [ˌdaɪəmənd həʊ'tel] **III U5,** 82
Discman ['dɪskmən] Discman **I U2,** 30
DLR [ˌdi:‿el‿'ɑ:] **I U4,** 55
Docklands Light Railway ['dɒkləndz ˌlaɪt 'reɪlweɪ] **I U4,** 55
Dynamo Moscow [ˌdaɪnəməʊ 'mɒskəʊ] **III U1,** 16
Eastenders [ˌi:st'endəz] **I U7,** 96
Embankment [ɪm'bæŋkmənt] **III U2,** 28
Emergency Room [ɪ'mɜ:dʒnsi ˌrʊm] **III U5,** 82
European Union [ˌjʊərə'pi:ən 'ju:njən] **III U3,** 55
FA Cup [ˌef‿eɪ 'kʌp] Pokal des englischen Fußballverbands, vgl. DFB-Pokal **III U1,** 15
Firestorm ['faɪəstɔ:m] **III U2,** 32
Flight Lab ['flaɪt ˌlæb] **II U2,** 23
Friar Tuck [ˌfraɪə 'tʌk] **II FA,** 110
Gelert ['gelət] **III U5,** 81
General Hospital [ˌdʒenrl 'hɒspɪtl] **III U5,** 87
GMT ['dʒi:em'ti:] **I U4,** 55
Great Fire [ˌgreɪt 'faɪə] **III U2,** 26
Great Tower [ˌgreɪt 'taʊə] **III U2,** 31
Greenwich Mean Time [ˌgrenɪdʒ 'mi:n taɪm] **I U4,** 55
Guy Fawkes [ˌgaɪ 'fɔ:ks] **I FA,** 114
Harrods ['hærədz] **II U2,** 23
Harry Potter [ˌhæri 'pɒtə] **II U1,** 11
Houses of Parliament [ˌhaʊzɪz‿əv 'pɑ:ləmənt] **I FA,** 114
ITV [ˌaɪti:'vi:] **III U5,** 82
James Bond [ˌdʒeɪmz 'bɒnd] **I FA,** 104
King William Walk [kɪŋ 'wɪljəm ˌwɔ:k] °**I U4,** 62
Kingsdale Comprehensive School ['kɪŋsdeɪl kɒmprɪ'hensɪv ˌsku:l] **III U4,** 66
Kitty ['kɪti] **III U5,** 95
Lady Ann Fitzwarren [ˌleɪdi‿æn fɪts'wɒrn] **I FA,** 108
Lady Richstone [ˌleɪdi 'rɪtʃstəʊn] **III U5,** 84
Leeds Castle [ˌli:dz 'kɑ:sl] **III U3,** 57
Little John [ˌlɪtl 'dʒɒn] **II FA,** 110
London Bridge [ˌlʌndən 'brɪdʒ] **III U2,** 32
London Dungeon [ˌlʌndən 'dʌndʒn] **III U2,** 26
London Eye [ˌlʌndən‿'aɪ] **III U2,** 26
London Knights [ˌlʌndən 'naɪts] **II U2,** 22
Madonna [mə'dɒnə] **III U2,** 29
Maid Marian [ˌmeɪd 'mæriən] **II FA,** 110
Man U ['mæn ju:] **III U5,** 82
Meridian Line [mə'rɪdiən 'laɪn] **I U4,** 54
Merlin ['mɜ:lɪn] **III FA,** 100
Monument ['mɒnjəmənt] **III U2,** 28
MTV [ˌemti:'vi:] **I U6,** 82
Naomi Campbell [ˌneɪəmi: 'kæmbl] **III U2,** 29
Napoleon [nə'pəʊliən] **II U5,** 62
Nessie ['nesi] **II FA,** 103
New Stone Age ['nju: ˌstəʊn ˌeɪdʒ] Jungsteinzeit **III U3,** 49
Nottingham Panthers [ˌnɒtɪŋəm 'pænθəz] **II U2,** 25
OC California [ˌəʊ 'si: ˌkælɪ'fɔ:niə] **III U5,** 82
Oz [ɒz] **II FA,** 114
Palace of Westminster [ˌpælɪs‿əv 'wesmɪnstə] **III U2,** 26
Queen Elizabeth [ˌkwi:n‿ɪ'lɪzəbəθ] **I U5,** 73
Radio Active [ˌreɪdiəʊ‿'æktɪv] **I U2,** 33
Ready Steady Cook [ˌredi ˌstedi 'kʊk] **III U5,** 82
Robbie Williams [ˌrɒbi 'wɪljəmz] **II U1,** 14
Robin Hood [ˌrɒbɪn 'hʊd] **II FA,** 110
Royal Family ['rɔɪəl 'fæmli] **III U2,** 26
Royal Observatory [ˌrɔɪəl əb'zɜ:vətri] **I U4,** 55
Rugby School [ˌrʌgbi 'sku:l] **III U1,** 8
Shakespeare ['ʃeɪkspɪə] **II U5,** 62
Sherlock Holmes [ˌʃɜ:lɒk 'həʊmz] **III U5,** 82

English – German

Spiderman ['spaɪdəmæn] **II U6,** 85
St James's Park [snt ˌdʒeɪmzɪz 'pɑ:k] **III U2,** 28
St Paul's Cathedral [snt ˌpɔ:lz 'kəθi:drl] **III U2,** 28
Superman ['su:pəmæn] **III U5,** 87
Supermouse ['su:pəmaʊs] **II U2,** 33
Taj Mahal [ˌtɑ:dʒ mə'hɑ:l] **III U1,** 13
Thames Festival Lantern Procession [ˌtemz 'festɪvl 'læntən prə'seʃn] **I U7,** 90
Thomas Tallis School [ˌtɒməs tælɪs 'sku:l] **I U1,** 10
Tiger ['taɪgə] **I U2,** 26
Titanic [taɪ'tænɪk] **III U3,** 45
Top of the Pops [ˌtɒp‿əv ðə 'pɒps] **III U5,** 82
Tower of London [ˌtaʊər‿əv 'lʌndən] **III U2,** 26
Tube [tju:b] **III U2,** 26
Urquhart Castle [ˌɜ:kət 'kɑ:sl] **II FA,** 102
Valentine ['væləntaɪn] **II U6,** 85
Weakest Link [ˌwi:kəst 'lɪŋk] **III U5,** 82
Wembley Stadium ['wembli 'steɪdiəm] **III U1,** 12
White House ['waɪt ˌhaʊs] **II U3,** 43
William the Conqueror [ˌwɪljəm ðə 'kɒŋkrə] **III U2,** 31
Wizard of Oz [ˌwɪzəd əv‿'ɒz] **°II U5,** 64
Wrigley Field Stadium [ˌrɪgli fi:ld 'steɪdiəm] **III U1,** 9

A

ab off [ɒf]
Abc alphabet ['ælfəbet]
Abend evening ['i:vnɪŋ]
am Abend in the evening [ˌɪn ði: 'i:vnɪŋ]
an diesem Abend that evening [ˌdæt‿'i:vnɪŋ]
heute Abend this evening [ðɪs 'i:vnɪŋ]; tonight [tə'naɪt]
zu Abend essen to have supper [hæv 'sʌpə]
Abendessen supper ['sʌpə]; tea [ti:]
zum Abendessen for supper [fə 'sʌpə]
abends in the evening [ˌɪn ði: 'i:vnɪŋ]
Abenteuer adventure [əd'ventʃə]
aber but [bʌt]
abfahren to leave [li:v]
Abfall rubbish ['rʌbɪʃ]
Abfälle rubbish ['rʌbɪʃ]
Abflug departure [dɪ'pɑ:tʃə]
abholen to collect [kə'lekt]; to pick up [pɪk‿'ʌp]
Abitur A-levels *(pl)* ['eɪlevlz]
abräumen von to get off [get‿'ɒf]
Abreise departure [dɪ'pɑ:tʃə]
abschalten to turn off [tɜ:n‿'ɒf]
abschließen to lock [lɒk]
abschrecken to frighten away [ˌfraɪtn‿ə'weɪ]
abschreiben to copy ['kɒpi]
absolut absolutely [ˌæbsə'lu:tli]
achten auf to watch [wɒtʃ]
Acker field [fi:ld]
addieren to add [æd]
Adresse address [ə'dres]
Aftershave aftershave ['ɑ:ftəʃeɪv]
Akku battery ['bætri]
Aktion action ['ækʃn]
aktiv active ['æktɪv]
Akzent accent ['æksnt]
Alarm alarm [ə'lɑ:m]
alle/alles all [ɔ:l]
alleine alone [ə'ləʊn]
alles everything ['evriθɪŋ]
Alphabet alphabet ['ælfəbet]
alphabetisch alphabetical [ˌælfə'betɪkl]
als as [æz; əz]
als *(Vergleich)* than [ðæn]
als *(zeitlich)* when [wen]
also so [səʊ]; well [wel]
alt old [əʊld]; ancient ['eɪnʃnt]
Alter age [eɪdʒ]
im Alter von of age [əv‿'eɪdʒ]
Amerikaner American [ə'merɪkən]
amerikanisch American [ə'merɪkən]
sich amüsieren to have a good time [ˌhæv‿ə gʊd 'taɪm]; to have fun [ˌhæv 'fʌn]
an at [æt; ət]; on [ɒn]
an sein to be on [bi:‿'ɒn]
anbieten to offer ['ɒfə]
anbringen to fix (to) [fɪks]
Andenken souvenir [ˌsu:və'nɪə]
andere/anderer/anderes other ['ʌðə]
ein anderer/eine andere/ein anderes another [ə'nʌðə]
ändern to change [tʃeɪndʒ]
anders different ['dɪfrnt]
Änderung change [tʃeɪndʒ]
Anfang beginning [bɪ'gɪnɪŋ]; start [stɑ:t]
anfangen to begin [bɪ'gɪn]; to start [stɑ:t]
Anführer/Anführerin leader ['li:də]
angeln to fish [fɪʃ]
Angeln fishing ['fɪʃɪŋ]
angreifen to attack [ə'tæk]
Angst haben (vor) to be frightened (of) [bi: 'fraɪtnd]
Angst machen to scare ['skeə]
Ich habe Angst. I'm scared. [aɪm 'skeəd]
ängstigen to worry ['wʌri]
anhaben to wear [weə]
anhalten to stop [stɒp]
anhören to listen ['lɪsn]
sich anhören to sound [saʊnd]
fest **anklopfen** to bang [bæŋ]
ankommen to arrive [ə'raɪv]
Ankündigung announcement [ə'naʊntsmənt]
anmalen to paint [peɪnt]
Anmerkung note [nəʊt]
annähernd nearly ['nɪəli]
Anorak anorak ['ænəræk]
Anregung suggestion [sə'dʒestʃn]
Anrufbeantworter answerphone ['ɑ:nsəfəʊn]
anrufen to call [kɔ:l]; to phone [fəʊn]; to ring [rɪŋ]
ansehen to look at ['lʊk‿ət]; to watch [wɒtʃ]
sich ansehen to look at ['lʊk‿ət]
anstatt instead of [ɪn'sted‿əv]
anstreichen to paint [peɪnt]
antippen to touch [tʌtʃ]
Antwort answer ['ɑ:nsə]; response [rɪ'spɒns]
Anweisung instruction [ɪn'strʌkʃn]
anziehen to put on [pʊt‿'ɒn]
sich anziehen to dress [dres]
Apfel apple ['æpl]
Apparat machine [mə'ʃi:n]
April April ['eɪprl]
Arbeit work [wɜ:k]
arbeiten to work [wɜ:k]
Arbeitsblatt worksheet ['wɜ:kʃi:t]
Arbeitsgemeinschaft club [klʌb]
Arbeitsstelle job [dʒɒb]
Architekt/Architektin architect ['ɑ:kɪtekt]
Arena arena [ə'ri:nə]
Ärger trouble ['trʌbl]
Argument argument ['ɑ:gjəmənt]
argumentieren to argue ['ɑ:gju:]
arm poor [pɔ:; pʊə]
Arm arm [ɑ:m]
Art kind [kaɪnd]; way [weɪ]
Artikel article ['ɑ:tɪkl]
Arzt/Ärztin doctor ['dɒktə]
zum Arzt gehen to see a doctor [si: ə 'dɒktə]
Assistent/Assistentin assistant [ə'sɪstnt]
Attraktion attraction [ə'trækʃn]
auch also ['ɔ:lsəʊ]; too [tu:]
sowohl … als auch as well as [əz 'wel‿əz]
auf at [æt; ət]; in [ɪn]; on [ɒn]; onto ['ɒntu:; 'ɒntə]; up [ʌp]
auf … zu towards [tə'wɔ:dz]
auf dem Land in the country [ˌɪn ðə 'kʌntri]
auf einmal suddenly ['sʌdnli]
auf Sendung on the air [ˌɒn ði‿'eə]
auf Wiedersehen goodbye [gʊd'baɪ]
auf … hinauf onto ['ɒntu:; 'ɒntə]
aufbauen to put up [pʊt‿'ʌp]
wieder aufbauen to rebuild [ˌri:'bɪld]
Aufblinken flash [flæʃ]
aufführen to perform [pə'fɔ:m]
Aufführung performance [pə'fɔ:məns]
Aufgabe exercise ['eksəsaɪz]
aufgeben to give up [gɪv‿'ʌp]
aufgehen to open ['əʊpn]
aufgeregt excited [ɪk'saɪtɪd]; nervous ['nɜ:vəs]
aufgeregt sein to be upset [bi: ʌp'set]
aufheben to pick up [pɪk‿'ʌp]
aufhören to finish ['fɪnɪʃ]; to stop [stɒp]
aufhören etw. zu tun to stop + -ing [stɒp]
aufhören mit to stop [stɒp]
aufmachen to open ['əʊpn]

German – English

aufnehmen to record [rɪ'kɔ:d]
aufpassen auf to look after [lʊk‿'ɑ:ftə]
sich **aufregen** to panic ['pænɪk]
aufregend exciting [ɪk'saɪtɪŋ]
Aufregung fuss [fʌs]
aufschauen to look up [lʊk‿'ʌp]
aufsetzen to put on [pʊt‿'ɒn]
aufspringen to jump up [dʒʌmp‿'ʌp]
aufstehen to get out of bed [ˌget‿aʊt‿əv 'bed]; to get up [get‿'ʌp]
aufsteigen to get on [get‿'ɒn]
aufstellen to put up [pʊt‿'ʌp]
auftragen *(Make-up)* to put on [pʊt‿'ɒn]
auftreten to perform [pə'fɔ:m]
aufwachen to wake up [weɪk‿'ʌp]
aufwecken to wake up [weɪk‿'ʌp]; to wake [weɪk]
aufzeichnen to record [rɪ'kɔ:d]
Auge eye [aɪ]
Augenblick moment ['məʊmənt]
im Augenblick at the moment [æt ðə 'məʊmənt]
in diesem Augenblick right now [ˌraɪt 'naʊ]
Augenbraue eyebrow ['aɪbraʊ]
August August ['ɔ:gəst]
aus from [frɒm]
aus … heraus out of ['aʊt‿əv]
eine **Ausbildung machen** to train [treɪn]
Ausbildung training ['treɪnɪŋ]
sich **ausdenken** to make up [meɪk‿'ʌp]
Ausflug trip [trɪp]
ausfüllen to fill in [fɪl‿'ɪn]
ausgeben to spend [spend]
ausgehen to go out [gəʊ‿'aʊt]
ausgraben to dig up [dɪg‿'ʌp]
ohne … **auskommen** to go without [ˌgəʊ wɪ'ðaʊt]
auslachen to laugh at ['lɑ:f‿ət]
im **Ausland** abroad [ə'brɔ:d]
ins Ausland abroad [ə'brɔ:d]
ausländisch foreign ['fɒrɪn]
auslösen *(Alarm)* to set off [set‿'ɒf]
Auslöser button ['bʌtn]
ausmachen to put out [pʊt‿'aʊt]
ausrauben to rob [rɒb]
Ausreißer/Ausreißerin runaway ['rʌnəˌweɪ]
sich **ausruhen** to rest [rest]
ausschalten to turn off [tɜ:n‿'ɒf]
ausscheren to swerve [swɜ:v]
aussehen to look [lʊk]
Aussehen look [lʊk]
außer beside [bɪ'saɪd]
außerhalb outside [aʊt'saɪd]
Außerirdischer/Außerirdische alien ['eɪliən]
Aussicht view [vju:]
aussteigen to get out [get‿'aʊt]
aussteigen aus to get off [get‿'ɒf]
Ausstellung exhibition [ˌeksɪ'bɪʃn]
Austausch exchange [ɪks'tʃeɪndʒ]
Australier Australian [ɒs'treɪliən]
australisch Australian [ɒs'treɪliən]
Auswahl choice [tʃɔɪs]
auswählen to choose [tʃu:z]
auswechseln to substitute ['sʌbstɪtju:t]
ausweichen to swerve [swɜ:v]
ausziehen to take off [teɪk‿'ɒf]
Auto car [kɑ:]
Autogramm autograph ['ɔ:təgrɑ:f]

B

Baby baby ['beɪbi]
Bach stream [stri:m]
Bäcker/Bäckerin baker ['beɪkə]
Backofen oven ['ʌvn]
Badeanzug swimsuit ['swɪmsu:t]
Badezimmer bathroom ['bɑ:θrʊm]
Badminton badminton ['bædmɪntən]
Bahnhof station ['steɪʃn]
Bahnsteig platform ['plætfɔ:m]
bald soon [su:n]
Ball ball [bɔ:l]
Banane banana [bə'nɑ:nə]
Bart beard [bɪəd]
Base base [beɪs]
Baseball baseball ['beɪsbɔ:l]
Basketball basketball ['bɑ:skɪtbɔ:l]
Batterie battery ['bætri]
Bauch stomach ['stʌmək]
bauen to build [bɪld]; to construct [kən'strʌkt]
Bauer/Bäuerin farmer ['fɑ:mə]
Bauernhaus farmhouse ['fɑ:mhaʊs]
Bauernhof farm [fɑ:m]
Baum tree [tri:]
Beamter/Beamtin officer ['ɒfɪsə]
beängstigend frightening ['fraɪtnɪŋ]
bedauerlich sad [sæd]
bedauern to feel sorry for [fi:l 'sɒri]
bedeuten to mean [mi:n]
Bedeutung meaning ['mi:nɪŋ]; sense [sens]
Bedienung waiter ['weɪtə]
Beeil dich! Hurry up! [ˌhʌri‿'ʌp]
beenden to finish ['fɪnɪʃ]
beerdigen to bury ['beri]
Beerdigung funeral ['fju:nrəl]
befestigen to fix (to) [fɪks]
befolgen to follow ['fɒləʊ]
befördern to carry ['kæri]
Beginn beginning [bɪ'gɪnɪŋ]; start [stɑ:t]
beginnen to begin [bɪ'gɪn]
begraben to bury ['beri]
behalten to keep [ki:p]
bei at [æt; ət]; with [wɪð]
beide both [bəʊθ]
Beifahrer/Beifahrerin passenger ['pæsndʒə]
Bein leg [leg]
beinahe almost ['ɔ:lməʊst]
zum **Beispiel** for example [ˌfər‿ɪg'zɑ:mpl]
sich **beklagen** to moan [məʊn]
bekommen to get [get]
belebt busy ['bɪzi]
beliebt popular ['pɒpjələ]
bellen to bark [bɑ:k]
Bellen barking ['bɑ:kɪŋ]
bemerken to notice ['nəʊtɪs]
sich stark **bemühen** to try hard [traɪ‿'hɑ:d]
benötigen to need [ni:d]
benutzen to use [ju:z]
beobachten to watch [wɒtʃ]
bereit ready ['redi]
berühmt famous ['feɪməs]
berühren to touch [tʌtʃ]
beschädigen to damage ['dæmɪdʒ]
beschäftigt busy ['bɪzi]
besichtigen to visit ['vɪzɪt]
besitzen to have got [hæv 'gɒt]
Besitzer/Besitzerin owner ['əʊnə]
besonders special ['speʃl]
besorgen to get [get]
besorgt sein to be worried [bi: 'wʌrid]
Besprechung meeting ['mi:tɪŋ]
besser better ['betə]
beste/bester/bestes best [best]
besteigen to climb ['klaɪm]
bestellen to order ['ɔ:də]
am **besten** best [best]
bestürzt sein to be upset [bi: ʌp'set]
Besuch visit ['vɪzɪt]
besuchen to see [si:]; to visit ['vɪzɪt]
Besucher/Besucherin visitor ['vɪzɪtə]
sich **beteiligen an** to enter ['entə]
betreten to enter ['entə]
Bett bed [bed]
beunruhigen to worry ['wʌri]
beunruhigt sein to be worried [bi: 'wʌrid]

bevor before [bɪ'fɔː]
bewachen to guard [gɑːd]
bewegen to move [muːv]
sich bewegen to move [muːv]
bezahlen to pay [peɪ]
Bild picture ['pɪktʃə]
Bildschirm screen [skriːn]
Bildung education [edʒʊ'keɪʃn]
billig cheap [tʃiːp]
Bindeglied link [lɪŋk]
Birne pear [peə]
bis to [tʊ; tə]; until [ʌn'tɪl; n'tɪl]
bis zu up to ['ʌp tə]
Bis dann! See you! ['siː jə]
ein **bisschen** a bit [ə 'bɪt]
bitte please [pliːz]
Bitte schön! Here you are! ['hɪə juː‿ɑː]
Bitte sehr! You're welcome. [jʊə 'welkəm]
bitten um to ask for ['ɑːsk fə]
blasen to blow [bləʊ]
Blatt leaf, leaves *(pl)* [liːf; liːvz]
blau blue [bluː]
Blei lead [led]
bleiben to stay [steɪ]
Bleistift pencil ['pensl]
Blick look [lʊk]
einen vernichtenden Blick zuwerfen to give … a dirty look [ˌgɪv‿ə dɜːti 'lʊk]
blind blind [blaɪnd]
Blitzen flash [flæʃ]
blöd stupid ['stjuːpɪd]
blond blond [blɒnd]; blond(e)-haired ['blɒndˌheəd]; fair [feə]
bloß only ['əʊnli]
Blume flower ['flaʊə]
Blut blood [blʌd]
Boden bottom ['bɒtəm]; ground [graʊnd]
Bohne bean [biːn]
Bonbon sweet [swiːt]
Boot boat [bəʊt]
borgen to borrow ['bɒrəʊ]
bösartig fierce [fɪəs]
böse angry ['æŋgri]
böse sein auf to be angry with [biː 'æŋgri wɪð]
Boss boss [bɒs]
Brand fire [faɪə]
brauchen to need [niːd]
(Zeit) brauchen to take [teɪk]
braun brown [braʊn]
Breakdance tanzen to break-dance ['breɪkdɑːnts]

brechen to break [breɪk]
brennen to burn [bɜːn]
brennen *(Licht)* to be on [biː‿'ɒn]
schwarzes Brett notice board ['nəʊtɪs bɔːd]
Brief letter ['letə]
Briefmarke stamp [stæmp]
Brieftasche wallet ['wɒlɪt]
Briefumschlag envelope ['envələʊp]
bringen to bring [brɪŋ]; to take [teɪk]
nach Hause bringen to take home [ˌteɪk 'həʊm]
britisch British ['brɪtɪʃ]
Brot bread [bred]
belegtes Brot sandwich ['sænwɪdʒ]
Brücke bridge [brɪdʒ]
Bruder brother ['brʌðə]
Buch book [bʊk]
buchen to book [bʊk]
Büchse tin [tɪn]
Buchstabe letter ['letə]
buchstabieren to spell [spel]
Bude stall [stɔːl]
bügeln to iron [aɪən]
Bumm! Crash! [kræʃ]
bunt colourful ['kʌləfl]
Burg castle ['kɑːsl]
Büro office ['ɒfɪs]
Bus bus [bʌs]
im Bus on the bus [ˌɒn ðə 'bʌs]
Busch bush [bʊʃ]
Bushaltestelle bus stop ['bʌs ˌstɒp]
Butter butter ['bʌtə]

C

Café café ['kæfeɪ]
Cafeteria cafeteria [ˌkæfə'tɪəriə]
Camping camping ['kæmpɪŋ]
Cartoon cartoon [kɑː'tuːn]
CD CD [ˌsiː'diː]
CD-Player CD player [ˌsiː'diː ˌpleɪə]
Celsius Celsius (C) ['selsiəs]
Charts charts *(pl)* [tʃɑːts]
Chef/Chefin boss [bɒs]
chinesisch Chinese [tʃaɪ'niːz]
circa about [ə'baʊt]
Clown clown [klaʊn]
Cola coke [kəʊk]
College college ['kɒlɪdʒ]
Comic comic ['kɒmɪk]
Comicheft comic ['kɒmɪk]
Computer computer [ˌkəm'pjuːtə]
cool cool [kuːl]
Cornflakes cornflakes ['kɔːnfleɪks]

aus **Cornwall** Cornish ['kɔːnɪʃ]
Couch couch [kaʊtʃ]; sofa ['səʊfə]
Countdown countdown ['kaʊntdaʊn]
Cousin/Cousine cousin ['kʌzn]
Curry *(Gewürz oder Gericht)* curry ['kʌri]

D

da there [ðeə]
da drüben over there [ˌəʊvə 'ðeə]
da ist there is [ðeər‿'ɪz]
da sind there are [ðeər‿'ɑː]
Dach roof [ruːf]
dank thanks to ['θæŋks tə]
danke thanks [θæŋks]; thank you ['θæŋk juː]
danken to thank [θæŋk]
dann then [ðen]
darauf zu towards [tə'wɔːdz]
quer **darüber** across [ə'krɒs]
das the [ðə; ði]; that [ðæt]
Das nenne ich … . That's what I call … . [ˌðæts wɒt‿'aɪ ˌkɔːl]
Datum date [deɪt]
dauern to take [teɪk]
Decke blanket ['blæŋkɪt]
dein/deine your [jɔː]
Dein … *(in Briefen)* Yours [jɔːz]
Deine … *(in Briefen)* Yours [jɔːz]
denken to think [θɪŋk]
der the [ðə; ði]
der/dem/den/die *(Relativpronomen)* who [huː]
der/dem/den/die/das *(Relativpronomen)* which [wɪtʃ]
deren whose [huːz]
derselbe/dieselbe/dasselbe the same [seɪm]
Desaster disaster [dɪ'zɑːstə]
deshalb that's why ['ðæts ˌwaɪ]
dessen whose [huːz]
Dessert dessert [dɪ'zɜːt]
Detektiv/Detektivin detective [dɪ'tektɪv]
deutsch German ['dʒɜːmən]
Deutscher/Deutsche German ['dʒɜːmən]
Dezember December [dɪ'sembə]
Dialog dialogue ['daɪəlɒg]
Diamant diamond ['daɪəmənd]
Diät diet [daɪət]
eine Diät machen to go on a diet [ˌgəʊ‿ɒn‿ə 'daɪət]
dich you [juː; jə]

German – English

Dichter/Dichterin poet ['pəʊɪt]
dick thick [θɪk]
die the [ðə; ði]
Diener/Dienerin servant ['sɜ:vnt]
Dienst service ['sɜ:vɪs]
Dienstag Tuesday ['tju:zdeɪ]
dies this [ðɪs]
diese/dieser/dieses this [ðɪs]
diese *(pl)* these [ði:z]
diese dort those [ðəʊz]
diese hier these [ði:z]
an diesem Abend that evening [ˌdæt‿'i:vnɪŋ]
digital digital ['dɪdʒɪtl]
Ding thing [θɪŋ]
dir you [ju:; jə]
direkt direct [dɪ'rekt]
Direktor/Direktorin director [dɪ'rektə]
Disko disco ['dɪskəʊ]
DJ DJ [ˌdi:'dʒeɪ]
Dokumentarfilm documentary [ˌdɒkjə'mentri]
dokumentiert on record [ɒn 'rekɔ:d]
Dokusoap docu soap ['dɒkju ˌsəʊp]
Dom cathedral [kə'θi:drl]
Donnerstag Thursday ['θɜ:zdeɪ]
Doppelgänger double ['dʌbl]
das **Doppelte** double ['dʌbl]
Dorf village ['vɪlɪdʒ]
dort there [ðeə]
Dose tin [tɪn]
Drama drama ['drɑ:mə]
dramatisch dramatic [drə'mætɪk]
draußen outside [aʊt'saɪd]
Drehbuch script [skrɪpt]
drehen to turn [tɜ:n]
drin inside [ɪn'saɪd]
dritte/dritter/drittes third [θɜ:d]
drücken to press [pres]
drucken to print [prɪnt]
drücken to push [pʊʃ]
du you [ju:; jə]
Du bist dran. It's your turn. [ɪts jɔ: 'tɜ:n]
dumm silly ['sɪli]; stupid ['stju:pɪd]; thick [θɪk]
Dummkopf idiot ['ɪdɪət]; silly ['sɪli]
dunkel dark [dɑ:k]
Dunkelheit dark [dɑ:k]
durch through [θru:]
quer durch across [ə'krɒs]
durchdrehen to get into such a state [getˌɪntə 'sʌtʃ‿ə 'staɪt]; to go bananas [ˌgəʊ bə'nɑ:nəz]
Durcheinander mess [mes]
durcheinander bringen to upset [ʌp'set]
Durchsage announcement [ə'naʊntsmənt]
durchschnittlich average ['ævrɪdʒ]
dürfen can [kæn]
nicht dürfen mustn't ['mʌsnt]
Dusche shower ['ʃaʊə]
DVD DVD [di:vi:'di:]
DVD-Player DVD player [di:vi:'di: 'pleɪə]

E

Ebene level ['levl]
echt real [rɪəl]
Es ist mir **egal.** I don't care. [aɪ dəʊnt 'keə]
Ehefrau wife, wives *(pl)* [waɪf; waɪvz]
Ei egg [eg]
eifersüchtig (auf) jealous (of) ['dʒeləs]
eigener/eigene/eigenes own [əʊn]
es **eilig haben** to be in a hurry [bi:‿ɪn‿ə 'hʌri]
ein/eine a, an [ə; ən]
ein paar a few [ə 'fju:]
einander each other [ˌi:tʃ‿'ʌðə]
Einband cover ['kʌvə]
Einbrecher/Einbrecherin burglar ['bɜ:glə]
einfach easy ['i:zi]
Einfall idea [aɪ'dɪə]
einflussreich important [ɪm'pɔ:tnt]
Eingang entrance ['entrənts]
eingängig catchy ['kætʃi]
einige a few [ə 'fju:]; any ['enɪ]; some [sʌm]
Einkauf shopping ['ʃɒpɪŋ]
Einkaufen shopping ['ʃɒpɪŋ]
Einkaufswagen trolley ['trɒli]
einladen to invite [ɪn'vaɪt]
Einladung invitation [ˌɪnvɪ'teɪʃn]
einmal once [wʌnts]
einsam lonely ['ləʊnli]
einschicken to send in [send‿'ɪn]
einschieben to put in [pʊt‿'ɪn]
einsetzen to put in [pʊt‿'ɪn]
einst once [wʌnts]
einsteigen *(Bus)* to get onto [get‿'ɒntə]; to get on [get‿'ɒn]
einsteigen in *(Auto)* to get into [get‿'ɪntə]
einstellen to set [set]
eintreten to enter ['entə]
Eintritt entrance ['entrənts]
Eintritt verboten! Keep out! [ki:p‿'aʊt]
Eintrittskarte ticket ['tɪkɪt]
Einzelkind only child ['əʊnli ˌtʃaɪld]
einzige/einziger/einziges only ['əʊnli]
Eis ice [aɪs]; ice-cream [aɪs'kri:m]
Eisbahn ice rink ['aɪs rɪŋk]
Eiscreme ice-cream [aɪs'kri:m]
Eishockey ice hockey ['aɪs ˌhɒki]
ekelhaft yukky ['jʌki]
Elefant elephant ['elɪfənt]
Ellbogen elbow ['elbəʊ]
Elle *(Längenmaß: 0,914 m)* yard [jɑ:d]
Eltern parents ['peərənts]
E-Mail e-mail ['i:meɪl]
Empfang reception [rɪ'sepʃn]
Empfangschef/Empfangschefin receptionist [rɪ'sepʃnɪst]
Ende end [end]
enden to end [end]
endlich finally ['faɪnli]
englisch English ['ɪŋglɪʃ]
enorm enormous [ɪ'nɔ:məs]
entkommen to escape [ɪ'skeɪp]; to get out [get‿'aʊt]
entlang along [ə'lɒŋ]
Geh ... entlang. Go down ... . ['gəʊ daʊn]
entlanggehen to go down [gəʊ 'daʊn]
entscheiden to decide [dɪ'saɪd]
Entschuldigung! Excuse me! [ɪk'skju:z mi:]
sich **entspannen** to rest [rest]
enttäuscht disappointed [ˌdɪsə'pɔɪntɪd]
entwerfen to design [dɪ'zaɪn]
Entzücken glee [gli:]
er he [hi:]
Erbe/Erbin inheritor [ɪn'herɪtə]
Erbse pea [pi:]
Erdkunde Geography [dʒi'ɒgrəfi]
Ereignis event [ɪ'vent]
erfahren to learn [lɜ:n]
Erfassung registration [ˌredʒɪ'streɪʃn]
erfinden to invent [ɪn'vent]; to make up [meɪk‿'ʌp]
Erfindung fiction ['fɪkʃn]
Erfolg success [sək'ses]
sich **erfreuen** to enjoy [ɪn'dʒɔɪ]
sich **erinnern (an)** to remember [rɪ'membə]
erklären to explain [ɪk'spleɪn]
erläutern to explain [ɪk'spleɪn]
wieder **erleben** to relive [ˌri:'lɪv]
erledigen to finish ['fɪnɪʃ]
erlöschen to go out [gəʊ‿'aʊt]
ermorden to murder ['mɜ:də]
erreichen to catch [kætʃ]; to reach [ri:tʃ]
erschrecken to scare ['skeə]; to upset [ʌp'set]

ersetzen to replace [rɪ'pleɪs]; to substitute ['sʌbstɪtju:t]
erst only ['əʊnli]
erstaunt surprised [sə'praɪzd]
erste/erster/erstes first [fɜ:st]
ersticken to choke [tʃəʊk]
erwarten to expect [ɪk'spekt]
erzählen to tell [tel]
Erzählung story ['stɔ:ri]
Erziehung education [edʒʊ'keɪʃn]
es it [ɪt]
es gibt there are [ðeər‿'ɑ:]; there is [ðeər‿'ɪz]
Es lautete .... It said .... [ɪt 'sed]
essen to eat [i:t]
Essen food [fu:d]
Essen zum Mitnehmen takeaway ['teɪkəweɪ]
Esszimmer dining room ['daɪnɪŋ rʊm]
et cetera etc. [ɪt'setrə]
etwa about [ə'baʊt]; around [ə'raʊnd]
etwas any ['enɪ]; anything ['eniθɪŋ]; some [sʌm]; something ['sʌmθɪŋ]
euch you [ju:; jə]
euer/eure your [jɔ:]
Euer ... *(in Briefen)* Yours [jɔ:z]
Eure ... *(in Briefen)* Yours [jɔ:z]
Euro *(Währung)* euro ['jʊərəʊ]
europäisch European [jʊərə'pi:ən]
Examen exam [ɪg'zæm]
Experiment experiment [ɪk'sperɪmənt]

F

Fackel torch, torches *(pl)* [tɔ:tʃ; 'tɔ:tʃɪz]
Fahne flag [flæg]
Fähre ferry ['feri]
fahren to drive [draɪv]; to ride [raɪd]
fahren *(Schiff)* to sail [seɪl]
Fahrer/Fahrerin driver ['draɪvə]; rider ['raɪdə]
Fahrplan timetable ['taɪmteɪbl]
Fahrrad bicycle ['baɪsɪkl]; bike [baɪk]
mit dem Fahrrad by bike [baɪ 'baɪk]
Fahrschein ticket ['tɪkɪt]
Fahrt journey ['dʒɜ:ni]
fair fair [feə]
Fakt fact [fækt]
in der **Falle sitzen** to be trapped [bi: 'træpt]
fallen to fall [fɔ:l]; to drop [drɒp]
fallen lassen to drop [drɒp]
falls if [ɪf]
falsch wrong [rɒŋ]
falsch machen to get ... wrong [get ... 'rɒŋ]
Familie family ['fæmli]
Fan fan [fæn]
fangen to catch [kætʃ]
Fänger/Fängerin catcher ['kætʃə]
fantastisch fantastic [fæn'tæstɪk]
Farbe colour ['kʌlə]; paint [peɪnt]
färben to dye [daɪ]
farbig colourful ['kʌləfl]
Farm farm [fɑ:m]
fast almost ['ɔ:lməʊst]; nearly ['nɪəli]
Fastfood-Restaurant burger bar ['bɜ:gə ˌbɑ:]
Februar February ['februəri]
Federball badminton ['bædmɪntən]
fehlen to be missing [bi: 'mɪsɪŋ]; to miss [mɪs]
Fehler mistake [mɪ'steɪk]
Feier party ['pɑ:ti]
eine Party **feiern** to have a party [ˌhæv‿ə 'pɑ:ti]
fein fine [faɪn]
Feind/Feindin enemy ['enəmi]
Feld field [fi:ld]
Fenster window ['wɪndəʊ]
Ferien holiday(s) ['hɒlədeɪ(z)]
Ferienhaus cottage ['kɒtɪdʒ]
Fernsehen TV [ˌti:'vi:]
Fernseher TV [ˌti:'vi:]
fertig ready ['redi]
festnehmen to arrest [ə'rest]
Festung fortress ['fɔ:trəs]
Feuer fire [faɪə]
Feuerstelle fire [faɪə]
Feuerwehr fire brigade ['faɪə brɪˌgeɪd]
Figur figure ['fɪgə]
Fiktion fiction ['fɪkʃn]
Film film [fɪlm]
filmen to film [fɪlm]
finden to find [faɪnd]
Finger finger ['fɪŋgə]
Firma firm [fɜ:m]; company ['kʌmpəni]
Fisch fish, fish *(pl)* [fɪʃ]
fischen to fish [fɪʃ]
Fischen fishing ['fɪʃɪŋ]
fit fit [fɪt]
Fläche area ['eəriə]
Flagge flag [flæg]
Flamme flame [fleɪm]
Flasche bottle ['bɒtl]
Fleck mark [mɑ:k]
Fleisch meat [mi:t]
fliegen to fly [flaɪ]
flüchten to escape [ɪ'skeɪp]
Flug flight [flaɪt]
Flugblatt leaflet ['li:flət]
Flughafen airport ['eəpɔ:t]
Flugzeug plane [pleɪn]
Flur corridor ['kɒrɪdɔ:]; hall [hɔ:l]
Fluss river ['rɪvə]
flüstern to whisper ['wɪspə]
flutartige Überschwemmung flash flood ['flæʃ ˌflʌd]
folgen to follow ['fɒləʊ]
folgend/folgender/folgende/folgendes following ['fɒləʊɪŋ]
Football American football [əˌmerɪkən 'fʊtbɔ:l]
Form form [fɔ:m]
Formular form [fɔ:m]
fortgeschritten advanced [əd'vɑ:nst]
fortschaffen to take off [teɪk‿'ɒf]
Foto photo ['fəʊtəʊ]
Fotos machen to take pictures [teɪk 'pɪktʃəz]
Fotoapparat camera ['kæmrə]
Fotografie photo ['fəʊtəʊ]
fotografieren to take pictures [teɪk 'pɪktʃəz]
Frage question ['kwestʃn]
fragen to ask [ɑ:sk]
fragen nach to ask for ['ɑ:sk fə]
französisch French [frentʃ]
Frau woman, women *(pl)* ['wʊmən; 'wɪmɪn]
Frau *(Anrede)* Miss [mɪs]; Mrs ['mɪsɪz]
frei free [fri:]
Freitag Friday [fraɪdeɪ]
fremd foreign ['fɒrɪn]
Fremder/Fremde alien ['eɪliən]; stranger ['streɪndʒə]
fressen to eat [i:t]
Freund/Freundin friend [frend]
Freund *(in einer Paarbeziehung)* boyfriend ['bɔɪfrend]
Freundin *(in einer Paarbeziehung)* girlfriend ['gɜ:lfrend]
freundlich friendly ['frendli]
Friede peace [pi:s]
frieren to be cold [bi: 'kəʊld]
frisch fresh [freʃ]
Friseur/Friseurin hairdresser ['heəˌdresə]
Frisur style [staɪl]
froh glad [glæd]; happy ['hæpi]
Frucht fruit [fru:t]
früh early ['ɜ:li]
Frühling spring [sprɪŋ]
Frühstück breakfast ['brekfəst]
frustriert frustrated [frʌs'treɪtɪd]
fühlen to feel [fi:l]

German – English

sich fühlen to feel [fi:l]
Führer/Führerin guide [gaɪd]; leader ['li:də]
Füller pen [pen]
Fünftel fifth [fɪfθ]
Funke(n) spark [spɑ:k]
funktionieren to work [wɜ:k]
für for [fɔ:; fə]
furchtbar frightening ['fraɪtnɪŋ]; horrible ['hɒrəbl]; terrible ['terəbl]
Fuß foot, feet *(pl)* [fʊt; fi:t]
Fuß *(Längenmaß: 30,48 cm)* foot, feet *(pl)* [fʊt; fi:t]
zu Fuß on foot [ɒn 'fʊt]
Fußball football ['fʊtbɔ:l]
Fußboden floor [flɔ:]
füttern to feed [fi:d]

G

Gabel fork [fɔ:k]
gälisch Gaelic ['geɪlɪk]
Gang corridor ['kɒrɪdɔ:]
Gang *(Menü)* course [kɔ:s]
ganz all [ɔ:l]; full (of) [fʊl]
im Ganzen in all [ɪn‿'ɔ:l]
Garderobe wardrobe ['wɔ:drəʊb]
Garten garden ['gɑ:dn]
Gärtner/Gärtnerin gardener ['gɑ:dnə]
Gast guest [gest]
Gastgeber host [həʊst]
Gate gate [geɪt]
Gebäude building ['bɪldɪŋ]
geben to give [gɪv]
Gebiet area ['eəriə]
gebrochen broken ['brəʊkn]
Geburt birth [bɜ:θ]
Geburtstag birthday ['bɜ:θdeɪ]
Gedicht poem ['pəʊɪm]
gefährlich dangerous ['deɪndʒrəs]
gefallen to please [pli:z]
Gefängnis prison ['prɪzn]
Gefühl feeling ['fi:lɪŋ]
gegen against [ə'genst]
Gegensatz contrast ['kɒntrɑ:st]
im Gegensatz zu in contrast to [ɪn 'kɒntrɑ:st tə]
sich **gegenseitig** each other [ˌi:tʃ‿'ʌðə]
Geheimnis secret ['si:krət]; mystery ['mɪstri]
gehen to go [gəʊ]; to leave [li:v]; to walk [wɔ:k]
… gehen to go + -ing [gəʊ]
Geh … entlang. Go down … . ['gəʊ daʊn]

Geist ghost [gəʊst]; mind [maɪnd]
gelangweilt bored [bɔ:d]
gelb yellow ['jeləʊ]
Geld money ['mʌni]
Geldbeutel wallet ['wɒlɪt]
Geldbuße fine [faɪn]
Geldstrafe fine [faɪn]
Gemälde painting ['peɪntɪŋ]
Gemüse vegetable ['vedʒtəbl]
genau exact [ɪg'zækt]; exactly [ɪg'zæktli]
genau genommen in fact [ɪn 'fækt]
genießen to enjoy [ɪn'dʒɔɪ]
genug enough [ɪ'nʌf]
genügend enough [ɪ'nʌf]
geöffnet open ['əʊpn]
Geografie Geography [dʒi'ɒgrəfi]
Gepäck luggage ['lʌgɪdʒ]
Gepäckaufgabe check-in ['tʃekɪn]
Gepäckwagen trolley ['trɒli]
Geplauder chat [tʃæt]
Geräusch noise [nɔɪz]; sound [saʊnd]
gerecht fair [feə]
Gern geschehen! You're welcome. [jʊə 'welkəm]
gern haben to like [laɪk]
gern mögen to love [lʌv]
Geruch smell [smel]
Gesamtschule comprehensive school [kɒmprɪ'hensɪv ˌsku:l]
Geschäft shop [ʃɒp]; store [stɔ:]
Geschäftsmann businessman, businessmen *(pl)* ['bɪznɪsmən; 'bɪznɪsmen]
geschehen to happen ['hæpn]
Geschenk present ['preznt]
Geschichte History ['hɪstəri]; story ['stɔ:ri]
geschieden von divorced from [dɪ'vɔ:st frəm]
geschockt shocked [ʃɒkt]
Gesellschaft company ['kʌmpəni]
Gesicht face [feɪs]
Gespenst ghost [gəʊst]
Gespräch dialogue ['daɪəlɒg]
Gestalt figure ['fɪgə]
Gestank smell [smel]
gestern yesterday ['jestədeɪ]
gestern Abend last night [lɑ:st 'naɪt]
gestern Nacht last night [lɑ:st 'naɪt]
gesund healthy ['helθi]
Getränk drink [drɪŋk]
Gewächshaus greenhouse ['gri:nhaʊs]
gewaltig huge [hju:dʒ]
Gewicht weight [weɪt]
gewinnen to win [wɪn]
Gewinner/Gewinnerin winner ['wɪnə]

gewöhnlich usually ['ju:ʒli]
Gitter grid [grɪd]
Glas glass [glɑ:s]
glauben to believe [bɪ'li:v]; to think [θɪŋk]
gleich the same [seɪm]
gleich *(zeitlich)* right away [raɪt‿ə'weɪ]
Glocke bell [bel]
Glück luck [lʌk]
du hast Glück you're lucky [ˌjʊə 'lʌki]
Viel Glück! Good luck! [ˌgʊd 'lʌk]
glücklich happy ['hæpi]; lucky ['lʌki]
Gold gold [gəʊld]
Mein **Gott!** My God! [maɪ 'gɒd]
Grab grave [greɪv]
Grabstein gravestone ['greɪvstəʊn]
Grad degree (°) [dɪ'gri:]
Gramm gramme (g) [græm]
Gras grass [grɑ:s]
grau grey [greɪ]
greifen to grab [græb]
Grieche/Griechin Greek [gri:k]
griechisch Greek [gri:k]
groß big [bɪg]; great [greɪt]; large [lɑ:dʒ]; tall [tɔ:l]
großartig fantastic [fæn'tæstɪk]; great [greɪt]; wicked ['wɪkɪd]
Größe height [haɪt]; size [saɪz]
Großstadt city ['sɪti]
grün green [gri:n]
Grund bottom ['bɒtəm]
Grundlinie back line [ˌbæk'lain]
Grundschule primary school ['praɪməri ˌsku:l]
Gruppe group [gru:p]
gruselig scary ['skeəri]
Gummi rubber ['rʌbə]
Gummistiefel rubber boots *(pl)* [ˌrʌbə 'bu:ts]
gut fine [faɪn]; good [gʊd]; well [wel]
Es geht uns gut. We're OK. [ˌwɪər‿əʊ'keɪ]
Guten Morgen! Good morning! ['gʊd 'mɔ:nɪŋ]
gut mit … umgehen können to be good with … [bi: 'gʊd wɪð]
ich bin gut in … I'm good at … [aɪm 'gʊd‿ət]
Gymnasium grammar school ['græmə ˌsku:l]

H

Haar, Haare hair [heə]
haben to have [hæv]; to have got [hæv 'gɒt]

Hafen port [pɔ:t]
Hähnchen chicken ['tʃɪkɪn]
halb half [hɑ:f]
zum halben Preis half-price [ˌhɑ:f'praɪs]
eine halbe Stunde half an hour [ˌhɑ:f‿ən‿'aʊə]
halb (drei) half past (two) ['hɑ:f pɑ:st]
Halbschwester half-sister ['hɑ:fˌsɪstə]
Halbzeit half-time [ˌhɑ:f'taɪm]
Hälfte half [hɑ:f]
Halle hall [hɔ:l]
Hallo! Hello! [he'ləʊ]
halten to keep [ki:p]
Haltestelle stop [stɒp]
Hand hand [hænd]
Hände weg! Hands off! [hændz‿'ɒf]
Handkarren trolley ['trɒli]
Handlung action ['ækʃn]
Handschuh glove [glʌv]
Handtasche handbag ['hænbæg]
Handy mobile ['məʊbaɪl]
hart hard [hɑ:d]; tough [tʌf]
Hass hate [heɪt]
hassen to hate [heɪt]
hätte gern would like [wʊd 'laɪk]
Haupt- main [meɪn]
Haus house [haʊs]
zu Hause at home [ət 'həʊm]
Hausaufgabe/Hausaufgaben homework ['həʊmwɜ:k]
Hausmeister/Hausmeisterin caretaker ['keəˌteɪkə]
Haustier pet [pet]
Heft exercise book ['eksəsaɪz ˌbʊk]
Heim home [həʊm]
Heimat home [həʊm]
heiraten to marry ['mæri]
heiß hot [hɒt]
Ich **heiße** .... My name is .... [maɪ 'neɪm‿ɪz]
Heizung heating ['hi:tɪŋ]
Held hero, heroes *(pl)* ['hɪərəʊ; 'hɪərəʊz]
Heldin heroine ['herəʊɪn]
helfen to help [help]
Helikopter helicopter ['helɪˌkɒptə]
hell fair [feə]
Helm helmet ['helmət]
Hemd shirt [ʃɜ:t]
(die Treppe) **herauf** upstairs [ʌp'steəz]
heraus out [aʊt]
herausfinden to find out [faɪnd‿'aʊt]
herausnehmen to take out [teɪk‿'aʊt]
Herbst autumn ['ɔ:təm]
herein in [ɪn]
hereinkommen to come in [kʌm‿'ɪn]
Herr *(Anrede)* Mr ['mɪstə]
herüberkommen to come over [kʌm‿'əʊvə]
herüberreichen to pass [pɑ:s]
um ... **herum** around [ə'raʊnd]
herumspringen to jump about [ˌdʒʌmp‿ə'baʊt]
sich **herumtreiben** to hang out [hæŋ‿'aʊt]
(die Treppe) **herunter** downstairs [ˌdaʊn'steəz]
herunter off [ɒf]
herunterfallen to fall [fɔ:l]; to fall off [fɔ:l‿ɒf]
herunterkommen to come down [kʌm 'daʊn]
herunterladen to download [ˌdaʊn'ləʊd]
Herzliche Grüße love [lʌv]
heute today [tə'deɪ]
heute Abend tonight [tə'naɪt]
heute Nacht tonight [tə'naɪt]
Hi! Hi! [haɪ]
hier here [hɪə]
Hilfe help [help]
hilflos helpless ['helpləs]
hilfreich helpful ['helpfəl]
Himmel sky [skaɪ]
(die Treppe) **hinauf** upstairs [ʌp'steəz]
hinauf up [ʌp]
die Treppe **hinaufrennen** to run upstairs [ˌrʌn‿ʌp'steəz]
hinaufschauen to look up [lʊk‿'ʌp]
hinausgehen to go out [gəʊ‿'aʊt]
hinauslehnen to lean out [li:n‿'aʊt]
sich hinauslehnen to lean out [li:n‿'aʊt]
hinausstellen to put out [pʊt‿'aʊt]
hineingehen to go in [gəʊ 'ɪn]
hinfallen to fall [fɔ:l]
hingehen to walk up [wɔ:k‿'ʌp]
hinlegen to lie down [laɪ 'daʊn]
sich hinlegen to lie down [laɪ 'daʊn]
sich **hinsetzen** to sit down [sɪt 'daʊn]
hinten at the back [ət ðə 'bæk]
hinter behind [bɪ'haɪnd]
Hinter- back [bæk]
hinterhergehen to follow ['fɒləʊ]
hinüber across [ə'krɒs]
hinübergehen to go over [gəʊ‿'əʊvə]
(die Treppe) **hinunter** downstairs [ˌdaʊn'steəz]
hinuntergehen to go down [gəʊ 'daʊn]
Hinweis clue [klu:]
hinzufügen to add [æd]
Hit hit [hɪt]
Hitparade charts *(pl)* [tʃɑ:ts]
Hobby hobby ['hɒbi]
hoch high [haɪ]; tall [tɔ:l]
hochheben to lift [lɪft]
Hochmoor moor [mɔ:]
hochspringen to jump up [dʒʌmp‿'ʌp]
Hochwasser flood [flʌd]
hochziehen to lift [lɪft]
Hockey hockey ['hɒki]
hoffen to hope [həʊp]
höflich polite [pə'laɪt]
Höhe height [haɪt]
Höhle cave [keɪv]
holen to get [get]
Holz wood [wʊd]
hölzern wooden ['wʊdn]
hören to hear [hɪə]
Horoskop horoscope ['hɒrəskəʊp]
Hose trousers *(pl)* ['traʊzəz]
kurze Hose shorts *(pl)* [ʃɔ:ts]
Hosentasche pocket ['pɒkɪt]
Hotel hotel [həʊ'tel]
Hubschrauber helicopter ['helɪˌkɒptə]
Huhn chicken ['tʃɪkɪn]
Hund dog [dɒg]
mit dem Hund spazieren gehen to walk the dog [wɔ:k ðə 'dɒg]
hundemüde dog-tired [ˌdɒg'taɪəd]
hundert hundred ['hʌndrəd]
Hunger bekommen to get hungry [get 'hʌŋgri]
hungrig hungry ['hʌŋgri]
Hut hat [hæt]

I

ich I [aɪ]
Ich heiße .... My name is .... [maɪ 'neɪm‿ɪz]
Ich nehme .... I'm having .... [aɪm 'hævɪŋ]
ich würde gern I'd like to [ˌaɪd 'laɪk tə]
ich würde lieber I'd rather [aɪd 'rɑ:ðə]
Idee idea [aɪ'dɪə]
Idiot idiot ['ɪdɪət]
ihm him [hɪm]
ihn him [hɪm]
ihnen them [ðem]
Ihnen you [ju:; jə]
ihr you [ju:; jə]
ihr/ihre her [hɜ:]; their [ðeə]; its [ɪts]
Ihr/Ihre your [jɔ:]

German – English

Ikone icon ['aɪkɒn]
im Gange sein to be on [biː‿'ɒn]
Imbiss snack [snæk]
immer always ['ɔːlweɪz]
immer noch still [stɪl]
im unteren Teil at the bottom [ət ðə 'bɒtəm]
in at [æt; ət]; in [ɪn]; into ['ɪntə]
in ... hinein into ['ɪntə]
indisch Indian ['ɪndiən]
Industrie industry ['ɪndəstri]
Information/Informationen information [ˌɪnfə'meɪʃn]
Informationszentrum information centre [ɪnfə'meɪʃn ˌsentə]
Inhalt content ['kɒntent]
Inlineskates skates *(pl)* [skeɪts]
Inlineskates fahren to skate [skeɪt]
innen inside [ɪn'saɪd]
innerhalb within [wɪ'ðɪn]
Insel island ['aɪlənd]
insgesamt in all [ɪn‿'ɔːl]
Inspektor inspector [ɪn'spektə]
Institut college ['kɒlɪdʒ]
Instruktion instruction [ɪn'strʌkʃn]
interessant interesting ['ɪntrəstɪŋ]
sich **interessieren für** to get interested in [get 'ɪntrəstɪd]
interessiert interested ['ɪntrəstɪd]
international international [ˌɪntə'næʃnl]
Internet Internet ['ɪntənet]
im Internet surfen to surf the Internet [ˌsɜːf ði‿'ɪntənet]
Internetauftritt website ['websaɪt]
Interview interview ['ɪntəvjuː]
interviewen to interview ['ɪntəvjuː]
irgendetwas anything ['eniθɪŋ]
irgendjemand anybody ['eniˌbɒdi]; anyone ['eniwʌn]
irgendwo anywhere ['eniweə]; somewhere ['sʌmweə]
irisch Irish ['aɪrɪʃ]
Italiener/Italienerin Italian [ɪ'tæliən]
italienisch Italian [ɪ'tæliən]

J

ja yes [jes]
Jacke jacket ['dʒækɪt]
Jackentasche pocket ['pɒkɪt]
Jagdhund hound [haʊnd]
Jagen hunting ['hʌntɪŋ]
Jahr year [jɪə]
Jahreszeit season ['siːzn]
Jahrgangsstufe year [jɪə]
Jahrhundert century ['sentʃri]
Jahrmarkt fair [feə]
Jahrtausend millennium [mɪ'leniəm]
Januar January ['dʒænjuəri]
Jazz jazz [dʒæz]
je each [iːtʃ]
jede/jeder/jedes each [iːtʃ]; every ['evri]
jeder (beliebige) anybody ['eniˌbɒdi]; anyone ['eniwʌn]
jeder everyone ['evriwʌn]
jemals ever ['evə]
jemand someone ['sʌmwʌn]; somebody ['sʌmbədi]
jene those [ðəʊz]
jenes that [ðæt]
jetzt now [naʊ]
jetzt gleich right now [ˌraɪt 'naʊ]
jeweils each [iːtʃ]
Job job [dʒɒb]
joggen to jog [dʒɒg]
Jugend youth [juːθ]
jugendlich teenage ['tiːneɪdʒ]
Jugendliche/Jugendlicher teenager ['tiːnˌeɪdʒə]; teen [tiːn]
Juli July [dʒʊ'laɪ]
jung young [jʌŋ]
Junge boy [bɔɪ]; lad [læd]
Juni June [dʒuːn]
Juwel jewel ['dʒuːəl]

K

Kalender calendar ['kæləndə]
kalt cold [kəʊld]
Kamera camera ['kæmrə]
Kamin fireplace ['faɪəpleɪs]
Kaminfeuer fire [faɪə]
Kampf fight [faɪt]
kämpfen to fight [faɪt]
Kampfrichter judge [dʒʌdʒ]
Kanal channel ['tʃænl]
Kanu fahren to canoe [kə'nuː]
Kappe cap [kæp]
Kapsel capsule ['kæpsjuːl]
kaputt broken ['brəʊkn]
kaputtmachen to break [breɪk]
Karotte carrot ['kærət]
Karte card [kɑːd]
Kartoffel potato, potatoes *(pl)* [pə'teɪtəʊ]
Kartoffelchip crisp [krɪsp]
Käse cheese [tʃiːz]
Kasten box [bɒks]
Katastrophe disaster [dɪ'zɑːstə]
Kathedrale cathedral [kə'θiːdrl]
Katze cat [kæt]
kaufen to buy [baɪ]
Kaufhaus department store [dɪ'pɑːtmənt stɔː]; store [stɔː]
Kaufhausdetektiv/Kaufhausdetektivin store detective ['stɔː dɪˌtektɪv]
Kautschuk rubber ['rʌbə]
kein/keine no [nəʊ]
keine Ahnung no idea [ˌnəʊ‿aɪ'dɪə]
keiner/keine none [nʌn]
Keks biscuit ['bɪskɪt]
Kelch cup [kʌp]
Kellergeschoss basement ['beɪsmənt]
Kellner waiter ['weɪtə]
kennen to know [nəʊ]
Kerl bloke [bləʊk]
Kette chain [tʃeɪn]
Kick kick [kɪk]
kicken to kick [kɪk]
Kilo(gramm) kilo (kg) ['kɪləʊ]
Kilometer kilometre ['kɪləʊˌmiːtə; kɪ'lɒmɪtə]
Kind child, children *(pl)* [tʃaɪld; 'tʃɪldrɪn]; kid [kɪd]
Kino cinema ['sɪnəmə]
Kirche church [tʃɜːtʃ]
Kiste box [bɒks]
klagen to moan [məʊn]
Klang sound [saʊnd]
klar clear [klɪə]
klären *(ein Problem)* to sort out [sɔːt‿'aʊt]
Klasse class [klɑːs]
Klassenarbeit test [test]
Klassenzimmer classroom ['klɑːsrʊm]
klatschen to clap [klæp]
Kleider clothes *(pl)* [kləʊθs]
Kleidergröße size [saɪz]
Kleiderschrank wardrobe ['wɔːdrəʊb]
Kleidung clothes *(pl)* [kləʊθs]
klein little [lɪtl]; small [smɔːl]
klettern to climb ['klaɪm]
klicken to click [klɪk]
Klingel bell [bel]
klingeln to ring [rɪŋ]
Es klingelt. The bell rings. [ðə 'bel rɪŋz]
klingen to sound [saʊnd]
Klippe cliff [klɪf]
klopfen to knock [nɒk]
fest klopfen to bang [bæŋ]
Klopfen knock [nɒk]
Kloster monastery ['mɒnəstri]
Klub club [klʌb]

knarren to creak [kriːk]
Knie knee [niː]
Knopf button ['bʌtn]
Kobold goblin ['gɒblɪn]
Koch/Köchin cook [kʊk]
Kochen cooking ['kʊkɪŋ]
komisch funny ['fʌni]
kommen to come [kʌm]; to get [get]
Komm./Kommt. Come on. [kʌm‿'ɒn]
Komödie comedy ['kɒmədi]
Kompanie company ['kʌmpəni]
Komparativ comparative [kəm'pærətɪv]
König king [kɪŋ]
Königin queen [kwiːn]
königlich royal ['rɔɪəl]
können can [kæn]
konnte/konnten could [kʊd]
könnte/könnten could [kʊd]
kann/könnte(n) vielleicht may [meɪ]
konstruieren to construct [kən'strʌkt]
Kontrast contrast ['kɒntrɑːst]
Konzert concert ['kɒnsət]
Kopf head [hed]
Kopfhörer headphones *(pl)* ['hedfəʊnz]
Kopfsalat lettuce ['letɪs]
kopieren to copy ['kɒpi]
kornisch Cornish ['kɔːnɪʃ]
Körper body ['bɒdi]
körperlich physical ['fɪzɪkl]
korrekt correct [kə'rekt]; right [raɪt]
Korridor corridor ['kɒrɪdɔː]
krabbeln to crawl [krɔːl]
Krach! Crash! [kræʃ]
Kraft power ['paʊə]
krank sick [sɪk]
Krankenhaus hospital ['hɒspɪtl]
Krankenpfleger nurse [nɜːs]
Krankenschwester nurse [nɜːs]
Krankenwagen ambulance ['æmbjələnts]
Krankmeldung sick note ['sɪk ˌnəʊt]
Kreis circle ['sɜːkl]
Kreuzfahrt cruise [kruːz]
Kricket cricket ['krɪkɪt]
kriechen to crawl [krɔːl]
Krimi detective story [dɪ'tektɪv ˌstɔːri]
Kriminalität crime [kraɪm]
Krone crown [kraʊn]
Küche kitchen ['kɪtʃɪn]
Kuchen cake [keɪk]
Küchenschrank cupboard ['kʌbəd]
Kuh cow [kaʊ]
sich **kümmern** to care [keə]
sich kümmern um to look after [lʊk‿'ɑːftə]
Kunde/Kundin customer ['kʌstəmə]
Kunst Art [ɑːt]
Kurier courier ['kʊriə]
Kurs class [klɑːs]
Kurve curve [kɜːv]
kurz short [ʃɔːt]
küssen to kiss [kɪs]
Küste coast [kəʊst]; seaside ['siːsaɪd]
Küstenlinie coastline ['kəʊstlaɪn]

L

Labor lab(oratory) [læb; lə'bɒrətri]
lächeln to smile [smaɪl]
lachen to laugh [lɑːf]
Laden shop [ʃɒp]; store [stɔː]
Lamm lamb [læm]
Lammfleisch lamb [læm]
Land country ['kʌntri]; land [lænd]; state [steɪt]
landen to land [lænd]
landesweit national ['næʃnl]
Landkarte map [mæp]
Landstraße road [rəʊd]
Landwirt/Landwirtin farmer ['fɑːmə]
lang long [lɒŋ]
langsam slow [sləʊ]
langweilig boring ['bɔːrɪŋ]
Laptop laptop ['læptɒp]
Lärm noise [nɔɪz]
lassen to leave [liːv]; to let [let]
Lasst uns .... Let's .... [lets]
Lassi *(Jogurtgetränk)* lassi ['lasɪ]
Laterne lantern ['læntən]
Lauf run [rʌn]
laufen to run [rʌn]; to walk [wɔːk]; to be on [biː‿'ɒn]
laufen gegen to run into [rʌn‿'ɪntə]
Läufer/Läuferin runner ['rʌnə]
laut loud [laʊd]
Es **lautete** .... It said .... [ɪt 'sed]
leben to live [lɪv]
Leben life, lives *(pl)* [laɪf; laɪvz]
am Leben alive [ə'laɪv]
lebendig alive [ə'laɪv]
Lebensmittel food [fuːd]
leer empty ['empti]
legen to put [pʊt]
sich legen to come down [kʌm 'daʊn]
lehren to teach [tiːtʃ]
Lehrer/Lehrerin teacher ['tiːtʃə]
leicht easy ['iːzi]
Tut mir **Leid.** sorry ['sɒri]
leihen to borrow ['bɒrəʊ]; to lend [lend]
Leinwand screen [skriːn]
leise quiet ['kwaɪət]; soft [sɒft]
Leiter ladder ['lædə]
lernen to learn [lɜːn]; to study ['stʌdi]
lesen to read [riːd]
letzte/letzter/letztes last [lɑːst]; final ['faɪnl]
leuchten to glow [gləʊ]
leuchtend brilliant ['brɪljənt]
Leute people ['piːpl]
Licht light [laɪt]
lieb dear [dɪə]
Liebe love [lʌv]
Liebe ... *(Anrede in Briefen)* Dear [dɪə]
Lieber ... *(Anrede in Briefen)* Dear [dɪə]
lieben to love [lʌv]
ich würde **lieber** I'd rather [aɪd 'rɑːðə]
Liebling pet [pet]
Lieblings- favourite ['feɪvrɪt]
Lied song [sɒŋ]
liefern to deliver [dɪ'lɪvə]
Lieferwagen van [væn]
liegen to lie [laɪ]
Liga union ['juːnjən]
lila purple ['pɜːpl]
Limonade lemonade [ˌlemə'neɪd]
Lineal ruler ['ruːlə]
Linie line [laɪn]
linke/linker/linkes left [left]
links left [left]; on the left [ɒn ðə 'left]
links abbiegen to turn left [tɜːn 'left]
Lippenpflegestift lip balm ['lɪp bɑːm]
Liste list [lɪst]
live live [laɪv]
Loch dump [dʌmp]
Löffel spoon [spuːn]
lokal local ['ləʊkl]
löschen *(Text)* to delete [dɪ'liːt]
löschen *(Feuer)* to put out [pʊt‿'aʊt]
lösen to solve [sɒlv]
losgehen *(Alarm)* to go off [gəʊ‿'ɒf]
Löwe lion ['laɪən]
Luft air [eə]
lustig funny ['fʌni]
sich lustig machen über to laugh at ['lɑːf‿ət]
Lyrik poetry ['pəʊətri]

M

machen to do [duː]; to make [meɪk]
eine Diät machen to go on a diet [ˌgəʊ‿ɒn ə 'daɪət]

German – English

sich lustig machen über to laugh at ['lɑ:f ət]
Spaß machen to be fun [bi: 'fʌn]
Macht power ['paʊə]
Mädchen girl [gɜ:l]
Magazin magazine [mægə'zi:n]
Magen stomach ['stʌmək]
Mahlzeit meal [mi:l]
Mai May [meɪ]
Make-up make-up ['meɪkʌp]
Mal *(zeitlich)* time [taɪm]
malen to paint [peɪnt]
Mama mum [mʌm]
man they [ðeɪ]; you [ju:; jə]
Manager/Managerin manager ['mænɪdʒə]
manchmal sometimes ['sʌmtaɪmz]
Mann man, men *(pl)* [mæn; men]
Mannschaft team [ti:m]
Mantel coat [kəʊt]
Mäppchen pencil case ['pensl ˌkeɪs]
Mappe folder ['fəʊldə]
Markstein landmark ['lændmɑ:k]
Markt market ['mɑ:kɪt]
Marmelade jam [dʒæm]
März March [mɑ:tʃ]
Maschine machine [mə'ʃi:n]; engine ['endʒɪn]
Mast post [pəʊst]
Mathematik Maths [mæθs]
Mauer wall [wɔ:l]
Maus mouse [maʊs]
Meer sea [si:]
Meeresküste seaside ['si:saɪd]
mehr more [mɔ:]
Mehrzahl plural ['plʊərəl]
Meile *(brit. Längenmaß)* mile [maɪl]
mein/meine my [maɪ]
Mein Gott! My God! [maɪ 'gɒd]
einer **Meinung sein** to agree [ə'gri:]
das **meiste** most [məʊst]
die meisten most [məʊst]
Menagerie menagerie [mə'nædʒri]
eine **Menge** a lot of [ə 'lɒt‿əv]
Menschen people ['pi:pl]
Menschenmenge crowd [kraʊd]
Menü menu ['menju:]
sich **merken** to remember [rɪ'membə]
merkwürdig strange [streɪndʒ]
Messe fair [feə]
Messer knife, knives *(pl)* [naɪf; naɪvz]
Meter metre ['mi:tə]
mich me [mi:]
Miesmacher/Miesmacherin wet blanket [wet 'blæŋkɪt]
Mikrofon microphone ['maɪkrəfəʊn]
Milch milk [mɪlk]
Milchmann milkman, milkmen *(pl)* ['mɪlkmən; 'mɪlkmen]
Million million ['mɪlɪən]
mindestens at least [ət 'li:st]
Mineral- mineral ['mɪnərəl]
Minestrone minestrone [ˌmɪnɪ'strəʊni]
Minute minute ['mɪnɪt]
mir me [mi:]
mit with [wɪð]
mitbringen to bring [brɪŋ]
miteinander together [tə'geðə]
mitnehmen to take [teɪk]
Mitspieler/Mitspielerin player ['pleɪə]
Mittagessen lunch [lʌntʃ]
Mittagszeit lunchtime ['lʌntʃtaɪm]
Mitte middle ['mɪdl]
mittel medium ['mi:diəm]
Mittel- middle ['mɪdl]
Mittelpunkt centre ['sentə]
Mitternacht midnight ['mɪdnaɪt]
Mittwoch Wednesday ['wenzdeɪ]
Möbel furniture ['fɜ:nɪtʃə]
Mobiltelefon mobile ['məʊbaɪl]
möchte gern would like [wʊd 'laɪk]
Mode fashion ['fæʃn]
Model model ['mɒdl]
Modell model ['mɒdl]
modisch trendy ['trendi]
mögen to like [laɪk]
gern mögen to love [lʌv]
möglich possible ['pɒsəbl]
Mohrrübe carrot ['kærət]
Molkerei dairy ['deəri]
Moment moment ['məʊmənt]
Moment mal! Hang on! ['hæŋ‿ɒn]
momentan at the moment [æt ðə 'məʊmənt]
Monat month [mʌnθ]
Mond moon [mu:n]
Montag Monday ['mʌndeɪ]
montags on Mondays [ɒn 'mʌndeɪz]
morgen tomorrow [tə'mɒrəʊ]
Morgen morning ['mɔ:nɪŋ]
am Morgen in the morning [ˌɪn ðə 'mɔ:nɪŋ]
am nächsten Morgen the next morning [ðə ˌnekst 'mɔ:nɪŋ]
Guten Morgen! Good morning! [ˌgʊd 'mɔ:nɪŋ]
Morgenappell assembly [ə'sembli]
morgens in the morning [ˌɪn ðə 'mɔ:nɪŋ]
Motor engine ['endʒɪn]
MP3 MP3 [empi:'θri:]
MP3-Player MP3 player [empi:'θri: ˌpleɪə]
müde tired ['taɪəd]
Müll rubbish ['rʌbɪʃ]
Mülleimer bin [bɪn]
Müllkippe dump [dʌmp]
Mülltonne bin [bɪn]
Mund mouth [maʊθ]
Museum museum [mju:'zi:əm]
Musical musical ['mju:zɪkl]
Musik music ['mju:zɪk]
müssen must [mʌst]; to have to ['hæv tə]; to need [ni:d]
mutig brave [breɪv]
Mutter mother ['mʌðə]
Mutti mum [mʌm]
Mütze cap [kæp]
Mythos myth [mɪθ]

N

nach after ['ɑ:ftə]
nach *(Uhrzeit)* past [pɑ:st]
nach to [tʊ; tə]
nach draußen outside [aʊt'saɪd]
nach drinnen inside [ɪn'saɪd]
nach Hause home [həʊm]
nach Hause bringen to take home [ˌteɪk 'həʊm]
Nachbar/Nachbarin neighbour ['neɪbə]
nachdem after ['ɑ:ftə]
Nachmittag afternoon [ˌɑ:ftə'nu:n]
am Nachmittag in the afternoon [ˌɪn ði: ˌɑ:ftə'nu:n]
nachmittags in the afternoon [ˌɪn ði: ˌɑ:ftə'nu:n]
Nachmittagstee afternoon tea [ˌɑ:ftənu:n 'ti:]
Nachricht message ['mesɪdʒ]; news *(sg.)* [nju:z]
Nachrichten news *(sg.)* [nju:z]
nachschlagen to look up [lʊk‿'ʌp]
nächste/nächster/nächstes next [nekst]
am nächsten Morgen the next morning [ðə ˌnekst 'mɔ:nɪŋ]
Nacht night [naɪt]
heute Nacht tonight [tə'naɪt]
nachts at night [ət 'naɪt]
Nachtisch dessert [dɪ'zɜ:t]; pudding ['pʊdɪŋ]
Nachtschwester night nurse ['naɪt nɜ:s]
nahe near [nɪə]; close [kləʊs]
in der **Nähe von** near [nɪə]
Nahrung food [fu:d]
Name name [neɪm]
Nase nose [nəʊz]

die Nase voll haben to be fed up [bi: ˌfed‿ˈʌp]
nass wet [wet]
national national [ˈnæʃnl]
Natur nature [ˈneɪtʃə]
natürlich of course [əv ˈkɔ:s]
Naturwissenschaft Science [ˈsaɪənts]
Nebel fog [fɒg]
neben beside [bɪˈsaɪd]; next to [ˈnekst tə]
nebenan next door [ˌnekst ˈdɔ:]
neblig foggy [ˈfɒgi]
Neffe nephew [ˈnefju:]
nehmen to take [teɪk]
Ich nehme .... I'm having .... [aɪm ˈhævɪŋ]
neidisch (auf) jealous (of) [ˈdʒeləs]
nein no [nəʊ]
nennen to call [kɔ:l]
Das nenne ich .... That's what I call .... [ˌðæts wɒt‿ˈaɪ ˌkɔ:l]
nervös nervous [ˈnɜ:vəs]
nett friendly [ˈfrendli]; nice [naɪs]
Netz net [net]
neu new [nju:]
Neuigkeit(en) news *(sg.)* [nju:z]
nicht no [nəʊ]; not [nɒt]
nicht einmal not even [nɒt‿ˈi:vn]
auch nicht not either [ˌnɒt ... ˈaɪðə]
noch nicht not ... yet [jet]
nichts nothing [ˈnʌθɪŋ]
nie never [ˈnevə]
nieder down [daʊn]
niederlegen to lie down [laɪ ˈdaʊn]
niemals never [ˈnevə]
niemand no one [ˈnəʊwʌn]; nobody [ˈnəʊbədi]
nirgendwo nowhere [ˈnəʊweə]
nirgendwohin nowhere [ˈnəʊweə]
Niveau level [ˈlevl]
noch still [stɪl]
noch ein/noch eine another [əˈnʌðə]
noch nicht not ... yet [jet]
Norden north [nɔ:θ]
normal normal [ˈnɔ:ml]
normalerweise usually [ˈju:ʒli]
Note *(in der Schule)* mark [mɑ:k]
Notfall emergency [ɪˈmɜ:dʒnsi]
Notiz note [nəʊt]; notice [ˈnəʊtɪs]
Notlage emergency [ɪˈmɜ:dʒnsi]
November November [nəʊˈvembə]
Nummer number [ˈnʌmbə]
nun now [naʊ]
nur only [ˈəʊnli]
nutzlos useless [ˈju:sləs]

O

ob if [ɪf]
oben above [əˈbʌv]; up [ʌp]; upstairs [ʌpˈsteəz]; at the top [ət ðə ˈtɒp]
oberer Teil top [tɒp]
oberhalb above [əˈbʌv]
obligatorisch compulsory [kəmˈpʌlsri]
Observatorium observatory [əbˈzɜ:vətri]
Obst fruit [fru:t]
obwohl although [ɔ:lˈðəʊ]
oder or [ɔ:]
offen open [ˈəʊpn]
offiziell official [əˈfɪʃl]
öffnen to open [ˈəʊpən]
sich **öffnen** to open [ˈəʊpn]
Öffnungszeiten hours [ˈaʊəz]
oft often [ˈɒfn]
ohne without [wɪˈðaʊt]
ohne ... auskommen to go without [ˌgəʊ wɪˈðaʊt]
Ohr ear [ɪə]
o.k. OK [əʊˈkeɪ]
Oktober October [ɒkˈtəʊbə]
Oma grandma [ˈgrændmɑ:]
Onkel uncle [ˈʌŋkl]
online online [ˌɒnˈlaɪn]
Opa grandad [ˈgrændæd]
Orange orange [ˈɒrɪndʒ]
Ordner folder [ˈfəʊldə]
Organisator/Organisatorin organizer [ˈɔ:gənaɪzə]
organisieren to organize [ˈɔ:gənaɪz]
Ort place [pleɪs]
örtlich local [ˈləʊkl]
Osten east [i:st]
Ozean ocean [ˈəʊʃn]
Ozeandampfer ocean liner [ˈəʊʃn ˌlaɪnə]

P

ein **paar** a few [ə ˈfju:]
Päckchen packet [ˈpækɪt]
packen to pack [pæk]
Paket packet [ˈpækɪt]
Palast palace [ˈpælɪs]
paniken to panic [ˈpænɪk]
Panter panther [ˈpæntθə]
Papa dad [dæd]
Paradies paradise [ˈpærəˌdaɪs]
Park park [pɑ:k]
Partner/Partnerin partner [ˈpɑ:tnə]
Party party [ˈpɑ:ti]
eine Party feiern to have a party [ˌhæv‿ə ˈpɑ:ti]
Pass passport [ˈpɑ:spɔ:t]
Passagier/Passagierin passenger [ˈpæsndʒə]
passen to fit [fɪt]
passen zu to match [mætʃ]; to go (together) with [ˈgəʊ wɪð]
Passkontrolle passports *(pl)* [ˈpɑ:spɔ:ts]
Patient/Patientin patient [ˈpeɪʃnt]
Pause break [breɪk]
PC PC [ˌpi:ˈsi:]
Pech bad luck [ˌbæd ˈlʌk]
peinlich embarrassing [ɪmˈbærəsɪŋ]
Pence *(Währung)* pence *(pl)* [pents]
Person person [ˈpɜ:sn]
Perücke wig [wɪg]
Pfad path [pɑ:θ]
Pfeife pipe [paɪp]
Pferd horse [hɔ:s]
Pflanze plant [plɑ:nt]
pflücken to pick [pɪk]
Pforte gate [geɪt]
Pfosten post [pəʊst]
Pfund *(Währung)* pound (£) [paʊnd]
Pfund *(Gewicht)* pound (lb) [paʊnd]
physisch physical [ˈfɪzɪkl]
pikant spicy [ˈspaɪsi]
pink pink [pɪŋk]
Pizza pizza [ˈpi:tsə]
Plakat poster [ˈpəʊstə]
Plan plan [plæn]
planen to plan [plæn]
Plattform platform [ˈplætfɔ:m]
Platz place [pleɪs]; room [ru:m; rʊm]
plötzlich at once [ət ˈwʌnts]; sudden [ˈsʌdn]; suddenly [ˈsʌdnli]
Plural plural [ˈplʊrəl]
Poet/Poetin poet [ˈpəʊɪt]
Poetry Slam *(Gedichtwettbewerb)* poetry slam [ˈpəʊətri ˌslæm]
Pokal cup [kʌp]
Polizei police [pəˈli:s]
Polizist policeman, policemen *(pl)* [pəˈli:smən; pəˈli:smen]
polnisch Polish [ˈpəʊlɪʃ]
Pommes frites chips *(pl)* [tʃɪps]
Pony pony [ˈpəʊni]
populär popular [ˈpɒpjələ]
Position position [pəˈzɪʃn]
Postamt post office [ˈpəʊst‿ˌɒfɪs]
Poster poster [ˈpəʊstə]
Postkarte postcard [ˈpəʊstkɑ:d]
praktizieren to practise [ˈpræktɪs]
Preis price [praɪs]
zum halben Preis half-price [ˌhɑ:fˈpraɪs]
pressen to press [pres]

German – English

prima brilliant ['brɪljənt]; cool [ku:l]
Prinz prince [prɪns]
privat private ['praɪvɪt]
pro per [pɜ:]
proben to practise ['præktɪs]
proben *(ein Theaterstück)* to rehearse [rɪ'hɜ:s]
probieren to try [traɪ]
Problem problem ['prɒbləm]
Programm channel ['tʃænl]; programme ['prəʊgræm]
Projekt project ['prɒdʒekt]
Prospekt leaflet ['li:flət]
Prüfung exam [ɪg'zæm]
Publikum audience ['ɔ:diəns]
Pudding pudding ['pʊdɪŋ]
Puder powder ['paʊdə]
Pulver powder ['paʊdə]
Punk punk [pʌŋk]
Punkt point [pɔɪnt]
punkten to score [skɔ:]
Punktestand score [skɔ:]

Q

quietschen to creak [kri:k]

R

Rad wheel [wi:l]
Rad fahren to cycle ['saɪkl]
Radiergummi rubber ['rʌbə]
Radio radio ['reɪdiəʊ]
Radiosendung radio show ['reɪdiəʊ ˌʃəʊ]
Radkranz rim [rɪm]
Rap rap [ræp]
rappen to rap [ræp]
Rasierwasser aftershave ['ɑ:ftəʃeɪv]
raten to advise [əd'vaɪz]; to guess [ges]
Rätsel mystery ['mɪstri]
rau tough [tʌf]
rauben to rob [rɒb]
Rauch smoke [sməʊk]
rauchen to smoke [sməʊk]
Raum room [ru:m; rʊm]
Reaktion response [rɪ'spɒns]
Realityshow reality show [ri'æləti ˌʃəʊ]
Recht haben to be right [bi: 'raɪt]
rechte/rechter/rechtes right [raɪt]
rechts right [raɪt]; on the right [ɒn ðə 'raɪt]
rechts abbiegen to turn right [tɜ:n 'raɪt]
Rede talk [tɔ:k]
reden to talk [tɔ:k]
reden mit to talk to ['tɔ:k tə]
Regal shelf, shelves *(pl)* [ʃelf; ʃelvz]
Regalbrett shelf, shelves *(pl)* [ʃelf; ʃelvz]
Regel rule [ru:l]
regeln *(ein Problem)* to sort out [sɔ:t‿'aʊt]
Regen rain [reɪn]
Regenguss shower ['ʃaʊə]
Regenschirm umbrella [ʌm'brelə]
Regisseur/Regisseurin director [dɪ'rektə]
Registrierung registration [ˌredʒɪ'streɪʃn]
regnen to rain [reɪn]
regnerisch rainy ['reɪni]
reich rich [rɪtʃ]
Reihe row [rəʊ]
reinigen to clean [kli:n]
Reis rice [raɪs]
Reise journey ['dʒɜ:ni]; trip [trɪp]; travel ['trævl]
reisen to travel ['trævl]
Reisepass passport ['pɑ:spɔ:t]
reiten to ride [raɪd]
Reiter/Reiterin rider ['raɪdə]
Religionsunterricht Religious Education (RE) [rɪˌlɪdʒəs‿edʒʊ'keɪʃn]
religiös religious [rɪ'lɪdʒəs]
Renn- racing ['reɪsɪŋ]
rennen to run [rʌn]
Rennen race [reɪs]
reparieren to fix (to) [fɪks]
Reporter/Reporterin reporter [rɪ'pɔ:tə]
reservieren to book [bʊk]
Respekt respect [rɪ'spekt]
Rest rest [rest]
Restaurant restaurant ['restrənt]
Restaurant mit Straßenverkauf takeaway ['teɪkəweɪ]
retten to rescue ['reskju:]; to save [seɪv]
Rettung rescue ['reskju:]
Rettungsschwimmer/ Rettungsschwimmerin lifeguard ['laɪfˌgɑ:d]
Rezept recipe ['resɪpi:]
Rezeption reception [rɪ'sepʃn]
Richter judge [dʒʌdʒ]
richtig correct [kə'rekt]; right [raɪt]
richtig machen to get … right [get … 'raɪt]
in **Richtung** towards [tə'wɔ:dz]
riechen to smell [smel]
riesig enormous [ɪ'nɔ:məs]; huge [hju:dʒ]; large [lɑ:dʒ]
Ring ring [rɪŋ]
etwas **riskieren** to take your chance [ˌteɪk jɔ: 'tʃɑ:ns]
Ritter knight [naɪt]
Rock skirt [skɜ:t]
Rolle part [pɑ:t]; role [rəʊl]
rosa pink [pɪŋk]
rot red [red]
rot werden to go red [gəʊ 'red]
Rücken back [bæk]
Rucksack rucksack ['rʌksæk]
rückwärtig back [bæk]
rufen to call [kɔ:l]; to cry [kraɪ]; to shout [ʃaʊt]
rufen *(Eule)* to hoot [hu:t]
Rugby rugby ['rʌgbi]
Rugbyschuh rugby boot ['rʌgbi bu:t]
Ruhe quiet [kwaɪət]
ruhig calm [kɑ:m]; quiet ['kwaɪət]
Run run [rʌn]
rund round [raʊnd]
Runde round [raʊnd]; run [rʌn]
Russe/Russin Russian ['rʌʃn]
russisch Russian ['rʌʃn]

S

Saal hall [hɔ:l]
Sache thing [θɪŋ]
Safe safe [seɪf]
sagen to say [seɪ]; to tell [tel]
Saison season ['si:zn]
Salat salad ['sæləd]
sammeln to collect [kə'lekt]
Samstag Saturday ['sætədeɪ]
Sand sand [sænd]
sandig sandy ['sændɪ]
Sandwich sandwich ['sænwɪdʒ]
sanft soft [sɒft]
Sänger/Sängerin singer ['sɪŋə]
sauber clean [kli:n]
säubern to clean [kli:n]
sauer sour ['saʊə]
Sauerkraut sauerkraut ['saʊəkraʊt]
Säugling baby ['beɪbi]
Schachtel box [bɒks]
Schaden harm [hɑ:m]
Schaf sheep, sheep *(pl)* [ʃi:p]
Schalter desk [desk]
Schatz *(Anrede)* dear [dɪə]
Schau show [ʃəʊ]
schauen to look [lʊk]

Schauplatz scene [si:n]
Schauspieler actor ['æktə]
Schauspielerin actress ['æktrəs]
sich **scheiden lassen** to divorce [dɪ'vɔ:s]
schenken to give [gɪv]
scherzen to joke [dʒəʊk]
Scheune barn [bɑ:n]
schicken to send [send]
Textnachricht schicken to text [tekst]
schieben to push [pʊʃ]
Schiedsrichter/Schiedsrichterin umpire ['ʌmpaɪə]; referee [ˌrefr'i:]
schief gehen to go wrong [gəʊ 'rɒŋ]
ein Tor **schießen** to score [skɔ:]
Schiff boat [bəʊt]
Schild sign [saɪn]
Schinken ham [hæm]
schlafen to sleep [sli:p]; to be asleep [ˌbi:‿ə'sli:p]
schläfrig sleepy ['sli:pi]
Schlafsack sleeping bag ['sli:pɪŋ ˌbæg]
Schlafzimmer bedroom ['bedrʊm]
Schlag knock [nɒk] shot [ʃɒt]; stroke [strəʊk]
Schlaganfall stroke [strəʊk]
schlagen to bang [bæŋ]; to bat [bæt]; to hit [hɪt]; to knock [nɒk]
k.o. schlagen to knock out [nɒk‿'aʊt]
Schläger bat [bæt]
Schlagmann/Schlagfrau batter ['bætə]
Schlagzeug drums *(pl)* [drʌmz]
Schlange queue [kju:]
schlecht bad [bæd]; sick [sɪk]
schlechter worse [wɜ:s]
schlechteste/schlechtester/schlechtestes worst [wɜ:st]
schleichen to crawl [krɔ:l]
Schleiereule barn owl ['bɑ:n‿aʊl]
schließen to close [kləʊz]
Schließfach locker ['lɒkə]
schließlich finally ['faɪnli]; in the end [ɪn ði:‿'end]
schlimmer worse [wɜ:s]
schlimmste/schlimmster/schlimmstes worst [wɜ:st]
Schlittschuhbahn ice rink ['aɪs rɪŋk]
Schloss castle ['kɑ:sl]
Schluss end [end]
zum Schluss in the end [ɪn ði:‿'end]
Schlüssel key [ki:]
schmackhaft tasty ['teɪsti]
schmecken to taste [teɪst]
Pizza schmeckt besser. Pizza is tastier. ['pi:tsə ɪz ˌteɪstɪə]

Schminke make-up ['meɪkʌp]
Schmuck jewellery ['dʒu:əlri]
Schmuggler/Schmugglerin smuggler ['smʌglə]
schmutzig dirty ['dɜ:ti]
schnappen to grab [græb]
Schnee snow [snəʊ]
schneien to snow [snəʊ]
schnell fast [fɑ:st]; quick [kwɪk]
schnüffeln to sniff [snɪf]
schnuppern to sniff [snɪf]
schockiert shocked [ʃɒkt]
Schokolade chocolate ['tʃɒklət]
schön beautiful ['bju:tɪfl]; fine [faɪn]; nice [naɪs]
schon already [ɔ:l'redi]
schottisch Scottish ['skɒtɪʃ]
Schrank cupboard ['kʌbəd]
einen **Schrecken einjagen** to scare ['skeə]
schrecklich frightening ['fraɪtnɪŋ]; horrible ['hɒrəbl]; terrible ['terəbl]
Schrei cry [kraɪ]
schreiben to write [raɪt]
Schreibtisch desk [desk]
schreien to cry [kraɪ]; to shout [ʃaʊt]
schreien *(Eule)* to hoot [hu:t]
Schritt footstep ['fʊtstep]
schüchtern shy [ʃaɪ]
Schuh shoe [ʃu:]
Schule school [sku:l]
Schüler/Schülerin pupil ['pju:pl]
Schulfach subject ['sʌbdʒɪkt]
Schulhof playground ['pleɪgraʊnd]
Schulklasse class [klɑ:s]
Schulranzen school bag ['sku:l bæg]
Schultasche school bag ['sku:l bæg]
Schuppen shed [ʃed]
Schuss gunshot ['gʌnʃɒt]; shot [ʃɒt]
Schüssel bowl [bəʊl]
Schusswaffe gun [gʌn]
schütteln to shake [ʃeɪk]
schwach weak [wi:k]
schwach werden to go weak [gəʊ 'wi:k]
Schwamm sponge [spʌndʒ]
schwarz black [blæk]
Schwein pig [pɪg]
Schweinefleisch pork [pɔ:k]
schwenken to wave [weɪv]
schwer heavy ['hevi]
Schwester sister ['sɪstə]
schwierig difficult ['dɪfɪklt]; hard [hɑ:d]
Schwierigkeit problem ['prɒbləm]
Schwimmbad swimming pool ['swɪmɪŋ ˌpu:l]

Schwimmbecken pool [pu:l]; swimming pool ['swɪmɪŋ ˌpu:l]
schwimmen to swim [swɪm]
Schwimmer/Schwimmerin swimmer ['swɪmə]
Schwimmreifen rubber ring [ˌrʌbə 'rɪŋ]
Sciencefiction science fiction [ˌsaɪəns 'fɪkʃn]
Scone *(Gebäck)* scone [skɒn]
Screenshot screen shot ['skri:n ˌʃɒt]
See lake [leɪk]
segeln to sail [seɪl]
sehen to look [lʊk]; to see [si:]
Sehenswürdigkeit attraction [ə'trækʃn]
sehr very ['veri]
Seife soap [səʊp]
Seifenoper soap [səʊp]
sein to be [bi:]
an der Reihe sein to be on [bi:‿'ɒn]
an sein to be on [bi:‿'ɒn]
sein/seine his [hɪz]; its [ɪts]
seit for [fɔ:; fə]; since [sɪnts]
seitdem since [sɪnts]
Seite page [peɪdʒ]; side [saɪd]
Sekretär/Sekretärin secretary ['sekrətri]
Sekunde second ['seknd]
selbst gemacht home-made [ˌhəʊm'meɪd]
selbstverständlich of course [əv 'kɔ:s]
selten seldom ['seldəm]
seltsam strange [streɪndʒ]
Sendung programme ['prəʊgræm]; show [ʃəʊ]
auf Sendung on the air [ˌɒn ði‿'eə]
September September [sep'tembə]
Serie series, series *(pl)* ['sɪəri:z]
Service service ['sɜ:vɪs]
sich **setzen** to sit down [sɪt 'daʊn]
sich setzen zu to sit with ['sɪt wɪθ]
Shorts shorts *(pl)* [ʃɔ:ts]
Show show [ʃəʊ]
sicher safe [seɪf]; sure [ʃʊə]
sichergehen to make sure [meɪk 'ʃʊə]
Sicherungskasten fuse-box ['fju:zbɒks]
Sicht view [vju:]
sie she [ʃi:]; her [hɜ:]
sie *(Mehrzahl)* they [ðeɪ]; them [ðem]
Sie you [ju:; jə]
siegen to win [wɪn]
Sieger/Siegerin winner ['wɪnə]
Siegtreffer winning goal ['wɪnɪŋ gəʊl]
Signal signal ['sɪgnl]
signalisieren to signal ['sɪgnl]
simsen to text [tekst]

German – English

singen to sing [sɪŋ]
Sinn sense [sens]
Sintflut flash flood ['flæʃ ˌflʌd]
Situationskomödie sitcom ['sɪtkɒm]
Sitz seat [si:t]
sitzen to sit [sɪt]
 in der Falle sitzen to be trapped [bi: 'træpt]
Sitzplatz seat [si:t]
Skateboard skateboard ['skeɪtbɔ:d]
skaten to skate [skeɪt]
SMS text message ['tekst ˌmesɪdʒ]
Snack snack [snæk]
so so [səʊ]
 so … wie … as … as [æz … æz; əz … əz]
so (schlimm) that (bad) ['ðæt bæd]
sobald as soon as [əz 'su:n‿əz]
Sofa couch [kaʊtʃ]; sofa ['səʊfə]
sofort at once [ət 'wʌnts]; right away [raɪt‿ə'weɪ]
sogar even ['i:vn]
Sohn son [sʌn]
solange as long as [əz 'lɒŋ‿əz]
solch such [sʌtʃ]
sollte/sollten should [ʃʊd]
Sommer summer ['sʌmə]
Sommerfest summer fair ['sʌmə ˌfeə]
Sonne sun [sʌn]
Sonnenbräune suntan ['sʌntæn]
sonnig sunny ['sʌni]
Sonntag Sunday ['sʌndeɪ]
sonst else [els]
sich **Sorgen machen** to worry ['wʌri]
sorgfältig careful ['keəfl]
Sorte kind [kaɪnd]
Souvenir souvenir [ˌsu:və'nɪə]
Spaghetti spaghetti [spə'geti]
spannend exciting [ɪk'saɪtɪŋ]
sparen to save [seɪv]
Sparschwein piggy bank ['pɪgi bæŋk]
Spaß fun [fʌn]
 Spaß haben to have fun [ˌhæv 'fʌn]
 Spaß machen to be fun [bi: 'fʌn]
 Viel Spaß! Have fun! [ˌhæv 'fʌn]
spät late [leɪt]
 später later ['leɪtə]
 zu spät late [leɪt]
spazieren gehen to go for a walk [ˌgəʊ fər‿ə 'wɔ:k]
Spaziergang walk [wɔ:k]
Speisekarte menu ['menju:]
Speisesaal dining room ['daɪnɪŋ rʊm]
spektakulär spectacular [spek'tækjələ]
speziell special ['speʃl]
Spiegel mirror ['mɪrə]
Spiel game [geɪm]; match [mætʃ]; play [pleɪ]
spielen to play [pleɪ]
 spielen *(Theater)* to act [ækt]
Spieler/Spielerin player ['pleɪə]
Spielfeld court [kɔ:t]; pitch [pɪtʃ]
Spielplatz playground ['pleɪgraʊnd]
Spielstand score [skɔ:]
Spielzeug toy [tɔɪ]
Spitze top [tɒp]
Sport sport [spɔ:t]
 Sport *(Schulfach)* Physical Education (PE) [ˌfɪzɪkl‿edʒʊ'keɪʃn]
 Sport machen to exercise ['eksəsaɪz]
 Sport treiben to do sports [du: 'spɔ:ts]
Sportfest sports day ['spɔ:ts deɪ]
Sportgeschäft sports shop ['spɔ:ts ʃɒp]
sportlich sporty ['spɔ:ti]
Sportplatz sports field ['spɔ:ts fi:ld]
Sportzeug PE kit [ˌpi:‿'i: kɪt]
Sprache language ['læŋgwɪdʒ]
sprechen to say [seɪ]; to speak [spi:k]; to talk [tɔ:k]
 sprechen mit to talk to ['tɔ:k tə]
Sprecher/Sprecherin speaker ['spi:kə]
springen to jump [dʒʌmp]
Staat state [steɪt]
staatlich state [steɪt]
Stadion stadium ['steɪdiəm]; arena [ə'ri:nə]
Stadt city ['sɪti]; town [taʊn]
Stadtplan map [mæp]
Stammkunde/Stammkundin regular ['regjələ]
Stand stall [stɔ:l]
Standbesitzer/Standbesitzerin stall holder ['stɔ:l ˌhəʊldə]
ständig always ['ɔ:lweɪz]
Star star [stɑ:]
stark hard [hɑ:d]; strong [strɒŋ]
Stärke power ['paʊə]
Start start [stɑ:t]
starten to start [stɑ:t]
Station station ['steɪʃn]
statt instead of [ɪn'sted‿əv]
stattfinden to take place [teɪk 'pleɪs]
Stau traffic jam ['træfɪk ˌdʒæm]
Steelband *(Band, deren Instrumente aus leeren Ölfässern bestehen)* steel band [ˌsti:l 'bænd]
stehen to stand [stænd]
stehlen to steal [sti:l]
steigen to climb ['klaɪm]; to rise [raɪz]
Stein stone [stəʊn]
Stelle place [pleɪs]
stellen *(Uhr)* to set [set]
sterben to die [daɪ]
Stern star [stɑ:]
Sternwarte observatory [əb'zɜ:vətri]
Stiefel boot [bu:t]
Stiefvater stepdad ['stepdæd]
Stil style [staɪl]
still quiet ['kwaɪət]
Stille quiet [kwaɪət]
Stimme voice [vɔɪs]
Stock stick [stɪk]
 im oberen Stock upstairs [ʌp'steəz]
 im unteren Stock downstairs [ˌdaʊn'steəz]
Stollenschuh rugby boot ['rʌgbi bu:t]
stolz auf proud of ['praʊd‿əv]
stoßen to knock [nɒk]; to push [pʊʃ]
 stoßen gegen to run into [rʌn‿'ɪntə]
Strand beach [bi:tʃ]
Straße road [rəʊd]; street [stri:t]
Strauch bush [bʊʃ]
Streich trick [trɪk]
streichen to paint [peɪnt]
Streit argument ['ɑ:gjəmənt]
streiten to argue ['ɑ:gju:]; to fight [faɪt]
 sich streiten to have an argument [ˌhæv‿ən‿'ɑ:gjəmənt]
streng strict [strɪkt]
strikt strict [strɪkt]
Stroh straw [strɔ:]
Stubenhocker couch potato ['kaʊtʃ pəˌteɪtəʊ]
Stück piece [pi:s]
studieren to study ['stʌdi]
Studio studio ['stju:diəʊ]
Stuhl chair [tʃeə]
Stunde hour ['aʊə]
 eine halbe Stunde half an hour [ˌhɑ:f‿ən‿'aʊə]
stundenlang for hours [fər‿'aʊəz]
Stundenplan timetable ['taɪmteɪbl]
Sturm storm [stɔ:m]
stürmisch stormy ['stɔ:mi]
suchen to look for ['lʊk fə]
Süden south [saʊθ]
Südwesten southwest [ˌsaʊθ'west]
Superlativ superlative [su:'pɜ:lətɪv]
Supermarkt supermarket ['su:pəˌmɑ:kɪt]
Suppe soup [su:p]
surfen to surf [sɜ:f]
 im Internet surfen to surf the Internet [ˌsɜ:f ði‿'ɪntənet]
Surfen surfing ['sɜ:fɪŋ]
süß sweet [swi:t]
Süßigkeit sweet [swi:t]

Sweatshirt sweatshirt ['swetʃɜ:t]
System system ['sɪstəm]
Szene scene [si:n]

T

Tabelle grid [grɪd]
Tafel board [bɔ:d]
Tag day [deɪ]
Einen schönen Tag noch. Have a nice day. [ˌhæv‿ə naɪs 'deɪ]
eines Tages one day [wʌn 'deɪ]
Tagebuch diary ['daɪəri]
täglich daily ['deɪli]
Talkmaster host [həʊst]
Talkshow talk show ['tɔ:k ˌʃəʊ]
Tante aunt [ɑ:nt]
Tanz dance [dɑ:nts]
tanzen to dance [dɑ:nts]
Breakdance tanzen to break-dance ['breɪkdɑ:nts]
tapfer brave [breɪv]
Tasche bag [bæg]
Taschendieb/Taschendiebin pickpocket ['pɪkˌpɒkɪt]
Taschengeld pocket money ['pɒkɪt ˌmʌni]
Taschenlampe torch, torches *(pl)* [tɔ:tʃ; 'tɔ:tʃɪz]
Taschenmesser penknife, penknives *(pl)* ['pennaɪf; 'pennaɪvz]
Tasse cup [kʌp]
tasten nach to feel for ['fi:l fə]
in der **Tat** in fact [ɪn 'fækt]
Tätowierung tattoo [tæt'u:]
Tatsache fact [fækt]
tauchen to dive [daɪv]
Tausch exchange [ɪks'tʃeɪndʒ]; swap [swɒp]
tauschen to change [tʃeɪndʒ]; to swap [swɒp]
tausend thousand ['θaʊznd]
Taxi taxi ['tæksi]
Team team [ti:m]
Technik Technology [tek'nɒlədʒi]
Tee tea [ti:]
Teenager teenager ['ti:nˌeɪdʒə]
Teil part [pɑ:t]
teilen to share [ʃeə]
teilnehmen an to take part in [teɪk 'pɑ:t‿ɪn]
Teilnehmer/Teilnehmerin an einem Poetry Slam slamster ['slæmstə]
Telefon phone [fəʊn]
telefonieren to phone [fəʊn]
Telefonnummer phone number ['fəʊn ˌnʌmbə]
Telefonzelle phone box ['fəʊn ˌbɒks]
Teller plate [pleɪt]
Temperatur temperature ['temprətʃə]
Tennis tennis ['tenɪs]
Terminkalender diary ['daɪəri]
Test test [test]
teuer expensive [ɪk'spentsɪv]
Textnachricht schicken to text [tekst]
Theaterstück play [pleɪ]
Thema subject ['sʌbdʒɪkt]; topic ['tɒpɪk]
Thriller thriller ['θrɪlə]
Ticket ticket ['tɪkɪt]
Tier animal ['ænɪml]
Tierpark zoo [zu:]
Tierpfleger/Tierpflegerin zookeeper ['zu:ki:pə]
Tiger tiger ['taɪgə]
Tipp tip [tɪp]
Tisch table ['teɪbl]
den Tisch decken to set the table [ˌset ðə 'teɪbl]
Tischtennis table-tennis ['teɪblˌtenɪs]
Titel title ['taɪtl]
Titelseite cover ['kʌvə]
Toilette toilet ['tɔɪlɪt]
toll brilliant ['brɪljənt]; great [greɪt]
Tomate tomato, tomatoes *(pl)* [tə'mɑ:təʊ; tə'mɑ:təʊz]
Ton sound [saʊnd]
Tonne *(Gewicht)* ton [tʌn]
Topf pot [pɒt]
Tor gate [geɪt]; goal [gəʊl]
ein Tor schießen to score [skɔ:]
Torpfosten goal post ['gəʊl pəʊst]
Torwart goalkeeper ['gəʊlˌki:pə]
tot dead [ded]
töten to kill [kɪl]
Tourist/Touristin tourist ['tʊərɪst]
Tradition tradition [trə'dɪʃn]
tragen to carry ['kæri]
Training practice ['præktɪs]; training ['treɪnɪŋ]
Transport transport ['træntspɔ:t]
Traum dream [dri:m]
traurig sad [sæd]
treffen to hit [hɪt]; to meet [mi:t]
sich treffen to meet [mi:t]
Treffen meeting ['mi:tɪŋ]
Trend trend [trend]
Treppe stairs *(pl)* [steəz]
die Treppe hinaufrennen to run upstairs [ˌrʌn‿ʌp'steəz]
Tresor safe [seɪf]
treten to kick [kɪk]
Tribüne platform ['plætfɔ:m]; stand [stænd]
Trick trick [trɪk]
Trikot jersey ['dʒɜ:zi]
Trillerpfeife whistle ['wɪsl]
trinken to drink [drɪŋk]
Trödelstand white elephant stall [ˌwaɪt 'elɪfənt stɔ:l]
tschüss bye [baɪ]
T-Shirt T-shirt ['ti:ʃɜ:t]
tun to do [du:]; to make [meɪk]
Tunnel tunnel ['tʌnl]
Tür door [dɔ:]
türkisch Turkish ['tɜ:kɪʃ]
Türklingel doorbell ['dɔ:bel]
Turm tower ['taʊə]
Turnhalle gym [dʒɪm]
Turnier competition [ˌkɒmpə'tɪʃn]
Turnschuhe trainers ['treɪnəz]
Türstufe doorstep ['dɔ:step]
Tüte bag [bæg]
Typ bloke [bləʊk]
tyrannisieren to bully ['bʊli]

U

U-Bahn underground ['ʌndəgraʊnd]
Übelkeit verspüren to feel sick [fi:l 'sɪk]
üben to exercise ['eksəsaɪz]; to practise ['præktɪs]
über above [ə'bʌv]; over ['əʊvə]; about [ə'baʊt]
überall all over [ˌɔ:l‿'əʊvə]; anywhere ['eniweə]; everywhere ['evriweə]
Überleben survival [sə'vaɪvl]
überprüfen to check [tʃek]
überraschend surprising [sə'praɪzɪŋ]
überrascht surprised [sə'praɪzd]
Überschrift title ['taɪtl]
Überschwemmung flood [flʌd]
flutartige Überschwemmung flash flood ['flæʃ ˌflʌd]
übrig left [left]
Übung exercise ['eksəsaɪz]
Übungsheft exercise book ['eksəsaɪz ˌbʊk]
Uhr clock [klɒk]
Uhr *(Zeitangabe)* o'clock [ə'klɒk]
Wie viel Uhr ist es, bitte? What's the time, please? [ˌwɒts ðə 'taɪm ˌpli:z]
umdrehen to turn [tɜ:n]
(sich) umdrehen to turn over [ˌtɜ:n‿'əʊvə]; to turn round [tɜ:n 'raʊnd]
Umfrage survey ['sɜ:veɪ]

German – English

Umgebung environment [ɪn'vaɪərnmənt]
umhauen to knock out [nɒk‿'aʊt]
umher around [ə'raʊnd]
umkehren to turn back [tɜ:n 'bæk]
Umschlag envelope ['envələʊp]
sich **umsehen** to look round [lʊk 'raʊnd]
umsteigen to change [tʃeɪndʒ]
umstoßen to upset [ʌp'set]
Umwelt environment [ɪn'vaɪərnmənt]
Umweltverschmutzung pollution [pə'lu:ʃn]
umziehen to move [mu:v]
unabhängig independent [ˌɪndɪ'pendənt]
und and [ænd]
Unfall accident ['æksɪdnt]
ungefähr about [ə'baʊt]; around [ə'raʊnd]
ungesund unhealthy [ʌn'helθi]
unglücklich unhappy [ʌn'hæpi]
unheimlich scary ['skeəri]; spooky ['spu:ki]
Uniform uniform ['ju:nɪfɔ:m]
Union union ['ju:njən]
Universität university [ˌju:nɪ'vɜ:səti]
uns us [ʌs]
unser/unsere our ['aʊə]
Unsinn rubbish ['rʌbɪʃ]
unten downstairs [ˌdaʊn'steəz]; at the bottom [ət ðə 'bɒtəm]; below [bɪ'ləʊ]
  unterer Teil bottom ['bɒtəm]
unter under ['ʌndə]
Unterführung tunnel ['tʌnl]
Untergeschoss basement ['beɪsmənt]
unterhalb below [bɪ'ləʊ]
sich **unterhalten** to chat [tʃæt]
Unterhaltung chat [tʃæt]
Unterricht class [klɑ:s]
unterrichten to teach [ti:tʃ]
Unterrichtsstunde lesson ['lesn]
unterschreiben to sign [saɪn]
unterstreichen to underline [ˌʌndə'laɪn]
Urlaub holiday(s) ['hɒlədeɪ(z)]
usw. etc. [ɪt'setrə]

V

Vater father ['fɑ:ðə]
Vati dad [dæd]
verändern to change [tʃeɪndʒ]
verängstigt scared [skeəd]
Veranstalter/Veranstalterin organizer ['ɔ:gənaɪzə]
Veranstaltung event [ɪ'vent]; session ['seʃn]
verärgert angry ['æŋgri]
Verbindung link [lɪŋk]
Verbrechen crime [kraɪm]
verbrennen to burn [bɜ:n]
verbringen to spend [spend]
Verdächtigter/Verdächtigte suspect ['sʌspekt]
Verein club [klʌb]
Vereinigung union ['ju:njən]
Vergangenheit past [pɑ:st]
vergessen to forget [fə'get]
vergleichen to compare [kəm'peə]
verhaften to arrest [ə'rest]
verheiratet mit married to ['mærid tə]
sich **verirren** to get lost [get 'lɒst]
sich **verirrt haben** to be lost [bi: 'lɒst]
verkaufen to sell [sel]
Verkäufer/Verkäuferin shop assistant ['ʃɒp‿əˌsɪstnt]
Verkehr traffic ['træfɪk]
verlassen to leave [li:v]
verletzen to hurt [hɜ:t]
verletzt hurt [hɜ:t]
Verletzung harm [hɑ:m]
verlieren to lose [lu:z]
  verloren gehen to get lost [get 'lɒst]
vermissen to miss [mɪs]
vermuten to guess [ges]
vernünftig sensible ['sensɪbl]
verpassen to miss [mɪs]
verregnet rainy ['reɪni]
verrückt crazy ['kreɪzi]; mad [mæd]
  verrückt machen to drive crazy [draɪv 'kreɪzi]
  verrückt nach … sein to be nuts about [bi: ˌnʌts‿ə'baʊt]
  verrückt werden to go bananas [ˌgəʊ bə'nɑ:nəz]
Versammlung assembly [ə'sembli]
verschieden different ['dɪfrnt]
verschlafen sleepy ['sli:pi]
Verschmutzung pollution [pə'lu:ʃn]
verschneit snowy ['snəʊi]
verschwinden to disappear [ˌdɪsə'pɪə]
verspätet late [leɪt]
versprechen to promise ['prɒmɪs]
Verstand mind [maɪnd]
verstecken to hide [haɪd]
  sich verstecken to hide [haɪd]
verstehen to understand [ˌʌndə'stænd]
Versuch experiment [ɪk'sperɪmənt]
versuchen to try [traɪ]
vertrauen to trust [trʌst]
Vertrauen trust [trʌst]
vervollständigen to complete [kəm'pli:t]
verwenden to use [ju:z]
verzeichnet on record [ɒn 'rekɔ:d]
Video video ['vɪdiəʊ]
viel a lot [ə 'lɒt]; much [mʌtʃ]
  viele many ['meni]
  viel/viele a lot of [ə 'lɒt‿əv]; lots (of) ['lɒts‿əv]
  Viel Glück! Good luck! [ˌgʊd 'lʌk]
vielleicht perhaps [pə'hæps]; maybe ['meɪbi]
Viertel quarter ['kwɔ:tə]
  Viertel nach quarter past ['kwɔ:tə pɑ:st]
  Viertel vor quarter to ['kwɔ:tə tə]
violett purple ['pɜ:pl]
Vogel bird [bɜ:d]
voll (von) full (of) [fʊl]
Volleyball volleyball ['vɒlibɔ:l]
völlig absolutely [ˌæbsə'lu:tli]
von from [frɒm]; of [ɒv; əv]
vor before [bɪ'fɔ:]; in front of [ɪn 'frʌnt‿əv]
  vor *(zeitlich)* ago [ə'gəʊ]
vorbei over ['əʊvə]
vorbeigehen an to pass [pɑ:s]
sich **vorbereiten** to get ready [get 'redi]
Vorführung exhibition [ˌeksɪ'bɪʃn]
Vorhersage *(Wetter)* forecast ['fɔ:kɑ:st]
Vormittag morning ['mɔ:nɪŋ]
vormittags in the morning [ˌɪn ðə 'mɔ:nɪŋ]
  vormittags *(Uhrzeit)* a.m. [ˌeɪ'em]
vorne at the front [ət ðə 'frʌnt]
Vorschlag suggestion [sə'dʒestʃn]
vorschlagen to suggest [sə'dʒest]
Vorschrift rule [ru:l]
vorsichtig careful ['keəfl]
Vorsingen audition [ɔ:'dɪʃn]
Vorspeise starter ['stɑ:tə]
Vorsprechen audition [ɔ:'dɪʃn]
sich (etwas) **vorstellen** to imagine [ɪ'mædʒɪn]
Vorstellung performance [pə'fɔ:məns]
Vortanzen audition [ɔ:'dɪʃn]
Vortrag talk [tɔ:k]
vorüber over ['əʊvə]

W

Wache guard [gɑ:d]
wachsen to rise [raɪz]

Wächter/Wächterin guard [gɑ:d]
etwas **wagen** to take your chance [ˌteɪk jɔ: 'tʃɑ:ns]
Wahl choice [tʃɔɪs]
wählen to choose [tʃu:z]
wahr true [tru:]
wahr werden to come true [kʌm 'tru:]
während *(+ Nomen)* during *(+ noun)* ['djʊərɪŋ]
während while [waɪl]
wahrscheinlich probably ['prɒbəbli]
Wahrzeichen landmark ['lændmɑ:k]
Waliser/Waliserin Welsh [welʃ]
walisisch Welsh [welʃ]
Wand wall [wɔ:l]
Wandtafel board [bɔ:d]
wann when [wen]
Warenautomat vending machine ['vendɪŋ məˌʃi:n]
warm warm [wɔ:m]
warten to wait [weɪt]
Warte mal! Hang on! ['hæŋ‿ɒn]
warten auf to wait for ['weɪt fɔ:]
Wärter/Wärterin zookeeper ['zu:ki:pə]
Warteschlange queue [kju:]
warum why [waɪ]
was what [wɒt]
Was ist los? What's up? [ˌwɒts‿'ʌp]
Was ist mit ...? What about ...? [wɒt‿ə'baʊt]
Was steht da? What does it say? [ˌwɒt dʌz‿ɪt 'seɪ]
waschen to wash [wɒʃ]
sich waschen to wash [wɒʃ]
Wasser water ['wɔ:tə]
Website website ['websaɪt]
Wechselgeld change [tʃeɪndʒ]
wechseln to change [tʃeɪndʒ]
wecken to wake [weɪk]
Wecker alarm clock [ə'lɑ:m ˌklɒk]
weg away [ə'weɪ]
Weg path [pɑ:θ]; way [weɪ]
Er ist auf dem Weg zu .... He is on his way to .... [ˌhi:‿ɪz‿ɒn hɪz 'weɪ tə]
wegbleiben to stay out [steɪ‿'aʊt]
wegbringen to take off [teɪk‿'ɒf]
weggehen to leave [li:v]
wegnehmen to take [teɪk]
wegräumen von to get off [get‿'ɒf]
wegrennen to run away [rʌn‿ə'weɪ]
weh tun to hurt [hɜ:t]
wehen to fly [flaɪ]
weich soft [sɒft]
weil because [bɪ'kɒz]
weinen to cry [kraɪ]
Weise way [weɪ]
weit far [fɑ:]
weit kommen to go far [gəʊ 'fɑ:]
es weit bringen to go far [gəʊ 'fɑ:]
weitergeben to pass [pɑ:s]
Weitsprung long jump ['lɒŋ ˌdʒʌmp]
welche/welcher/welches what [wɒt]; which [wɪtʃ]
Welle wave [weɪv]
Wellenreiten surfing ['sɜ:fɪŋ]
Welt world [wɜ:ld]
wem who [hu:]; whom [hu:m]
wen who [hu:]; whom [hu:m]
wenige few [fju:]
weniger less [les]
wenigstens at least [ət 'li:st]
wenn if [ɪf]; when [wen]
wer who [hu:]
werden to become [bɪ'kʌm]; to get [get]
werden/werden nicht *(futurisch)* will ('ll), won't [wɪl; wəʊnt]
werfen to throw [θrəʊ]
Werfer/Werferin pitcher ['pɪtʃə]
Werkstatt workshop ['wɜ:kʃɒp]
wertvoll valuable ['væljuəbl]
wessen whose [hu:z]
Westen west [west]
Wettbewerb competition [ˌkɒmpə'tɪʃn]
wetten to bet [bet]
Wetter weather ['weðə]
Wettkampf match [mætʃ]
Wettlauf race [reɪs]
einen Wettlauf machen to run a race [ˌrʌn‿ə 'reɪs]
wichtig important [ɪm'pɔ:tnt]
widerhallen to echo ['ekəʊ]
wie *(Vergleich)* like [laɪk]
wie as [æz; əz]
wie how [haʊ]
Wie alt bist du? How old are you? [haʊ‿'əʊld‿ɑ: ju:]
Wie geht es dir/Ihnen/euch? How are you? [ˌhaʊ‿'ɑ: ju:]
Wie heißt du? What's your name? [ˌwɒts jə 'neɪm]
wie viele how many [haʊ 'meni]
Wie viel kosten ...? How much are ...? [ˌhaʊ 'mʌtʃ‿ɑ:]
Wie viel kostet ...? How much is ...? [ˌhaʊ 'mʌtʃ‿ɪz]
Wie viel Uhr ist es, bitte? What's the time, please? [ˌwɔts ðə 'taɪm ˌpli:z]
Wie wäre es mit ...? What about ...? [wɒt‿ə'baʊt]
wieder again [ə'gen]
wieder erleben to relive [ˌri:'lɪv]
wiederherstellen to rebuild [ˌri:'bɪld]
auf **Wiedersehen** goodbye [gʊd'baɪ]
wild wild [waɪld]
willkommen welcome ['welkəm]
Willkommen in ... Welcome to ... ['welkəm tə]
willkommen heißen to welcome ['welkəm]
Wind wind [wɪnd]
windig windy ['wɪndi]
windsurfen to surf [sɜ:f]; to windsurf ['wɪnsɜ:f]
winken to wave [weɪv]
Winter winter ['wɪntə]
winzig tiny ['taɪni]
wir we [wi:]
Wirbel fuss [fʌs]
wirklich real [rɪəl]; really ['rɪəli]
wissen to know [nəʊ]
Wissenschaft Science ['saɪənts]
Wissenschaftler/Wissenschaftlerin scientist ['saɪəntɪst]
Witz joke [dʒəʊk]
Witze machen to joke [dʒəʊk]
wo where [weə]
Woche week [wi:k]
in der Woche a week [ə 'wi:k]
pro Woche a week [ə 'wi:k]
Wochenende weekend [ˌwi:k'end]
wohin where [weə]
Wohltätigkeit charity ['tʃærɪti]
Wohltätigkeitsverein charity ['tʃærɪti]
wohnen to live [lɪv]
wohnen bei to stay with ['steɪ wɪð]
Wohnung flat [flæt]
Wohnzimmer living room ['lɪvɪŋ rʊm]
Wolf wolf, wolves *(pl)* [wʊlf; wʊlvz]
Wolke cloud [klaʊd]
wolkig cloudy ['klaʊdi]
Wolldecke blanket ['blæŋkɪt]
wollen to want (to) ['wɒnt tə]
Workshop workshop ['wɜ:kʃɒp]
Wort word [wɜ:d]
Wrack wreck [rek]
wunderschön beautiful ['bju:tɪfl]
Wunsch wish [wɪʃ]
wünschen to wish [wɪʃ]
würde(n) would [wʊd]
Wurf throw [θrəʊ]
Wurst sausage ['sɒsɪdʒ]
Würstchen sausage ['sɒsɪdʒ]
würzig spicy ['spaɪsi]
wütend furious ['fjʊəriəs]; mad [mæd]

Z

zäh tough [tʌf]
Zahl number ['nʌmbə]
zahlen to pay [peɪ]
Zahn tooth, teeth *(pl)* [tu:θ; ti:θ]
Zauberer wizard ['wɪzəd]
Zeh toe [təʊ]
Zeichen sign [saɪn]; signal ['sɪgnl]
ein Zeichen geben to signal ['sɪgnl]
Zeichentrickfilm cartoon [kɑ:'tu:n]
zeichnen to design [dɪ'zaɪn]; to draw [drɔ:]
zeigen to show [ʃəʊ]
Zeile line [laɪn]
Zeit time [taɪm]
Du liebe Zeit! Good grief! [gʊd 'gri:f]
Zeitalter age [eɪdʒ]
Zeitschrift magazine [mægə'zi:n]
Zeitschriftenhändler/ Zeitschriftenhändlerin newsagent ['nju:sˌeɪdʒənt]
Zeitung newspaper ['nju:sˌpeɪpə]
Zelt tent [tent]
Zelten camping ['kæmpɪŋ]
Zentimeter centimetre ['sentɪˌmi:tə]
Zentrum centre ['sentə]
zerbrechen to break [breɪk]
zerbrochen broken ['brəʊkn]
zerstören to destroy [dɪ'strɔɪ]
ziehen to pull [pʊl]
Ziehen tug [tʌg]
Ziel goal [gəʊl]
Zimmer room [ru:m; rʊm]
zirka around [ə'raʊnd]
zittern to shake [ʃeɪk]
Zoll customs *(pl)* ['kʌstəmz]
Zoll *(Längenmaß: 2,54 cm)* inch [ɪnʃ]
Zoo zoo [zu:]
zu to [tʊ; tə]
zuerst at first [ət 'fɜ:st]; first [fɜ:st]
zuflüstern to whisper ['wɪspə]
zufrieden stellen to please [pli:z]
zufrieden sein mit to be pleased with [bi: 'pli:zd wɪð]
Zug train [treɪn]
zugehen auf to walk up to [wɔ:k‿'ʌp tə]
Zuhause home [həʊm]
zuhören to listen ['lɪsn]
zumachen to close [kləʊz]
zunächst at first [ət 'fɜ:st]
zunehmen to rise [raɪz]
Zunge tongue [tʌŋ]
zuordnen to match [mætʃ]
Zupfen tug [tʌg]
zurück back [bæk]
zurückgehen to turn back [tɜ:n 'bæk]
zusammen together [tə'geðə]
zusammenfügen to match [mætʃ]
Zusatz extra ['ekstrə]
zusätzlich extra ['ekstrə]
Zuschauer/Zuschauerin viewer ['vju:ə]
Zustand state [steɪt]
zustimmen to agree [ə'gri:]
zweimal twice [twaɪs]
zwingend compulsory [kəm'pʌlsri]
zwischen between [bɪ'twi:n]

In the classroom

What you can say ...

... when you arrive and leave:	
Good morning, Mrs/Mr	Guten Morgen, Frau/Herr ... .
I'm sorry, I'm late.	Tut mir Leid, dass ich mich verspätet habe.
What are we going to do today?	Was machen wir heute?
I'm sorry, I've forgotten my exercise book.	Tut mir Leid, ich habe mein Heft vergessen.
What's for homework, please?	Was haben wir als Hausaufgabe auf?
See you next time.	Bis zum nächsten Mal.
Have a nice weekend.	Schönes Wochenende!
Goodbye./Bye.	Auf Wiedersehen./Tschüs.

... if you want to be polite:	
I'm sorry (to bother you), but could I please borrow your mobile/... ?	Entschuldige, (dass ich dich störe,) aber kann ich bitte dein Handy/... ausleihen?
I'm sorry about my homework/... .	Es tut mir Leid wegen meiner Hausaufgaben/... .
I'm sorry (that) I'm late.	Entschuldigung, dass ich zu/so spät komme.
Oh, I'm sorry!	Oh, Entschuldigung/Verzeihung!
That's OK./ No problem.	Macht nichts./Nichts passiert.
That's no problem.	Kein Problem.
Wait, I'll help you.	Warte mal! Ich helfe dir.
Thanks./Thank you (very much).	Danke! Vielen Dank!
I'll carry those books for you, Miss.	Ich trage Ihnen die Bücher, Frau ... .

... if there is a problem:	
How are you?	Wie geht es dir?
Are you feeling ill?	Fühlst du dich krank?
What's the matter with you?	Was fehlt dir denn?
I'm fine, thank you.	Gut, danke.
I'm not feeling well.	Ich fühle mich nicht gut.
I've got a headache.	Ich habe Kopfweh.
Can I open the window, please?	Darf ich bitte das Fenster öffnen?
Can I go to the toilet, please?	Darf ich bitte auf die Toilette gehen?

... if you want to ask for help:	
Can you help me, please?	Können Sie mir bitte helfen?
I don't understand this.	Ich verstehe das nicht.
What do we have to do?	Was müssen wir denn machen?
What's that in English / German?	Was heißt das auf Englisch / Deutsch?
Can I say: ...? / What does ... mean?	Kann ich sagen: ...? / Was bedeutet ...?
How do you do this exercise?	Wie macht man diese Übung?
Is this right? I'm not sure.	Ist das richtig? Ich bin nicht sicher.
Sorry, I don't know.	Tut mir Leid, das weiß ich nicht.
Can you write it on the board, please?	Können Sie das bitte an die Tafel schreiben?
Can I ask a question, please?	Kann ich bitte eine Frage stellen?
Pardon? Can you repeat the question / sentence, please?	Wie bitte? Können Sie die Frage / den Satz bitte wiederholen?
Can you play the CD again, please?	Können Sie die CD bitte nochmal abspielen?
Can we do another example, please?	Können wir noch ein Beispiel machen?

... if you have a discussion:	
What do you think?	Was meinst du?
In my opinion	Meiner Meinung nach ... .
I think you are right/wrong.	Ich denke, du hast recht/Unrecht.
On the one hand ... , on the other hand	Einerseits ... , andererseits ... .

... if you work together:	
Can I work with ... ?	Kann ich mit ... zusammenarbeiten?
Can I have your ... ?	Kann ich mal dein/e/n ... haben?
Whose turn is it?	Wer ist dran?
What are we going to do first?	Was machen wir als Erstes?
Let's write ... on our poster.	Schreiben wir ... auf unser Poster.
Let's put this picture here.	Setzen/Kleben wir das Bild hier hin.
You can be ... and I'll be	Du kannst ... spielen und ich werde ... spielen.
Let's act the story/play a game.	Lasst uns die Geschichte/ein Spiel spielen.

... if you give a talk:	
Today I'd like to talk about	Heute möchte ich über ... reden.
Here you can see	Hier seht ihr ... .
On the left/right	Auf der linken/rechten Seite ... .
I hope you liked the talk.	Ich hoffe, euch hat mein Vortrag gefallen.
Are there any questions?	Habt ihr Fragen dazu?

... if you want to talk about stories/poems/songs:	
I like/don't like this story/poem/song/game.	Diese Geschichte/Dieses Gedicht/Lied/Spiel gefällt mir/ gefällt mir nicht.
I think it's good/interesting/brilliant/funny/really exciting.	Ich finde sie/es gut/interessant/toll/ witzig/wirklich spannend.
I think it's sad/boring/terrible.	Ich finde sie/es traurig/langweilig/schrecklich.
It was OK but I've read better ones.	Sie/Es ist ganz nett, aber ich habe schon bessere gelesen.
I don't think this is right/wrong.	Ich glaube nicht, dass dies richtig/falsch ist.

What the teacher says to you

Questions	
Excuse me. Could you ... ?	Entschuldigung, könntest du ... ?
Could you help me, please?	Könntest du mir bitte helfen?
What's the problem?	Was ist das Problem?/Was ist los?
What's happening in the picture?	Was passiert (gerade) im Bild?
What do you know about poetry slams/... ?	Was wisst ihr über 'poetry slams'/... ?
What do you think of ... ?	Was haltet ihr von ... ?
Have you got any other ideas?	Habt ihr andere/sonstige Ideen?
Can you find the mistakes?	Könnt ihr die Fehler entdecken?
What does ... mean?	Was bedeutet ... ?

Instructions	
Be careful with the word order/... .	Achtet auf die Satzstellung/... .
Make a grid (like this).	Macht eine Tabelle (wie diese).
Match the questions/pictures with the answers/ sentences.	Ordnet den Fragen/Bildern die Antworten/Sätze zu.
Read the definitions.	Lest die Definitionen.
Define these jobs/... .	Erklärt diese Berufe/... .
Discuss with a partner.	Diskutiert mit einem Partner/einer Partnerin.
Give three reasons.	Nenne drei Gründe.
Find the places on the map.	Sucht die Orte auf der Karte.
Close your books, please.	Macht eure Bücher zu.
Don't forget to check your spelling.	Vergesst nicht, die Rechtschreibung zu prüfen.
Give your talk to the class.	Halte dein Referat vor der Klasse.
Present your poster/DVD to the class.	Präsentiere dein Poster/deine DVD vor der Klasse.

List of irregular verbs

to **be** [bi:]	**was/were** [wɒz/wɜ:]	**been** [bi:n]	sein
to **become** [bɪ'kʌm]	**became** [bɪ'keɪm]	**become** [bɪ'kʌm]	werden
to **begin** [bɪ'gɪn]	**began** [bɪ'gæn]	**begun** [bɪ'gʌn]	beginnen, anfangen
to **bet** [bet]	**bet** [bet]	**bet** [bet]	wetten
to **build** [bɪld]	**built** [bɪlt]	**built** [bɪlt]	bauen
to **blow** [bləʊ]	**blew** [blu:]	**blown** [bləʊn]	blasen
to **break** [breɪk]	**broke** [brəʊk]	**broken** ['brəʊkn]	(zer)brechen; kaputtmachen
to **bring** [brɪŋ]	**brought** [brɔ:t]	**brought** [brɔ:t]	bringen, mitbringen
to **burn** [bɜ:n]	**burnt** [bɜ:nt]	**burnt** [bɜ:nt]	(ver)brennen
to **buy** [baɪ]	**bought** [bɔ:t]	**bought** [bɔ:t]	kaufen
to **catch** [kætʃ]	**caught** [kɔ:t]	**caught** [kɔ:t]	fangen
to **choose** [tʃu:z]	**chose** [tʃəʊz]	**chosen** ['tʃəʊzn]	wählen, auswählen
to **come** [kʌm]	**came** [keɪm]	**come** [kʌm]	kommen
to **cut** [kʌt]	**cut** [kʌt]	**cut** [kʌt]	schneiden
to **dig up** [dɪg‿'ʌp]	**dug up** [dʌg‿'ʌp]	**dug up** [dʌg‿'ʌp]	ausgraben
to **do** [du:]	**did** [dɪd]	**done** [dʌn]	machen, tun
to **draw** [drɔ:]	**drew** [dru:]	**drawn** [drɔ:n]	zeichnen
to **drink** [drɪŋk]	**drank** [dræŋk]	**drunk** [drʌŋk]	trinken
to **drive** [draɪv]	**drove** [drəʊv]	**driven** ['drɪvn]	fahren
to **eat** [i:t]	**ate** [et / eɪt]	**eaten** ['i:tn]	essen, fressen
to **fall** [fɔ:l]	**fell** [fel]	**fallen** ['fɔ:ln]	fallen, herunterfallen, hinfallen
to **feed** [fi:d]	**fed** [fed]	**fed** [fed]	füttern
to **feel** [fi:l]	**felt** [felt]	**felt** [felt]	fühlen, sich fühlen
to **fight** [faɪt]	**fought** [fɔ:t]	**fought** [fɔ:t]	kämpfen
to **find** [faɪnd]	**found** [faʊnd]	**found** [faʊnd]	finden
to **fly** [flaɪ]	**flew** [flu:]	**flown** [fləʊn]	fliegen
to **forget** [fə'get]	**forgot** [fə'gɒt]	**forgotten** [fə'gɒtn]	vergessen
to **get** [get]	**got** [gɒt]	**got** [gɒt]	kommen, bekommen; werden
to **give** [gɪv]	**gave** [geɪv]	**given** ['gɪvn]	geben, schenken
to **go** [gəʊ]	**went** [went]	**gone** [gɒn]	gehen
to **hang out** [hæŋ‿'aʊt]	**hung out** [hʌŋ‿'aʊt]	**hung out** [hʌŋ‿'aʊt]	sich herumtreiben
to **hear** [hɪə]	**heard** [hɜ:d]	**heard** [hɜ:d]	hören
to **hide** [haɪd]	**hid** [hɪd]	**hidden** ['hɪdn]	verstecken, sich verstecken
to **hit** [hɪt]	**hit** [hɪt]	**hit** [hɪt]	schlagen, treffen
to **hold** [həʊld]	**held** [held]	**held** [held]	halten
to **hurt** [hɜ:t]	**hurt** [hɜ:t]	**hurt** [hɜ:t]	verletzen, weh tun
to **keep** [ki:p]	**kept** [kept]	**kept** [kept]	(be)halten
to **know** [nəʊ]	**knew** [nju:]	**known** [nəʊn]	wissen, kennen
to **lay** [leɪ]	**laid** [leɪd]	**lain** [leɪn]	legen
to **learn** [lɜ:n]	**learnt** [lɜ:nt]	**learnt** [lɜ:nt]	lernen
to **leave** [li:v]	**left** [left]	**left** [left]	lassen, verlassen, abfahren
to **lend** [lend]	**lent** [lent]	**lent** [lent]	leihen
to **let** [let]	**let** [let]	**let** [let]	lassen
to **lie** [laɪ]	**lay** [leɪ]	**lain** [leɪn]	liegen
to **lose** [lu:z]	**lost** [lɒst]	**lost** [lɒst]	verlieren
to **make** [meɪk]	**made** [meɪd]	**made** [meɪd]	machen, tun

to **mean** [mi:n]	**meant** [ment]	**meant** [ment]	bedeuten, meinen
to **meet** [mi:t]	**met** [met]	**met** [met]	treffen, sich treffen
to **put** [pʊt]	**put** [pʊt]	**put** [pʊt]	setzen, stellen, legen
to **read** [ri:d]	**read** [red]	**read** [red]	lesen
to **rebuild** [ˌri:ˈbɪld]	**rebuilt** [ˌri:ˈbɪlt]	**rebuilt** [ˌri:ˈbɪlt]	wieder aufbauen, wiederherstellen
to **ride** [raɪd]	**rode** [rəʊd]	**ridden** [ˈrɪdn]	fahren, reiten
to **ring** [rɪŋ]	**rang** [ræŋ]	**rung** [rʌŋ]	klingeln; anrufen
to **rise** [raɪz]	**rose** [rəʊz]	**risen** [ˈrɪzn]	steigen, wachsen, zunehmen
to **run** [rʌn]	**ran** [ræn]	**run** [rʌn]	rennen, laufen
to **say** [seɪ]	**said** [sed]	**said** [sed]	sagen, sprechen
to **see** [si:]	**saw** [sɔ:]	**seen** [si:n]	sehen; besuchen
to **sell** [sel]	**sold** [səʊld]	**sold** [səʊld]	verkaufen
to **send** [send]	**sent** [sent]	**sent** [sent]	schicken
to **set** [set]	**set** [set]	**set** [set]	stellen, einstellen
to **shake** [ʃeɪk]	**shook** [ʃʊk]	**shaken** [ˈʃeɪkn]	schütteln, zittern
to **show** [ʃəʊ]	**showed** [ʃəʊd]	**shown** [ʃəʊn]	zeigen
to **sing** [sɪŋ]	**sang** [sæŋ]	**sung** [sʌŋ]	singen
to **sit** [sɪt]	**sat** [sæt]	**sat** [sæt]	sitzen
to **sleep** [sli:p]	**slept** [slept]	**slept** [slept]	schlafen
to **smell** [smel]	**smelt** [smelt]	**smelt** [smelt]	riechen
to **speak** [spi:k]	**spoke** [spəʊk]	**spoken** [ˈspəʊkn]	sprechen
to **spell** [spel]	**spelt** [spelt]	**spelt** [spelt]	buchstabieren
to **spend** [spend]	**spent** [spent]	**spent** [spent]	verbringen, ausgeben
to **stand** [stænd]	**stood** [stʊd]	**stood** [stʊd]	stehen
to **steal** [sti:l]	**stole** [stəʊl]	**stolen** [ˈstəʊln]	stehlen
to **swim** [swɪm]	**swam** [swæm]	**swum** [swʌm]	schwimmen
to **take** [teɪk]	**took** [tʊk]	**taken** [ˈteɪkn]	nehmen, mitnehmen, bringen
to **teach** [ti:tʃ]	**taught** [tɔ:t]	**taught** [tɔ:t]	lehren
to **tell** [tel]	**told** [təʊld]	**told** [təʊld]	erzählen, sagen
to **think** [θɪŋk]	**thought** [θɔ:t]	**thought** [θɔ:t]	denken, glauben
to **throw** [θrəʊ]	**threw** [θru:]	**thrown** [θrəʊn]	werfen
to **understand** [ˌʌndəˈstænd]	**understood** [ˌʌndəˈstʊd]	**understood** [ˌʌndəˈstʊd]	verstehen
to **upset** [ʌpˈset]	**upset** [ʌpˈset]	**upset** [ʌpˈset]	erschrecken, durcheinander bringen, umstoßen
to **wake** [weɪk]	**woke** [wəʊk]	**woken** [ˈwəʊkn]	(auf)wecken
to **wear** [weə]	**wore** [wɔ:]	**worn** [wɔ:n]	anhaben, tragen
to **win** [wɪn]	**won** [wɒn]	**won** [wɒn]	gewinnen, siegen
to **write** [raɪt]	**wrote** [rəʊt]	**written** [ˈrɪtn]	schreiben

Lösungen Check-out

Unit 1 – Seite 20

1 Things people do

2. Do Sue and Barbara **play baseball**? – No, but they **often play volleyball**.
3. Does Marcia **enjoy sports**? – No, but she **always enjoys music**.
4. Does Mr Brown **buy a computer magazine**? – No, but he **usually buys a sports magazine**.
5. Does Rob **ride his bike to the stadium**? – No, but he **rides his bike to the park at weekends**.
6. Do the fans **take Cincinnati Reds flags** to a game (with them)? – No, but they **always take Chicago Cubs flags** (with them).

2 Wrong facts

1. That's wrong. A football team **never has** 15 players. A **rugby team** has 15 players. (A football team has 11 players.)
2. That's wrong. Derrek Lee **never** plays for the Cincinnati Reds. He plays for the **Chicago Cubs**.
3. That's wrong. Beach volleyball players **never** use arm signals. They use **hand** signals.
4. That's wrong. In baseball the pitcher **never** tries to hit the ball with a bat. The **batter** tries to do this.
5. That's wrong. Volleyball players **never** wear helmets. They always wear **shorts and a T-shirt**.
6. That's wrong. In football the players **never** pass and catch the ball. They do this in **rugby**.
7. That's wrong. They **never** play beach volley ball in a field. They play it **on sand/in a court**.
8. That's wrong. In tennis a referee **never** says the score. An **umpire** says the score.

3 A description: A crazy tennis match

Mustersätze: Three players **are looking** at a flower on the court. A person/man **is taking** a picture (of them). A boy **is carrying** a lot of tennis balls. A player/woman **is drinking** a lemonade/a coke/something. The people **are watching** the others on the court. They **are laughing**. The umpire **is going** bananas/**is shouting**. (He's **saying** they should start the game/leave the court … .) A man **is carrying** an umbrella. A cow **is eating** grass/**is standing** on the court. The players **are wearing** T-shirts and shorts. The man with the camera **is wearing** a hat.

4 Mixed bag: No test tomorrow

1. goes	3. is learning	5. work/ learn	6. is	8. is trying	10. doing
2. is sitting	4. does		7. playing	9. is	11. is packing

Unit 2 – Seite 38

1 At the Science Museum

a) Last Saturday it **was** Jamie's birthday. Jamie and his friends **went** to the Science Museum. They **took** the Underground there. The trip **wasn't** long so they **got** to the museum early. They **bought** their tickets and **decided** to go to the flight lab first because they **didn't** want to wait in the long queues later. They really **liked** it. Then they **wanted** to see the old Concorde but they **couldn't** find it. They **asked** a man in uniform. He **was** very nice and **showed** them where to go. Before they **left,** they **visited** the Museum shop. There **were** lots of interesting things there and fantastic posters, too. Jamie's friends **gave** him a great present: He **could** choose something from the shop! He **chose** a model of his favourite car.

b) 2. They didn't watch a science film, they went to the Science Museum.
3. They didn't go there by bus, they went by Underground.
4. They didn't steal the tickets, they bought them.
5. They didn't want to have a snack first, they wanted to go to the flight lab.
6. They didn't hate the flight lab, they really liked it.
7. They didn't visit the toilets, they visited the museum shop.
8. Jamie didn't get a poster from his friends, he got a model of his favourite car.

2 Can you remember?

a) 1. When did the Great Fire happen?
2. Where did the pickpocket steal the rucksack?
3. Why did the people go to the river?
4. How did Reg meet David Beckham?
5. Where did Pru work before she started at Accent?
6. Who did James, the milkman, get cakes or sweets from?
7. What did Suzanne hate until she became a courier?
8. When did they build the Tower of London?

b) 1. The Great Fire happened in 1666.
2. He stole it at Marble Arch.
3. They wanted to escape from the fire (in boats).
4. He met David Beckham because he once took him to the airport (in his taxi).
5. She worked in a post office before she started at Accent.
6. He got cakes or sweets from his customers.
7. She hated helmets until she became a courier.
8. They built it in the 11th century.

3 A class photo

ones; one; one; one; ones; ones; one

4 Mixed bag: A terrible trip to London

1. came	5. got	9. had seen	13. were	17. didn't feel	21. had bought
2. had	6. went	10. went	14. had left	18. went	22. looked
3. was	7. was	11. were	15. went	19. didn't look	23. were
4. forgot	8. got	12. didn't like	16. was	20. wanted	

Unit 3 – Seite 56

1 A day trip

1. can; 2. needn't; 3. can't, 4. needn't; 5. needn't; 6. can; 7. can; 8. can; 9. needn't; 10. can

2 Rules on a ferry

2. You must listen to the announcements.
3. You mustn't put your feet on the seats.
4. You must keep out of the engine room.
5. You mustn't throw away your bottles/throw your bottles away.
6. You must take them/the bottles back.
7. You mustn't leave your luggage anywhere.

8. You must keep your luggage with you.
9. You mustn't dive off the ferry.
10. You mustn't carry animals or plants (with you).

3 Must I?

a) 1. You: Mum says I must learn my French. Must I do it now?
Dad: No, you needn't. You can learn it **next week.**
2. You: Mum says I must wash the car. Must I do it now?
Dad: No, you needn't. You can wash it tomorrow.
3. You: Mum says I must clean my shoes. Must I do it now?
Dad: No, you needn't. You can clean them this afternoon.
4. You: Mum says I must do the shopping. Must I do it now?
Dad: No, you needn't. You can do it after lunch.
5. You: Mum says I must walk the dog. Must I do it now?
Dad: No, you needn't. You can do it after supper.
6. You: Mum says I must feed the cat. Must I do it now?
Dad: No, you needn't. You can do it in an hour.

b) 1. You: Dad says I can learn my French **next week.**
Mum: No, you can't. You must do a test on Monday.
2. You: Dad says I can wash the car tomorrow.
Mum: No, you can't. You must help the neighbour (then).
3. You: Dad says I can clean my shoes this afternoon.
Mum: No, you can't. You must go swimming (then).
4. You: Dad says I can do the shopping after lunch.
Mum: No, you can't. You must buy some things for lunch.
5. You: Dad says I can walk the dog after supper.
Mum: No, you can't. You must go to bed early.
6. You: Dad says I can feed the cat in an hour.
Mum: No, you can't. You must do it a once.

4 A word puzzle

1. A **cruise** ship is … . 2. A **smuggler** is a person **who/that** takes things that they mustn't take to another country. 3. A **port** is a place (town/village) **which/that** is on the coast. 4. A **canoe** is a (kind of) boat **which/that** you can use on a small river. 5. A **ferry** is a (kind of) ship **which/that** can also take cars. 6. A **passenger** is a person **who/that** goes on a boat, ship, ferry, bus, train or plane (or in a car). 7. The **sea** is water **which/that** meets the land at the coast/beach.

5 Mixed bag: English isn't always English

1. that	3. that	5. that	7. that	9. that
2. that	4. that	6. whose	8. whose	10. that

6 A visit to Leeds Castle

1. Last summer we went to South England for a holiday./
We went to South England for a holiday last summer.
2. On the day after we arrived, it was rainy./ It was rainy on the day after we arrived.
3. So we didn't want to take the train down to the coast on that day.
4. Instead of that we went to Leeds Castle in the morning./
In the morning we went to Leeds Castle instead of that.

5. At ten o'clock the owner showed us the different rooms of the castle./
   The owner showed us the different rooms of the castle at ten o'clock.
6. They built the first castle buildings there over a thousand years ago./
   Over a thousand years ago they built the first castle buildings there.
7. Today people from all over the world visit this fantastic castle in Kent./
   People from all over the world visit this fantastic castle in Kent today.

Unit 4 – Seite 74

1 Work for it!

a) 2. Dad: If you paint the garage door, I'll give you five pounds.
   3. Your aunt and uncle: If you do our shopping, we'll give you three pounds.
   4. Your brother: If you deliver my papers (for me), I'll give you five pounds.
   5. Your grandma: If you clean my windows, I'll give you four pounds.
   6. Mrs Howard: If you read to me, I'll give you three pounds.

b) 2. If I paint the garage door for my dad, he'll give me five pounds.
   3. If I do my aunt and uncle's shopping (for them), they'll give me three pounds.
   4. If I deliver my brother's papers (for him), he'll give me five pounds.
   5. If I clean my grandma's windows (for her), she'll give me four pounds.
   6. If I read to Mrs Howard, she'll give me three pounds.

2 If, if, if …

2. If Mum's still at work, I'll do the shopping for her.
3. If you're busy, I won't ask for your help right now.
4. If you aren't careful, you'll have an accident on your bike.
5. If my parents are angry, they won't give me my pocket money.
6. If you're sad, we'll go and see a funny film.
7. If you take my CD once more, you'll be sorry!
8. If she doesn't turn off that yukky music, I won't help her with her homework!

3 Myself, yourself …

1. Maybe I should teach myself French/Turkish.
2. I wash myself at 7:30 in the morning.
3. She dresses herself in the bedroom.
4. He can see himself in a/the mirror.
5. They hear themselves in a/the tunnel.
6. You can hurt yourselves on the wall/if you climb over the wall.
7. We can help ourselves at a self-service café.
8. It cleans itself.

4 Mixed bag: She'll be surprised!

1. part, 2. won, 3. own, 4. she, 5. want, 6. perform/slam, 7. fans/friends, 8. across, 9. lots, 10. favourite, 11. slam/perform, 12. band, 13. that, 14. know, 15. play, 16. performance, 17. will

Unit 5 – Seite 94

1 Have they got any …?

1. Have you got **any DVDs**? No, sorry, we haven't got **any DVDs** but we've got **some CDs**.
2. Have you got **any newspapers**? No, sorry, we haven't got **any newspapers** but we've got **some magazines**.
3. Have you got **any books**? No, sorry, we haven't got **any books** but we've got **some comics**.
4. Have you got **any sports posters**? No, sorry, we haven't got **any sports posters** but we've got **some Bollywood posters**.
5. Have you got **any birthday cards**? No, sorry, we haven't got **any birthday cards** but we've got **some postcards**.
6. Have you got **any exercise books**? No, sorry, we haven't got **any exercise books** but we've got **some diaries**.
7. Have you got **any coke**? No, sorry, we haven't got **any coke** but we've got **some lemonade**.
8. Have you got **any camera batteries**? No, sorry, we haven't got **any camera batteries** but we've got **some torch batteries**.
9. Have you got **any banana ice-cream**? No, sorry, we haven't got **any banana ice-cream** but we've got **some chocolate ice-cream**.
10. Have you got **any pencils**? No, sorry, we haven't got **any pencils** but we've got **some pens**.

2 Anybody for a cup of tea?

1. I'm just making some tea – **anybody** else for tea?
2. Did you see Derek with Fiona? I'm sure there's **something** in the air!
3. You're not going **anywhere** until you've cleaned your room!
4. I'm still hungry. Isn't there **anything** left to eat?
5. If you don't have **anybody** who can help you, just call me at the weekend.
6. I know **somebody** has to lose. But why must it be me?
7. I've lost my TV magazine. Have you seen it **anywhere**?
8. We won't tell **anybody** our plans yet because we want them all to be surprised.
9. I dropped my mobile down the toilet – and there isn't **anything** funny about that!
10. I saw a great poster of that film **somewhere** in town.
11. **Something** strange happened to Dave when he was on his way to the cinema.
12. I don't think **anything** has gone wrong. They've probably just missed their train.

3 While the burglar was stealing …

a) 2. Mark and his girlfriend **were dancing** at a disco.
3. Mr Bell **was driving** a night bus.
4. Jenny **was sitting** in a cinema.
5. Grandpa Bell **was walking** the dog.
6. Kitty and Birdy **were sleeping** (in the kitchen).

b) 1. Mrs Bell **wasn't visiting** her sister in Cornwall. She **was flying** to Australia.
2. Mark and his girlfriend **weren't having** a meal. They **were dancing** at a disco.
3. Mr Bell **wasn't walking** the dog. He **was driving** a night bus.
4. Jenny **wasn't staying** at a friend's house. She **was sitting** in a cinema.
5. Grandpa **wasn't sleeping**. He **was walking** the dog.

4 Mixed bag: The story never ends

1. who, 2. at, 3. thought, 4. dead, 5. While, 6. sports, 7. go, 8. turned/wanted, 9. go, 10. didn't, 11. didn't, 12. getting

Lösungen Try it out!

Try it out! 1 – Seite 24–25

A Reading

1

a. bike race
b. accident
c. July
d. countries
e. races
f. competition
g. the green jersey
h. important

2 d. the man with the shortest time for all the races.

3

a. helmets
b. times
c. crashed

B Language

a. cycling fans talk **about** the 'Tour'.
b. the most famous bike race **in** the world
c. most **of** them are not really bad
d. crashed **at** 88 kilometres an hour
e. must wear helmets **during** the race
f. different groups **of** races
g. the man **with** the most points
h. the race **for** the yellow jersey

C Mediation and communication

You: Er **braucht** einen **Helm**, aber er will **keinen kaufen**.
Er möchte ihn nur **übers Wochenende ausleihen**.
You: That's **no problem**. He has **some old ones** here. **Try them**.
You: Der **blaue Helm** ist zu **groß** aber der **rote Helm passt** ihm sehr gut.
Kann er ihn bis **Montag ausleihen**?
You: She **isn't here** on Monday but **Tuesday is OK**.

D Listening

1. 10 kilometres from Paris.
2. It is raining.
3. Because they must wait for their new bikes.

E Writing

1

On Saturday afternoon a team from Breitdorf Youth Club had their first beach volley ball match this year and they won! They played against a team from Stuttgart so it wasn't easy. But they stayed cool and scored three points in the last five minutes.

2

I think that's right. There are lots of sports which are fun. Sports needn't be dangerous. People who do dangerous sports often have accidents and they can die.

Or

I think that's wrong. Dangerous sports are more exciting. They are only dangerous if you aren't careful.

Try it out! 2 – Seite 42–43

A Reading

1

a. right
b. right
c. wrong
d. wrong
e. right
f. right

2

a. It's for teenagers.
b. She thinks it is a great idea and it's fun.
c. They worry about drugs, bullying and healthy food.

B Language

a. interesting
b. young
c. great
d. healthy
e. friends
f. questions

C Skills

a. arbeitet
b. funktioniert nicht
c. arbeitsfähig
d. arbeitslos
e. Büroarbeit

D Mediation and communication

You: Meine Freundin **möchte wissen**, wie sie **morgen** zum **Stadion** kommt.
You: When do you want to **leave** here?
You: Sie **muss um 2 Uhr** am Stadion sein.
You: You can **take the bus**. It leaves at **24 minutes past one** from the **front of the school**.

E Listening

traffic jams, bullying, drugs, noise

F Writing

1

Hi, Brad, I have just read about a website for young people in London. They can find out about events in the city and get information on transport there. They can also write to it if they have a problem but don't want to talk to their parents or teachers about it.
Young people write the texts. I think it's a great idea.
I'll send you the address if you like. Yours, Max

2

I think it's right. A lot of pupils have problems and need to talk about them. It's an easy way to give pupils and parents information quickly.
Or
I think it's wrong. All school websites are boring. Lots of kids aren't interested in a website at school. They only want to play computer games.

Try it out! 3 – Seite 60–61

A Reading

1

a. Hastings
b. The Isle of Wight
c. The Isle of Wight
d. The Isle of Wight
e. Hastings
f. The Isle of Wight

2

a. a day
b. the dangerous life of a smuggler
c. the history of smuggling
d. 'Smugglers Adventure'
e. the 'ghost' of a smuggler
f. strange noises

B Language

a. scared b. hard c. noises d. largest e. cycle

C Skills

1

a. smuggler b. life-sized c. slave

2

a. A place where you can see old things like pictures and jewels.
b. A person on a ship who robs other ships and often kills the people on them.
c. A place which has got a lot of dark halls and tunnels.

D Mediation and communication

a. In **Gandria.**
b. No. It opens on **13th April**.
c. The **history of customs** from the middle of the **19th century**.
d. **Check** your **passport** or **money** and look for things that a **smuggler** has put in a **car**.
e. No, we can only get there **by boat**.

E Listening

a. 3 Scotland b. 2 Hastings c. 2 castles d. 1 English e. 3 windsurf

F Writing

1

There have been pirates and smugglers on the south coast of England for more than 700 years. They had a very hard life and it was dangerous, too. In Hastings the smugglers used the caves on the coast. In the past they smuggled brandy, gold and slaves. But today they smuggle other things like wild animals and drugs. Some smugglers smuggle people, too.

2

I think it's right. Some museums with old pictures are boring but there are some very exciting museums, too. They have videos and interesting exhibitions. You can have a great day in a good museum.

Or

I think it's wrong. The only museums that I know are really boring. They are old and dark and have lots of strange pictures or funny old furniture.

Try it out 4! – Seite 78–79

A Reading

a. Tamil Nadu in India
b. matches
c. windows
d. hurt
e. strong
f. money
g. school
h. parents
i. child labour
j. ten years ago

B Language

1

a. comes
b. have to
c. earn
d. feel
e. leave
f. happen

2

a. factory b. matches c. parents d. child labour

C Mediation and communication

a. In einem Zimmer ohne Fenster in einer Fabrik in Indien.
b. Sie stellt Streichhölzer her.
c. Sie muss arbeiten, weil ihre Familie das Geld braucht.
d. Weniger als 50 Cent pro Tag.
e. Nein. Es passiert in vielen anderen Ländern auch.

D Listening

1. She hasn't done her Maths homework.
2. She hasn't got anything to wear to a party.
3. Her best friend isn't speaking to her.
4. Her hair looks terrible.

E Skills

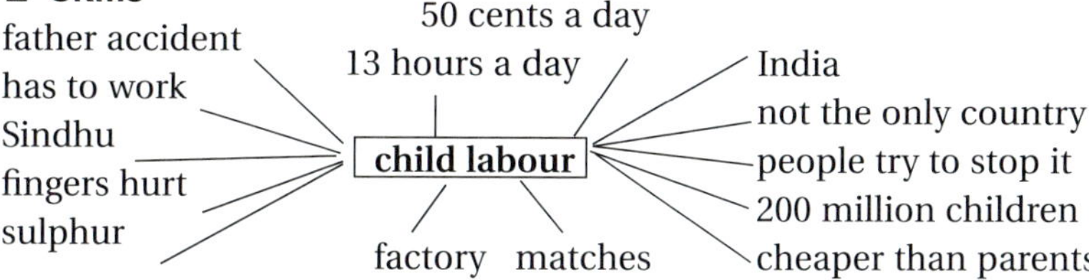

F Writing

1

There is child labour in many countries in the world. More than 200 million children do child labour. Some of the children like Sindhu work in factories for 13 hours a day. They make matches. They feel tired and their fingers hurt because the sulphur is very hot. But they have to work. They should not be in the factories but the owners want them to work. They are cheaper than their parents.

2

I think that's right. Their families often need the money, so they have to work. They don't earn as much as their parents and they sometimes work 13 hours every day. They can't go to school and the factories are unhealthy.

Or

I don't think that's right. Sindhu and her friends get money for their work. Sindhu has a home and parents. Some children are alone in the world.

Lösungen Grammatik

Unit 1

G1

We **play** football/basketball/… in a club. Our team **has got** … players. We **have** practice once/two days a week/… a week/every Monday/… . We **wear** shorts and T-shirts and trainers. The name of our club **is** … .

G2

1. What is Nutty **doing**?
2. He **is riding** on a tiger.
3. **Is** Jack **riding**, too?
4. No, he **isn't**. He**'s falling** into the water.
5. And what **is** Jane **doing**?
6. She**'s playing** beach volleyball.
7. What **is** the elephant **wearing**?
8. It**'s wearing** a swimsuit.

G3

1. Jack usually **plays** football but today he**'s jumping** through the trees.
2. The fish usually **go** swimming but today they**'re playing** volleyball.
3. Jane usually **goes** shopping but today she**'s climbing** a tree.
4. The lion usually **sleeps** under a tree but today she**'s catching** her lunch.

Unit 2

G4

The police **stopped** a pickpocket in London. What **did** he **get**? He **got** five wallets but he **didn't get** much money. Where **did** they **catch** him? The **caught** him at Monument.

G5

Nutty: Look. All these hats are in my shop.
Jane: Which **ones** are your favourites?
Nutty: The **one** on the left is expensive. It's £15. The **one** next to it is cheap.
It's the cheapest **one**. And the **one** on my head is the most beautiful **one**.

G6

… After he **had eaten** breakfast, he **made** a big chocolate cake for his friends. When he **had finished** the cake, he **put** it on the table. … After he **had waited** for two hours, he **was** very sad. … After he **had packed** his rucksack, he **went** to the river. Two hours later he **went** home and **opened** the front door. When he **opened** the door, he **heard** his friends say, 'Happy Birthday!'

Unit 3

G7

We **must** escape! We **can't** go through the trees. We **can't** take the helicopter. We **must** get across the river but we **needn't** swim. We **can** take the boat. We **mustn't** wait. We **must** hurry up!

G8

1. People **who** live in tree houses don't usually have windows.
   Leute, die in Baumhäusern wohnen, haben für gewöhnlich keine/selten Fenster.
2. A panther is an animal **which** can climb trees.
   Ein Panter ist ein Tier, das auf Bäume klettern kann.

3. The panther **whose** name is Pat likes to visit Jack in the tree house.
   Der Panter, der Pat heißt (dessen Name Pat ist), besucht Jack gern im Baumhaus.
4. But other animals **which** are frightened always hide behind the cupboard.
   Aber Tiere, die Angst haben, verstecken sich immer hinter dem Schrank.

G9

1. Every day Jane swims in the river.
2. One morning she sees a lion under the trees.
3. Five minutes later an elephant arrives at the river.
4. Two minutes later Jane is on the elephant.

Unit 4

G10

1. I promise I'**ll help** you.
2. I'm sure it'**ll rain** tomorrow.
3. I think my friend **will wait** for me.

G12

1. If my parents **move** to another place, I'**ll be** unhappy (angry/happy/...)/ I'**ll** miss my friends.
2. If it **rains** tomorrow, I **won't go** to the pool/I'**ll stay** at home/I'**ll go** to the cinema.
3. If you're late for the lesson, you'**ll get** more homework/you'**ll have** to stay here for an hour after school.

G14

1. I can do this **myself**.
2. She fell off her bike and hurt **herself**.
3. Cats always clean **themselves**.
4. We can see **ourselves** in the mirror.

Unit 5

G15/16

1. There are **some** great films on TV tonight.
2. Are there **any** soaps on BBC1?
3. Have you seen the TV magazine **anywhere**?
4. **Somebody** has taken it.
5. You can't find **anything** in this house!

G17

1. What **were** they all **doing**? Nutty **was washing** his T-shirt.
2. Jane and Jack **weren't washing** their T-shirts, they **were playing** the drums.
3. The tiger **was sitting** in the tree. He **was eating** a banana.

G18

1. When Jack **went** to bed, Jane **was thinking** about a new tree house.
2. While Jack **was sleeping**, Jane **was working**.
3. When Jack **woke** up, Jane **was smiling**.
4. While Jane and Jack **were sitting** in their new tree house, Nutty **was collecting** wood for his house.

G19

1. Yesterday I **was allowed to** watch TV.
2. Yesterday I **had to walk** the dog.
3. Last week I **didn't have to** go to school.
4. On Sunday I **wasn't able to** play football.

Text- und Bildquellen

Textquellen:
S. 33: Brad Arnold, Robert Todd Harrell, Christopher Lee Henderson, Matthew Darrick Roberts © Songs of Universal; für D, CH, A: Universal/MCA Music Publishing GmbH, Berlin;
S. 43: PONS Orange Line Wörterbuch © Ernst Klett Sprachen GmbH, Stuttgart;
S. 51: Sting © GM Sumner; für D, CH, A: EMI Music Publishing Germany GmbH Co KG, Hamburg;
S. 69: Linda Perry © für D, CH, A: Famous Music Publishing Germany GmbH Co KG, München

Bildquellen:
Umschlag: Corbis (Ole Graf/zefa), Düsseldorf;
Vorsatz: London Transport Museum, London; **S. 4:** Avenue Images GmbH (Corbis RF), Hamburg; MEV, Augsburg; Fotofinder (Caro/ Oberhäuser), Berlin; Avenue Images GmbH (Image Source), Hamburg; **S. 5:** Alamy Images RM (David Pearson), Abingdon, Oxon; Ingram Publishing, Tattenhall Chester; Fotosearch RF (Photodisc), Waukesha, WI; Seuffert, Felix, Hannover; **S. 6:** defd, Hamburg; Corbis (Ralf-Finn Hestoft), Düsseldorf; Corbis (Rick Doyle), Düsseldorf;
S. 8: Getty Images (John Gichigi), München; defd, Hamburg;
S. 9: Avenue Images GmbH (Corbis RF), Hamburg; Corbis (S. Carmona), Düsseldorf; Chicago Uncommon (Dawn M. Mikulich), Chicago IL; Alamy Images RM (Kim Karpeles), Abingdon, Oxon;
S. 10: Getty Images (Photographer's Choice/Lang), München;
S. 11: Corbis (Icon SMI/Goren), Düsseldorf; Getty Images (David Rogers), München; MEV, Augsburg; **S. 12:** Getty Images (stone/David Pfeifroth), München; JupiterImages (RF/photos.com), Tucson, AZ; Getty Images (taxi/John Terence Turner), München; Getty Images RF (PhotoDisc), München; Alamy Images RM (Jeff Morgan), Abingdon, Oxon; **S. 13:** Kessler-Medien, Saarbrücken; CSI, New Delhi; iStockphoto (RF/Galina Barskaya), Calgary, Alberta; Getty Images (The Image Bank/Joe Patronite), München; **S. 14:** Fotosearch RF (Stockbyte), Waukesha, WI; Ingram Publishing, Tattenhall Chester; Getty Images (Mike Powell), München; **S. 15:** Alamy Images RM (Jiri Rezac), Abingdon, Oxon; Getty Images (Mike Hewitt), München; Picture-Alliance (epa/Martyn Hayhow), Frankfurt; **S. 16:** Getty Images (Hulton Archive/Topical Press Agency), München; Getty Images (Hulton Archive/Hutton), München;
S. 17: Science & Society Picture Library, London; **S. 18:** Klett-Archiv (Steinle), Stuttgart; Getty Images RF (PhotoDisc), München; Fotosearch RF (PhotoDisc), Waukesha, WI; Avenue Images GmbH (Corbis RF), Hamburg; **S. 19:** Getty Images (Prior), München; Chicago Uncommon (Dawn M. Mikulich), Chicago IL; Fotosearch RF (Stockbyte), Waukesha, WI; **S. 20:** MEV, Augsburg; **S. 24:** Picture-Alliance (epa/Breloer), Frankfurt; **S. 26:** Fotofinder (Caro/ Oberhäuser), Berlin; **S. 27:** Picture-Alliance (Writtle), Frankfurt; Alamy Images RM (Sullivan), Abingdon, Oxon; Fotofinder (Freelens Pool/ Kutt), Berlin; Corbis (Fisher), Düsseldorf; Corbis (Blair), Düsseldorf; Fotofinder (Vario Press/Unkel), Berlin; **S. 28:** London Transport Museum, London; **S. 29:** Picture-Alliance, Frankfurt; Fotofinder (Picture News/Vedde), Berlin; Fotofinder (Keystone/Schulz), Berlin; Alamy Images RM (Angel Terry), Abingdon, Oxon; Corbis (Reuters/Evans), Düsseldorf; Getty Images (Cole), München; Corbis (REUTERS/Ian Hodgson), Düsseldorf; Getty Images (MS Kim), München; Fotofinder (Schapowalow/SIME), Berlin; **S. 30:** Fotofinder (Arco/Scholz), Berlin; Nickwoodphoto, Clapham Common; Nickwoodphoto, Clapham Common; **S. 31:** Avenue Images GmbH (Image Source), Hamburg; Historic Royal Palaces, Surrey; Historic Royal Palaces, Surrey; Avenue Images GmbH (Corbis RF), Hamburg; Alamy Images RM (AA World Travel), Abingdon, Oxon; Alamy Images RM (Mary Evans Pict. Lib), Abingdon, Oxon; Fotofinder (Schapowalow/Heaton), Berlin; Fotofinder (Widmann), Berlin;
S. 32: Fotofinder (Bridgeman/Stapleton), Berlin; Fotofinder, Berlin;
S. 33: Historic Royal Palaces, Surrey; Alamy Images RM (Alex Segre), Abingdon, Oxon; www.britainonview.com, London; Alamy Images RF (RF), Abingdon, Oxon; Getty Images (Photonica/AB), München;
S. 34: Getty Images (taxi/Moskowitz), München; The Ceres Partnership, Dunsden, Reading; Fotosearch RF (Photodisc), Waukesha, WI; **S. 35:** Masterfile (Woodhouse), Düsseldorf; Image 100 (RF), Berlin; **S. 36:** Getty Images (taxi), München; Getty Images (Vincent), München; **S. 37:** Harper Collins Publishers, New York;
S. 38: Alamy Images RM (David Pearson), Abingdon, Oxon;
S. 39: Klett-Archiv (Preker-Franke), Stuttgart; Getty Images (DK Stock/Hung), München; **S. 42:** Bananastock RF, Watlington/Oxon;
S. 45: Alamy Images RM (David Pearson), Abingdon, Oxon; Corbis (Ric Ergenbright), Düsseldorf; Ingram Publishing, Tattenhall Chester; iStockphoto (RF/Irwin), Calgary, Alberta; **S. 46:** Alamy Images RM (Nick Hanna), Abingdon, Oxon;
S. 48: iStockphoto (RF/Woodworth), Calgary, Alberta; **S. 49:** Corbis (RF), Düsseldorf; **S. 50:** Avenue Images GmbH (Stockbyte), Hamburg;
S. 51: iStockphoto (RF/Hidden), Calgary, Alberta; **S. 54:** Alamy Images RF (RF/fotosonline), Abingdon, Oxon; MEV, Augsburg;
S. 55: etric/Press; Avenue Images GmbH (Index Stock), Hamburg; Alamy Images RM (David Lyons), Abingdon, Oxon; Alamy Images RM (Photofusion), Abingdon, Oxon; Avenue Images GmbH (Corbis RF), Hamburg; **S. 57:** Argus (Peter Frischmuth), Hamburg; iStockphoto (RF), Calgary, Alberta; **S. 58:** Alamy Images RM (Paul Thompson Images), Abingdon, Oxon; iStockphoto (RF/Antonopoulos), Calgary, Alberta;
S. 59: iStockphoto (RF/Jon Helgason), Calgary, Alberta;
S. 60: www.discoverhastings.co.uk; iStockphoto (RF/chrissie shepherd), Calgary, Alberta; **S. 62:** Fotosearch RF (Photodisc), Waukesha, WI; **S. 63:** Visum (Georg Schoenharting), Hamburg; Seuffert, Felix, Hannover; **S. 67:** Corbis (Little Blue Wolf Productions), Düsseldorf; **S. 69:** Alamy Images RF (RF/Design Pics), Abingdon, Oxon; Avenue Images GmbH (Stockbyte), Hamburg; **S. 73:** Getty Images (Photonica/Olaf Tiedje), München; **S. 76:** Alamy Images RM (Janine Wiedel Phot.), Abingdon, Oxon; Alamy Images RM (Rachael Bowes), Abingdon, Oxon; **S. 78:** terre des hommes Deutschland e.V., Osnabrück; **S. 80:** defd, Hamburg; **S. 81:** Alamy Images RM (Ange), Abingdon, Oxon; Argus (Mike Schröder), Hamburg; Corbis (Ralf-Finn Hestoft), Düsseldorf; Alamy Images RM (ACE), Abingdon, Oxon; **S. 83:** Alamy Images RM (Ilianski), Abingdon, Oxon;
S. 87: Alamy Images RF (RF), Abingdon, Oxon; iStockphoto (RF), Calgary, Alberta; Corbis (Rick Doyle), Düsseldorf; **S. 93:** JupiterImages (RF/photos.com), Tucson, AZ; **S. 96:** Alamy Images RM (Ashley Cooper), Abingdon, Oxon; **S. 99:** Alamy Images RM (Edifice), Abingdon, Oxon; Alamy Images RM (Guillen Phot.), Abingdon, Oxon;
S. 111: Reuen, Sascha, Essen; Klett-Archiv (Hamida Aziz), Stuttgart;
S. 118: Getty Images (Malte Christians), München;
S. 119: Avenue Images GmbH (Image Source), Hamburg; **S. 120:** Corbis (Chuck Savage), Düsseldorf; **S. 121:** defd, Hamburg; **S. 143:** Comstock, Luxemburg; Corel Corporation, Unterschleissheim; **S. 148:** MEV, Augsburg; **S. 149:** Comstock, Luxemburg; Alamy Images RM (Sullivan), Abingdon, Oxon; **S. 153:** MEV, Augsburg; **S. 154:** Comstock, Luxemburg;
S. 161: Comstock, Luxemburg; iStockphoto (RF), Calgary, Alberta;
S. 167: Comstock, Luxemburg

Every effort has been made to trace the proper owners of the copyrighted material. However, in a few cases, this may have proved impossible despite repeated enquiries. The publishers would be glad to hear from any further copyright owners of material reproduced in this book.

LONDON
CAMDEN TO
Camden Market
Regent's Park
Outer Circle
Albany Street
Hampstead Road
Park Road
Maida Vale
SHERLOCK HOLMES
Sherlock Holmes Museum
Madame Tussaud's
Marylebone Road
Gloucester Place
Baker Street
Westway A40
Edgeware Road
Wigmore Street
Oxford Street
Oxford Circus
Bond Street
Regent Street
Marble Arch
Notting Hill Carnival
NOTTING HILL
Bayswater Road
Hyde Park
Piccad
Circu
The Serpentine
Rotten Row
Piccadilly
Green Park
Kensington Road
Buckingham Palace
National History Museum
Brompton Road
Sloane Street
Heathrow Airport
Cromwell Road
Victoria Station
Brompton Road
Fulham Road
King's Road
Wimbledon
Chelsea Embankment
Grosver